THE SALES MANAGER'S TROUBLESHOOTER

JOHN CEBROWSKI
CHARLIE ROMEO

PRENTICE HALL

Library of Congress Cataloging in Publication Data

Cebrowski, John.
    The sales manager's troubleshooter / by John Cebrowski, Charlie Romeo.
        p.   cm.
    Includes index.
    ISNB 0-13-673476-6 (case)
    1. Sales management. 2. Sales personnel. I. Romeo, Charlie. II. Title.
HF5438.4.C4 1998
658.8'1—dc21   98-17529
                                                                      CIP

Printed in the United States of America

10 9 8 7 6 5 4 3 2 1

ISBN 0-13-673476-6 (case)

ISBN 0-13-673476-6

9 780136 734765   90000

ATTENTION: CORPORATIONS AND SCHOOLS

Prentice Hall books are available at quantity discounts with bulk purchase for educational, business, or sales promotional use. For information, please write to: Prentice Hall Special Sales, 240 Frisch Court, Paramus, New Jersey 07652. Please supply: title of book, ISBN, quantity, how the book will be used, date needed.

PRENTICE HALL
Paramus, NJ 07652

A Simon & Schuster Company

On the World Wide Web at http://www.phdirect.com

Prentice Hall International (UK) Limited, *London*
Prentice Hall of Australia Pty. Limited, *Sydney*
Prentice Hall Canada, Inc., *Toronto*
Prentice Hall Hispanoamericana, S.A., *Mexico*
Prentice Hall of India Private Limited, *New Delhi*
Prentice Hall of Japan, Inc., *Tokyo*
Simon & Schuster Asia Pte. Ltd., *Singapore*
Editora Prentice Hall do Brasil, Ltda., *Rio de Janeiro*

ACKNOWLEDGMENTS

A sincere thank you to our distinguished Advisory Board of sales, marketing, legal, and human resource managers whose insights and experience were deeply appreciated. The Board included Dan Campbell, Dennis C. Carpenter, Mike Daley, Peter A. Garbis, Robert J. Guerra, Al Harrison, Thomas E. Johnson, Gregory E. Kent, Carol King, Suzanne Kitchel, Bruce Michelson, Paul Procaccini, Edward J. Sulick, James Waldron, and J. Christopher Warner.

The Board's confirmation of the problems, guidance and suggestions on how to treat the problems, editing, and proofreading of the drafts was a considerable aid and helped keep us on track.

We also extend our appreciation to Catharine Cebrowski, Elizabeth Cebrowski, Brett Fenwick, Dr. Elizabeth Hudgins, Larry Kincaid, Maribeth Llopiz, Rev. Daniel Mode, Kristin Niro, Bob Portland, and John Romeo, who provided expertise for specific elements or answers to technical questions.

Our wives, Amanda and Elaine, read and reviewed numerous problems. Their observations and opinions were always fitting. We greatly appreciated their encouragement when we got bogged down and their patience with personal trade-offs over the many months of writing.

Thanks go to our literary agent, Michael Snell, who provided valuable and patient counsel at the beginning as the book concept and proposal took shape.

Special acknowledgment

We declare, first and foremost, that the foundation for our sales and sales-management success was laid a long time ago by two fathers, John S. Cebrowski, and Charles P. Romeo, Sr., whose presence and guidance was always noticed but not always recognized. Their example of integrity, interpersonal skills, work ethic, and sales professionalism is woven throughout this book. This book is dedicated to them.

ABOUT THE AUTHORS

John and Charlie have known each other since 1974 when both lived in Glastonbury, Connecticut and were selling and managing for Digital Equipment Corporation out of their Meriden office. Each have traveled different professional courses, but both have gone to each other for advice and counsel, and the professional and personal relationship has endured and grown through the years. This book is a manifestation of an idea voiced back then that "some day we have to do something together." This book is the "something."

John is now President of Sales Builders, Inc. A five-year-old consulting and retained executive search firm in Fairfax, VA that specializes in marketing and sales. Prior to Sales Builders, John was General Manager of Sales and Distribution for Solarex Corporation where he established a worldwide distribution and direct sales network. He also successfully led sales organizations for Xerox Corporation, US Surgical Corporation, and General Electric Medical Systems.

His articles have appeared in *Executive Excellence, Sales and Marketing Strategies & News,* the *Journal of Business & Industrial Marketing,* and *Business Resource Report.* He is an adjunct professor at Pace University's World Trade Institute in New York.

John received his MBA in Marketing from Northwestern University (Kellogg), and a BFA in Industrial Design from the Rhode Island School of Design.

Charlie is currently Sales Vice President for Digital Equipment Corporation's Multi-Vendor Customer Services Group in Lexington, MA. For more than twenty years Charlie has successfully managed sales operations that range from small teams that sell to large accounts, to large teams that sell to small accounts. He has managed sales efforts that were confined to local territories and others that were global in nature. He has significant experience selling both products and services to and with sales partners.

Staff experience as a sales planning manager and sales development manager adds corporate level and business issue insights.

Charlie received his BS in economics and mathematics from the University of Massachusetts, and completed the executive MBA program at Babson College.

CONTENTS

INTRODUCTION

"What are you going to do for me this month?"

"So—when do we get the contract?"

"I want MORE—NOW!"

"Can't you get your people to do any better?"

Sound familiar? Of course it does. The bottom line of *The Sales Manager's Troubleshooter* is all about results because sales management is all about The Numbers. "Sales results are the ultimate measurement of effectiveness for sales managers, and effective problem solving is a major aid toward making the numbers."

Problems can cause you to lose momentum, sap your energy, consume scarce time, wreck your career, hit your bank balance, disrupt your agenda, aggravate you miserably, rob you of excitement—and we're sure—cause a lot of other headaches. But you're paid big bucks to solve them. *The Sales Manager's Troubleshooter* intends to help you do that.

No two sales-management arenas are the same, and similar problems have unique twists. Even if issues arise repeatedly in the same organization, new circumstances and new players make every sales-management problem unique. As a result, suggested handling of the problems in this book is comprehensive, and the delivery of the information permits selective application.

Solving sticky, uncomfortable problems is often an unwelcome chore, but problem solving can also be exciting and rewarding. It is a great feeling of accomplishment to face off against a tough issue and come out a winner.

THREE DELIVERABLES IN THE BOOK

One, the *integrity* of approaches and actions, is intended to create long-term winning scenarios for you, your people, your organization, and your customers, clients, and sales partners.

Two, the possible actions are *practical and extensive*, allowing you to customize them around your own management style.

Three, the material is in *an easy reference* format—an off-the-shelf manual of ready-to-implement ideas.

Four Ways to Use the Book

1. *As a reactionary tool.* "I've got a tough issue on my hands. I wonder what these guys say that can stir my problem-solving juices." Pick up *The Troubleshooter* when you're in the throes of wrestling with a toughie.

2. *As preventive medicine.* "How can I *prevent* these problems from happening in the first place?"—or—"Oh, *that* situation could happen to me; I think I better read it."—or—"Let's see what I can learn in order to eliminate nasty surprises." Scan through *The Troubleshooter* to anticipate problems and minimize situations that lead to problems.

3. *As a training aid.* "I need to develop the problem-solving skills of our sales managers." The Problems can act as classroom case studies, small-group discussion topics, and as a reference for individual manager coaching. The material can add substance to sales-meeting agendas or formal training sessions.

4. *As a reminder of the day-to-day activities that made you successful in the first place.* "I knew that technique, but I've forgotten about it." The detailed suggestions in *The Troubleshooter* can rejuvenate the building blocks of your early achievements.

How the Book Is Organized

The Problems

The problems have been confirmed by research with sales managers such as you and have been segmented into 14 easy-to-identify parts.

There are more problems out there than are in the book, but we focus on the top priorities, giving you a broad treatment of each.

The Format

The treatment of each problem follows a similar six-part format:

1. The Story
2. Temptations
3. What Happened Here . . . ?
4. Options
5. Possible Actions
6. Lessons

THE STORY: This is a brief vignette to create a picture of the situation—a jumping-off point. While The Story behind your version of the problem is no doubt different, the material that follows the story will have similar application. We expect that you'll be thinking of options and possible actions before you even finish these quick scene-setting intros. And that is exactly our objective—to get your problem-solving juices flowing.

TEMPTATIONS: The aim of including Temptations is to recognize the reality of human nature and suggest to you not to succumb to irrational impulses but to engage in rational problem solving. Yielding to temptations often exacerbates problems.

Stone-cold analytical response is not the only way to solve a problem and neither is hot, shoot-from-the-hip backlash. Sales management is all about people, so problem solving is a balanced blend of logic and sensitivity. It is important to recognize and accept the emotional reactions for what they are—natural frustration or anger that must be managed and factored into your solutions.

WHAT HAPPENED HERE . . . ? This section highlights a list of possible factors that led to the problem. It is intended to get you thinking about what else—beyond what was revealed in the story—could have led to the problem. Our aim is to present an array of possibilities to stimulate reflection to help you identify underlying motives.

There are always multiple sides to a problem, and What Happened Here . . . ? strives to identify many of the culprits. The more potentialities you can recognize, the greater the likelihood of solving the problem.

OPTIONS: This section presents reasonable courses of action. Some Option sections lead off with strategic questions that must be answered before an option can be chosen. The option we select to follow will be obvious and is consistent with our intent to follow a high-integrity road of win-win problem solving.

POSSIBLE ACTIONS: This is a stride-by-stride comprehensive outline of concrete steps to solve the problem. You may find it appropriate to follow all the steps or select only certain elements to integrate with your own thoughts.

In reality, the number of Possible Actions are almost infinite. We present thoughts that should be bedrock considerations in your solution. Take the Possible Actions and blend them into your style and situation.

LESSONS: Comments in this concluding section emphasize take-away messages from the material, relate growth provided, or suggest final steps to avoid repetition of the problem. Lessons offer a final opportunity for contemplation.

CHECKLIST

There is a comprehensive checklist of 21 points on page 521 to consider in solving your problems. The checklist is intended to be used to support any of the problems by acting as a reminder of additional matters to consider. It is also a tickler intended to be used as a guide for unusual situations that the book does not address.

YOUR FEEDBACK AND INPUT OPPORTUNITY

A voluntary survey suggestion form on page 523 gives you the opportunity to be a part of the next edition.

Do you have additional thoughts to enhance the existing problems? Would you like to suggest a new sales-management problem for the next edition? Fax or e-mail it in.
We would like to hear from you.

THE BOTTOM LINE

The Sales Manager's Troubleshooter shortens the problem-solving learning curve and provides creative and logical organization to the sales-management problem-solving process.
The book will do these six things for you:

1. It will give you more time for *selling and coaching*.
2. It will enable you to exhibit improved *leadership and management*.
3. It will *reduce risks* associated with personnel management.
4. It will help you *look good* through improved credibility and integrity of action.
5. It will *position you* for increased responsibility and reward.
6. And most important, it will *help you achieve* the numbers.

IN CONCLUSION

When you take this book off the shelf you will find something to help you.

John and Charlie

part one

TROUBLESHOOTING THE EXECUTION PROBLEM

Execution is a singular problem in Part 1. It is a fundamental sales-management requisite. The ability and need to execute is common to the remaining 100 problems. Execution is what ultimately gets you to solutions of your problems.

Whatever problem is worth solving at all is worth solving well.

Execution stands on its own.

1–1 THE PROBLEM:

Your ability to personally execute is not what you would like it to be.

THE STORY

Julie glanced over her sales plan and final results, thinking that there were many things that had not been accomplished. She had this gnawing feeling that the year could have been better, although she would never admit that to anyone.

She thought to herself, "If I had done some of the things I had planned to do, I probably would have been able to make the President's Club trip to Hawaii." As it was, she missed by one percentage point.

"I know what to do. I've been to all the seminars and read all the books. Everything they say is true. But it's one thing to know that stuff and another thing to do it," Julie thought.

Right then and there she made a resolution to herself to improve her execution next year.

TEMPTATIONS

The temptations associated with execution are always detracting and self-defeating.

Denigrate yourself

"I'm just not good enough. I don't think I've got what it takes."

Rationalization

"Considering the hand I was dealt, I did all right this year. I should be happy."

Shortcuts

"There have got to be some tricks I'm missing. I've got to become a better gamester."

It's a better idea to put a stake in the ground just slightly beyond your current grasp and then commit to bust your butt to reach it.

WHAT HAPPENED HERE ...?

Julie is not satisfied. That's a great starting point for anyone to improve execution. Many sales managers would probably be happy to trade places with Julie.

Something is eating at Julie. She probably doesn't completely understand it, and it's not likely anyone else ever will either. These cravings are sometimes impossible to articulate.

Julie may have read an item or watched a program that stirred something inside her.

Her manager or one of her people may have made a comment that she interpreted as a challenge.

A peer whom she perceives as inferior may have surpassed her.

Execution is not so much about time utilization, personal organization, or priorities as it is about something a lot deeper.

OPTIONS

You have only two options with this problem.

1. Hold what you've got. You may be happy with the status quo. You could convince yourself that you are a model of execution excellence. Don't reach any farther.
2. Commit and work to improve your execution.

   It's a binary decision. This is simple. So far.

POSSIBLE ACTIONS

Execution is *both* the act *and* the manner of doing something.

1. Do it.
2. And do it well. (You *must* concern yourself with the quality side of execution.)

This problem deals with *both* doing something and doing it well. Remember the Nike ads on TV that proclaimed, "Just do it?" Well, that's a great motto, but it is only half the story.

Why is execution so important?

- How many times have you heard yourself or someone else say, "I could have done that."
- And the other person says, "Well, why didn't you do it?"
- And the first person provides a laundry list of excuses and rationalizations that are too long for this book.
- How many times have you heard yourself or someone else say, "I could have done better."
- And the other person says, "Well, why didn't you?"
- And the first person again adds to the laundry list.

Execution is what gets you to the numbers and next year's President's Club trip, and it makes you feel much better about yourself in the process.

Closing the gaps between knowing and doing is what this problem is all about. The gap between *believing* you know what to do and *actually* doing it and the gap between doing it *mechanically* and doing it in the *best possible way* is also what this problem is all about.

There Are Three Levels of Execution

1. You do something because you have to do it, for example, writing your monthly report, or on the personal level, going to the dentist.
2. You do something because you want to do it, for example, coaching your people, or on the personal level, taking your family on that long-promised vacation.
3. You do something because you'd be extremely frustrated if you couldn't do it, for example, building personal relationships with strategic customers, or on the personal level, playing golf every Saturday morning.

Your job as a sales manager is to get yourself and all of your people to the 3-level and close the gaps with every aspect of your job. Is that realistic? Probably not, but that's *the goal* with execution. Bottle the feeling of the Saturday-morning golf game and work to transpose it to every element of the job.

If you broke up your sales-management job into little pieces, you could put each piece on one of those three levels. So the problem becomes how to get the ones to be twos, and the twos to be threes.

How to Close the Gaps

First things first. You must make a personal commitment that you want to execute better. How do you normally make a personal decision or resolution, one that sticks? Most personal decisions and resolutions never amount to much. What makes you think this one will stick? Here are four ideas to help your execution resolution stick. First,

- Tell all your people about it, especially people who have power or authority over you, such as your boss.
- Proclaim the resolution publicly. There's nothing like standing up in front of the sales unit and laying your feelings on the line.
- Put the resolution in writing for all to see on a regular basis. Formal disclosure works wonders. A simple catchphrase, similar to "Just do it," posted everywhere, is also effective.
- Think back in your own life. What else worked for you with major resolutions? Employ those tactics.

Second, associate and build relationships with people whose personal execution is at the highest levels. They should become your new colleagues and maybe at some point your friends.

Third, place yourself within personal and professional organizations that have a reputation for execution. Longer term, if that means moving on, move.

Fourth, acquire the following behaviors that promote execution excellence.

Behavior Requisites for Execution Excellence

Aside from closing the gaps, the goal of execution excellence is to reach the limits of your God given gifts and talents. Everyone was dealt a different hand or has different limits of execution.

There are seven requisites to reach those limits. The internalization and application of these seven behaviors, at the highest possible level of intensity, can help get your execution to the 3-level and close the gaps. We've included some examples.

1. *Hard work.* The sales manager is a physical and mental investor. Sweat is not a problem. There is a willingness to engage, mix it up, to do whatever it takes, to get dirty, whatever the circumstances. Example: Neil Armstrong, Jimmy Carter, or Madeleine Albright.

2. *Hunger.* The manager has a deep desire for victory, fulfillment, achievement, or recognition. He or she is not satisfied and wants something real bad. Example: Charles Lindbergh, Roberto Goizueta, or the gold medal-winning 1980 U.S. Olympic ice-hockey team.

3. *Openness to improvement.* The manager is willing to open herself up and say, "Hey, I want help." The manager understands that she doesn't know it all, that others may have valuable insights. People who execute well are lifelong students of their profession. Example: Ted Williams, Beverly Sills, or Dave Thomas.

4. *Single-mindedness.* The sales manager can easily push away conflicting activities. There is no feeling of guilt or remorse for having missed out on something. Tunnel vision keeps other things from being obstacles. The manager understands that something else may have to suffer in the process. Example: Bill Gates or Gary Kasparov.

5. *Passion.* The sales manager has a compelling drive to do what needs to be done. No one, or no schedule, has to tell him what to do. Passion gets the manager out of bed early to do it. Passion means the manager eagerly and enthusiastically migrates to that activity. He loves what he is doing. Example: Mother Teresa, Martin Luther King, Jr., or Lee Iacocca.

6. *Maverick.* The sales manager can comfortably and confidently act independently. She is a self-reliant thinker, not risk-averse, and doesn't let the opinions of others hold her back. Any grief in the process rolls off her back. Example: Jack Welch, Harry Truman, or Tom Peters.

7. *Pride.* The manager's self-esteem doesn't let her settle for anything but the best. Execution is all about your personal standards, about what is personally acceptable. Example: Colin Powell, Meryl Streep, or Joe Montana.

These behaviors ignite top-level execution and are within everyone's reach. When you think about adopting these behaviors, think about this Oscar Wilde quote, "Moderation is a fatal thing. Nothing succeeds like excess."

Models to Learn From

Execution doesn't demand supreme gifts such as a Michael Jordan or other famous people noted above have. Execution means taking the gifts that *you were given* and pressing yourself to utilize them to the fullest, as Jordan and the others have done.

Look closer to home for models.

For example, we have a friend who is so particular and proud of her pie crusts that if the texture of the dough isn't just right she'll trash the effort, start over, and go through three or four more batches of dough until it is right. Just imagine if you and your people had that level of standard in your sales work. How many sales unit plan drafts are you willing to trash until you get it right?

What models in your personal and work life can you think of? Look at all those models, talk to them if you can, and ask why and how they are able to do the things they do in the manner they do them. Be ready to probe behind the humble responses.

Add those behaviors to your management style.

Recognize the Negative Forces that Inhibit Execution

In spite of what many of your colleagues may say about wanting you to be successful, many would just as soon have you stay and wallow with them in mediocrity.

- *Fatigue*. Example: "Julie, we've been at this for three hours, and we're all tired. We don't need to proof the proposal again."
- *Others who urge you to compromise*. Example: "Julie, why do you keep spending your time on that presentation? It looks good enough as it is."
- *Others who don't want you to leave them behind*. Example: "Julie, I left my forecast in this format. You don't need to do anything more to yours."

You can also be your own worst enemy in regard to execution excellence.

- *Fear of failure*. Example: "People will doubt my ability or lose confidence in me if this doesn't work."
- *Lack of an open mind*. Example: "I don't need anyone else's inputs. What could *they* possibly know about *my* situation."
- Lack of introspection. Example: "I know myself well enough."

Keep the seven behaviors and your personal models in your mind's eye to beat these negative forces.

Final Thought

As a sales-unit manager, one of your jobs is to get your people to improve their execution along with you. Why not put this subject on your next sales-meeting agenda.

LESSONS

Execution is the difference between grand success and missing by one percentage point. All of the requisite behaviors of execution excellence already reside inside you. All you need to do is light your spirit of execution to bring them out.

This is not really a problem. This is an opportunity. Take advantage of it.

Just do it, and do it well.

part two

TROUBLESHOOTING PLANNING AND STRATEGY PROBLEMS

2–1 THE PROBLEM:

You are unsure which markets and customers deserve attention.

THE STORY

Jim had been a successful sales manager for a few years and had just been recruited as a district sales manager for a firm in a different industry. He had been asked to take over one of the company's larger and more promising districts. It was a challenge he relished.

Unfortunately, Jim's predecessor had been unsuccessful and this plum of a district had not produced up to expectations. There was little wonder why. As Jim interviewed each of his new salespeople, he found that although each of them had a well-defined territory, there was no guidance given regarding the markets or customers to target. Direction and plans were virtually nonexistent, and customer satisfaction was at an all-time low.

Jim knew that all eyes were on him and expectations were high.

TEMPTATIONS

When you are at war (and sales *is* war), and your enemy (the competition) is coming over the horizon, you cannot have your army (your sales unit) wandering around in the forest.

Wariness

"Think I'll wait and see how things develop. This is too big to mess up. They don't expect miracles overnight."

Wait to be spoon-fed

"I'm sure the people in corporate marketing will tell me everything I need to know."

Cookie-cutter

"I'll just do the same things as the other sales managers. It will be safer that way."

With the cost of sales and marketing ammunition nowadays, there isn't a minute or a nickel to waste.

WHAT HAPPENED HERE ...?

No one knows. That's why Jim was hired for this position.

Some sales managers tend to let their people pick the low-hanging fruit and spend little time with key customers or investing in new markets. Eventually, this lack of direction and targeting will catch up to them and they will begin to fail. That may be what happened.

There could be staffing, deployment, strategy, and training issues in this district that are awesome. The potential list is almost endless. This could be one tough nut to crack.

OPTIONS

There are several options Jim could employ.

1. Jim could opt to focus on execution of *specific sales activities* in order to make a quick impact, for example, presentation skills and presentation execution.
2. He could opt to spend maximum time in the field *coaching*, passing on his exceptional skills. For example, he could concentrate on coaching questioning and closing techniques.
3. He could decide to try to improve *operationally*. For example, he could concentrate on management processes, such as pipeline, forecasting, and planning.
4. Since this is a plum situation, Jim could spend some time identifying *where* his people should concentrate their efforts to minimize wandering in the forest.

All the options are viable, but answering the where question first ensures that he will maximize the effect of all his other efforts. Where becomes a logical first step.

POSSIBLE ACTIONS

As a rule, product development loads the gun, marketing aims it, and sales fires it. It sounds as if Jim needs to work with marketing in the aiming phase of the process.

But First

It is important that Jim ensure that his top accounts are cared for in a professional manner. Therefore, the first thing he must do is identify the sales unit's top accounts. For whatever reason, in most industries, 80 percent of the total revenue for a sales unit is generated by approximately 20 percent of its customers. Jim understands the 80/20 rule and must teach it to his sales unit.

The ratio may be slightly different for Jim's team, but that's okay. Jim's task is to get his people and prior sales data together and determine the top accounts, those that generate 80 percent of the revenue. Having the salespeople participate in the effort embeds the process and the concept.

1. Stack-rank all accounts by last year's, or an average of the last two or three years', total sales (largest at the top).

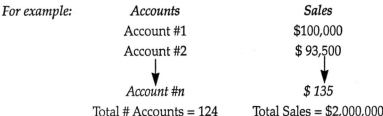

For example:

Accounts	Sales
Account #1	$100,000
Account #2	$ 93,500
Account #n	$ 135
Total # Accounts = 124	Total Sales = $2,000,000

2. Calculate 80 percent of Total Sales: $.8 \times \$2,000,000 = \$1,600,000$

3. Add the Sales column from the top of the list (Account #1) until you equal or exceed 80 percent of Total Sales. For example, assume accounts #1 to #26 = $1,680,250.

Those 26 accounts are the accounts that produced 80 percent of the business in one of the territories (26 equals 20.6 percent of 124). The process is the same in all territories.

Each salesperson now has a top-account list. If there happens to be any uncovered accounts, Jim must ensure that he has a salesperson assigned to each of them. Each of Jim's salespeople must then visit each top account and ask *at least* three questions:

1. "What do you appreciate about the way our firm meets your needs?"
2. "What open issues, or new issues, would you like us to resolve?"
3. "Are you looking at alternative suppliers of our products and services, and why?"

The answers to these questions *and any other questions* Jim deems appropriate should be submitted to him along with a simple account profile, likely available on his people's laptops.

- Account's name, business type, contacts, and major users
- Account's products and services, and how our product or service is integrated into theirs
- Key accomplishments last year
- Quantitative goals and qualitative objectives for this year, plus sales efforts in progress
- The contact(s) that provided the answers to the three or more questions

This information will allow Jim to contact the customer directly, *as needed*, and will be the beginning of a comprehensive, top-account database-and-action plan. (Referencing Problems 2–5, on planning, and 6–3, on customer retention, may provide additional ideas.)

Then, Jim has to make sure his team has a plan to address the issues identified by the three questions. This could be done in a team meeting where each team member discloses his or her customers' answers.

It is a good bet that there will be quite a bit of similarity in responses, and therefore the team can together define strategies and actions. All the salespeople should also inform

Jim and their peers how they plan to deal with those issues that are unique to their accounts.

Finally, Jim has to make sure he incorporates these action plans into his operational process and ask each salesperson to report on the plan's progress periodically. Jim should also visit every one of these accounts as soon as possible, giving priority to those that are concerned about how they are being serviced or are at risk.

> The bottom line of this exercise: *It is not only important to determine* where *attention is demanded, but* what *the attention should amount to.*

Next: New Markets and Prospects

Successful sales teams do not stop with their installed base. They aggressively open new accounts because they know that is the only avenue to long-term growth and success. The "products" are the items sold by Jim's company.

The next question Jim needs to answer is, "What markets should we attack?"

Corporate Direction

Generally speaking, corporate marketing (assuming Jim's firm has that function) will give sales teams guidance regarding where to sell. Often this information is on target but presented at a macro level and therefore limited in tactical value. The fact is, corporate marketing is not just thinking about Jim's sales team when they pull market information together. They are thinking about all of the sales teams across the company and around the world.

What Jim must do is localize the guidance and data he receives from marketing.

Segment the Market

Most often, marketing will segment a broad market into smaller submarkets. For example:

- Broad market: Health care
- Submarkets: Hospitals, clinics, and doctors offices

Use corporate's segmentation wherever possible. If you have not received segmented information, you will have to segment the market yourself. Your marketing people can be helpful in this process. Segmentation helps focus sales efforts and can save time and expense.

The Optimum Customer

Jim's next step is to define the *optimum customer* for the company's products in each segment. This is the customer with whom they would have the highest probability of closing quickly and profitably. Jim could consider the following attributes when defining this optimum customer:

- *Total revenues or whatever best "sizes" customers in his industry*: example: firms with annual revenues exceeding $50 million, or hospitals of 200 or more beds
- *Total number of employees*: example; law firms with 50 or more lawyers
- *Work performed*: example; firms that do their own machining
- *Technology*: example; firms that utilize a LAN, or Local Area Network
- *Profitability*: example; businesses that operate on gross margins of 20 percent or more
- *Competitive positioning*: example; all locations using competitor "A's" services

Optimum customers may have two or more attributes to further focus sales efforts.

Size the Segments

Jim now needs to determine *how many* optimum customers exist in his district by *market segment.* This can be done by utilizing some or all of the lists, directories, and databases that are available for the industries to whom he sells. For example:

- Dun & Bradstreet—comprehensive and most used, but least selective
- American Business Information—general business information
- Moody's—banking
- Computer Intelligence—computer industry
- Dorenfest—health care

There are many others. Jim needs to determine the best list or database for his needs. Here again, his marketing department, a marketing consultant, an independent market-research firm, associations to whom his company belongs, various government agencies, a librarian, or even a telemarketer using the Yellow Pages can be a big help.

Listen to Your Gut

Experience has taught Jim's team where and why they have been successful in the past. Those lessons must be compiled and thought must be given to how they can be replicated with optimum customers in the submarkets. This is simply a subjective braindump. Jim must write down the assessments and suggestions of his people. Oprah Winfrey puts it this way, "Follow your instincts. That's where pure wisdom manifests itself."

Gather More Information

However, the old proverb, "measure twice, cut once," also has value. Experiential information should be reinforced. It behooves the team to gather more information about the submarkets. They can do that by calling on a sampling of potential customers, using focus groups composed of customers from the three market segments, or some of the resources noted earlier. They must agree on what information they will gather. For example;

- What are the customers' needs, constraints, issues, and objectives?
- Do the products and services Jim's people offer fit? Where and why?
- What competitors are entrenched and what ones are vulnerable?

Build a Matrix

Armed with all the instinct and hard data the team should now create a simple matrix.

Products	Market Segments		
	Hospitals	*Clinics*	*Doctor's Offices*
A	Red	Green	Green
B	Green	Yellow	Yellow
C	Yellow	Red	Green
D	Green	Yellow	Red
E	Green	Green	Green
F	Red	Red	Yellow

The market segments are those that marketing provided or that analysis told Jim were sizable and worthwhile to pursue due to the number of optimum customers.

The team now needs to color in every box of the matrix.

GREEN.   Where there is a strong match between the optimum customers needs and the company's products, where there is a propensity to buy, where competitive positioning is not that strong, and all other attributes are generally favorable and leaning in Jim's direction.

YELLOW.   Where the match is there, but is not that strong or the attributes are less than favorable.

RED.   Where the match does not exist, other attributes are not favorable, or both.

Now, at a glance, Jim and his team know exactly where they must focus their time and build sales strategies to develop new business.

He now has a *process* to tell him what markets and customers deserve attention. This process of targeting new customers and markets must be frequently repeated—the rate at which Jim does it is a function of his business's strategy, its products and service offerings, and market dynamics.

LESSONS

Never forget who brought you to the dance. Your top 20 percent that produce 80 percent of your revenues must be managed and nurtured with the utmost care.

Continually invest effort in building an understanding of your markets and never be satisfied with the resources you employ to build that understanding. Keep turning the rocks for more resources and more data. Understanding permits growth. And growth is imperative to the firm's and your personal long-term success. Work closely with your marketing colleagues in that effort and ensure that your market development efforts become a continuing management process.

2-2 THE PROBLEM:

You do not know what competition is doing.

THE STORY

Sarah always made it a point to have a snappy conference call with her salespeople late every Friday afternoon. The sharing benefited the whole sales unit.

The last couple of Fridays she had noticed that the pressure from a certain competitor had suddenly escalated, inflicting increased losses on Sarah's team and causing her people to request larger-than-usual allowances to combat them.

"What are they up to?" she inquired.

"I don't know." "I can't tell." "I haven't figured it out yet." "They're messing around with my good customers." And so it went around the horn.

"For crying out loud, you can't tell me we don't know *anything*," Sarah countered.

This is crazy, I can't tolerate this, she thought to herself after the call.

TEMPTATIONS

When the bad guys start doing stuff and having an impact that you don't understand, it is easy to get goosey and jumpy.

Allege foul play

"They're obviously not playing fair, or must be engaged in an illegal business practice."

Strike blindly

"I'll discount so deep that they'll have to buy the business."

> *Attack someone*
> "The clowns in marketing should have forewarned us, but as usual, they're asleep."

Competition loves senseless responses. It feeds their egos and their cash flow.

WHAT HAPPENED HERE . . . ?

You flat-out don't know. Admission of that fact is the best answer right now.

Sarah's loss rate has increased to a point where it is beginning to hurt. At least she is fortunate that she has a miniprocess, the conference call, to catch these happenings early.

Maybe this is a new competitor on the scene, and Sarah's people have not had time to create counter strategies. Or, maybe, they have not taken this player seriously enough.

The competitor could be under new aggressive leadership, and an array of changes in strategy, pricing, products and services, promotion, customer service, and other sales and marketing variables could have been launched under Sarah's unsuspecting nose. Possibly an old competitor has learned some new tricks.

It could be that Sarah's products are not as competitive in the industry as they once were. It has been said that when this occurs, *real selling* must begin.

Sarah's people could be losing because they have become complacent. Complacency can creep up on a sales unit insidiously if its products have enjoyed a significant competitive advantage in the past.

Sarah may have neglected competitive training. She may not have taught her people that proactive competitive information gathering is essential or coached them on all the tricks associated with intelligence collection.

OPTIONS

This is a two-edged sword. On one edge, Sarah doesn't know what her competition is doing, so she has *no options* other than to find out—*fast*.

On the other edge, she has to reverse the slide immediately in spite of little or no information.

POSSIBLE ACTIONS

What you don't know can hurt you.

Why Do You Need to Understand Competitive Messages and Actions?

Competitive information is imperative. You can't formulate strategies and plans, differentiate yourself, combat hostile approaches, or challenge and refute claims about something you don't know. And you certainly can't make the numbers. It seems obvious, but it's oft forgotten.

Get Your Heads Together

You must have a plan.

Competitive intelligence gathering is a corporate matter, not just a sales-organization matter. However, that doesn't mean you should wait to be spoon-fed. Salespeople have their eyes, ears, and laptops closer to the market than anyone, just as people in other functions are privy to some hot competitive info through their own contacts.

Get together people from sales, marketing communications, market development, services marketing, product development, MIS, customer service, and other functions that have access to competitive information. Brainstorm ideas on "who" will gather "what" from "where" and "how" it will be compiled, assessed, distributed, and utilized. Agree on competitive info-gathering objectives and plans and how they will fit into everyone's management processes. Appoint leadership and meet regularly to assess results and challenge yourselves to continually do better. Following are four key elements of your plan.

1. *Management process.* Scrutinize your sales-management process top-down, from the corporate suite to the street, because competitive-information gathering is a subset of the process. Competitive-information gathering will be only as strong as your overall sales-management processes.

Front-line sales managers should regularly receive guidance from up top on what competitive questions to ask salespeople during pipeline or other operational reviews and add their own experience-based questions. Ask salespeople to submit articles, ads, literature, quotes, and any other material they can gather as a part of their periodic reports. Utilize your sales-force automation package to gather and submit information on a real-time basis. Hold your people more accountable and tighten the overall process. Sarah had a process, but it may not have been thorough or demanding enough.

Your management process must also include comprehensive loss reviews. Every loss to a competitor is an opportunity to learn and must be viewed by all in that context. Do not whip your people with a loss report. It might be the last one you get.

2. *Wage war.* Make competition expose themselves. (Remember, this is a two-edged sword.) The best competitive information-gathering systems are offensive, going into the holes after competition, not sitting idly by waiting to pick up scraps of information. Attack competitors' installed base with a well-planned campaign. You will learn about the competitors and keep them occupied at the same time. You will also win some business and have some fun in the process. Katharine Hepburn said, "Enemies are so stimulating," and that is exactly the point of this effort.

3. *Ask your customers.* Relationships transcend competition—*almost* all the time.

In many cases, it is both appropriate and wise to interview customers. Many will take the time to tell you who has approached them and detail a near miss you experienced. Expect the candor in these situations to vary. Customers can help, *but* . . . overly intrusive searching for information implies fear and trepidation. Be careful you don't send those signals.

4. *Fine-tune your tactics.* Make it a sales-unit exercise to discuss and expand the following list.

- Read competitors' ads in local and national periodicals, closely watch their ads on TV, and carefully listen to the ones on the radio. Their salespeople are being told to emphasize the same messages that the ads contain. Marketing messages are consistent. You can count on it. Therefore, you can prepare responses. For example: If ads say, "Call our local office for a demonstration," you can bet that the competitive salespeople are concentrating on giving demonstrations and have received extra training on demo skills. Your response may become one of sharpening your own demo skills.
- Study what your competitors are saying and emphasizing at trade shows and exhibitions. Whatever they showcase is what you can expect to see in the field and in the stores.
- Your people probably run into competitive salespeople by accident. Where were they observed, what were they doing, what were they carrying, and what other impressions did they make? Those can be valuable signals.
- Buy a single share of stock in a competitor. You will get all the info you ever wanted. A cheaper way is to talk to your broker, call their PR office, go to the library, or call-up their website.
- Look at product displays and point-of-purchase displays in stores. Their content, placement, graphics, and words are your competition.
- Some prospects will offer competitive proposals or quotations for your review, but expect that in some cases your quotes will be shown with equal ease.
- Search out disgruntled competitive customers. They are a wealth of information.
- Certain consumer reports and industry periodicals compare products. Read the comparisons and prepare answers.
- Keep a close eye on all the display want ads in the paper. They provide early warning of what your competitors are planning. Look at ads for *all* positions, not just sales. New people bring new ideas and foster changes.
- Appoint someone in the sales unit to regularly play "adversary" for each major competitor at meetings and during strategy sessions. Employ the intensity of the *Top Gun* movie.
- Train your people intensively on the competition's products, services, and strategies. Knowledge begets more questions. Don't get complacent because you're #1.

Practice Makes Perfect

Are you familiar with the simple computer matrix game called Minesweeper that asks you to find hidden "mines" without blowing yourself up? If you've ever played it, you've probably noticed that practice makes you better. Competitors lie hidden the same way. Constant probing for competitors by your entire sales unit will expose tendencies in the competition the same way a Minesweeper player discovers tendencies with mine placements.

If Competition Is Smart

Competition will do things quickly, with little or no forewarning and then change approaches again before you have the ability to respond to the first attack. Your information-gathering and management processes therefore must be constant and dynamic to enable you to react.

The Dark Side

Don't be naive and believe that everybody plays by the rules. Some firms have espionage programs, although no one would ever call them that or ever admit to them. Now that competition is global, vigilance is more important than ever, because the business practices in many places are ruthless. There are people from all over the world who are hungry for information about your firm and its products and technologies. Piracy is a fact of business life. Departing executives vacuum files. Never forget that there are two sides to competitive intelligence gathering. Do not assume that you are immune from attack.

It is easy to cross the boundary from aggressive intelligence gathering to questionable and unlawful practices. Keep everyone on the right side of the line. A regular review of do's and don'ts and corporate practices with your in-house counsel or outside attorney is time well spent.

A Final Warning

Arrogance and complacency are fatal diseases. Don't ever feel so confident about yourself that you slough off worrying about competition or look only at their warts. Remember that the seeds of destruction are sown in self-satisfaction in the best of times.

LESSONS

Competitive information gathering is drudgery and hard work. It is one of the first things forgotten in the midst of day-to-day pressures, so it takes resolute leadership and management-process discipline to keep it from slipping.

Salespeople or sales managers who have little or no competitive information to contribute don't have a full understanding of their role. It cannot be assumed that salespeople know how or where to look for competitive information. Train them where and how to look.

Training on competitive products, services, and strategies must be comprehensive and continuous.

Competitive information gathering is a challenge to management and sales rep integrity that must be regularly counseled and managed.

2-3 THE PROBLEM:

You are wrestling with deployment options and decisions.

THE STORY

Maxine was a new division sales manager assigned to cover geography never adequately managed. The division's responsibilities included rural and urban areas, heavy industrial pockets, light manufacturing, high tech, and transportation hubs. A hodgepodge.

She had inherited 14 people of various tenure, talents, and titles. The competition was active and well entrenched, and the market share was well below company targets.

The company had not been pleased with the results coming out of this area for some time, which is why Maxine was put in the position. She had been told to take whatever actions she felt were prudent and profit enriching. Part of the analysis and plan she set for herself was to take a look at deployment.

TEMPTATIONS

This is a problem that is often masked. Managers see performance issues and attack visible and traditional targets without looking under the rocks. Looking for real causes and opportunities should keep you from these temptations.

Throw darts

"I'll spread everybody out to make sure we're covering all the bases and all the turf."

Kick butt

"What we need here is an iron hand and some accountability."

Corporate lock-step

"I'll do what the rest of the corporation is doing; it seems safe, and it seems to be working." or "Who am *I* to suggest anything different?"

Deployment is one of your major decisions. Where—and how—you put your people on the sales playing field can have a huge impact on your results.

WHAT HAPPENED HERE . . . ?

Maxine got thrown into a situation like thousands of other sales managers and is faced with a simultaneous problem and opportunity. No one starts with a clean slate, unless you are fortunate to be dealing with a brand-new business and a brand-new product.

Competitive pressures, pricing and margin erosion, customer turnover and sales personnel turnover, customer complaints, a high cost of sales, stagnant productivity, and market-share decline are all signals that you should review, and possibly revamp, your deployment scheme.

OPTIONS

The problem is how to place your finite resources for optimal results. You have X number of people with different skills and experience and you must array them for the best possible effect. At one end of the deployment spectrum you can take a homogeneous approach to deployment, and at the other end of the spectrum you can take a microdeployment approach. There are many options in between.

Microdeployment is breaking up your area of responsibility into the smallest number of differentiated pieces and matching your people to those microsegments for the purpose of differentiation and fulfilling customer expectations to the fullest. Customers place a premium on organizations who thoughtfully deploy their people in order to optimally solve their problems. Microdeployment is attractive, but it is cost prohibitive to all but those with the deepest pockets.

Here are common deployment options, with some strengths and weaknesses.

- Deployment by the *size* of customers is common. Examples of this approach include international-account, national-account, and major-account programs where the biggest, most complicated multilocation customers get special attention.

    +'s: This is a well-proven sales concept. Customers appreciate the coordination, customization, and total value possible with these programs. Volume and share growth accrue to well-run programs. The highest-level relationships are possible.

    -'s: The lack of commitment from top management, poorly designed compensation programs, a lack of coordination and communication, a lack of role definition of the participants, and parochial management can be major roadblocks. Pricing and margin erosion is also likely because of both customer demands for the best deals, and competitive pressure because these customers represent huge chunks of business. These programs require strong team-oriented management.

- You can deploy by *types of customers,* or what is termed vertical selling. Vertical selling is the assignment of your salespeople to specific industries, markets, or customer classes. For example, a salesperson or a sales team would concentrate on telecommunications customers, on financial-services customers, or on agribusiness customers within a certain area.

+'s: Customers like this approach because salespeople possess broad and deep knowledge of their business, their processes and problems, and applications of your products and services. The credibility of these sellers is high, and the sellers are also highly motivated because they know they are expert at what they do.

-'s: The cost of knowledge training and skill development can be high, unless you recruit from the vertical markets. Your flexibility in moving your people around is limited, and recruiting can be time consuming and expensive.

- You can deploy your people resources with a combination of *specialists* and *generalists*. A small percentage of your people can be made into experts, or specialists with certain products, technologies, or customer types to support the generalists. This approach works well with very complex products, services, and technologies, and where there are multiple product lines.

  +'s: This is a proven concept where specialist resources can operate from both headquarters and the field, supporting hot spots of opportunity. Customers benefit from expertise and solutions on an as-needed basis.

  -'s: The cost of specialists may be prohibitive and compensation-plan design can be tricky. The specialist's planning and time utilization must be monitored closely. Customers may develop a poor impression of the generalist because of diminished perceived value. Roles can get to be confusing. The specialist's understanding of individual customer needs is limited, so there must be close cooperation and communication between the generalist and the specialist in account planning.

- You can deploy by *teams*. Team selling is selling and servicing a customer with more than one person. Teams can be made up of various sales, service, technical, credit, design, and production people. The teaming potential is not limited and includes teaming with allied vendors and sales partners.

  +'s: Customers like teams because they imply strength, and they get questions and issues answered quickly. Groups can unearth problems, offer solutions, and build a network of relationships that no individual could. And buyers are now *buying* as teams.

  -'s: Customers may see all the people as extra costs, and the makeup of a team requires deft decision making. Team selling can confuse customers if roles are not defined. There is the potential for redundancies, which are perceived as waste. Compensation plans are a challenge to create and manage.

- You can consider deploying some of your resources *inside as a telesales* function.

  +'s: This is a highly effective deployment option for prospecting, providing a technical-support hotline, and conducting customer surveys. It works well with simple or commodity products, and with after-sale parts-and-supplies sales. The approach also lets you start your new hires inside to develop their business and product knowledge. This can be a cost-effective deployment, permitting you to focus your outside people.

-'s: The approach is impersonal, although relationships can be built if the same people regularly contact the same customers. Lack of coordination between the inside and the outside staff can lead to confusion. Roles and responsibilities must be well defined. Telesales, or telemarketing, has been abused through low levels of professionalism and can also be viewed as intrusive by many customers.

- You can deploy by *geography*, assigning salespeople to buildings, towns, cities, counties, states, regions, and countries. Geographical deployment works well with commodity or simple products or where you have a finite number of customers widely dispersed. Databases and computer mapping tools are now available to help with these decisions.

  +'s: This is a well-proven deployment scheme that is easy to manage. The option ensures that you're covering all the turf. It is easy to spot weak territories and weak reps.

  -'s: It takes constant review of the market because businesses move and growth rates vary by area, so there is a need to regularly shift boundaries to keep everyone in balance. The sales manager must be very active in the field.

- You can deploy your people by the *number of customers* they are responsible for managing. It is a simple approach that can work well with many commodity and consumer products. Experience may have proven to you that a good rep should be able to handle X number of customers. Databases and computer-mapping tools are also useful for this scheme.

  +'s: You can vary the number of customers, creating smaller or larger territories, using the smaller ones for new reps and the bigger ones for experienced reps. Productivity measurements are easier, and it is easy to spot weak territories and weak reps.

  -'s: There is no provision for special attention or application of expertise. The sales manager usually fills that role.

- You can deploy by *prospects versus existing customers*. The "hunters-versus-farmers" approach is common. Some salespeople are better at, and enjoy, digging for new customers. The thrill of the hunt is rewarding. Other sales types are more people oriented and are better suited to tilling the relationship and growing and maintaining the business.

  +'s: This approach permits you to maximize your sales talents. Many salespeople like it. You can grow markets and businesses more quickly, and customer retention is likely to be higher.

  -'s: You don't have a continuous relationship. You need a simultaneously firm and flexible criteria for handover of the new business, and the handoff still has the potential of being clumsy, and the customer may feel manipulated in the process. Two different compensation methodologies must be compatible and fair. You don't broaden or completely develop your people when you use this scheme. Some salespeople may see the approach as personally limiting and abusing. High turnover is possible.

- Deploying your people *by products* enables you to have some folks selling certain products, and some folks selling other products. This approach works well where a supplier has a few highly differentiated product lines or services.

  +'s: Customers appreciate the special in-depth knowledge that salespeople possess. In situations where the customer contacts are very technical, comprehensive product and technology know-how is effective.

  -'s: You may have two or more people calling on the same customers at the same locations. The customer may view the redundancy as wasteful and costly. Your T&L and personnel costs will likely be higher.

- The usage of *sales partners* is a marketing as well as a sales-management decision. Sales partners are wholesale distributors, VARs (Value-Added Resellers), dealers, retailers, and independent sales agencies. This is an attractive option that goes beyond the deployment choices with your own people, but is included here because you and your people will be managing the sales partners.

  +'s: Sales partners possess detailed local market and customer knowledge and product expertise. They can supply a level of support and responsiveness impossible to achieve by the supplier, can add value and services, sell from inventory, and can reduce your cost of sales. Sales partners are particularly effective with simpler products, in developing markets, and internationally. This option also moves sales costs from the fixed line to the variable line.

  -'s: You can't control independent sales partners as you can a direct sales force. You have less understanding of the final market and customer, and your margins are lower.

- Finally, a hybrid deployment is an option. This is the use of two or more of these deployment schemes. This is very common. The more hybrid you become, the closer you get to microdeployment.

  +'s: This approach does the best job of satisfying customers.

  -'s: The hybrid approach is the most difficult to manage because it is the most complex. Higher-priced sales managers require broader and deeper skills.

There are other marketing alternatives to get to the customer, such as the Internet and direct mail, but our problem addresses personal selling options.

POSSIBLE ACTIONS

Initial Understanding

Your goals and objectives must be clear, particularly the long-term ones. Deployment decisions must be made for the long term because redeployment is often difficult and costly. Sales-deployment strategies should also be consistent and supportive of overall corporate-marketing strategies.

You must have a thorough understanding of your constraints. What are your expense limits? How many people are you currently allocated, and how many are you likely to have down the road? How much support is available in terms of computer and communications technologies, and office, warehouse, floor-space, and other resources?

Consider how your competitors deploy their people. They may or may not be doing it well. *Deployment is an opportunity to differentiate yourself.*

Deployment decisions benefit from a group approach. Always approach and solve this problem as a management team. Marketing can be particularly helpful with these decisions. The following simplified thought processes are intended to encourage analysis.

THOUGHT PROCESS #1: Identify the primary values of your customers. Based on the strengths and weaknesses of various deployment options, which deployment option do you think can best meet important values of *your* customers? Develop a matrix to make some judgmental fits. For example, if product knowledge is critical to your customer, is one deployment option clearly better than others?

THOUGHT PROCESS #2: Execute an analysis of the strengths, weaknesses, and potential of all your direct reports. Potential is the key. What is your assessment of the responsibilities your people can *grow* into handling, given the necessary coaching and training? Does this analysis give you any ideas? In what deployment option would each of your people fit best? For example, if you have a couple of reps who are engineers, could they be support specialists, helping the generalists?

THOUGHT PROCESS #3: Break your sales process and transaction process down into finite steps. Ask yourself what deployment option, or person, can best meet each step. The same person doesn't have to handle every step. Does this give you any ideas? For example, if a key part of your sales process is writing and presenting a proposal, can you turn one or two people into inside sales-support staff concentrating on writing proposals?

THOUGHT PROCESS #4: Cost out your options, even if they are just estimates. Get help from your marketing and financial staff. This analysis will help you understand the profitability associated with each deployment option.

There is an analytical element to sales management, and these thought processes are just meant to stir your thinking. Analysis will strengthen your decision making.

Execution

Deployment moves can be disruptive. Detailed implementation plans and training, not only within the sales unit, but with every department that is touched by sales activities and actions, are necessary. You will find in actual practice that you will *transition* into new deployment schemes, not jump into them. Deployment actions take time. Be ready to accept modifications in form and in kind as you go forward with your implementation.

Track results and measure the impact of deployment changes.

LESSONS

Customer values and needs change, competition and markets evolve, and new technologies emerge. Just as in sports, always think about moving your players to more advantageous positions because of changes in the environment. Deployment decisions are always unfinished.

Deployment engineering is like widening an existing highway. Sales, or traffic, must still flow while you're in the construction process.

Consider *all* your options. Don't stick with an option simply because you personally are comfortable managing that option. Push your own personal boundaries.

Creative deployment is one of the best ways to squeeze incremental market shares from places where there doesn't seem to be any more potential.

Create an expectation among your people that deployments are fluid, not cut in stone. It makes future modifications easier.

Don't walk into management assignments with deployment options fixed in your mind. Give yourself time to understand your customers, markets, and staff.

2-4 THE PROBLEM:

You do not have an effective, differentiating sales-unit strategy.

THE STORY

Roger was in the midst of his monthly sales meeting. The agenda was unfolding nicely, and Roger's boss was in attendance, thoroughly enjoying the give-and-take.

Just prior to the meeting breakup, Thornton, an eager, bright-eyed sales trainee, who had just returned from basic sales training at corporate headquarters, asked his first question of the day. "Roger," he asked cautiously, "what is our unit's sales strategy for the next period?" Everyone in the room, particularly Roger's boss, turned and leaned forward to hear Roger's wisdom. Roger paused, gathered his thoughts, and spoke, ". . . ."

At the end of the meeting, Roger's boss stopped him and gave him a unsettling head nod for the feeble answer to Thornton's question. Nothing further needed to be said.

TEMPTATIONS

Strategy is the horse your sales unit is going to ride to the winner's circle. Your people are looking for direction and leadership in this regard. Be careful of the following traps.

> *Miss the point*
>
> "Yes, splendid point, Thornton. Our strategy is to close harder and more often."
>
> *Huff and puff*
>
> "Our strategy is to *win*! We're the best sales unit in the division, and we're going to blow everyone's doors off."
>
> *Smoke and mirrors*
>
> "We'll be using a benchmarking matrix in conjunction with our quality deployment hierarchy and the cognitive dissonance associated with the parameter estimates."

Here is a better response and starting point: "The essence of strategy is choosing to perform activities differently than rivals do," Michael Porter, Harvard Business School.

WHAT HAPPENED HERE . . . ?

You were unprepared and caught off guard. It happens all the time.

Face it, Roger doesn't have a strategy, and if it were inspiring or effective he would be proud of it, and he would have belted it out.

Other signs that a sales manager doesn't have an inspiring or effective sales unit strategy include the following:

1. The unit's results are weak or below expectations.
2. The manager has no written sales-unit plan, or has a plan that is disorganized and not utilized.
3. The manager is not sleeping well, worrying about competition and worrying about his job.
4. The unit's activities are shot-gunned. The sales unit is splattering the countryside and customers with random activities.
5. Other people characterize the sales unit as reactionary. There is little proactive focus.
6. The sales unit's members seem to be drifting independently of each other.
7. The manager and his people are frazzled, always tired, or bellyaching.

Perhaps Roger's personal expectations are modest. Sales leaders who don't desire to excel typically don't have unit strategies.

Roger may not understand what a sales unit strategy is and why it is important, or he just can't think of one. Perhaps he may think that he needs something grand, or he's looking for something unrealistically creative. He may be caught up in an activity trap, believing a lot of activity is the sole key to results.

Perhaps Roger is not aware of the sheer power of effective sales-unit strategies, or no one ever trained or coached him on the subject.

Maybe Roger's manager never suggested the need for a strategy. Some sales-management goal sheets unfortunately don't spell out strategy development as a requisite.

OPTIONS

There are two interrelated problems here. One, Roger may not have a strategy in the first place. And two, if he did have one, it's not inspiring or effective.

He has two options.

1. Leave well enough alone and continue as he is.
2. Create a break-out, bust-it-open sales-unit strategy. His choice is obvious.

POSSIBLE ACTIONS

Roger must first make sure he clearly understands his firm's business and marketing strategies and the sales-unit strategy of his immediate manager. Strategies cascade down the organization. Roger's efforts must be *consistent* with those above him. Consistency does not mean sameness. *Consistency means that his sales unit's strategy reinforces and complements their efforts.*

Why Do You Need a Strategy?

You need to *focus* the sales unit and provide *direction* to exceed plan while staying within your expense and resource constraints.

A Definition

A sales-unit strategy is a central theme or emphasis around which you gather your people. It is a rallying point, a focal point of activity, or a focus of sales-unit firepower. It is a concrete activity, skill, or attitude that is emphasized to win business.

It is not philosophy or a mission statement.

A strategy is a simple statement—a phrase, a couple of sentences—easy to grasp and easy to memorize. It is something the sales unit will lean on.

Sales strategies often flow from a company's unique strengths or resources, or the special skills and knowledge of the sales-management team.

Here are some examples.

- "The sales team strategy is to jointly develop sales proposals with our many small original equipment manufacturers (OEMs) who lack these particular skills in satisfying their customers. Our efforts support our business strategy to emphasize the partnering relationship with our OEMs."

- "The group's sales strategy is in-depth product knowledge and technical expertise. By acting as consultants we meet our customers' need for information and leverage our business's unique technologies."
- "Our sales-unit strategy is to take advantage of our factory automation and quality processes by bringing as many prospects on factory visits as possible. We know that when prospects see our capabilities it impresses them, and they then choose to buy from us."

Those three examples follow the success formula.

The Formula

An effective sales-unit strategy that focuses people's energy and brings in the business is based on the 3D formula: *Differentiation, Dominance,* and *Demand.*

DIFFERENTIATION.   Differentiation means that you are filling a gap or niche not covered by the competition or your peers. Or, you are doing *something* at a level of intensity or level of uniqueness that they are not doing, or cannot match. You are making your sales approach look different from any other supplier, and that difference can be preserved.

Differentiation implies that *you understand* competition's activities so that you can perform activities differently. There is no sense creating and executing a strategy that replicates competition.

DOMINANCE.   Dominance means you execute your differentiation *so well* that you rule or control by superior power. You rise above everyone else. You execute a sales activity at a level of professionalism that gains you a regional, national, or international reputation. Dominance implies the highest level of sales-effort quality. You are a recognized expert.

DEMAND.   What you choose to dominate, and how you choose to differentiate yourself, must be important to customers, clients, and sales partners. The strategy must meet *demand.* It must have value for the customer. It must be appreciated. That's why it is important to have an in-depth understanding of what is important to your customers, clients, and sales partners.

More strategy examples that meet the 3D criteria.

- "My sales unit's strategy is to give the most comprehensive product demonstrations because customers value the demos. By doing so, we will differentiate ourselves in the industry."

    This sales strategy could complement a marketing strategy based on product capabilities.
- "Our sales-unit strategy is to be known for our courtesy and civility to customers. Our customers demand it, and by being more courteous than anyone else, we will differentiate ourselves on the floor."

This sales strategy could complement a corporate strategy based on customer service.

- "The sales team's strategy is to give benchmark presentations because buying teams make the decisions in our industry, and they demand comprehensiveness."

  This sales strategy could complement a marketing strategy based on corporate image.

- "Our sales-unit strategy is to utilize state-of-the-art sales-force automation technology in order to meet our customers' demand for information."

  This sales strategy could complement a business strategy based on speed.

In each of these examples, the sales manager knows that his or her strategic focus is in *demand*, that the unit intends to *dominate* with a certain activity, and that this activity will *differentiate* the sales unit from competition. He or she also knows the sales unit is consistent with the company. Sales units can have more than one strategy, but they should all follow the same formula.

Approaches

Here are some suggestions to stimulate your strategic thinking and aid you in developing a strategy and keeping it inspiring and effective.

1. Look at every step of your sales cycle. Is there *one* step in which you can dominate? Is it possible to add style, flair, or small touches that differentiate a certain step?
2. Copy a strategy from another industry. Look for a winning sales strategy in another venue.
3. Talk to marketing. Marketing people are good at strategy development.
4. Look at the commercials on TV and read the ads in magazines and trade journals. Look for the strategy within the messages. Many are obvious; some are subtle.
5. Buy a book on business or marketing strategy.
6. Read the business section of your local newspaper and read the business dailies looking for the strategies in the success stories.
7. Shop, even if you're not in consumer products. Cruise the malls and superstores and look for the strategy behind the way people promote, merchandise, and sell.
8. As hard as it can sometimes be, listen to the telemarketers that call and try to understand the strategies behind their scripts.
9. Read your junk mail. It's not junk. It's loaded with strategic ideas you can borrow.
10. Talk to your boss and ask about his or her strategy. Make sure you understand it.

This problem is not meant to be solved by you as an individual. Put the subject on the agenda of your next sales-unit meeting. Get the whole team involved in the creative process.

LESSONS

A sales strategy alone cannot carry the day. It is a key to open the door. You still have to walk through it.

A strategy should be so simple and so focused as to be unmistaken by anyone. Strategies that have to be explained in great detail or be backed up with data, charts, and graphs are not strategies, they are behavioral rationalizations.

The 3D formula never changes, but your market segments, customers, clients, and sales-channel partners are in flux. Your company's products, services, and technologies change. Your company's resources, finances, infrastructure, and people change. Competition changes. As a result, you always need to be rethinking your strategies. Modify your strategies because of what's going on around you, not because someone told you to do so.

You'll know you have an effective strategy when all of your people clearly articulate and crisply execute the sales unit's strategy, you begin receiving compliments from peers, executive management comes to visit you, and your results go through the roof.

2–5 THE PROBLEM:

You've been told your sales plans are inadequate.

THE STORY

Tracy walked into her office on Monday morning and found her district's sales plan for the next reporting period back on her desk. It was loaded with red marks. "This is not complete." "Give me more." "Doesn't meet our challenges." "Please resubmit next Monday."

It knocked the wind out of her sails. She was disappointed—and mad. She had other plans for this week. Fun stuff. As she looked through the document she could see that Alex, her GM, had really chopped it up.

Now, what was she going to do, she agonized.

TEMPTATIONS

Planning is a sales management core competency. Don't surrender to any of these impulsive temptations.

Make up a story
"Alex, I gave this to one of my people as a management-development exercise. I should have told you that. I'll take it from here."

Embellish

"I'll just throw in a few words and numbers here and there and get back to real work."

Feint a higher priority

"Alex, we're in the middle of that big RFQ [Request-for-Quotation]. Can I get back on this at the end of the month? You don't want us to blow this big deal, do you?"

Virtually all sales managers seem to have a resistance to paperwork, but plans are not paperwork. Better to think of them as intellectual roadmaps.

WHAT HAPPENED HERE . . . ?

Tracy may have thought that sales plans were meant for the drawer. Possibly no one had ever scrutinized her plans before.

Tracy may have believed that this planning business is just a top-management exercise.

A new top executive may have surprised everyone with new planning expectations, or maybe Tracy never worked for a manager who valued planning. Her boss's management style may be different from hers.

Perhaps she thought that only the numbers matter. Maybe no one ever taught her how to write plans, or she never witnessed the correlation between great plans and great results.

Perhaps, like some sales managers, Tracy just doesn't like to write, or can't type, or is intimidated by her PC. She may be saying to herself, 'They're paying me for coaching and selling, not for writing. She may not understand that planning is strategic and tactical thinking, not writing. Planning is an intellectual exercise, not a mechanical exercise.

Any or all of the above may be at play here. Do they sound familiar?

OPTIONS

Tracy has three options.

1. She has a due date. She can fix the sales plan, fully answering Alex's questions, giving it the time and attention it deserves.

2. Another option is to stop everything and nail it. Create a picture-perfect plan. But starting from scratch may not be a viable option because of the time constraint.

3. A third option is a combination of the two. Do the best possible job in the time remaining, but then come back to Alex with a totally updated plan after you've had time to talk to your people, other staff members, and to really study the matter.

Sales planning is a learned skill. Managers who are naturally comfortable with problem solving, creativity, and organization are usually comfortable with it, but it's something everyone can master. If you're serious about a career in management—any kind of management—it is worthwhile to sharpen this skill. It does have a very positive effect on promotability.

POSSIBLE ACTIONS

Calm down. Rearrange the calendar. It's time to get to work.

A Personal Assessment

Think about what you did. Ask yourself what's good or bad, aside from what Alex pointed out. If you're honest, you'll agree with the critique. You'll know where you tried to cut corners and where else you can make improvements. All plans can benefit from a second chance.

Get Clarification

Go back and ask for more details. Ask Alex to share an outline or a model. See if you can uncover further expectations. Probe. Perhaps Alex will share another manager's effort or a past plan of his own. The interchange will provide ideas and focus and will improve the end product.

Use Your Resources

Other sales managers in your organization may have ideas. You could even meet as a team if they are having the same problem. Perhaps a colleague in marketing or finance will share some tips. Additionally, there are some great paperback books on writing business and marketing plans, and they're not expensive. Invest in a few and look up the section on sales plans, often hidden within the marketing section. Take the same approach with a book on sales management.

Don't Forget "Flow"

Plans can be written only *after* you have your sales goals in hand and *after* you have a strategy in mind. That sequence is imperative. Goals and strategy will obviously appear in your plan.

Get Your Team Involved

A sales manager should always get the inputs of staff members. Ask for their ideas while sharing the following characteristics of effective sales plans. You could also delegate select portions of your plan for them to create and have them submit their own sales plan in a format consistent with yours. That's always a good idea, but if you do that, *coach them* on their planning.

Characteristics of the Best Sales-unit Plans

Sales-unit plans should be personal. There are no hard-and-fast rules, but we do strongly suggest some proven *format, content,* and *style* ideas that you can integrate into your plans. The following apply at all sales-management levels.

1. SUGGESTED FORMAT.   Matrices filled with bullets work well with sales-unit plans. The format encourages conciseness, and it is easily upgradeable and easy to work from. A matrix can be created for each major objective or goal. Each objective should highlight the who, what, where, when, why, how, how much, and results expected. A matrix is customizable and readable and can be kept in your PC or laptop. Here is a simple example:

Statement of Major Objective or Goal

Description of activity	Rationale	Timing	Responsibility	Issues	Resources needed	Costs/ expense	Expected results
Sub-activity A							
Sub-activity B							

Not every element of a plan can be in this format, but matrices can be the dominant format. Remember, planning is thinking, not writing. Generate the key thoughts first.

2. SUGGESTED CONTENT.   The following major sections are requisites. The detailed topics in each section can vary widely. This list is meant to stimulate thinking. Even with matrices forming a major portion of your plan, there are places where your judgment will suggest written material. Also, with many topics, detailed attachments are apropos, so we've put a * with subjects where attachments would be helpful. Priorities will vary by firm, so possible content is listed alphabetically.

Executive Summary

The executive summary is the last part of the plan to be written. In five to ten sentences it should convey the situation, goals, objectives, strategies, and key activities.

Analysis

Analyze subjects that apply to your business. Describe the current status and potential impacts of these items

- The economy
- Your industry
- Trends
- Key political issues
- Your markets
- New technologies
- Key legislative issues
- Strengths and weaknesses
- Competition
- Currency valuations
- Environmental issues
- Obstacles and threats

Communications

Describe communications vehicles you will use and show samples, agendas, and formats, if possible. Discuss communications policies both inside and outside your business.

- Sales meetings
- Newsletters
- E-mail and voice mail
- Planned special guests
- Video conferencing
- Bulletins
- Informal team building activities

Compensation

This is a complex area and usually deserves a *separate* plan. It is included here as a reminder of its importance.

- The Basic Plan*: Describe strategy, format, and administration.
- Incentives: Discuss commissions, bonuses, draws, and other variables.
- Long-term rewards: Discuss equity, stock options, savings programs, and others.
- Plan revisions: State how effectiveness will be monitored and exceptions managed.

Controls

This is a description of the tools and processes you will use to monitor performance and how and when they will be utilized. Sample formats make good attachments with most of these items.

- Business reviews*
- Performance reviews*
- Contingency handling
- Individual plans*
- Business indicators that will be monitored
- Pipeline reviews and management*
- Regular sales-plan updating
- Forecast*
- TQM process integration
- Sales process audits
- Other management processes
- Quarterly, monthly, weekly reports*

Customers

This is a description of the customer/client base, with their priorities and issues

- Major customer classes and segments and subsegments
- Beta sites, collaborative customer sites, or trial accounts
- Major-account identification and plan
- National-account identification and plan
- Vertical markets
- Customer-retention plan
- At-risk accounts
- New-customer plans

Expenses

A detailed layout of all costs associated with your sales unit

- Operating budgets, by line item*
- Budgets by sub-units or individuals*
- Capitol expenditures*
- Reporting processes
- Spending authorizations and control mechanisms

Inter-Team Teamwork

Detail who and how you and your people will integrate these resources into your sales activities.

- Technical service
- Physical distribution
- MIS or IT management
- Product-business groups
- Executive management
- Accounts receivable

- Telesales
- The factory
- Human resources
- Credit management
- Software development

- Customer service
- Inside sales-support staff
- Marketing
- Product engineering
- Quality management

Organization

Steps you will take to build and strengthen your organization and your people. (Attach an organization chart.)

- New hires planned or anticipated
- Deployment plan
- Training of all types
- Your personal development plan

- New-hire criteria and search processes
- Performance-problem management
- Job responsibilities and roles
- High-potential employee management

Recognition/rewards

Actions you will take to recognize individuals, subunits, and the sales unit.

- Management awards
- Special incentives
- Performance awards
- President's Club or other corporate recognition

- Perks
- Commendations
- Teamwork awards

Results

Items that you will measure against goals or objectives—on a daily, weekly, monthly, quarterly, or annual basis.

- Revenue*
- Sales*
- Market shares*
- Key sales activities
- Qualitative goals and objectives
- Orders*
- Profitability*
- Inventories*
- Products, product lines, or SKU* performance
- Bookings*
- Margins*
- Returns*

Sales Partners

Actions you will take to improve coordination and results with your sales partners.

- Selection processes and planned additions.
- Support programs
- Contracts or agreements
- Training
- Communication programs
- Policy generation and enforcement
- Costs, margins, and terms
- Terminations

Selling

Describe major activities that will bring in the business.

- Presentation formats and guidelines
- Special targeted contacts and level of contact
- Procedures for RFQs and RFPs
- Lead management program
- Promotion plans
- Sales aids and collaterals
- Proposal formats, reviews, and signoffs
- Quotation guidelines and formats
- Demonstration protocols
- Trade show and exhibit participation
- Seminars and open houses
- Special"sale"plans

Strategies

Discuss your strategy or strategies, and other direction-giving messages.

- Vision and direction
- Strategies for various markets and customer classes
- Differentiating actions planned
- Key concepts and customer messages to employ

Technology

Describe technology that you will use, its application, and how it will benefit the customer and the corporation. Also discuss plans for evaluating and acquiring new technology.

- Website
- Sales-force automation software
- Electronic Data Interchange (EDI)
- Laptops/PC's
- Custom product-design or services software
- Presentation devices

3. SUGGESTED STYLE.   Aside from the hard content, top-level sales, marketing, and corporate executives get a "feel" for the strength of a sales-unit plan by how it's written and the presence of "softer" ingredients. If management doesn't see or feel these ingredients, red flags go up in their minds. Weave these threads into your plans.

1. *Readability:* Managers want an easy read. They want a simple structure, heavy on bullets, graphics, visuals, charts, facts, and figures—and short on prose. There are no points for poundage. Descriptive prose is mandatory, but should be succinct and meaningful. The plan should be well organized. Plan hygiene—the spelling, grammar, and so forth, is expected to be flawless. The quality of a plan says a lot about the writers commitment to *quality execution.*

2. *Understanding:* It should be abundantly clear that the writer understands the business, the environment in which the firm is operating, the firm's constraints, the larger objectives, his or her markets and customers and that he or she understands competitive products, services, and strategies.

3. *Research:* Managers would hope to see references to other people, customers, and third parties that had been solicited for opinions or data. Research implies depth and thoroughness. Research offers proof without the asking. Superficiality doesn't sit well at the top.

4. *Focus:* They want you to focus on products, services, issues, processes, and people that are relevant to both the company at large and to your markets and customers. They would rather see depth in a few key areas than an attempt to cover everything in an incomplete fashion. Most would accept a plan that indicated "further planning needed" on second- or third-tier subjects.

5. *Priorities:* Priorities should be rationalized. Managers would look for the thought processes that established the priorities, and they would hope that the plan's priorities would be consistent with the organization at large.

6. *Creativity:* Innovativeness, new ideas, suggestions, calculated risks, and a streak of boldness should be present. They don't want to read history, excuses, blandness, old tired lines, aged bromides, and "this is the way it's always been." The presence of creativity is an indicator of attitude and aggressiveness. Yes, they're looking for pragmatism, but it should not be the dominant flavor. Challenges to the status quo would be looked on favorably.

7. *Specifics:* Managers want to see hard numbers, dates, percentages, probabilities, ranges, quotations, impressions, data, whatever. They don't want to see mush, and if someone appears to be saying safe things in abundance it is an immediate red flag.

8. *Resources:* They want to be shown who and what are needed to get the plan accomplished. It is critical that they see teamwork and collaboration.

9. *Issues:* They want to be shown the major hurdles that are in your way and want to see suggestions on how to go over or around the hurdles, or indications of a process you will initiate to try and solve the issues. If you want their help, say so in the plan. Indicate what other help would be appreciated. If there are things inhibiting achievement, they should be discussed.

10. *Investment needs:* This is not the same as resources. This implies people, money, facilities, equipment, and so on, that would be helpful to facilitate achievement of the plan.

11. *Commitments:* You should commit to results: Number 1, you should commit for yourself and for your organization, and managers would like to see how your sales unit bought into the commitment. You should also commit to timing and to activities that will lead to results.

12. *Recommendations:* You need to offer recommendations—for next steps, for specific actions, for programs, for investment, for hiring, for training, for market development, for products, for pricing—whatever. Prioritize your recommendations. Rationalize the recommendations. Cost-out the recommendations, if possible.

13. *Workability:* Finally, they would look for a plan that is realistic and that can be a good day-to-day management tool. Workability is reflected in format, its ability to be communicated to peers and superiors, and the presence of all the preceding attributes. Also, can the plan stand on its own? A plan's ability to be executed without its author is a good test of workability.

Document It

Put it on the screen or on paper with gusto and personally present it. Expect the give-and-take of a presentation to help you tune it further.

LESSONS

You will understand your business, feel more integrated, and feel more confident about yourself, your sales unit, and your direction. A thorough plan lightens your load.

Planning gets more important the higher you go. The sooner you master the art, the quicker you'll position yourself for additional responsibility.

Writing a sales-unit plan forces you to plan out, as well as down and up. The plan, first and foremost, should help you deliver value to your customer base and sales partners. Secondarily, it should be useful throughout your own organization.

Solid sales-unit plans set a good example for salespeople and specialists who should have plans for territories, individual sales opportunities, and special responsibilities.

Planning causes you to stop and think. It is the most worthwhile reflective activity that you will engage in, and it forces you out of your activity trap.

2–6 THE PROBLEM:
You do not have a priority model.

THE STORY

"Abner, good morning, hold on while I get rid of the other call."

"Hello, Eunice? Sam here again. Can I call you back, its my rep in Orlando on the other line? Thanks. Bye."

"Abner, I'm back . . . oops . . . hold just a second, my boss just walked in."

"Sam, where is your trade-show plan? I'm sitting down with the marketing people in two minutes."

"I'll bring it in as soon as I'm off the line," Sam quickly responds.

"Abner, whew, okay, how are you? Whoa, one of my reps just stuck his head in. I'll call you back on the car phone in ten minutes. Thanks."

Damn, Sam thinks to himself as he runs out, it's like this all the time.

TEMPTATIONS

The demands on a sales manager can get to be unbearable at times. When you are doing so many things there is a temptation to take short cuts or make illogical moves.

Surrender

"I'll do the best I can, but a lot of this stuff will just have to slide. I'll take the heat."

Drop a critical activity

"I'm just not going to be able to spend much time in the field anymore."

Take the phone off the hook

"Betty, I'm not in if anyone calls this morning."—or—"If that's Abner, I'm out."

A priority model is a framework that mitigates this kind of reactionary management.

WHAT HAPPENED HERE . . . ?

Sam is out of control, careening towards who-knows-where.

The normal pace of business in Sam's firm could be a zillion miles an hour. There are some industries and businesses that operate that way, making prioritization hypercritical.

Perhaps Sam is a new sales manager who hasn't found his groove yet, or he could be an experienced manager confused by the rapid changes around him. Maybe he has refused to buy into the firm's sales-force automation system or management processes.

Odds are that Sam has no written sales-unit plan.

The ripples from an overly demanding or disorganized boss may be a factor, or priorities have not been communicated from above. Also, Sam's manager may be negligent for not having observed or counseled him on his efficiency and work style.

Corporate cultures that don't have formal communications protocols or aren't process-driven can wreck havoc with *all* managers' priorities.

Strong and demanding personalities in other business functions could be making life tough for all the sales managers in the firm.

Sam's firm may be operating with fewer resources due to cost cutting, and he finds himself doing more things himself. All the more reason to follow a priority model.

OPTIONS

You have two options with this problem.

1. Continue to tolerate the situation you are enduring. Surprisingly, some sales managers thrive on lack of order and a frantic pace.

2. Change your priority model, prioritize your activities, and manage your sales unit rather than letting it manage you.

POSSIBLE ACTIONS

Stop. Step back and reexamine what you're doing and how you're performing the job.

Why?

The best place for Sam to start is ask himself *why* he is having this problem. A self-assessment that includes the potential causes highlighted in What happened here . . . ? plus others that he can identify must be accomplished. Unless the causes of the problem are addressed, the problem will remain, regardless of other actions. Sam must also admit to personal negative tendencies that hurt his organization and prioritization.

Priorities Are Special

Activities represent everything you do on a daily basis, *all* the ingredients of your job. Priorities are priorities because they represent the select few activities that you *must* execute in a given time period. The key word here is *must*. There are no options with priorities. Nothing. Zero. Zip. Priorities *must* be executed before anything else.

Priority means "earlier in time, preceding something else, precedence in order of rank, or the having of certain rights before another." Implicit in the word priority is choices and trade-offs. If you execute your priorities you still have a lot of other work left to do, but you have executed your most important tasks.

One Priority Model

Priorities vary by management level. The priorities of a vice president of sales and the priorities of an area sales manager are different because their jobs are different, but they have one priority in common.

The #1 priority at any level of sales management:

PEOPLE

Your staff is your #1 priority. Without a full and capable team you are helpless.

Building and developing your sales unit organization is your #1 priority. Always was, always will be. Your organization is your foundation. People sell—not computers, not brochures, not ads, nor direct mail pieces. All the rest is marketing, very valuable in its own right, but all those activities are not personal selling.

It's called "personal selling" because *people* do it. People are your foundation, and because foundations erode, people is a never-ending #1 priority. So hiring, training, and coaching should get top attention.

After putting your foundation in place, the following will form the rest of your hierarchy of priorities. It should be no surprise that customers, clients, and sales partners come next.

Many of your activities will affect more than one layer of the hierarchy. That multiplier effect should be a signal to you. Priorities that touch multiple levels should be higher on your list.

Your   Sales   Unit   Organization
Activities that meet the needs of customers, clients, and sales partners
Activities important to the management of your company.
Activities and expectations on the boss's agenda.
Your personal activities.

If you like, take this model and tune it to meet your situation and style. Keep it simple. Your model becomes the basis of your day-to-day activity management.

What Motivates You?

Sales managers tend to do what they like to do, what provides personal satisfaction, and what they are good at. It is imperative to recognize that your personal motivations may be at odds with this five-level hierarchy. It takes self-discipline to give preference to other people's priorities and to integrate the activities of other people into your agenda. Notice where your personal activities are in the hierarchy. Dead last.

A Second-Priority Model

Your day is full of activities, some important, some urgent, and some both. All of your activities could fit into one of these four quadrants. The first-priority model helps you *define* what is important. This second-priority model helps you *execute* what is important.

Quadrant 1: URGENT and *IMPORTANT*	*Quadrant 2: IMPORTANT,* *but not* **URGENT**
There are times when you'll be in this quadrant, usually because something in quadrant 2 became hot. Something popped up. For example: Hiring is important. If you suddenly have an open slot, it now becomes both important and urgent. Quadrant 1 stuff is stuff that has to happen today. It is okay to do urgent things but they should be important. And don't play mind games with yourself, telling yourself that the urgent stuff in quadrant #3 is important.	This is the quadrant where you want to work and live. Your goal should be to stay in this quadrant and look at the other three quadrants from this vantage point. Concentration on the important things keeps you above the fray. If you force yourself to live in Quadrant 2, then Quadrant 1 becomes easy to define. Quadrant 1 becomes something in Quadrant 2 that suddenly must be done with speed.
Quadrant 3: URGENT, *but not* **IMPORTANT**	*Quadrant 4: Not* **IMPORTANT** *and not* **URGENT**
Working on items in this quadrant is simply keeping busy. Many sales managers enjoy working in this quadrant because they enjoy checking things off lists of things to do. It feels good. It can become addictive. You love telling everybody what you did. Focusing on urgent activities causes you to lose sight of important activities. The feeling is, if it's urgent, it must be important. Wrong. This quadrant is a trap.	You're wasting your time if you are doing anything in this quadrant. Maybe you made a mistake. If you find yourself in this quadrant a lot maybe you should fire yourself.

(Source: *First Things First*, Steven R. Covey, Fireside)

Quadrant 2 is the key. Put this model on the white board in your office, or in your PC. Turn it into a working model. Someplace visible is best. You want reps and other managers to see this. It will cause them to respect you and your time and to firm up their own priority models.

Formal Priority Guide

You should have one key document that can help with your priority choices.

Your goal sheet. What is written on the *annual goal and objective sheet* you and your manager completed at the beginning of the year? Those goals are surely weighted and prioritized. It would be fair and proper to treat that goal sheet as a sacred cow.

Food for Thought

Here are ten questions to help you further identify and clarify priorities.

1. If your manager were executing your job, what would he or she do first? Second? Third? Do those things.
2. On what would your people prefer that you concentrate? Ask them if you don't know. Do those things.
3. What do you have a reputation for doing well? Do those things to keep your reputation intact because your reputation is priceless.
4. What are the habits and priorities of other top-performing sales managers? To the extent that they fit your style, copy and integrate those things.
5. Why were other people promoted? The activities and efforts that led to their results were affected by their priorities. Consider doing similar things.
6. What are the criteria for recognition, rewards, or bonuses at the end of fiscal periods? The activities that lead to those awards are priorities. Do those things.
7. What obstacles and problems are gnawing at your firm that your creativity and initiative can help remove? Attack those things.
8. What behaviors do the managers above you appreciate when they are stressed? Execute those behaviors and activities with deftness and priority.
9. What crises do you see on the horizon, or what dilemmas do you anticipate advancing toward the horizon? Take the long view as well as the short. Begin to attack those things.
10. What concepts, products, issues, or processes do you hear top management referring to on a regular basis? Make the same items your priority.

Final Points to Keep Disciplined

Sales management is a constant struggle of trade-offs. These final points can help your priority decisions.

- Break up your big *important* priorities into digestible pieces, eating the elephants one bite at a time.
- Let your people and other managers know what your priorities are. The value of sharing lies in the fact that they are less likely to intrude and will understand why you come to them for assistance. Discipline begets discipline.
- Work hard to develop a reputation as your firm's most prioritized sales manager. Others will meet your expectations, and prioritization will become a self-fulfilling prophecy.
- Keep the number of your goals and objectives to a minimum. Goal dilution leads to jumbled priorities.
- Beat procrastination by placing your most challenging *important* tasks at the top of your priorities.
- Prioritize your customer and sales-partner contacts. Circumstances and market conditions make certain customers more *important* than others at times.
- Empower your people and delegate *important* selected tasks.
- Managing from a detailed, working sales-unit plan aids identifying what is *important*.

LESSONS

You must have a personal priority model. It will serve as an effectiveness anchor. Share it with your people and colleagues and live by it.

Sales management is a never-ending stream of personal choices. Choices and options are colored by personal preferences that only you can manage. A model helps you make choices.

Sales-management work is cyclical. Priority management becomes more of a priority in times of heightened activity. Build and refine your model in times of lessened activity. Carry the lessons and habits to periods of elevated activity.

In the end, it boils down to executing according to your model.

part three

TROUBLESHOOTING LEADERSHIP PROBLEMS

3–1 THE PROBLEM:

You do not have a sales-management philosophy
or guiding principles.

THE STORY

Frank and Bill were both sales managers who had come up through the ranks together, weathering many storms and supporting each other along the way. At best, business was, "okay" at the moment, but neither was 100 percent comfortable with his personal circumstances.

Their usual Saturday-morning tennis match had just concluded. Sitting on the court, tired and sweaty and reflecting on the latest challenges they were both facing, Frank said, "Bill, what do you believe it would take for you and me to be *really* successful sales managers? I mean *r e a l l y* successful! Deep down inside, what do you *believe is really important?*"

After a moment's thought, Bill replied, "Well, money! Luck! Some people in my unit who were more ambitious! Heck, I don't know, if I knew I wouldn't be sitting here!"

TEMPTATIONS

Frank's question strikes at the need for inner direction and focus. The frustration of not having principles to lean on sometimes causes sales mangers to yield to easy temptations.

Make one up

"Ahem. Well, I believe that if we work closer with our clients . . . I mean . . . if we listen to what their problem is . . . you know . . . their real need . . . maybe we can do a better job of servicing them . . . you know what I mean?"

Repeat someone else's philosophy

"I was reading that new sales-management best-seller, you know the one, and it said . . ."

Joke

"Frank, I'm going to hit you with my racquet, can't we relax for a minute?"

You may think that jesting, snappy one-liners can hide the truth, but that's not the case.

WHAT HAPPENED HERE . . . ?

These two sales managers are like reeds in the wind—with very shallow roots.

Frank's friend was caught off guard, and he was unprepared. He was lucky that it was not one of his own people or his own manager who asked the question. The honest answer is, "I have no idea. Let's talk about it."

Perhaps Bill never stopped to think about what made him tick, or what drove him, or what he believed in, in regard to sales management.

Perhaps Bill's life and his work may have been chugging comfortably along, and he never felt the need to ask himself this basic question. The answers may be there, but he has never organized and utilized the thoughts to his advantage.

The fact that Frank is groping for core beliefs, basic truths, or credos is a sure sign that he doesn't have a sales-management compass, but understands its value.

OPTIONS

There are three options here.

1. Admit that you don't have any core beliefs, that you never thought about it, that you don't believe it's that important, and leave it at that.
2. State what you *do* feel to the best of your ability, without ruffles or flourishes, and take any lumps in the process.
3. Admit to yourself that if you *did* have some bedrock sales-management principles you could articulate, you'd live by them, and probably achieve greater success.

POSSIBLE ACTIONS

If you're having trouble with the word "philosophy," substitute "guiding principles." Don't think of this as management style or strategy, think of this problem as your *core sales-management beliefs*.

Grab a paper and pen or turn on your PC.

Why Do You Need Guiding Sales-Management Principles?

There are many reasons, some of which follow:

1. They give you a strong sense of who you are and what you stand for.
2. A philosophy or guiding principles give you the ability to maintain your own personal values and beliefs in the face of conflict.
3. They serve as a foundation to fall back on in times of stress or disorientation.
4. Guiding principles anchor you, enabling you to withstand threats to your integrity.
5. They give you a feeling of self-direction, providing comfort in knowing exactly how you are going to get to your destination.

6. They strengthen your self-confidence, something your people will pick up on.

7. They heighten your feeling of self-empowerment.

8. Guiding principles provide a sense of freedom.

9. Principles permit you to serve as a beacon for others who are searching for guidance. They give your people, your colleagues, and your superior something to latch on to and make them more comfortable with you.

10. And finally, as Mark Twain said in his own inimitable manner, "Few things are harder to put up with than the annoyance of a good example."

What would you add to the list?

Think About the Principles You Already Possess

Here are some ticklers to get you going:

If *we* went to the people who work for you and asked them, "What does _____(your name)____ deeply believe in?—or—What does he or she stand for?" What would *they* say? Would the answer be consistent across your organization? What would you *want* them to say?

In answer to the following three questions, what would *you* say?

1. "After __ X __ years of sales management experience I've come to believe that _____, and _____."

2. "My experience as a sales manager has shown me that _____ _____ are the most important elements of the job."

3. "I believe that sales management excellence is based on _____ _____."

Document Your Deep-seated Beliefs

For example: One of the authors' guiding principles has to do with hiring. The author's core principle about hiring is to *hire fiber-laden talent.* Fiber is the essential substance, strength, and character of a person—integrity, honesty, sincerity, perseverance, and work ethic. *We believe* that these intangibles are enduring and have withstood the tests of time and lead to hiring and sales success. You can have guiding principles in regard to many different aspects of sales management:

For example, training: What do you believe?

For example, leadership: What do you believe?

For example, relationships: What do you believe?

For example, teamwork: What do you believe?

For example, innovation: What do you believe?

For example, empowerment   What do you believe?

In regard to _____: What do you believe?

You can have as many principles as experience has proven to you are valuable.

Consider writing down a philosophy about a key management challenge. For example: The authors' philosophy regarding "How to manage for sales growth" includes the following nine points. What would be your answer to the same question?

Our List	**Your List**
How to manage for sales growth	*How to manage for sales growth*
Lead with courage and discipline.	?
Set goals and expectations.	?
Create and execute plans.	?
Build a great team.	?
Train fanatically.	?
Focus on $-producing activities.	?
Engage your resources.	?
Manage relationships.	?
Work with upbeat intensity.	?

We believe in our list deeply because it is based on *our* experience.

If you want to borrow some from our list, be our guest. Your list doesn't have to agree with ours. Your list is *your* list. *What do* you *deeply believe?* The objective is to get to the point that come whatever, *you* will believe in and live by your own sales-management philosophy. You can have a list or a statement for any major sales-management subject or challenge you choose. *Write down what you stand for and what is genuinely important to you.* The exercise is revealing and embedding.

Your axioms, guiding principles, or philosophies don't have to reflect any grand theoretical schemes. As a matter of fact, short and simple is best.

Philosophies and guiding principles take time to build, like the pyramids. They come block by block. The sales manager with 25 years of experience should have assembled many more blocks than the sales manager with two months of experience.

These beliefs change over time, are influenced by the people around you, both superiors and subordinates, and by what you read, hear, and experience. Your core principles are always evolving. Some will stay with you forever, and some may come and go rather quickly.

Engage Your Deep-seated Beliefs to Strengthen Them

Execute sales-management actions based on your beliefs. (Walk-the-talk is the popular slogan.)

Make management decisions on the basis of your bedrock beliefs, regardless of what others may value or pressure you to do.

Tell someone about your personal sales management beliefs. You'll find that is a powerful way to clarify and test your principles. It is amazing what can happen in the translation from mind to words—how you may hesitate and equivocate. You'll find that the more you articulate and engage your beliefs, the smoother they will become, the more confident you will get, and the more consistently you will live and manage by them.

LESSONS

This thought process will cause you to reexamine what you stand for. These guiding principles, or deep-seated beliefs, will rub off on those around you. Strength of conviction is contagious.

The people around you may not totally agree with all of your principles, but they will respect you and respect the fact that you have them—and they may be inspired to firm up their own.

Your principles will anchor you and enable greater and consistent success. You will feel much better about yourself for having sales-management philosophies and guiding principles.

3–2 THE PROBLEM:

You want to instill higher expectations and "raise the bar."

THE STORY

Lance's sales unit has never missed its monthly or yearly goals in the three and a half years that Lance has been the district manager. And he has a few plaques to prove it.

Lance was a sports nut who had been the conference high-jump champion in high school, and he marveled at the heights that the current Olympic athletes were now clearing. Javier Sotomayor of Cuba had cleared 8' 1/2"! Wow! It was incredible that the number kept creeping higher, and it caused him to think about how he could instill some of that "creep" into his sales unit.

In spite of his performance, he was frustrated. Why can't *we* be the top sales team in the world this year, he dreamed?

TEMPTATIONS

Moving to the top is the hardest thing in sales management. That last little bit of result seems to take more energy than anything before it. These temptations are legendary, but are not the answer.

Kick butt

"Look at those big-time coaches. They're screaming and in the face of their people all the time. If it fires up prima donna athletes, it can work for me."

Send everyone to a sales evangelist

"I think I'll enroll the team in some of those razz-ma-tazz conferences to juice them up."

Big bucks

"An incentive program will do the trick." or "The commission rate is the problem."

The best approach is to carefully engineer that last bit of success. And the word "engineer" is most appropriate because it takes precision and planning to get to the top.

WHAT HAPPENED HERE . . . ?

Lance has grown uncomfortable with plain-vanilla success and is looking to make a quantum leap, or at least to inch his way up.

Lance's own competitiveness or desire to excel could be pushing him, or maybe he saw someone else win top honors and deep down inside he believes he is better than that person. Also, others around Lance may be striving to surpass him, and that has lit his fire.

Maybe Lance's boss challenged him to do better.

Perhaps Lance just has a personal dream. High standards are often inspired by deep indescribable drives.

On the down side, Lance may be feeling some pressure because his company is cutting back, and he knows that only the top sales managers will be retained.

Going over the top has eluded many, but it can be done.

OPTIONS

Your options are very simple.

Do you *really* want this? How *badly* do you want to do this? Are you willing to invest the effort?

YES or NO!

POSSIBLE ACTIONS

Go for it! Quantum leaps in high-jump heights occurred when there was a major change in the basic technique from the scissors to the western roll and then to the Fosbury flop. Most improvements through the years have been incremental, based on fine tuning and better training. Whether it's world-class high jumping or world-class sales management, the top performers have followed the same path of utilizing both big and little ideas.

Develop an Adoptable Dream

You need to identify where you want to take the sales unit. Do you remember the speech when Dr. Martin Luther King, Jr., said, "I have a dream . . ."? It was powerful, wasn't it? Your dream should display the same ambitious attitude. Having that attitude and doing something with it are two different things, however.

Dreams must be adopted by the people in your sales unit. If they are not adopted they will lack the power and leverage sales-unit members can bring to bear.

How do you make a dream adoptable? The dream must represent the sales unit as a whole but be tailored to each salesperson, by showing how attainment of the dream will help each individual get to his or her personal goals or have it satisfy his or her personal ambitions.

An adoptable sales-unit dream should be able to be articulated simply and quickly. It should be memorable. It can weld a sales unit together fast and firm.

Go and rent a videotape of Dr. King's speech. Play it at your next sales-unit meeting. Share your dream for the sales unit at the same time.

Personal Commitment

The sheer act of raising the bar can be a little scary. You are putting yourself on the line, exposing yourself. Are you sure you want to go ahead with this? Everyone is watching. There is no shame in leaving it where it is. It's more comfortable leaving it where it is, at a height you know you can clear. Maybe you want to pursue another problem instead of this one?

Setting high expectations casts you as a leader. Setting *lofty* expectations or pursuing a lofty dream implicitly casts you as a more courageous leader. As Robert Louis Stevenson said, "Keep your fears to yourself, but share your courage with others." Share your adoptable dream.

Create a High-Expectations Plan Based on Attitudes, Behaviors, and Activities

Your dream requires a cultural transformation. Recognize that transformations take time. If you treat your path to higher expectations as a journey rather than as an event or a program, you're more apt to be successful.

In order to get the sales unit to a higher level, your task is to identify what supports and what inhibits that transformation in terms of attitudes, behaviors, and sales-unit activities.

Your objective is then to alter the attitudes, behaviors, and activities of your people by altering *your own* attitudes, behaviors, and activities.

Ask your staff for their contribution and involvement in setting the higher standards and expectations. "What would we have to do to achieve the dream?" Involvement fosters buy-in.

Some key elements of your plan could include the following:

- Your expectations should be as measurable as can be, but qualitative expectations are just as valuable.

- Your new expectations should be specific, understandable, and easily identifiable. Others should be able to look at the new results and say, "Yes, he did it."

- In creating the new expectations, start from *both* the market side and your corporate side. Your expectations should support and satisfy both sets of stakeholders. Set expectations that are in the best interest of the entire business, so that when you need help, everyone will say, "Of course," because they see the benefit across the board.

When you raise the bar you will be changing the way things get done, and you are changing everyone's comfort zones along the way. Gradual but steady raising of the bar is a good way to get long-lasting, constant results.

Attitudes that Enable Higher Expectations

In order to get incredible things done, display the following supporting attitudes, not the inhibiting ones:

Supporting Attitudes	Inhibiting Attitudes
Belief. Exhibit a strong belief in your people. Let them know that you believe that they can do what they previously thought they couldn't. No one in the world operates at his or her full capacity.	Nagging doubt
Knowledge. It's important to know yourself, your people, your constraints, your strengths—and above all—know that it can be done.	Uncertainty

Assumptiveness. Introduce higher expectations matter-of-factly. New expectations announced with drama and drum rolls usually inspire fear or disbelief. Quietly assume you'll succeed.	Caution and reserve
Focus. A laser-beamlike single-mindedness of purpose will keep you on track.	A shotgun mentality
Craving. Crave ideas, creativity, initiative, quality, and other concepts to which you are deeply committed.	Contentment with the status quo

What other attitudes can you add to the list?

Inhibiting attitudes are often the opposite of supporting attitudes, but may include other negative dispositions as well.

Behaviors that Enable Higher Expectations

In order to get extraordinary things done (or set world records) modify and monitor your personal behaviors.

Supporting Behaviors	**Inhibiting Behaviors**
Share your power by enabling and empowering your people to act.	Have your people seek permission for everything.
Act as a leader, articulating the dream, identifying destinations, setting direction, and inspiring your people over the rough spots.	Manage everything tightly.
Let your people see that you set high expectations for yourself, and then set about performing.	Avoid the risk of exposing yourself.
Bring infectious vitality and passion for your people, products and services, and company to enliven the environment.	Measure your personal effort so as to not go overboard.
Trust your staff. Trusting them with the BIG STUFF and bigger responsibilities builds confidence in their ability to succeed.	Be wary and cautious of everyone and everything. Go slow.
Be a rabid coach providing helpful ideas and suggestions to help everyone over the hurdles.	Let them figure it for themselves.
Communicate progress, what's working and what's not working, and reiterate the higher standards over and over.	Assume they get tired of hearing it all.

Regularly throw out renewed individual and group challenges to keep raising the bar.	Exhibit little faith in the value of continuing pursuit.
Measure activities as well as results. People work on what is being measured.	People work if you squeeze them.
Be candid and forthright about shortfalls and problems, holding the team accountable and persevering in the face of stubborn challenges.	Accept a few excuses.
Work and results that you *accept* without challenge, comment, or feedback automatically becomes the new standard. Inspect what you expect. Word will get around with what you accept or reject.	Don't plan any rigorous scrutiny of activities or results.
Set an example of excellence in *all* things. Let your people see that the sum total of all the *little things* adds up to high expectations with the big things.	Just stay focused on the bottom line.
Reach into your leadership bag of tricks to cajole, flatter, sweet-talk, coax, prod, challenge, entice, or persuade as necessary. Everyone and every expectation takes something different.	Stay holed up in the office.
Let your team know how much you appreciate them. Accentuate and recognize the positive aspects of little and big contributions along the way.	Their compensation plan is sufficient reward.
Proudly hold up and display the sales-unit's achievement of new standards. Celebrate a little and broadcast the results.	Revel in the personal glory.
Keep your higher level of expectations self-sustaining with your interest. High-expectation cultures thrive on ever-present leadership.	Assume that momentum will keep things going.
Be consistent in your actions, processes, and expectations	Deviate as needed.

What other behaviors would you like to add to the list?

Activities that Enable Higher Expectations

All standard-raising plans need these elements.

Supporting Activities	Inhibiting Activities
Train for excellence. If all aspects of training are treated with rigor, intensity, and high standards, then the achievement of higher expectations is more likely.	Keep everyone out there selling.
Tear your sales cycle and transaction cycle apart into little pieces. Rigorous focus on improving *all* activities and sales processes, measured against benchmarks, will enable higher expectations.	Just focus on closing the deals.
Establish and maintain a working atmosphere that relies heavily on teamwork and team activities. The synergy will fuel everyone's fire.	Salespeople are too individualistic to operate as teams.

What other activities would you add to this list?

The Results

People will rise to meet your expectations and together achieve the dream. You just have to communicate the dream and set the expectations, and support your people with enabling attitudes, behaviors, and activities.

When you've stopped raising the bar, or pursuing a dream, you've stopped.

LESSONS

You and your sales unit will never have more fun, personal reward, and memories than those times when you've decided to go for it. You will discover that the effort was well worth it. *You all* surprise yourselves and expand your boundaries in the process.

Your personal commitment and willingness to invest and make sacrifices will ultimately be the factor in how high you raise and how often you clear the bar.

3–3 THE PROBLEM:
The sales unit lacks teamwork and cohesiveness.

THE STORY

Louise had been on the job for a month as the new district manager, carefully collecting observations. She had noted many things, including little or no sharing of war stories between the salespeople, only a courteous relationship with the inside sales staff; no strategy-and-tactics discussions among the account managers; no extracurricular meetings after hours, the office staff clearing out punctually at 5:00; little talk of personal activities, and so on.

The district wasn't setting any records, and at her first sales meeting she sensed that they all had that what-in-the-world-are-we-here-for feeling as they came into the conference room. She had shared her goals, values, and expectations, but there were very few questions.

Louise was trying to figure out how to get this team together. She needed to light the fire.

TEMPTATIONS

A cohesive, vibrant team environment is a product of leadership. Environments can tell you a lot about the skills and priorities of leaders. We won't suggest the following approaches to Louise.

Blame the predecessor
  "Joe certainly screwed things up. How in the world did these people ever work with him?"

Nah
  "These people probably think that teamwork is touchy-feely stuff." or "Teamwork is great if we were playing basketball, but this is sales."

Cheerlead
  "Let's play a tape every morning or pipe in some music."

It is difficult not to scream when you see a lack of synergy among capable individuals. Teamwork makes it easier to improve processes, be a tougher competitor, and win more often.

WHAT HAPPENED HERE . . . ?

Obviously, little or nothing happened here in regard to building a team. Teamwork is highly visible. You can also hear it and sense it.

Teamwork is getting more difficult to build because of a reduced sense of loyalty, a belief that people will not be with an organization for the long haul, and the increased concern with satisfaction of self. The effectiveness of the team concept in sales is binary. It either works exceedingly well or it doesn't, because it emanates from the capabilities of the immediate manager, who either has, or doesn't have, team-building skills. Fortunately, the skills required to build a team can be learned.

What happened here may be that Louise's predecessor was not the best leader, didn't value teamwork, or tried some things that backfired. Teamwork doesn't screech to a halt when an effective leader leaves.

It may be that this district's geography is dispersed, that they have gone to a virtual-office concept, or that new computer and communications tools are keeping them apart. A physically dispersed team leads to an emotionally dispersed team if there are no compensatory steps taken.

Perhaps the folks in this district never or infrequently met as a team, or did anything as a team.

It may be that the elite few who are capable of being superstars on their own (so they think) see a teamwork effort as a drag, as a distraction, as a time waster, and have pooh-poohed previous efforts.

There is both interteam teamwork and intrateam teamwork. It looks as if both may be missing in our story. Interteam teamwork gets people from allied departments and business functions working closely with you. Intrateam teamwork gets your own people cooperating and coordinating. They must go together.

OPTIONS

Louise has two options.

1. She could leave this issue the way it is, try to blow through this assignment quickly, and get on to something bigger and better. It's been done. Some risk there, of course.

2. She could commit to improve teamwork, in one of two ways.

   One, she could address this at some later time, after straightening out personnel, sales channel, market, retention, performance, expense, or other issues.

   Two, she could attack the environment now, build the teamwork and cohesiveness, and use that energy to help solve *all other* issues.

You commit to the teamwork concept, or you don't, because it takes a lot of time and effort. There is no middle ground.

Some people may argue that the teamwork concept doesn't count for much in sales, but given similar talent, strong individuals working closely together for common goals can always outperform strong individuals who are in it for themselves. It's human nature.

POSSIBLE ACTIONS

Start with your customers and clients in mind when considering teamwork actions. If your team-building actions don't ultimately benefit customers and clients, put the proposed action aside. It's certainly okay to have a few things in the plan just for the sales unit, but first things first.

The Demonstration of the Value of Teamwork

Do you really believe that sales units that work together as teams perform better? You probably do. However, if you're not 100 percent convinced of that fact, be aware that your efforts will likely be transparent and your people will think that anything you say or do is a self-serving sham.

The vast majority of salespeople understand the value of teamwork. Messages on the value of teamwork have been coming at them from all sides for years, and the messages are true.

The value of teamwork is not the problem. The problem is demonstrating to your people *how* they can work together as a team. That's your job.

Set an Example

Talk "team." Speak positively about your co-managers and co-workers, regardless of level and function. Talk to your co-managers and boss frequently and make sure your people witness it. Let them see you asking people at all levels for their opinions. Tell your people how you successfully solved a problem by working with peers and other staff members. Show your people that you value the opinions and contributions of others, *and show them that you reciprocate to an equal or greater degree.* Teamwork is not self-serving. Teamwork is enterprise-serving.

Act team. Engage your own people frequently, and let the rest of the staff witness the fact that you respect the accumulated knowledge and talent of everyone in the sales unit. Stir everyone's intellect and energy together. When they see that, they'll be more apt to follow your example. Jack Welch, CEO of General Electric, said it this way in *Fortune's* Leadership Lessons, "I think that any company that's trying to play in the 1990's has got to find a way to engage the mind of every single employee. Whether we make our way successfully down the road is something only time will tell—but I'm as sure as I've ever been about anything that this is the right road."

The breadth of your team-building plan depends on your current situation and how far you want to take your sales unit. The more the sales unit is bonded the more benefits accrue to the sales unit and individual members. The most successful sales units have a continuing emphasis on creating ways for people to collaborate. Frankly, your effort will reflect your strength of conviction about teamwork.

Tips and Techniques

Here are some ideas to help build a cohesive team.

- Ask a subteam of two or three individuals to make a presentation at a sales-unit meeting.
- Encourage team sales calls, utilizing people in and outside the sales unit where the situation warrants.
- Say what's on your mind, good or bad. Speaking out encourages contribution in return. Utilize what you hear.
- Have your team help create the sales unit's plan, a forecast, or a meeting agenda.
- Tout detailed examples of successful teamwork from other parts of the company. Show the results.
- Make joint assignments for collateral responsibilities, such as new-hire training.
- Delegate a couple of your people to represent the sales unit at special events and meetings and have them make reports.
- Obtain hats, shirts, or other paraphernalia with company and team logos.
- Display pictures of the team in newsletters and in the office.
- Hoist banners or create a hall of fame with plaques and trophies. Cut loose and celebrate together.
- Be accessible and interested in what all team members have to say.
- Share win-loss analyses for the benefit of all.
- Show equal dignity and respect for every individual that reports to you regardless of his or her title or responsibilities.
- Ask the team for their suggestions on a wide array of business subjects that can benefit the company, not just the sales unit.
- Call individuals into your office frequently to ask their opinion about an issue.
- Train your people as a group, rather than in fragments.
- Invite outsiders to your sales-unit meetings to demonstrate a value for their opinions. Utilize selected contributions.
- Foster team-versus-team competition with another sales unit.
- Ask several people, in and outside the sales unit, to join strategy and problem-solving discussions.
- Adopt a team name or a motto and print and post it prominently. Use the team name, not the manager's name, in reports and documents.
- Ask management to make performance awards to the sales unit, not to you personally.
- Support your people vigorously. Go to the wall. Fight for their needs and let them see you bloodied.
- Put team-related success stories on the E-mail, in a newsletter, or discuss them at meetings.
- Regularly share breakfasts or lunches in small groups, or as a complete sales unit.

- Jointly approach and solve a major competitive threat.
- Execute team problem solving and team-strategy development sessions.
- Reinforce and personally recognize the positive things the team is doing.

Create your own list. The list becomes your team-building plan. These same tips and techniques are as useful with your independent sales agencies, distributors, dealers, and retailers as they are with your direct staff. Sales partners also want to feel that they belong to your sales unit team.

Rules

Here are seven teamwork-building rules to live by:

1. *Exhibit a constant willingness to give of yourself.* Your generosity of time, energy, and intellect communicates commitment to teamwork. Your giving should *always* out-weigh your seeking and receiving.
2. *Exhibit a constant search for opinions and help.* It will be a demonstration that you value people and ideas.
3. *Experiment.* Try new team-building ideas. Stick with what works and drop unsuccessful approaches.
4. *Be impatient.* The sooner you get your people working as a team the better off you all will be.
5. *Be aware of differences.* The same team-building approaches may not work in all environments.
6. *Look at successful teams in all areas of your business and personal life.* Discern why they are successful.
7. *It never stops.* Team building is a continuing process—an evolution—changing as the environment and membership changes.

LESSONS

It takes a conscious effort to build a team. It doesn't happen by itself.

Other managers draw competency conclusions about you from the level of teamwork they observe and experience. They are more likely to respect and support sales units and individuals within those sales units who work well together

Team identity and belonging is a powerful force. There is a special pride in being part of a closely knit team. There is a special comfort in times of personal stress or unit challenge. Everyone feels better and performs better.

Sales managers lead sales teams. They don't steer a group of individual sales reps. That's called herding. Herding is done from the back and the sides. Leading is done from the front.

3–4 THE PROBLEM:
Morale is bad.

THE STORY

Tony's sales-unit was just barely making its targets, plodding along, but there was no fire in anyone's eyes.

This place feels like a morgue, Tony thought to himself one day. He was smart enough to recognize that morale was in the pits, but he was unsure why or what to do about it.

Catching a couple of his people in the office late the same day, he asked, "How's everything going?"

"We're still alive" and "Who the hell knows?" were the two forgettable responses that were like a slap in the face. He stopped, flushed with anger, and committed to himself on the spot that this had to come to a halt immediately.

TEMPTATIONS

When everyone's chin is on the floor and you have just gotten a wake-up call, it can be tempting to act impulsively.

Self-righteousness
   "It can't be me! I've been busting my butt! These people need to bust theirs."

Point fingers
   "If this company didn't keep changing its policies, we'd be okay."

Clean house
   "It's time to fire the whole lot and bring in some winners."

Sales managers who pride themselves in building and keeping morale at a high level constantly work at it because they understand that *morale is extremely fragile*. They know the slightest issues at the wrong time can put their sales unit into a tailspin.

WHAT HAPPENED HERE . . . ?

It looks as if Tony took his eye off his people. There are many things that can wither the morale of your people if you are not watching and reacting.

A lack of vision or clear strategy within Tony's company could have caused his people to feel uneasy. Salespeople expect clear direction.

Tony's firm might have product problems that have allowed his competition to regain beachheads that his people had fought hard to win.

Possibly Tony's products are suffering from quality or delivery problems. As a result, his reps have had to sell the same deal over and over. This translates into less new opportunity selling time, less business, and ultimately less money.

Often, people's morale suffers when they feel that there are few, if any, career-advancement opportunities available to them in the organization.

It could be that Tony's comp program has problems, or his people are not getting paid accurately, or on time.

Maybe the reps' job security is threatened. Corporate downsizings deflate morale.

Tony's sales unit may be in close physical proximity to other sales units that are riding high. It can be depressing to be around others who are feeling good about themselves all the time. It is easy to start feeling sorry for yourself when other teams are winning and having fun.

Maybe Tony forgot the power of recognition, pats on the back, and simple thank-yous.

Goals in Tony's sales unit may be unrealistic, spawning a defeatist attitude.

Maybe Tony has been overconcentrating on managing and has forgotten about leading.

Salespeople can get down when they perceive that the boss doesn't want to be bothered, that they are not liked or trusted, that they perceive a lack of respect, or they sense that the boss doesn't have confidence in them.

This is a problem where it is extremely important that you make an extra effort rooting out these and other potential causes, because causes and actions are immutably intertwined. *The very act of digging sends a strong message to your people that you care and that you value them.*

OPTIONS

You've got two options. Your choice depends on your personal level of satisfaction.

1. You could choose to ignore the problem. The fact is that your sales unit is barely making its targets, and the problems that are causing poor morale may not be in your control. You could say that morale was always very good in the past, and you have no reason to believe that it will not return as soon as things outside your control are corrected.

2. On the other hand, you may feel that the morale problems are adversely affecting your team and that performance will ultimately suffer. Your attrition rate may increase if you do not address the issues now.

POSSIBLE ACTIONS

You can have bad morale in a squeaky-clean environment. You can have great morale in the face of adversity. It takes leadership to enable great morale to flourish in all situations. "Morale is when your hands and feet keep on working when your head says it can't be done." So said a U.S. admiral several years ago.

Diagnosis

The best way to find the issues is to ask your people—and not though a memo or a survey. You need to *look them square in the eye*. They need to trust that you will not use what they tell you against them. If you have established an environment of trust with your people, they will tell you what they think the issues are. If you have not established trust, now is the best time to start. It is a good bet that if you find that they do not trust you, you are well on your way to determining the cause of bad morale. Leadership cannot exist without trust.

CONTROLLABLES AND UNCONTROLLABLES.   If you look back at the "what happened here . . ." list and the issues your people identify, it is obvious that you can quickly and personally affect some items, but not others.

Examples of controllables may be compensation, goals, attitude, recognition, direction, and training.

Examples of uncontrollables may be product quality, product specifications, pricing, delivery, and downsizing. *But*, you have a voice with uncontrollables. There is nothing to which you cannot add your two cents. Remember, you are a sales manager, so you have an implicit advantage. You can make yourself effectively and tactfully heard inside. It is no guarantee things will change, but you must let your people see you making the effort.

IS THERE A BAD INFECTION GOING AROUND?   There are people in every organization, both in and out of the sales unit, who like to point up the painful side of issues and events. It is a part of their nature. They carry their attitude like a disease and they have a negative affect on morale. These are the people who usually see the glass as half empty, rather than half full. Salespeople are susceptible like everyone else.

These people have labels. We are sure you are familiar with them all.

- *Bullies:* These are thugs from other departments who enjoy browbeating your people.
- *Desk-jockeys:* From the comfort of a spacious office and a hot cup of coffee they have no clue to the reality of life on the outside, but they "know" it's a piece of cake.
- *Doomsayers:* Their world is ending tomorrow. It makes no sense to change anything.
- *Naysayers:* Their vocabulary is laced with "nope," "that's-a-negative," "never," "nix," "by no means," and "absolutely not."
- *Needlers:* These are frustrated sales wannabes that nag and goad you and your people because they secretly believe they could do your job better than you.
- *Insurrectionists:* They are ticked-off at the company and want you to join their cause.

- *Candy-coaters:* These people smile deceitfully and say, "Oh, you poor thing, I hope things get better."
- *Mutineers:* These are the most dangerous, because they are informal peer leaders inside your own sales unit.

Regardless of their rank, you must identify these people, speak to them, isolate your staff from them (if they're outsiders), respectfully ask them to change their ways, or ask for their cooperation. If that doesn't work, their superiors need to be notified.

IS THERE A POWER SHORTAGE?   There are two kinds of people—energy takers and energy givers.

Candidly, are you personally energizing or deenergizing your own sales unit?

Who are the people around you who energize you and your sales unit? Who are the ones who sap your individual and collective energy? Identify them all. Strengthen your relationships with the givers and distance yourself from the takers.

Remember that relationships can energize you to do more than you and your sales unit can do alone, which brings us to the next point.

DO YOU NEED A SPECIALIST?   When you are dealing with uncontrollables, it helps to get help for a morale power boost.

For example:

- If lengthy deliveries are battering morale, invite the manager of production control to listen to your people and then address the sales unit with details of issues and steps being taken to solve the problem.
- If downsizing is a threat, invite a senior executive to listen, address the sales unit, clear the air, and share the reality of the situation.
- If there is a problem with a product, invite a product-marketing manager to listen for inputs and to share the product development plans.

Notice that in all cases the common thread is that the invited specialist must *listen.*)

Draft a Plan

Building morale is your job, but ask your sales unit for their ideas to help you develop a plan of attack for those aspects of morale to which all of you can contribute, for example, competitive threats or the need for additional resources.

Help your sales unit to come up with the ideas. Stir their creative juices and ensure that what they come up with is simultaneously realistic and pushes the boundaries of possibilities. It is important that the plan you develop has a chance of making a difference. Pie-in-the-sky ideas that are not feasible will eventually frustrate your people and actually do more to damage morale than to improve it.

Many times you cannot totally solve the issues that are creating poor morale. (We assume that if you could solve them completely, you would.) However, just the act of attempting to solve these issues goes a long way in improving morale. That's leadership.

Never let the sales unit see you act as a victim in the creation or execution of your plan.

How to turn morale around?

1. Lead the creation and maintenance of a make-it-happen *climate* where you and your people can achieve your personal and business goals.
2. Execute, or influence, the *exact opposite* of all the issues identified in What happened here . . . and identified through questioning your people.
3. Dedicate yourself to *executing the plan* that your people helped generate.

It takes concentration, your positive attitude and example, constant awareness and effort, and a fighting spirit and confidence that says "I won't let anything get me—or us—down."

Report Back to the Sales Unit

Keep your people aware of your progress. You may not always be successful in completely solving the issues, but you will minimize them or find ways to avoid them. In all cases, you improve the trust relationship with your people. That alone can improve the sales unit's morale.

Lessons

The major lesson is that courageous leadership is the foundation of good morale.

Constantly create opportunities to look your people in the eye. Ask them how they feel about what you and the company are doing. Watch their eyes. Listen carefully to the words they use to answer you. The stronger the words, the stronger the feelings.

Watch and listen for changes. If you sense a negative trend, jump on it immediately. Try to catch problems early in their life cycle. They are much easier to solve when they are young.

This problem teaches you that morale is a controllable and that much of the control is in your hands. Even in the face of corporate adversity, a good sales manager can make a positive impact with a creative morale-building plan and have a high-morale sales unit.

Solving this problem is a reminder that good morale is a positive, infectious spirit that must constantly be nurtured. Left uncared-for, good morale drifts to become indifferent or bad morale.

3–5 THE PROBLEM:

Your people are not sufficiently empowered.

THE STORY

Every morning Sharon, a zone sales manager, arrived at her office with all the best intentions. She knew what she wanted to accomplish and couldn't wait to get at it.

Unfortunately, today, like almost every other day, Sharon could hear her phone ringing as she walked down the hall toward her office. It was John, one of her sales reps, asking for Sharon's approval to "call high" at one of his accounts. After spending ten minutes getting all of the details, Sharon gave John her approval.

Between the phone calls and a full mailbox, 6:00 P.M. came very quickly. As usual, Sharon did not do anything she had set out to do. Leaving the office, she said aloud, "The good news is that I'm involved in the business and helping my reps succeed . . . or am I?"

TEMPTATIONS

Temptations associated with this problem are on different ends of the spectrum. Managers tend to either feed this habit, or to act recklessly to kill the habit.

Fry yourself

"I'll just have to go to a 70-hour week and put a business-phone line in my home."

or

Cold turkey

"That's it! Starting tomorrow, no more calls. Becky, tell the reps I'm busy and don't disturb me if they call. They can sink or swim on their own."

Lack of understanding of what empowerment means sometimes contributes to a manager's hesitancy to let go. Empowerment is not wholesale abrogation of responsibility. It is simply enabling and authorizing people to do what they are capable of doing.

WHAT HAPPENED HERE . . . ?

It is very easy to feel good about filling your work time with interruptions from subordinates. You feel wanted, involved, and important.

The fact is, your overall team yield is lower than it could be because of your reps' needs to involve you every step of the way. If your people were working in a more independent fashion you could have more sales campaigns in progress at any given time, and the overall sales cycle could be shortened significantly.

So why do they come to Sharon for their short-term direction? Maybe Sharon has staged the environment in such a way that they feel they *must* come to her for everything. For example:

- It appears Sharon may be *methods*, rather than *results* oriented. She probably gets too involved in *how* her people approach the sale?
- Sharon probably doesn't give her people full responsibility for a sales campaign, but rather keeps the responsibility and just assigns them tasks.
- When her people ask for direction, or come in with a problem, maybe Sharon goes directly into a "preaching" mode telling them exactly what to do.
- It seems likely that Sharon has never told her reps that it is okay for them to think and act for themselves.

Maybe Sharon is a new manager, and all this participation amounts to showing-off, in other words, an ego trip. It is a fault in experienced managers as well.

Sharon may not have enough confidence in her people to allow them to run by themselves. This often happens when sales managers possess extensive product and technology expertise and have a lot of experience. The thought is, my level of knowledge is the only acceptable level.

In any case, Sharon's teams' overall production depends, to a great extent, on her availability and judgment. As a result, she has little time to work on those items that could improve the overall effectiveness of her team. She's probably late submitting forecasts and reports to her management, not to mention that her vacations (if she has time to take them) are most likely spent on the phone to the office.

Sharon is probably never more than an arm's length away from her beeper or cellular phone.

Sharon may be happier if she left managing and went back to selling.

OPTIONS

Sharon's options are bounded on the *left* by staying in complete control and bounded on the *right* by fully empowering her people.

If Sharon wants to be like most effective sales managers, she will find a comfortable position in the middle. However, the best sales managers have found that leaning towards the *right* (toward empowerment) is much more effective. Sharon's options are to decide where she wants to position herself. Sharon is on a sliding scale, on which she controls her movement.

POSSIBLE ACTIONS

This is difficult because it involves *admission* to oneself that the current style is not working. The end of the Story signals that Sharon recognizes this important fact. That's good.

Check Your Confidence

Oftentimes the level of sales-rep empowerment is directly related to the level of confidence the manager has in her people's ability to act independently. The fact is, a manager must first have confidence in herself, before she can have confidence in her people. The manager must believe that she can deal with any situation that could possibly arise out of her people's acting independently. Until the manager has that self-confidence, she cannot have confidence in her people, or even worse, give them the confidence they need to succeed independently.

Sharon cannot give her people something she does not have, so the first step is to develop her personal confidence. That can come only from a deeper understanding of sales management. Outside training and coaching from the boss may be called for.

Then Sharon must begin to relinquish control in a few limited situations. This will allow her to deal with the transition issues and prove to herself that she, and they, can handle it. Truthfully, Sharon will be surprised how easy it is. She'll kick herself for not doing this sooner.

Start Slowly

Just as Sharon is going to be reluctant to give up control, her people are going to be reluctant to take it. Let's face it. If they have worked in a high-control environment for some time, many will not know how to handle the transition.

First, Sharon must let them know what she is up to. She must tell them that she believes that they can handle more responsibility and that she plans to help them accept it. She must tell them that she understands that it will be difficult for all of them, but if they work on it together, everyone will benefit.

Next, she should come up with a simple catchphrase that everyone can identify with. For example:

"Better to beg for forgiveness, rather than plead for permission."

Whatever Sharon picks, she should make it visible, but not trite. Putting the catchphrase on all of her written communications and on the wall in her office helps. If she wants to have the thought of empowerment in the front of *their* minds, Sharon needs it in front of hers as well.

Next, pull the team together and ask them to come up with some sales or marketing initiatives that they believe would improve their individual and collective performance.

Jointly agree on a couple of ideas and assign the ideas to miniteams to completely plan, design, implement, and manage. Sharon can set herself up as a consultant in this process, track the results diligently and be sure to credit her people when presenting results of these initiatives to upper management. Even better, she can let her people present their ideas and results themselves.

Next, wean them slowly but deliberately. When asked for advice, give it freely. But give advice only on *their* ideas and plans. Be careful not to provide solutions.

When posed with a scenario, ask, "What do you recommend?"

If their solution is not on target or superficial, do not criticize them, but coach them. Initiate dialogue with questions such as these examples:

"While preparing your solution, did you consider . . . ?" or "Have you talked to Susan? She had a similar situation recently and might be able to give you some ideas."

Help *guide* your people not only to the solution of their current problem but to a methodology that will help them improve their overall problem-solving skills. There is an old saying that goes "If you give a man a fish, he eats for a day. If you teach him to fish, he'll eat for a lifetime." This saying is one-hundred percent applicable to sales.

Be patient. Most of the time Sharon will know the solution to the problem or the correct strategy to use well before her rep knows it. Guard against telling the rep what to do for the sake of expediency unless he or she is in the middle of a time-critical situation. Even then, *share your thought process*, not just the answer. The time Sharon spends with her people today will pay off manyfold in the future.

Take every opportunity to coach in this manner. During staff meetings and strategy sessions pose hypothetical what-if questions. Listen to the responses and guide the thought process with questions.

Finish Briskly

Reward innovative behavior. When your people solve a difficult problem or come up with a clever approach, applaud their efforts and allow them to share their concepts with the rest of the sales unit.

Do not reprimand a rep for making a mistake or losing a sale. Sit down with the individual and review the approach and the thought process. Turn negative situations into positive learning experiences. This is especially important if the rep was acting in an appropriate manner throughout the process or sales campaign. You do not want to shake the confidence of a rep, or of others who are watching for your reactions and approval.

If you do these things consistently, you will be well on your way to the *right* side of the spectrum—empowering your people to start taking initiative.

Create an Operating Envelope

As you begin to move your people to the right, it becomes important to clearly define what you expect from them.

In Problem 3–1 the setting of guiding principles and personal beliefs are discussed. You may find a reading of that problem helpful here. You need to develop a guiding principle regarding empowerment. For example, we strongly believe the following elements are the critical ingredients of empowerment . . . its definition . . . the ingredients in our envelope.

- To think independently, synthesizing the facts, and exercising good judgment
- To generate innovative approaches to sales strategies and solutions
- To be accountable, or answerable, for decisions and actions

Add others that fit your understanding and beliefs regarding empowerment. Give yourself time. You have to be able to tell your people what you believe regarding empowerment and what behaviors you expect.

Then listen for areas in which you continually have to give counsel. That is a signal that you haven't communicated a key area of empowerment. Update your guiding principle regarding empowerment with that experience.

Set Up an Operational Discipline

In the past, Sharon was involved in most of the deals. Because of this, she may not have needed much operational discipline or management processes. Now, she will not be as involved in most deals. Therefore, she will need to regularly test the water. For each rep, she may want to keep her eyes on the following: Your list will vary.

- Performance-to-sales goal
- Performance to forecast
- Pipeline status
- Customer satisfaction
- Days outstanding for payment

The added discipline and management process will help Sharon remain confident that things are going as planned, or tell her where she needs to be more involved.

Moving to the right, empowering your people, is hard work but well worth it. You will be amazed at how much time you will have to devote to other priorities.

LESSONS

The more horses you have pulling the cart, the faster and farther it will go.

In a right-dominated sales-management model, your people are out in front, with you, pulling as hard as they can. Whereas in a left-dominated model, they are sitting in the cart while you do all the pulling. Quite honestly, if they are good people, they probably are not even enjoying the ride.

3–6 THE PROBLEM:
Your directives and strategies are unduly challenged.

THE STORY

Joyce began to feel uncomfortable during her last sales-unit meeting, when Howard, one of her best reps and clearly a peer leader, started pushing back extremely hard on a directive Joyce felt was important for the overall success of the group. Howard was so vocal and adamant that others joined him, while some supported Joyce's position, turning it into a free-for-all.

"All right, all right, Howard, that's it," Joyce finally yelled in exasperation.

Joyce quickly moved the discussion to a less controversial subject, despite the fact she never gained closure on the original topic. Everyone could see Joyce's obvious displeasure. The meeting broke up in a glum atmosphere.

TEMPTATIONS

Public put-downs, particularly by subordinates, are unacceptable and can cause any manager to react irrationally. The nature of the problem creates two sets of related temptations.

Real-time temptations. The heat of the moment and the pressure of all those eyes glued on you can cause regretful reactions.

Scream

"I DON'T WANT TO HEAR ANOTHER WORD, NOW CUT THE NONSENSE."

Cave-in

"All right, all right, you win, we'll do it your way."

After-the-fact temptations. There is also a long-term gnawing worry about ongoing damage to your authority and credibility that could lead you to negatively reassert yourself.

Retaliation

"Howard, I don't care what your sales are. If you ever do that again, you're history."

Eliminate meetings

"That's the last time I'll ever let them gang up on me."

You never know if you'll fully recover from such an episode.

WHAT HAPPENED HERE . . . ?

A good rep appears to have exhibited poor judgment by crossing the fine line between respectful challenge and insubordination. Howard could be a very savvy guy, and his inputs may be legitimate, but his emotional delivery blots out the value of his contribution.

In this case, maybe Joyce did not have the time to let her team aid in the development of her idea. Because of this, they felt the need to guide her through the thought process after the fact, and it got out of hand.

Open environments require rules and regulations that govern the interchange of ideas. Maybe Joyce has not spent the time to clearly establish the ground rules.

Joyce's people may not understand the difference between nonnegotiable issues, such as *"should* we do it?" and non-negotiable issues, such as *"how* do we do it." The "should" question has already been answered in Joyce's mind. The sales unit must now concentrate its inputs on the negotiable question, "How do we do it?"

Joyce may not have defined the behaviors she values, so that her people understand how to react in certain situations.

Howard may be retaliating for a previous grievance he had with Joyce, and is consciously trying to make Joyce look bad.

In spite of Howard's performance, the chemistry between the two may never have been good. Howard may hold little respect for Joyce.

Finally, the power of peer leaders to embolden other less-capable group members has had an effect on the chemistry and camaraderie of the sales unit. Joyce probably struggled a long time to build those dynamics, and they may have taken an irreparable hit.

OPTIONS

Joyce has four problems-within-the-problem to wrestle with. One, address Howard's behavior. Two, settle on the environment she wants in the sales unit. Three, communicate the parameters of the environment. Four, build up from the ashes of the destructive behavior.

Her options with each problem depend on her personal objectives. In Joyce's case, her objectives are to be treated with respect, ensure civility in the sales unit, and foster an open environment.

PROBLEM #1:   Every sales manager has a different threshold of tolerance for challenge. Joyce's relationship with, and respect for, the challenger, and the way the challenge was issued, has a lot to do with her tolerance and reaction. Joyce must pull Howard aside and tell him how she feels and what behaviors she expects in the future. Her options are to be as soft as putty, firm but fair, or tough as nails.

PROBLEM #2:   Since Joyce's objective is an open environment, her only options have to deal with how open is open? She could keep open discussion a part of her style but discipline those who speak out against her. Or, recognizing that challenge is a healthy part of open environments, she could engineer an environment that allows her people to voice their opinions without creating a free-for-all.

PROBLEM #3:   Joyce's options here relate to how she communicates the environment. There are two elements of communication. The short-term element deals with the words she chooses to use in front of the team. In that process, she must make Howard look like a part of the solution, not a villain. The long-term element deals with the integrity of her personal actions.

PROBLEM #4:   Joyce's options are to rebuild on her own, or to look for ways to integrate the leverage of Howard, the peer leader, to strengthen the sales-unit's comeback.

In any case, Joyce needs to deal with this situation swiftly and decisively if she is to keep the team welded together, reestablish her personal standing, and be effective in the future.

POSSIBLE ACTIONS

Leadership is not easy. Your personal style will, more than anything else, define your leadership style.

Deal with Howard

This meeting should be held right after the sales unit meeting breaks up. A counseling approach will do more good than an emotional confrontation. Be candid and specific. Focus on Howard's behavior, not the items that were under discussion in the sales unit meeting. Get agreement from Howard that he understands and will adhere to your counseling.

Open Environments

Don Shula, former coach of the Miami Dolphins football team, once said that a river without banks is just a puddle. In creating an environment that encourages openness, you need to clearly define and communicate those "banks" if you expect good ideas to flow.

Define the Banks of the River

The banks of your open-environment river are your own personal philosophy or guiding principles about open environments.

Here are some examples of principles in which we strongly believe, that define our banks for open environments.

1. *Respect for the individual.* People and their ideas, regardless how different, deserve everyone's respect.
2. *Teamwork.* Sales units working as a team come up with the best approaches and best answers to problems and opportunities. Active solicitation of ideas from all team members helps teams win and ultimately gain glory for individuals.
3. *Innovation.* New and clever ideas that aid the objectives of the sales unit are welcomed.

4. *Passion—with perspective.* Ideas tempered by a clear perspective of the overall team situation, business needs, and business constraints are essential.

Add to, or modify this list to create banks of your own. However you define your personal banks, *you must strongly believe* in them. (Problem 3–1 talks about building a management philosophy and guiding principles. You may find it helpful.)

Valued Behaviors also Define Your Banks

It is important that you clearly let your people know what type of behavior you expect and value. Elements of behavior that we believe are imperative for open environments include:

- Everybody is treated with courtesy.
- Teammates are allowed to completely communicate their thoughts and ideas.
- Attempt to see the positive in every idea put on the table.
- Dead horses need not be beaten.

Once again, modify this list to incorporate *your beliefs* and suit your own style. These principles and valued behaviors, or banks, when communicated and managed within a sales unit, set the proper tone for open environments.

Communicate the Banks of Your River

At this point, only Joyce knows what her threshold for tolerance of challenge is and what her banks and values are. Her task is to communicate the banks, values, and threshold, via words and actions, to her sales unit. The best way is to simply stand up in front of the sales unit and lay it all out. People expect and respect the communication of boundaries and rules.

Reinforce your banks and values visibly on chalkboards, chartpads, E-mails, memos, or however else you choose. Then watch the behavior, contribution, and sales results improve.

Rebuild and Be Consistent

Confide in Howard from the beginning of your bank-building process. It would not surprise us if a top performer of Howard's capability and astuteness sensed the value of volunteering to apologize in front of the sales unit. If that doesn't occur, ask him for other rebuilding ideas.

Now that you have defined how "the river" will run, you must continually reinforce the valued behavior. Thank people for innovative ideas. Openly recognize the team when they are working well with one another. Thank everybody for taking part in the formulation of a good action plan. Give the team credit for the idea when you are presenting it to your boss.

On the other hand, clearly and swiftly deal with individuals who are not playing by the rules. For example, if the story were to repeat itself with another player: "Jack, we have heard you. Now let others voice their opinions." If that does not work, take a ten-minute break and step out into the hall. Let Jack air his concerns. Then let him know that you respect his ideas (even though you may not agree with him), but you are concerned that he is not playing by the rules.

An open management style, although appearing casual, requires a significant amount of structure.

LESSONS

The major lesson of this problem is that your people expect you to provide clear boundaries—or banks. They do not know how to react if you do not tell them.

Of course, the best approach is to take preemptive action by communicating your open-environment principles and values before this problem attacks you.

If you invite an open environment, you need to be prepared to deal with people who do not agree with your direction or strategy. Disagreement is generally healthy. If it becomes disruptive or abusive, the value of disagreement is lost.

Effectively leading sales units in an open environment is hard work, but it is more gratifying and profitable than the alternative.

3–7 THE PROBLEM:

You must rally your people around an enormous sales goal.

THE STORY

It is early in the fourth quarter of the fiscal year, and Karen's team is ahead of its plan. As a matter of fact, she is on the verge of having the best year of her career.

Karen's boss, Bart, calls her into his office one day, and after exchanging some pleasantries he got serious and said "Karen, we need to begin thinking about next year. I just received my sales goal, and it isn't a pretty picture."

Right about then her hands begin to sweat.

Bart continued, "You are my strongest team, and therefore I need you to pick up more than your fair share." Bart then handed Karen a piece of paper with a number on it. She reads the number in disbelief and asks if this is really her number or an estimate of the U.S. national debt. They both laugh nervously.

TEMPTATIONS

After you've experienced the fatigue and euphoria that accompanies the view from the top of a mountain you've just scaled, straining to see the top of a much higher mountain can lead to feelings of hopelessness and despair.

Surrender

"We can't make this number. I am not even going to try. This is impossible."

Whine

"You've got to be kidding. C'mon, give me a break, Bart. I carried the load this year."

Haggle

"I can stretch to 85 percent of this number, but not the whole thing. How about if we do some reallocating with the other managers? Even the national budget gets negotiated."

As a rule, it is best not to overreact in these situations. Remember a couple of things:

1. What you say now could affect your relationship with Bart and your peers forever.
2. Your salespeople are always taking their lead from you. If they see you overreacting and complaining, you can bet that they will follow suit when it is time for you to give them their sales goals.

WHAT HAPPENED HERE . . . ?

Usually, when a sales unit gets a larger-than-expected target it is because the company needs the revenue or has reason to believe that the revenue is achievable. Budgets are not developed and assigned for punitive purposes. The upside is that the boss has great confidence in Karen.

Consider the following possibilities:

- Corporate expenses are too high, and the only way to avoid another layoff is to generate more revenue.
- Management wants to make the numbers look good because the company will be offered for sale.
- Executive management is under intense pressure to satisfy stockholder or board-of-director expectations.

- Karen's firm is losing market share, and management has decided to make some aggressive pricing and promotional moves to stop the slide.
- Marketing is about to introduce a new line of products intended to leapfrog the competition.
- Karen's boss may be trying to make a name for himself in the company by committing to a large growth budget.
- A mistake could have been made. Karen's potential may have been overestimated due to a miscalculation.

  In any case, it is now Karen's problem to deal with.

OPTIONS

There are four options with this problem.

1. Karen could expend all her time and energy trying to get her number reduced. This is usually not a fruitful exercise. At the end of the day, Karen's boss would then have the problem of redeploying the "difference" to Karen's peers. He is upset, her peers are upset, and she has to start watching her backside. It's not healthy.
2. Karen could decide to pedal faster. This is the run-and-pray approach. It can work if the percentage increase is not too large or if Karen's people are underutilized.
3. Karen could stretch her people and then polish her whip. Again, this can work, but only for a short time. Karen's reps will work for only so long with the sword of Damocles hanging over their heads.
4. Finally, Karen can decide that although the number is near impossible, she is going to find a way to make it. As Winston Churchill once said to the people of England: "This was their finest hour." And it may well be Karen's finest hour.

POSSIBLE ACTIONS

Enormous sales goals take enormous leadership. You must convert the burden of an enormous sales goal into the energy required to achieve it.

Adopt a Can-do Attitude

First and foremost, develop and internalize a can-do attitude by outlining a rough draft of possible strategies and action steps in your mind. Without this attitude, you will not be able to convince your people that they can succeed. You might not know precisely at this point *how* you are going to make the budget, but you must not doubt that you *will* make it.

A can-do attitude springs from self-confidence and a healthy response to challenge, not from cheerleading or immature enthusiasm.

Only when you have confirmed your confidence (however shaky it may be) can you give the enormous sales goal to your people. Remember, you can never give something, tangible or intangible, to someone unless you first possess it. Please take your time with your attitude-building process because everything that follows depends on it. You want to have your people see you as a living embodiment of Dr. Florence Sabin's quote, "If I didn't believe the answer could be found I wouldn't be working on it."

Check Morale

Pray that it is good. Play up the team's current performance, voice your belief that they can do anything, and get them pumped up to a mind-set for dealing with what is coming. Your own style and relationships with your people will be your best guide. Don't be manipulative, but feed and reinforce their self-confidence.

If your team's morale is not good, you are in deeper difficulty. Problem 3–4 suggests that morale is fragile and that turnarounds take time. Attack and correct the morale problem first.

Armed with a can-do attitude and an understanding of the sales unit's morale, it's now time for Karen to talk to Bart.

Test for Accuracy

First, make sure Bart understands that you are committed to finding a way to make the goal.

Let him know that your objective at this moment is understanding and confirmation. You must understand the parameters that were used to set Bart's budget and your budget, so that you can communicate the logic and rationale to your people.

If you can find an error in corporate's logic, your boss may be able to get his budget reduced, and in turn yours may be reduced proportionately. It is important that this testing be focused on the implications associated with your sales unit and not on your personal agenda.

Once you have satisfied your understanding and confirmation needs, *let it be*.

Protect the Current Fiscal Period

There is a risk that needs to be addressed. (Assuming that Karen goes public with the number, or the number becomes known.) Karen and her people are in the midst of closing out a dynamite year. She does not want anything to distract her people from their goal of finishing on top. When they find out what their budgets are going to be for the next period, they could:

- Throw up their hands and start looking for a new job,
- Waste time trying to convince Karen that the number is too high and needs to be adjusted,
- Plan ahead by sandbagging this year's orders so that they have a jump-start on the next period. (The authors are assuming that Karen, herself, will not sandbag.)

Typically, sales-compensation programs are most lucrative once salespeople exceed their goal. Since Karen's team is doing well, they probably (she hopes) will not slow down.

Regardless of the reps' knowledge of the next period's budget, if you have an incentivized sales force, stay close to your less-than-100-percent performers as the year comes to an end. If you have a salaried sales force, stay close to your greater-than-100-percent performers.

Karen should start the process of getting ready for the next period while keeping the number in her pocket for as long as possible. There is no upside in sharing it prematurely.

Involve Your People

Individually and collectively, ask everyone to begin thinking about the next period while they are closing the current period. This is time well spent. They will feel they are part of the system.

Do not share the enormous sales goal. It could boggle their minds and thought processes. Ask them to think about trends, strategies, tactics, major opportunities, new markets, competitive targets, priorities, and all the other elements important to your business. The objective at this point is to set the stage for a *more comprehensive planning process* than normal.

Calculate Your Run Rate

The next thing to do is determine the run rate of your sales unit. Run rate is the number that you would *normally expect* to be assigned for the next period. Different sales organizations calculate run rates differently, but generally a sales manager would consider the current year's forecasted end point, minus any one-time large deals, plus the industry growth rate (or your company's growth rate in the area), plus new one-time deals.

Here is an example. The numbers are purely illustrative:

Current year's forecasted end-point	$10,000,000
Minus one-time large deals, if any. Example: One deal @ 1,000,000	-1,000,000
	9,000,000
Plus the industry growth rate. Example: 10%	900,000
Plus new one-time large deals, if any. Example: One deal @ 1,250,000	1,250,000
New run rate	$11,150,000

Now compare your sales unit's run-rate number to your enormous sales goal. The difference is referred to as the "delta." Example: run rate of $11,150,00 versus enormous sales goal of $17,00,000. The delta is $5,850,000. (This level of delta can make anyone sweat.)

Leading, managing, and selling

You are *compelled* to pursue excellence in the way you lead, manage, and sell in order to beat an enormous sales goal. The best approach is to mirror the Olympic motto: "*citius, altius, fortius,*"—or—"faster, higher, stronger." Every element of your work must be a leap to world-level standards.

Your objective becomes finding ways to chip away at the delta until it is zero.

Now's the Time

Share the enormous sales goal with your sales unit—*at a time and place and in a forum*—that will serve as the beginning of your long-term assault on the goal. Orchestrate this campaign launch thoughtfully. This is a new experience for everyone. Get everyone in the boat securely.

Share your aforementioned can-do attitude.

The Starting Point

Where are you going to sell? Targeting possible customers to whom to sell, *more precisely than past efforts*, will help reduce the delta. It makes no sense to attack an enormous sales goal without more and better market data. Existing customers is a good first step. Next, the availability and use of innumerable information sources such as mailing lists, directories, sophisticated databases, state and government databanks, and others is imperative. This is a team effort. Utilize marketing staff, outside researchers and consultants, associations, government agencies, and other resources relevant to your business. Leadership in locating and gathering this information will vary from firm to firm. Karen and her people must be a part of the process, contributing their own market knowledge and opinions, not just being spoon-fed the data.

Make estimations as to the improvements in run rate provided by precision targeting. For example: Precision targeting could reduce the delta from $5,850,000 to $3,850,000.

Deployment Initiatives

The question that needs to be asked is: "Can we improve our expected run rate by changing how we are currently organized and deployed?" (Review Problem 2–3 on deployment for ideas.) Consider options that are natural extensions of your current organization and focus. It is best to steer clear of revolutionary changes because they could consume precious time and resources.

Once you have drafted some deployment alternatives, put up a strawman proposal to your sales unit and give them an opportunity to react to it. *The objective of the exercise is to get everyone thinking how the sales unit can maximize sales by altering its deployment.* In spite of salespeople's reticence to change, they will appreciate the involvement, and you will be the recipient of many helpful points and considerations.

As the sales unit reviews and reacts to the straw proposal, make estimations as to the sales improvements to run rate. (This is not an exact science.) Once completed, calculate a new delta. For example, the sales unit, through new deployment schemes, may be able to reduce the delta from 3,850,000 to 2,000,000.

Tactical Initiatives

Since the delta is still positive, you now need to brainstorm with your sales unit and plan other initiatives to eliminate the remaining delta. Some examples could include:

1. Conducting special training.
2. Using new market-development tools such as a website or a targeted direct-mail campaign.

3. Launching a revitalized support "toolbox" for your sales partners and resellers.

4. Creating selling and buying incentives around certain products or for certain types or classes of customers.

5. Expanding services you previously provided for free, and then charging moderate fees.

6. Introducing new financing options.

7. Bundling products and/or services in new and creative ways.

8. Implementing sales-force automation processes to improve productivity.

9. Expanding export sales in new countries if off-shore markets are in your purview.

Develop realistic estimates of how much each initiative will reduce your delta. For example, the selection of initiatives 1, 4, and 7 may reduce your remaining delta from $2,000,000 to zero.

Set Your Rep's Goal Sheets

Most often, the sales manager would distribute her sales unit's total number to her reps letting them collectively carry the complete nut. (Problem 4–3 would be a good guide at this point.)

However, Karen may feel that passing out the entire goal to her people would demoralize them. She may want to hold some back. If so, she *must ensure* that the company's compensation plan rewards overperformance and that every rep knows that she is depending on him or her to overperform in order for the sales unit to win. The budget methodology choice is never easy. Karen can get some inputs and guidance from her boss on this important call.

Create Operational Discipline

Karen needs to ensure that everybody in the sales unit is continually focused on the right activities. Operational discipline, through a *modified* management process, will allow her to monitor and manage her people's activities. *There must be a more precise execution of the management processes that accompany an attack on an enormous sales goal.*

WARNING: DO NOT MAKE THE MANAGEMENT PROCESS BURDENSOME. An example of a simple process is as follows:

- Set an appropriate cycle for business reviews. The time segment represents your firm's standard reporting period. The review frequency represents how often during the time segment you meet with each sales rep. The frequency must be greater than usual.

Suggestion:

Time Segment	Review Frequency
Quarter	Biweekly
Month	Weekly

Design a simple format for everyone to follow during the reviews.

Suggestion:

- Forecast for the current time segment and performance to date against the forecast
- New opportunities in the pipeline, how they were identified, and plans to identify others
- Issues and roadblocks that need to be resolved to close specific opportunities
- Major sales activities planned and resources and tools needed
- What's working and what's not working

Focus on the "help" aspect of your management process and the reviews will not be looked upon as a burden.

Accelerate Your Personal Pace

Throughout the period of the enormous sales goal, provide your reps with decisions, opinions, and ideas at a level of speed they have never seen before.

LESSONS

This problem teaches you that you must transform the pressures of an enormous sales goal into the energy and processes required to achieve it. When faced with an enormous sales goal you must lead and manage at a higher level of intensity and with classical precision.

Keeping your organization at full strength with top-quality people and integrating their intellectual assets and energy fully can minimize trauma associated with enormous sales goals.

Johnny Miller, world-famous PGA golfer, who early in his career was compared to Jack Nicklaus, said, "When I got to the top of the mountain I enjoyed the view, but when Jack Nicklaus got to the top of a mountain he looked for a higher mountain to climb." If you adopt an attitude of always looking for higher mountains, when one comes along you're more apt to be able to scale it.

part four

TROUBLESHOOTING MANAGEMENT PROBLEMS

4-1 THE PROBLEM:
You are having a hard time finding top-notch people.

THE STORY

It was 3:00 P.M. and Eric had been interviewing candidates since 8:00 in the morning to fill the two open slots on his team. The fact that he had candidates to interview was the good news. The bad news was that this was the fourth day of intensive interviewing, and he had not found anyone who was up to his standards to join his team. Where are the good ones, he kept thinking.

The pressure to hire some new reps was growing.

"Eric, how is it going?" his boss queried him during a break in the interviewing.

I didn't need to be jabbed with that needle, Eric thought to himself.

Eric was clearly under the gun. Panic was starting to set in.

TEMPTATIONS

The temptations at times like this are all variations of the same frightful theme—compromise.

Create excuses

"This candidate's track record is only fair, but it sounds as if he was not treated fairly in these past two positions."

Go backwards

"That person I talked to yesterday was sort-of, kind-of a maybe. I'll bring her back."

Revamp your specifications

"Maybe I am not being realistic and should revise my profile and standards."

Never, never, never yield to hiring subpar people just because the pressure is on.

WHAT HAPPENED HERE . . . ?

You have two gaping holes in your organization, and you cannot find qualified candidates.

There are many reasons for having open slots:

- Eric's company has experienced a sharp upturn in business.
- A new product has been introduced, and the company wants Eric to hire people specifically to sell it.

- Eric may have just opened new territories.
- Eric's sales unit may be experiencing higher than normal attrition for reasons of reorganization, changed strategies, financial performance, or competitive raiding.
- Eric's leadership and management style may not be conducive to holding people.
- Eric's industry, company, or products and services may not be attractive compared to other job alternatives.

Whatever the reason for the openings, Eric is having difficulty filling them. There are only five reasons for not being able to find *top-qualified* people.

1. Eric has waited until he has an opening to begin the search. He forgot sales-management Rule #1, which is to *recruit all the time.*
2. Eric may be in a rut. He may be looking in the same old tired and worn-out places where he has always looked and may be using the same old search tools.
3. Eric may be trying to do this all alone, not using the resources in his company.
4. Eric's message to the marketplace may be flawed. The words, values, attributes, and deliverables he is using to describe his company and the open positions may not be attractive to *top people* in the job market or be competitive with other firms.
5. Eric may not be able to recognize a top candidate if he saw one. As Elbert Hubbard, the American author once said, "There is something rarer than ability. It is the ability to recognize ability."

OPTIONS

Eric has two options.

1. He could continue along the search path he's on and hope and pray that he finds some good people. In so doing, Eric could accept running behind his sales plan as he is, or he could make some adjustments by providing extra help to his top people while his search is underway.
2. Or, he could try to increase the number of high-quality applicants available to him.

The choice seems obvious, but that's not the way it always goes.

POSSIBLE ACTIONS

This is Eric's big chance to improve his sales unit.

Think for a Minute

First of all, top quality people *are* out there. You know that.

Second, what are you looking for? As silly as that question sounds, can you *precisely articulate* what a top-quality candidate looks like, so you'll know one when you see one?

Third, if you're not getting the *quality* of candidate you want, you're doing something wrong. You're a savvy sales manager who knows where the warts are in your own industry and business, in your firm's hiring practices, and in your own interviewing processes. Admit the suboptimal approaches and messages you are clinging to and commit to changing them.

Finally, you are offering a "package" to a prospective employee, a package in the broad sense, not a package in the compensation sense. There are two aspects to that package: the substantive contents and the pretty wrapping and bow. It is your job to contribute to making both aspects of that package as attractive as can be.

Put Yourself in their Shoes

You probably consider yourself a top-quality sales manager. What would *you* look for in packages that you would examine, or that would attract you to discuss another opportunity? Here are some examples of what *top sales professionals of all ranks* want to see, feel, and believe, and all of this must be communicated just to get them to come in your door.

- *Environments:* "I want an environment based on integrity and professionalism."
- *Attitude:* "I want to work with a committed, positive, and confident group of people that have a clear view of where they are going."
- *Leadership:* "The management team should be courageous, forward-looking people who communicate bedrock values."
- *Technology usage:* "I want to have access to the latest computer and communications technologies and to have the firm committed to technology usage and leadership."
- *Compensation:* "Top compensation that rewards top performance is important."
- *Recognition:* "I want to be recognized for my efforts, both in and outside the firm."
- *Freedom:* "I'd like a culture where I can express myself, where innovation is welcome."
- *Growth:* "I want an organization committed to planned growth that affords future personal opportunities."
- *Development:* "Exposure to quality training programs is essential."
- *Contribution:* "I want to make a significant contribution to the enterprise and the ecosystem in which it operates."
- *Intellectual challenge:* "I want to be exposed to new concepts so that I can grow, and I'd hope to be able to reciprocate with ideas of my own and have them listened to."
- *Operational excellence:* "I want a firm engrossed in TQM, BPR, JIT, and other proven management processes, and one that always has its eye out for new processes."
- *Equity (if you're a small business):* "I'd like a piece of the action if you want me to pour my heart and soul into this."
- *Responsibility:* "Give me something significant to do, let me run, and hold me accountable."
- *The employment process:* "I would hope to be treated with hospitality and respect throughout an organized hiring proceeding."

Does your package contain these points, and do your interviewing team members communicate these points? The attributes of your package should be consistent with the attributes top candidates desire.

Three key points:

1. What *top people* look for, and the degree to which they must see it, is not the same as what everyone else looks for and needs.
2. Firms tend to draw people who are mirror images of the image the firm portrays.
3. Packages of attributes to draw top-quality people are not developed overnight.

Here are some suggested actions to increase the *flow* of top-quality applicants.

Advertise

Do you have a human resources department? If the answer is yes, get their help to craft and place *carefully word-smithed* ads that reflect the package or culture you want to communicate. Use a combination of tried-and-true and new newspapers, magazines, or professional journals. If Eric's firm has a homepage on the World Wide Web, they can advertise there as well.

Human resources can drive and help manage the whole process. They can suggest places to run ads, and they can be invaluable in the screening process.

Without an HR department, a sales, marketing, or organization consultant can help.

Search Firms

Both retained executive-search firms (in virtually all cases) and contingency firms (in some cases) can be an excellent source of high-quality candidates. However, you cannot just go to them when you have a need. You must build a close working relationship with one or two firms in your area by meeting with them on a regular basis. Make sure that they know exactly what type of people you are looking for by providing them with a detailed, written, prioritized profile, and a description of the package you offer.

Give your search contacts immediate and detailed feedback on every candidate they send you. If they see you compromise your profile, you can expect a continuing flow of compromised candidates. In general, treat your search and contingency firms as a specialty arm of your own organization. They funnel the best candidates to those clients with whom they have the best relationships.

Advertise Internally

Another effective way to find strong candidates is to send a memo or E-mail to a wide distribution within your own company (in large firms with diversified operations). Keep the memo brief. Explain the job(s) you have open and the characteristics of the perfect candidate.

Ask the recipients to forward the names of any people they know who fit your needs and may be interested in the open position.

This approach has two benefits:

1. You tap into the personal networks of the people on the distribution list.
2. In a nonthreatening way you are letting others in your company know of your needs in case they themselves have an interest.

Be sure to act swiftly with any candidates who come to you through this route. Remember to keep the person who recommended the candidate in the loop at all times.

Tap Your Personal Network

The same memo you used earlier could be sent, in the form of a letter, to your personal, non-company network, for example, people you have worked with in the past, members of your country club, church, neighbors, friends, and so on. All those contacts have personal networks of their own that can be tapped into.

Here again, act swiftly, keep your network informed of results, and express gratitude for their assistance.

Network

As you travel on business, talk to customers and sales partners, work trade shows, and attend seminars always make it a point to mention the fact that you are looking for people and provide a summary of what those people look like. Also ask people who have been recently hired to recommend candidates. The benefits are obvious.

Trainee Program

Don't overlook the option of hiring good raw recruits, as well as veterans. Balance in a sales unit is essential. It is good to have younger, less-experienced people working alongside seasoned professionals. Both groups benefit from the experience. Setting up a trainee program is not easy, but if done correctly can pay significant dividends. Key things to think about include:

- Invest in and develop a well-led, well-managed, and comprehensive training program that encompasses your company, products and services, and sales skills. *Rigor is the key*.
- Staff your training program with your best people. Let excellence feed excellence.
- Set up a formal mentor/protégé program utilizing your top people.

Corporate Communications

Remind the people who are responsible for all your firm's external communications that the messages and values communicated in all formats and media have a direct impact on recruiting for *all* positions, not just sales. Every phone contact, ad, press release, and sales collateral says something about the desirability of working for your firm, as well as your products and services.

LESSONS

Hiring is your most important task as a manager. Never stop looking for top-notch candidates, regardless of your current needs. It takes carefully crafted messages, recruiting campaigns, and company cultures to lure and hire top-notch people. You can't hire what you can't bring in the door. Ultimately, these two lessons will be your best approach to minimize this problem.

Work with the rest of your management team to build a sensitivity to how your firm is perceived on the outside. Ensure that the package of attributes you finally communicate and offer are consistent with the needs and values of *top-notch* people.

4–2 THE PROBLEM:
You are struggling to decide which candidate to hire.

THE STORY

Peter was a new regional sales manager for a firm in a hot technology sector that was experiencing explosive growth. One of his priorities at the moment was to fill a couple of sales-engineer positions.

He was bleary-eyed from the 172 resumés and all the screening he had gone through in the past two months. He was close to making one decision, but it was a tough call because there were several good people. Frankly, they were all beginning to look alike.

"Peter," his VP asked in the midst of his agonizing, "how are you doing? How many slots have you still got open? We need to fill these positions ASAP. We need the business."

He knew it was time to make some "calls."

TEMPTATIONS

Hiring decisions are the most important decisions a sales manager makes. There isn't a close second. The challenges of hiring can lead to these self-proclaimed realistic decisions.

Compromise

"It looks as if two of these may work out, in spite of a little glitch. And if they don't, well, I'll just fire them and get others. I just can't wait any longer."

Throw darts

"Heck, they all look alike. They all have great backgrounds. I can't go wrong."

Prejudice

"Whoa, here's one that graduated from my alma mater. All Wildcats are great."

American author Mary McCarthy offers this: "If someone tells you he is going to make a 'realistic decision,' you immediately understand that he has resolved to do something bad."

WHAT HAPPENED HERE . . . ?

It sounds as if Peter has gotten a great response from his ads and employment agencies.

Perhaps he understands the magnitude of the decisions and is just afraid to pull the trigger. Maybe deep down inside Peter recognizes that he started a process for which he didn't prepare adequately or execute with the diligence he knows it requires. Maybe he lost sight of what he is looking for or never knew adequately what he was looking for in the first place.

Maybe Peter is thinking that if he looks just a little longer and a little harder he'll find some better alternatives, alternatives who will be obvious, who seem to be risk-free. Familiar feelings?

When a sales manager thinks about the type of person he would like to hire, a mental image of capabilities and attributes comes to mind. That image could be based on experience, beliefs and values, observations, the recommendations of peers and superiors, or a combination of factors. Many managers make sales and sales-management hiring decisions based on nothing more than that image. In a few lucky cases it works. But in many instances it leads to problems ranging from mild disappointment to cases of financial and personal disaster.

OPTIONS

There are four things you can do at this point, each requiring as much help as you can get.

1. You can make some decisions based on the interviews you have conducted.
2. You can bring several of the top candidates back in for another round of discussions.

3. You could crank up your current efforts and keep looking. Maybe run the ads again or go to another agency.

4. You could call time-out and go back to the beginning and examine your methodology to make sure you're doing *everything* as cleanly and thoroughly as possible. It may prevent you from making some bad decisions.

Peter has decided to explore the fourth option.

POSSIBLE ACTIONS

Pull yourself together and focus. It is time to draw up (or redraw) a hiring plan. Base the plan on the 5P-selection formula: *preparation, profile, process, precaution,* and *pick*, which will enable you to assemble the best possible sales unit. Big winners are competent and uncompromising with all five steps.

An important part of this process is not only to help you choose a candidate, but also to help you understand why you chose whom you did.

The responsibility for establishing and setting the standards and ground rules for the 5P process must come from the top sales executive in the firm. In smaller businesses, VPs, general managers, or company presidents who actively head up sales efforts should lead this effort. Implementation leadership then lies with the hiring sales manager.

The 5P process is intentionally detailed because of the seriousness of the subject. We recognize the reality that hiring is both an art and a science and that you may have limited time and resources, but use this process to the fullest extent possible.

The First P: Preparation

Before you even begin the search and interview process there are several things that need to be documented.

1. Think about your customers and buyers and discern what *they* would want in the sales people who will be working with them. Customers and buyers prefer to deal with people like themselves, people who mirror their values and can be responsive to their needs.

2. Characterize your best people. Why are they good? What do they do? Write down the capabilities, skills, and attributes of your best staff members. The outline helps define what you are looking for.

3. Ensure that you have an up-to-date, realistic job description, not the file-drawer variety. Have current staff, human resources, and your boss challenge it. You can't look for people and know whether you have a fit if you can't specify the shape and size of the hole you're trying to fill. Even if your firm doesn't have or doesn't use job descriptions, write down all the things the new salesperson is expected to do. The document acts as an interview checklist.

4. Think about diversity of age, gender, and race in your organization. An unbalanced sales force may be costing you business. Extremes in sales unit makeup should be avoided. As an example, consider how the top sports teams benefit from a good balance of rookies and veterans.

5. Review the following basic ingredients of sales success, with which you are certainly already familiar. There is general agreement among researchers and sales executives that these are time-proven attributes that form a core of competencies in salespeople.
   - *Empathy,* which translates into the ability to listen, understand, be responsive, and build relationships.
   - *Ego drive,* which translates into self-confidence, a strong belief in self, and the drive that makes people self-starters.
   - *Resiliency,* which translates into the ability to bounce back and refuse to fail.
   - *Discipline,* which translates into organization, planning, and a willingness to invest extensive time and effort.
   - *Achievement,* which translates into self-motivation and a continuing quest to succeed.
   - *Competitiveness,* which translates into unyielding persistence and a hunger to win.
   - *Caring,* which translates into a desire to serve, to help, and to solve problems.

6. Obtain some interview coaching, or buy a book on the subject. Ask your human-resources staff, employment agency, or search firm for suggestions. Most are masters.

7. Take a team approach to the hiring process. Pull together a group of people who touch the customer during the course of day-to-day business, such as marketing, customer service, and technical-service people, plus human resources. Diversity in your selection team breeds interviewing thoroughness. Three to four people is probably sufficient, but even a single additional mind and hand is a big help.

The Second P: Profile

Now you're ready to prepare a profile.

Brainstorm. Get your team together and define *in detail* what the new hires should look like. The written profile is a specification for the job. That spec will probably contain 8 to 15 criteria that include everything from the aforementioned core competencies to education, type and amount of experience, prior employers, languages, and computer competency.

A profile that includes all the critical success factors you identified in your preparation phase combined with these additional brainstormed items will ensure that nothing falls between the cracks.

When creating the profile, segment it into the three areas of knowledge, attributes, and skills to ensure completeness. Here are some additional sales-success factors to consider in your profile. Add as you like.

Knowledge is what the candidate should already know.	Attributes are the personal qualities, characteristics, and traits required to sell effectively.	Skills are the natural or acquired talents the candidate already possesses.
Self knowledge is important *because* this is a measure of maturity, and understanding of capabilities. *Specific knowledge* has to do with markets, certain types of customers, technologies, selling, or products.	*Integrity, Attitude, Judgment, Civility, Creativity, Organization, Balance, Stamina, Energy, Image, Work ethic*	*Speaking, Listening, Planning, Writing, Cross-cultural capability, Closing, Managing relationships, Political astuteness, Computer and communications technologies*

Next, prioritize your profile. There are two ways you can do that.

One, you can create a *qualitative* model. Have the selection team rank the profile criteria. As an example, assign an *A* to the most important criterion, *B* to the next most important criterion, *C* to the least critical criterion. This prioritization will let you grade each candidate with an "excellent," "good," "fair," or "poor," making your selection easier and rational.

A simplified *qualitative* profile evaluation sheet could look like this:

Criteria	Excellent	Good	Fair	Poor	Comments
1st Criterion = A	X				
2nd Criterion = B		X			
3rd Criterion = B				X	
4th Criterion = C		X			
5th Criterion = C		X			
Total					

Two, you can create a *quantitative* model. Again, rank the criteria and assign a weight to each one, for example, from a top score of 5 down to a low score of 1. Then rate each of your candidates on a scale of 5, 4, 3, 2, and 1 against your weighted list. Thus, 5 points for a 5-level criterion yields 25 points, the maximum; 3 points for a 2-level criterion yields 6 points. A total will give you scores for each candidate.

A simplified *quantitative* profile evaluation sheet could look like this:

Criteria	5	4	3	2	1	Total	Comments
1st Criterion = 5	X					25	
2nd Criterion = 4		X				16	
3rd Criterion = 4				X		8	
4rd Criterion = 2		X				8	
5th Criterion = 2		X				8	
Total						65	

An important part of this analysis is not to just help you pick a candidate, but also to help you understand why you feel good or bad about a candidate.

Test your profile against your existing sales people. The action serves as a reality check. How well do they meet the profile? This test will help you make sure that your profile is useful. You should find a correlation between current top performers and the profile.

In the end, the profile should represent a sincere reflection and detailed description of the kind of people and capabilities you want in your firm. Finally, discipline yourself to update your profile on an annual basis. The environment is always changing.

The Third **P:** *Process*

Create a process checklist. The checklist is a simple one-page matrix that identifies all the steps in the hiring process, the people who will take part, and the timing. A process ensures thoroughness. It should follow a logical sequence and request confirmations and sign-offs.

A simple process checklist could look like this. Adjust it to meet your needs.

Activity	Responsibility	Timing	Comments	Sign-off
Initial contact				
Resume review				
Initial interview				
Second interview				
Facility tour				
Headquarters interview				
Additional executive interview(s)				
Reference check				
Compensation negotiation				
Employment agreement				
Review and sign-off				
Offer letter sent				
Offer accepted				

Share your process with your candidates from the beginning. It will display your professionalism and differentiate you from other firms they may be considering.

The Fourth P: Precautions

Here are six precautions to take before making your picks.

1. There is a tendency to hire in your own image, and that can be dangerous. Diversify, rather than clone. A diversified sales team calling on a diversified customer base can provide a competitive advantage.

2. The bar that you expect candidates to clear is often the measure of your self-image of skill and capability. Many managers use themselves as the benchmark, and while they may be *good*, it may prevent them from hiring *even better* people. Don't be afraid to hire people *better* than you. As President Kennedy once said, "A rising tide raises *all* boats."

3. Give yourself time in spite of other short-term pressures. Hiring decisions follow you for a very long time—well past your tenure with the firm.

4. Be cautious of first impressions, even though research has demonstrated that first impressions are key to hiring. Interviewees are smarter and better prepared these days. They have received coaching from outplacement firms or career counselors. Also, sales and sales-management applicants are expert at making a good first impression because that is inherent to the sales profession. Make sure the impression holds during follow-up interviews.

5. Candidates also have priorities, and a company profile of their own to match, particularly those who are employed. They have a shopping list that includes compensation plans, your management style, training and development, support, resources, promotional opportunities, potential mergers and acquisitions, downsizing history, expense guidelines, and other concerns—and none are reticent to share their questions. Many candidates have been burned with previous employers. Hiring managers must be prepared for scrutiny and probing questions. Don't lose a great candidate because you can't answer his or her questions.

6. Sell yourself hard in the process because you don't want to lose a potential star. You are competing for the best people. It's a free-agent world. Expect that the candidates are talking to others. Sell your company—its mission, values, expectations, and standards; its products and services; its commitment to research and development, to technology, and to growth; and its strength in the market. Come across as serious, knowledgeable, enthusiastic, candid, and having integrity. Even if the candidate turns down your offer, he or she will likely go home to talk with friends and colleagues about this great company he or she just

interviewed—and the person the candidate talks to may be the potential superstar you are looking for.

The Fifth P: Pick

Decision time. Armed and confident with thorough preparation, a solid profile, a scrupulous process, and mindful of the precautions, the picking now becomes almost self-evident. The best candidate may leap off the page at you.

Get the selection team together again.

- Look at the data, the evaluations, the interview comments, and the observations.
- Listen to everyone. Give yourself time.
- Factor in the chemistry and the gut-level feelings that are so important to hiring decisions. Balance the analytical thinking with subjective fit because you are hiring people, not machines.
- *You* make the decision.
- Document the discussion. Use the comments to go back and tweak your profiles and processes for the next position to be filled.

At the end of the day, put the horses in the barn.

LESSONS

No hiring decisions are better than bad hiring decisions.

Recruiting and hiring never stop. Create these comprehensive processes *now* so that you can use them again in the future. The initial investment keeps paying dividends.

You can use the 5P-selection process in your search for sales partners as well as your own staff.

Hiring is an art as well as a science. The best decisions are a combination of gut, chemistry, logic, and analysis. In the end, you'll choose people that you feel good about, and over the years you'll learn what makes you feel good about people.

Final suggestion: You can turn a great hire into a *fantastic* hire with an intensive, well-organized orientation- and -training period. You may want to refer to that effort as the sixth P, Priming.

And always remember what Ambrose Bierce, another American author, said, "A man is known by the company he organizes."

4–3 THE PROBLEM:
You are unsure how to assign equitable sales goals.

THE STORY

Susan, Elaine's best rep, asked her for some of her time late one Friday afternoon. It seems Susan was concerned that her new sales goal would be too high—again.

"Boss," Susan said diplomatically, "you've always made it a practice of taking our previous year's results and adding a growth factor to determine next year's quota. Right?"

"Right," Elaine agreed.

"I don't think that's fair," Susan went on, "especially for someone like me who goes the extra step to bring in the extra business. Your approach penalizes me each year."

Elaine assured her that this year would be different. Susan seemed to buy into Elaine's comment and left. Elaine leaned back, thinking, I've got to come up with something better.

TEMPTATIONS

When you know you're going to be faced with inevitable challenges, and no one is going to be happy with his or her sales goal, there is the temptation to take a sneaky way out.

Play the "equality" card
> "I'll just peanut-butter-spread the budget by dividing my total goal by the number of reps I have and assign each person that number."

Reward and revenge
> "I'll give Susan a break and load up a couple of the troublemakers."

It's not a big deal
> "Hey, the market changes so quickly it doesn't really matter who gets what."

It does matter who gets what because people's understanding and respect for a process is often reflected in their commitment and results, and you are impacting their compensation.

WHAT HAPPENED HERE ... ?

It sounds as if Elaine has been taking the easy way out in the past. Many managers do exactly that. There may be some businesses where the my-percentage-is-your-percentage approach is appropriate. It's simple, and it can work.

The problem with Elaine's method is that it does not take into account major nonrecurring wins or losses that happened throughout the year, may under- or overestimate potential of a territory, and to some extent, rewards poorer performers and penalizes better performers.

Perhaps Elaine is in a rut because this is the way the company has always done it. Her manager may never have questioned her methodology, no other rep may have questioned it before Susan, and Elaine may have been focusing on other matters.

Elaine may not have the initiative or the interest to delve into the subject. After all, assigning sales goals is not what you'd call a pleasurable management task.

OPTIONS

There are many ways to assign budgets. This *is* a complex subject. The best approach depends on your particular situation.

The fact is, budget setting is not an exact science. You can apply science and logic to ensure to at least the 80 percent level that each of your people has an equal opportunity to be successful. After that, your gut and experience must take over.

There are many factors that influence budget setting. For example:

- Geography
- The current installed base
- Upside potential
- The existing pipeline
- Planned marketing and promotional activities

- New-product launches
- Competitive positioning and areas of strength
- Experience levels of the reps
- Customer movement and investments
- Number and experience of partners in the territory

Each of these factors (and others important in your business) impact the reps' ability to achieve their sales goals. Your job is to confirm *your* factors, set the most equitable sales goals possible, and then help each of your reps exceed those goals.

Let's begin with some philosophy. Elaine needs to decide how she is going to break up the load she is carrying.

1. Is she going to deploy 100 percent of the quota on her reps?
2. Is she going to deploy more than 100 percent on her reps to guard against individual shortfalls and attrition?

3. Is she going to deploy less than 100 percent on her reps and therefore depend on their overperformance (typically at an accelerated commission rate) to carry her over the line?

Each approach has merit and can be successful. It really depends on Elaine's style and corporate policies as to which one she chooses.

Once she has determined the total sales goal to be deployed, she has some options:

1. The smooth peanut-butter spread is an option.
2. Elaine's historic approach, the my-percentage-increase-is-your-percentage increase is a second option.
3. Elaine could try to evaluate the potential of each of her reps' territories and set sales goals accordingly. Let's take this approach to address Susan's concern.

POSSIBLE ACTIONS

First, get organized with your current sales goals, historic data, market information, and your PC or pen and paper. Next, confirm how you want to deploy, or place, your people. For the sake of this Problem, assume that your people's assignments remain unchanged.

Establish Some Ratios and Definitions

The following points will be referred to in this budgeting process.

Average yield = total budget ÷ total number of reps. Example, if your budget is $16,000,000 and you have 14 sales reps, then average yield is $16,000,000 ÷ 14 reps = $1,142,857 per rep. Average yield serves as a comparative reference point.

Growth percent = the growth from last year's actual results compared to this year's budget, shown as a percentage. Example, this year's $16,000,000 budget minus last year's actual results of $14,000,000 = $2,000,000. $2,000,000 ÷ $14,000,000 = 14.29% growth from last year's actual results. Growth percentage is also a comparative reference point.

Installed base (or IB): Every territory has a set of customers that can be relied on to do business with your company every year. This is the steady year-after-year business that comes in like clockwork, *not the total business.* This steady business is your *installed* base. It is important to keep track of this number from year to year. In most businesses it usually runs between 70 and 80 percent of the total business for the year. Some accounts will fall off the list and others will be added over time.

Installed base trend: This number is a percentage and indicates the rate an installed base is growing or decreasing in value year to year. Installed base trend is an historic number that can easily be computed if you keep good records. For example, the installed base last year was $12,000,000, and two years ago it was $11,000,000. The *installed base trend* is then ($12,000,000 - $11,000,000) ÷ $11,000,000 = +9.1%. Over those two years your IB grew 9.1%. Keep track of your IB every year and compute your IB trend. Over time, the trend will give you a good feel for how your IB is growing or declining.

Percent of installed base: This is the percentage of your total budget that is installed base. For example, if your total installed base is $12,000,000 with a new budget of $16,000,000, then the percent *of installed base* is 75 percent.

The delta: Delta is the difference between your installed base and your budget. For example, $16,000,000 - $12,000,000 = a $4,000,000 delta. You can almost always count on a delta, meaning your new budget is greater than your installed base. (If your installed base equals or exceeds your new budget, thank God, and get ready to count the money.)

Now you need to build a goal for each of your reps by distributing your installed base and the delta equitably.

Confirm Each Territory's Installed Base

You should now calculate the installed base and the installed-base trends for each of your people.

This is accomplished by assigning each account in your installed base to one of the sales reps. If you have several years of data, you can also calculate the installed base trend for each sales rep. Note, however, that trending data are most accurate over a large base of accounts and therefore may not be dependable at the rep level.

Once you have confirmed the installed-base numbers for your reps, you should trust them. Some of those year-in-year-out accounts will produce well. Others will not. At the end of the day, the installed base number should happen, unless:

1. There is a product or technology leap by a competitor.
2. Your company is about to introduce a killer product of its own.
3. Your products are entering the downside of their product life cycle.
4. The industries and markets served, or the general economy, turns sour.

More often than not, if you believe the installed-base numbers and do not try to over-analyze them, you will not be disappointed.

Installed-base Growth

Some portion of your delta will be obtained through growing the installed base. The installed-base trend for each rep is a good guideline for you to use when assigning an installed-base growth number to each rep. As stated before, it is most desirable to have an installed-base trend for each of your reps. You then need only to apply the percent growth to each rep's installed-base number. If you don't, or can't, develop an individual territory trend, apply your sales unit's installed-base-trend percent to each of your rep's installed base.

> The *new installed-base* number is last year's installed base times the *installed-base trend*. As an example, if Susan has an IB of $900,000 and an installed-base trend of 25 percent, then her new IB number will be $900,000 x 25% = $225,000, added to the $900,000 = $1,125,000.

By the time you repeat this calculation for all of your sales reps you may discover that the $4,000,000 delta has been allocated. However, odds are, you probably have a sizable amount left to allocate. Using our example, assume there is still $2,000,000 to allocate.

Territory Upside

It is now time to determine each sales rep's potential in the noninstalled-base accounts in the sales unit's area of responsibility. This is where the science ends and the artistry begins. However, there are ways to add science to the artistry.

First, determine how much business was produced above and beyond the IB accounts in previous years. This number is simply total sales in a territory minus the installed base. In Susan's case, let's say it was $1,250,000 - $900,000, or $350,000. It is an indicator of the rep's efficiency and not necessarily territory potential.

Second, define the *optimum customer* for your goods or services. This is the customer to whom you would have the highest probability of selling your products.

Consider the following attributes when defining an optimum customer:

- Total revenue
- Total number of employees
- Growth, actual or estimate
- Industry

- Available applications
- Competitive situation
- Propensity to buy your product
- Other attributes of your choice

Where possible, assign ranges to the attributes, for example:

Total revenues $100 million - to - $1 billion
Total number of employees 500 - to - 5000

Third, determine the *average value* of a sale to a new customer. Look back a year or two to get the information. It is as simple as determining the total amount of business you received from noninstalled-base customers divided by the total number of transactions.

Fourth, determine the number of optimum customers in each rep's territory. This can be accomplished by using some of the many lists that may be available for the industries to which you sell, for example, Dunn & Bradstreet and Computer Intelligence (CI). Lists and databases exist for many industries. There is also a Book of Lists that could help you determine the most appropriate source of data for your business. In addition, for some businesses, the Yellow Pages can be a good source of information.

Make sure that you conduct your search using the attributes of your optimum customer. This will ensure that you get the most accurate picture of a territory's potential.

There are several desktop mapping tools that may help you to visualize the density of optimum customers on a territory-by-territory basis. They would also help you compare potential between territories and determine if there are any patterns you could take advantage of. Decision-support tools such as this can be invaluable in budget deployment as well as with direct-marketing programs.

The total upside potential of each territory can then be calculated by multiplying the number of optimum customers in a territory times the average sale value.

Your job now consists of distributing the remainder of your delta in an equitable fashion considering the upside potential of each territory. The more potential, the more upside a rep would get. Assume that the upside potential in Susan's territory is 10 percent of the sales unit's total potential. She would then get 10 percent of the remaining $2,000,000, or an additional $200,000 upside goal. Susan's new sales goal would be the $900,000 installed base, plus the $225,000 from IB growth, plus the $200,000 upside, for a total of $1,325,000. Her percent of installed base would be $900,000 ÷ $1,325,000, or 68 percent.

At this point, you should be able to calculate and distribute the remainder of the $2,000,000. The next step is to chart the data.

Reality Check

Create a spreadsheet that looks like the example on page 110. Illustrative numbers from the discussion for Susan, plus other hypothetical numbers, have been inserted. (See page 110)

A spreadsheet will allow you to compare the size and relative fairness of each rep's proposed budget. Generally, more difficult budgets will be characterized by low IB trends, low-percent IBs, and high-growth percentages.

The column labeled "Compensation at 100%" is extremely important. It represents the amount of money each of your reps would earn if they achieved 100 percent of the proposed budget. You can now, by evaluating the potential earning power and relative difficulty of what you planned for your reps, make any adjustments you feel are necessary.

Communicate

You are now ready to communicate the results of your analysis to your reps. If you have performed the analysis described here, your task will be somewhat easier. However, discussing new budgets with sales reps is always exciting, if not challenging.

As long as there are reps and managers, new and more imaginative arguments to lower a budget are sure to emerge every year.

Sales reps, like golfers, have figured out that you win or lose every match prior to striking the first ball. A golfer tries to negotiate a favorable handicap, and a sales rep tries to negotiate a favorable budget. As the manager, you would be disappointed if a rep did not.

Sales rep	Last year's results	Installed base	IB trend	New IB	Upside	New sales goal	% IB	Growth %	Compensation at 100%
Susan	$1,250,000	$900,000	25%	$1,125,000	$200,000	$1,325,000	68%	6%	$41,000
Rep #2	$1,450,000	$1,070,000	21%	$1,294,700	$230,000	1,524,700	70%	5.2%	$46,000
Rep #14	$825,000	$600,000	23%	$738,000	$102,000	$840,000	71%	2%	$34,000
Sales unit totals	S14,000,000	$12,000,000	22%	$14,640,000	1,360,000	$16,000,000	75%	14.29%	
Sales unit average yield	$1,142,857								

LESSONS

The primary lesson of this problem is to keep excellent records. Understand the data that are required to set good budgets and make sure that you have the discipline to collect it in the current year. This will make next year's budgeting that much easier. After a few years, the availability of trending information will make the job easier yet.

Expect your people to negotiate with you. Do not think less of them when they try to convince you that the number you have in mind is outrageous.

Your people will respect you for your due diligence, even though they may not be pleased with the final numbers.

This approach was developed for a territory-oriented sales-force deployment. It works equally well for other deployment schemes.

4–4 THE PROBLEM:
Leads are not being followed up and managed.

THE STORY

Cay was catching up on her E-mail one morning when a message from Barney, one of the product managers, soured her mood. The syrupy "Dear teammate" intro raised a red flag.

The message accused Cay and her salespeople of "not following up on the *Highly Qualified* leads my group has sent to you and your team." The words "delinquent," "commitment," "team player," "corporate priority," and other hot buttons were liberally sprinkled in the message." We've invested a lot of money and time in . . . ," the message went on.

Barney claimed that he had sized the opportunity represented by those leads to be close to $216,000. Barney was always precise. Barney also suggested Cay's "performance to quota could be significantly higher if your people would only call on these qualified customers."

And, as usual, Cay noted that Barney was kind enough to copy her boss on the message.

TEMPTATIONS

Lead management has a rich subculture all its own, and it so often fuels a distressing competition between sales and marketing.

Return the hostile fire

"Dear Barney: These leads are useless. Come and see me when you get your act together." cc: The world.

Claim higher priorities

"Dear Barney: The team has been assisting the CEO with a confidential pilot project."

Deprive him of any satisfaction

"I'll kill him with silence. We'll do our job, but he can sit and stew."

Better to think of lead follow-up and management more like dentistry. New technologies and processes have made both activities virtually painless for all parties.

WHAT HAPPENED HERE . . . ?

It appears that frustrations are quite high on both sides of the fence. Barney believes that he is providing top-notch leads to Cay's people. Cay's people think that the leads are junk, and the only thing they know about the prospects is that they could fog a mirror when they filled out the bingo cards.

The worse thing is, there may be some truth in both viewpoints.

In many cases, a marketing department measures its effectiveness by the number of leads it provides to a sales force. These leads often are in response to campaigns that offer a giveaway for information. Sometimes they come from trade shows that use a variety of gimmicks to entice people to fill out questionnaires. Marketing then adds some priority to the leads such as urgency (hot, warm, cold) and potential dollar value and distributes them. The next thing the sales force hears is the constant high-pitched whine of Marketing asking about the status of each lead.

Salespeople, on the other hand, are measured on deals closed. There are no hot, warm, or cold deals, just in-the-pipeline or closed deals. Salespeople are notoriously bad at administrative work and therefore frustrate the marketing department with the lack of timely and quality feedback on the leads provided. Leads that do not immediately turn into opportunities often find their way to the circular file.

Salespeople also lose confidence in a lead source. If they uncover an abundance of tire-kickers and literature-seekers early in a batch of leads, they will discard the remainder of the leads. They will also most likely ignore future leads from that source.

Unfortunately, a sales rep's concept of a *Highly Qualified* lead is one with a purchase order attached.

As you can see, the viewpoints are not compatible. It takes strong management and a lot of discipline to bridge this gap. It is worth bridging, however. Your yield per rep will increase, and your cost of selling will decrease.

OPTIONS

There are only two options.

1. Cay could assume that the relationship between marketing and sales is going to be strained and do nothing to rectify it. As one sales manager said, "If our marketing department were in charge of marketing sushi, it would be called "good dead fish."
2. Cay could work closely with Barney to help both of them develop the campaigns required to generate the leads her sales unit needs to be successful.

If Cay chooses the path of involvement, she will need to develop and execute a closed-loop lead-tracking process that both her team and Barney can buy into.

POSSIBLE ACTIONS

First of all, lets get one thing straight. Responses from marketing campaigns are just that, responses. They do not turn into leads unless you put some effort into them.

The work that is required is not easy. It is tedious and must be performed by skilled people. However, responses cost a lot of money to generate. If you wisely spend a *little more* money, the responses can be turned into *highly qualified leads*. Then your sales people will gain confidence, their yields will improve, your costs will go down, and your overall sales revenue will increase. All it takes is a sound lead-nurturing and lead-tracking process.

Work Collaboratively

Cay and Barney need to work together in all aspects of lead generation and lead follow-up. It starts with the campaigns that are developed. Both departments need to agree on exactly what is required. That includes what markets and what customers in each market are to be targeted, what specific contacts within each customer, and what type of media should be used to communicate with these people. It is then important for Cay and Barney to agree on *how* and *to what sales channel* the responses from these campaigns are to be distributed.

The process that is developed has to satisfy the needs of both marketing and sales in order to be truly successful.

Involve Your Sales Reps

As with many other aspects of sales management, up-front involvement of Cay's people will improve the quality of the end product as well as the commitment of her people to execute. She must ask them to help with campaign development and make sure they understand the overall goals and how Cay feels the campaign will help them personally. She should ensure they know the roll-out plan for the campaign. They should also know (if possible) which customers in their territory will be touched by the campaign.

It is a good idea to have them experience the campaign firsthand. If it is a direct-mail campaign, send them the mailer. If it is telemarketing oriented, have them called by the telemarketer, and so on.

The more Cay's people know about the campaign that generated the responses, the more effective they will be during the follow-up phase. Cay will know she's successful when her salespeople view the leads as uncashed commission checks.

Qualify, Qualify, Qualify

Each response needs to be qualified to be turned into a lead before it is given to a sales rep. This can be accomplished most effectively and efficiently with telemarketing, whether by Cay's own telemarketing group or one that her firm contracts from the outside. An experienced telemarketer can weed out the tire-kickers and literature-seekers quickly.

Once the telemarketers have determined the real potential buyers, they can begin to determine timing, that is, when a potential customer intends to buy. This takes more skill and preparation than the initial screening process.

Cay and Barney will need to work closely with the telemarketers to ensure that they understand the goal and essence of the campaign. Together, all three should develop a script and a series of questions that will help the telemarketers determine who is serious and who is not. The script should also help the telemarketer to determine *when* they plan to buy, *how much* they plan to spend, what *criteria* they plan to use to choose a vendor, *who* the final decision maker is, and so on.

It is recommended that you work with the same telemarketing firm right down to the same individuals, if possible, for all your campaigns. Once you have developed a good working relationship, the quality of the information you receive will improve significantly.

Nurture

The process of further qualifying serious buyers includes determining when they plan to start their buying cycle. If it is determined that the time is *now*, the response turns into a lead and should be fired electronically to your selling channel immediately.

If the prospect is not ready, the telemarketer should not pass the response on to Cay's people. The lead should be left with the telemarketer to nurture. The telemarketer will develop a relationship with the potential customer during the nurturing phase, periodically keeping in touch. The telemarketer could supply the prospect with different collateral pieces during this prepurchase time frame.

Eventually the time will be right, the customer will be ready to begin the buying cycle, and the response turns into a lead and is passed to one of Cay's salespeople or a sales partner. *The farther into the sales cycle she and Barney can wait before they engage a salesperson, the better off they are. The rep's enthusiasm to follow up will be higher, the yields will be higher, and sales costs will be lower.*

Databases and Reporting

All responses from a campaign should be kept in a database. It is up to Cay and Barney what information is kept, beyond customer demographics, but the following is recommended.

- Product type
- Types of services
- Lead campaign name and number
- Response date to initial inquiry
- Current status
- Response disposal, identifying reason
- Literature sent; when, what was it, to whom

- Dollar value of opportunity
- Lead being worked/nurtured
- Lead eliminated or delayed, identifying the reason
- Lead lost to competition, identifying the competitor
- Lead date, the date it was turned over to a sales rep
- Sales rep or sales partner name
- Close date or date purchase order received

Barney can now produce reports that will turn this data into real information for everyone. For example: Total responses by campaign. Total leads by sales rep (or by partner). Responses that turned into leads. Responses that turned into purchase orders.

This will allow Cay and Barney to determine

- What type of campaigns work well.
- What type of customers are responding to the campaigns.
- How many leads are going to which salespeople.
- Which salespeople are following up on the leads they have been given.

The options are unlimited. The key is that both managers determine the best set of reports for each of them to improve processes, productivity, and results.

Close the Loop

Too often lead tracking systems end when the lead is given to the sales rep or sales partner. This is unfortunate because some of the most important information about the campaign and leads is lost. It is, however, understandable because the task of following up with salespeople to learn the status of the lead can be difficult. As mentioned before, salespeople do not enjoy doing administrative work, and they do not like people prying into their business.

Cay's process must include an easy way for her reps to tell her the status of each lead they have received. One way to do this is to generate a report titled "the status of leads by sales rep" on a monthly basis. Simply have your reps pencil in or keystroke status updates. An administrator or the telemarketer can then compile these updates into the database. The method Cay and Barney use will depend on the tools available.

The type of information you gain by closing the loop can include numerous options, including:

Campaign Effectiveness
- Total responses
- Responses that turned into leads
- Total sales dollars vs. campaign cost

Sales Effectiveness
- Total leads closed
- Average dollar value per lead
- Number of leads given to partners

This information can help Cay and Barney to determine what type of campaigns to run in the future and what training Cay may need for her salespeople.

Integrate with Your Pipeline System

If Cay spends the time and money to turn a response into a lead, she should expect that her salespeople will take it seriously. Therefore, the leads must be entered into her pipeline system and receive the same scrutiny as other pipeline opportunities.

Share Successes

Be sure to communicate all wins from a campaign. Give credit to the process and people that turned that response into a lead. Cay and her people will quickly figure out that marketing *can* help and that this new process is generating worthwhile *highly qualified leads*.

LESSONS

Lead generation and management is a sales and marketing team effort. The ability to generate highly targeted programs, the availability of sophisticated software and communications tools, and efficient telemarketing practices can make lead programs highly profitable.

Sales staff must be an integral part of lead-generation programs from the beginning.

Effective qualifying and lead nurturing will enable you to pass on qualified leads later in the sales process, using your sales people for what they're best at—closing orders.

4–5 THE PROBLEM:

You do not have an effective "pipeline" process.

THE STORY

"Cortland, I'm under pressure to put in a 'bet my badge' forecast to headquarters and I need a *guaranteed* sales number from your sales unit for the upcoming quarter," Kathy gravely said.

As the Regional Sales Manager, Kathy was in the midst of getting the word out to all her district managers.

"I know we usually go over forecasts monthly," she went on, "but I guess corporate has some real problems. Hope your pipeline is in good shape."

Whew, this sounds serious, Cortland thought to herself. Pipeline? Who knows what I've got out there. As Kathy went on describing the critical nature of the request, Cortland wasn't listening because she knew she was in deep soup.

"Cortland, I need your answer by noon tomorrow," Kathy concluded.

TEMPTATIONS

The frustration that accompanies a lack of information can be very stressful, especially when you know it is self-inflicted pain. Self-protection mechanisms often pop up to make matters worse.

Throw a dart

"I'll toss in a low number to hedge my bet. I'll look like a hero when we blow by it."

Play Jeopardy

"Kathy, if you give me the answer you're looking for to make *your* number, I'll build a story to back you up."

Jerk the sales unit around

"Lottie, tell everyone I want them in the office promptly at 7:30 in the morning for an emergency meeting—no excuses!"

Candor is a better approach. Your boss may not like the answer, but she'll respect it.

WHAT HAPPENED HERE . . . ?

You have ignored one of the most fundamental elements of sound sales management, managing your "pipeline." This is a wake-up call.

A pipeline is, in its simplest form, a list of *all* the deals—*all of them*—regardless of their status, that Cortland's salespeople are working on. The emphasis is upon *working on*—at some stage in Cortland's firm's sales process. Just being aware of a potential deal does not qualify the deal for the pipeline. As with a real pipeline, someone has to place something *in it* before it can flow through and out the other end. It's a wonderful metaphor. The sales pipeline is a document or sales-force automation application that contains key information about the deals being worked on.

A pipeline is not a forecast. The pipeline is a list of possibilities—all the known opportunities that are at some stage of development in your sales process. Only some of the opportunities in the pipe will feed the forecast. Not everything that flows out of the end of the pipeline will be a win. Some will be losses, some will evaporate, and some will start the process all over again. *The pipeline is a measure of potential.*

A *robust* pipeline is one of the best indicators of the health of a business, which is why Kathy suggested that Cortland look at her pipeline. A pipeline is often the only mechanism that allows a sales manager to forecast his or her sales volume with any amount of accuracy.

The fact is, Cortland has no way of knowing how solid her forecast can be because she does not have a sound pipeline to base it on. She obviously has not spent time on it.

It may be that Cortland treated the process sloppily because she did not understand its value. Perhaps she wasn't trained properly on its implementation, or Kathy may have treated the subject casually in the past.

Cortland's firm may not be process oriented. Poor pipeline management is a sign that other sales management processes may be out of whack as well.

Business may have been good in the past, and the sales managers may have become lax with their pipeline-and-forecasting processes. Good times have a habit of doing that.

Just like a real pipeline, there can be leaks in a sales pipeline. Leaks happen when sales managers don't watch what's going on and opportunities just seep mysteriously into the sand. Regular and intense scrutiny prevents leaks. Stories about leaks can fill another book.

OPTIONS

Cortland has two problems here.

One, what is she going to do in the short term in order to give Kathy a respectable number? For that we refer her to Problem 4–6, "You must submit a weak sales forecast to your boss." She'll also have to use the pipeline she has, as weak as it may be.

Two, she has to start immediately on firming up her pipeline process. Her effort may help with the short-term forecast, and it will certainly help with future forecasts. Since this is bet-your-badge time, there are no other options.

POSSIBLE ACTIONS

Who Is This For, Anyway?

First, a pipeline is for salespeople. It is a tool to help them manage their territories or accounts—to keep track of all their potential. Implicit in this acknowledgment is the fact that they should play a role in defining the pipeline's content, the methodology and tools used to track it, and be held accountable for its accuracy.

Second, a pipeline is for sales management. It is a tool to help them coach and manage.

Third, a pipeline aids managers in all other business functions. It gives them a sense of what is on the horizon—good or bad. Corporate management's responsibility is to analyze and act on what the pipeline is telling them and feed resultant plans back to the sales organization.

Where Are You?

Cortland needs to have a conversation with herself about what she's doing or not doing related to managing the pipeline. It's likely she knows what to do, but hasn't been executing it. If she has doubts about how to manage the process she's got to go to Kathy immediately and say, "Hey, I think I need a quick refresher." The signal may cause Kathy to pull all the district sales managers in.

Engineer the Pipeline

Cortland needs to confirm with Kathy what information is needed in the forecast, to ensure that her pipeline delivers what's required.

Next, she needs to contact all her people and tell them to update their pipeline by a certain time and confirm what information should be included. *The quality of pipelines is inversely proportional to the amount of information tracked.* She should ensure the pipeline contains only information that is absolutely required by her reps and by her for the forecast.

Respectable pipeline content could include the following:

- Sales rep's name
- Industry or major market segments or customer classes you serve

- Product being sold
- Estimated dollar value of transaction

- Competitor(s)

- Step of the sale, the point your rep is at in the sales process, or sales cycle associated

- Customer's name
- Customer location, in order to differentiate between multiple opportunities with the same firm
- Support services being sold
- Projected close date, and requested delivery date
- Percent probability of winning the opportunity, using standardized probabilities of sales management's choice
- Comments, issues, or obstacles associated with the opportunity.

You should add or delete suitable data for your business, ensuring you engineer it for the benefit of your sales unit.

Sales Force Automation Tools

There are numerous sales force automation programs that will simplify the entry-and-edit process for your sales unit. They also allow easy roll-up of the individual pipelines of your reps into one pipeline for your entire sales unit. Purchasing a standardized tool or having one customized for your firm is an excellent investment.

Build It!

Cortland needs to instruct her people to update their pipeline using the sales unit's current tool. She needs to take an over-the-shoulder *coaching approach* on this first go-round to make sure everyone grasps the idea and is entering raw data as they should.

If her software tool changes or is modified, close coaching must continue.

It's Time for Some Massaging

The value of pipelines lies in converting the raw data into useful reports. This is where your software comes in. Remember, a pipeline is a measure of potential. Good engineering up front, and massaging of the raw data, will enable you to develop highly useful reports to let you know everything that is on the horizon. Sample reports could include:

Total pipeline by rep

Total pipeline by product or service

Total pipeline by competitor

Total pipeline by industry, market, or customer class

Total pipeline by week, month, or quarter

Total pipeline by sales channel

Total pipeline by virtually any combination or permutation you may want. However, don't over do it and hold your ground against having inside managers talking you into pipeline report inflation.

Well-thought-out reports can help you make a variety of management decisions that go far beyond a forecast. For example,

- A reduction in potential in a certain product area may indicate a need to cut back production, redesign product, make packaging changes, or make a pricing change.
- A dominance of one competitor in your pipeline may suggest the need for a special training session.

How Much Is Enough?

Cortland will soon find out the relationship between the magnitude of a rep's pipeline and their actual sales for a fiscal period. This is an amazingly consistent ratio and one of the primary benefits of an accurate pipeline. History will tell you how large a rep's pipeline needs to be to support his forecast. For example, if history says that a rep needs three times his forecast in the pipeline to be successful and he is forecasting $1,000,000, he had better have at least $3,000,000 in his pipeline or the chances of failure are high.

What to Ask Reps About Their Pipeline

This is a critical topic. *Remember, a pipeline is not a forecast.* If you treat a rep's pipeline like a forecast, you will never have an accurate pipeline because salespeople are reluctant to share their total activity list with management because they do not want to be *grilled* about opportunities that are not closeable in the near future. If you interrogate your reps about their pipeline, it will shrink down to just those few opportunities that they want you to ask them about.

Ask questions from a pipeline viewpoint, not a forecast viewpoint. For example:

- "Marie, what activities do you have planned this week to increase your pipeline?"
- "How do you explain the decrease in product X opportunities in your pipeline?"

- "How do you think your pipeline will trend in the next six months?"
- "Aside from some recent orders, what's happened to cause your pipeline to shrink?"
- "What marketing strategies would give your pipeline a boost?"
- "The deals you're chasing seem much smaller than the rest of our sales unit. How can we uncover some larger deals?"
- "The banking segment of your pipeline is really declining. What needs to be done to reverse the decline?"
- "I see you have phenomenal success in building potential in the X application market. How about sharing your approach with the rest of the sales unit?"

An accurate pipeline and good reports can be an outstanding management tool.

A Cautionary Note

Pipelines have a personality all their own:

- Pipelines will get smaller near the end of the fiscal year. This is because your reps are focusing on closing business and not on building or updating their pipeline. Also, they never want to have a robust pipeline during budget-setting time.
- Pipelines will not be up to date if you do not pay clockwork-like attention to them.
- Your reps' pipeline accuracy will suffer if you do not make it easy for them to add, delete, and update opportunities. (This goes back to the importance of the engineering.)
- Pipelines are a reflection of the sales manager's style.

Close the Loop

Your pipeline process must contain a close-the-loop discipline to identify final disposition. Reason codes track why a particular result occurred. Each opportunity will sooner or later be:

- LOST to the competition. Reason codes could be "why," and to what competitor.
- WON. Reason codes could be "why," and against what competitor.
- DELAYED by the customer. Reason codes should identify "why."
- ELIMINATED by the customer. Reason codes should identify "why."

It is important that you *force* the discipline to appropriately close out each entry. The word "force" is used on purpose. Your reps will not automatically do this on their own.
Some final keys:

- Do not let any entry slip unnoticed from the pipeline. (This is the leakage referred to earlier.) If work ceases, have your rep assign a final disposition.

- Question all deals whose step of the sale does not increase over a reasonable time frame.
- Watch out for the "Delayed" and "Eliminated" disposition code. They are sometimes euphemisms for "Lost."

Once you are assured that your reps close the loop, reports such as the following are useful: "Deals won by industry or product." "Deals lost to a specific competitor, or for a certain reason, such as availability, price, or specifications."

All this information can help you manage your people and your business.

Integrate Your Pipeline into Other Processes

The better you are able to integrate your pipeline into other processes, the more accurate the pipeline will be. For example:

- *Sales leads:* Have them all placed directly into a rep's pipeline. This will help ensure that your reps are following up on the leads and give you a final disposition of each lead. This is also an easy way for you to judge the effectiveness of your marketing campaigns.
- *Sales-support allocation:* Ensure that all resource deployment is directed toward pipeline opportunities. For example, do not assign sales-support resources to an opportunity unless the opportunity appears on the rep's pipeline.

LESSONS

Your pipeline is the data foundation to managing your sales unit. It is your highest information-gathering priority because it feeds many processes and decisions, such as budgeting, deployment, training, forecasting, and resource allocation. The comfort that accompanies thorough understanding of what and how much is in the pipeline will also reduce day-to-day stress.

If you spend time managing your pipeline, you will save you more time on other matters, reduce fire drills, and set an excellent example for your salespeople's territory and/or account management.

You will understand your business and your markets very well and be a more valued management asset to your employer.

4–6 THE PROBLEM:
You must submit a weak sales forecast to your boss.

THE STORY

As a regional sales manager, Don's forecasts are routinely thorough because he knows that his manager, Vito, the division sales VP, is a stickler for accuracy and planning. Don and his team have always been comfortable with the format of the report, and they understand how this information is vital to everyone. Don had begun to assemble the inputs for his monthly forecast, which was due in three days, when he discovered that he was looking at a disaster. At first glance, it looked as if this unpleasant surprise would be less than 50 percent of his objective—far, far below expectations. The timing couldn't be worse. It was the last month of the quarter.

TEMPTATIONS

Forecasting is both an art and a science. At times like this the "art" aspect of forecasting can get out of control. Don't let it—and don't let any of these temptations unfold.

Smoke and mirrors
  "We're a class act. We'll suck it up and make it happen. Watch the magic."

Attack
  "I warned those ivory-tower bozos in marketing that the price increase would zap us!"

BS
  "We'll inflate the forecast a wee bit, hope we can pull off some surprises, and rationalize the results with a soft-market story at the end of the period."

Honest and accurate forecasts are a reflection of your total business acumen and integrity. "Always do right. This will gratify some people and astonish the rest." So said Mark Twain.

What Happened Here . . . ?

Don was blindsided, that's what happened. What he *does know* is that he shouldn't have been surprised.

Somehow he was lulled into complacency by his own people or his own success. Don may have taken his eye off the ball and assumed it would be business as usual. A lack of scrutiny of his people's inputs and the lack of his own due diligence seems to have ambushed him. Unquestioning repetitiveness may have finally caught up with him.

Poor prospecting and no process or accountability for continuing market development could be the culprit. Perhaps he is not conducting periodic pipeline reviews. Don's forecasting protocols or his attitude about forecasting may be flawed.

Sandbagging by one or more of his reps—to position themselves for the next period—is a distinct possibility.

New competitive strategies or competitive promotional actions could have been in force, and Don was waylaid by them.

Certainly, some market segments or major customers could have gone sour.

Don really has three issues here. One, how is he going to deal with the reality of the forecast itself? Two, how did this happen? And, three, what is he going to do to recover? He needs to address all three simultaneously.

Options

In response to the first issue—how is he going to deal with the forecast—he has two options. He's honest and calls the forecast as it is, or he fudges it. Whether he fudges it a little or fudges it a lot doesn't matter; the bottom line is he has decided to fudge it—not to tell the whole story—and that is double jeopardy. There is no middle ground. This is an integrity check. Don's call.

In response to the second issue—how did this happen—he has only one option. Dig. Fast and deep. He needs to critically review his business-tracking and forecasting methods. The players. The process. The timing. The prioritization he gives it.

In response to the third issue—what is he going to do to recover—he needs a creative, team-formulated fill-the-gap recovery plan.

Possible Actions

Calm down. Stop thinking about the reprimand you'll hear from Vito and start thinking about the problem. Establish and communicate a we've-got-a-job-to-do challenge to your people. Don't waste time anguishing over couldas and shouldas.

Sound the Alarm

Tell Vito you've discovered you're in trouble, before the forecast is submitted. Don't let his reading of the forecast be the first indication of a problem. Provide an estimate of the forecast. Also supply a *rough outline* (verbal or written) of a fill-the-gap plan along with the early warning and let him know you'll attach a detailed fill-the-gap plan to your final forecast. *A fill-the-gap plan details how Don will get from his current position to his final forecasted position.* That final forecasted position may or may not be his sales goal for the period. Regardless, it is imperative he have a plan on how he is going to get to his forecast.

Talk to the salespeople again. Provide both an outline of situation questions you want answered about the market and customers and an outline for fill-the-gap plans. Let them know you'll be back to them (individually or in group format) at a specified time, to finalize and rationalize the forecast and design individual and team fill-the-gap plans.

What Happened Outside?

It's time for a little analysis. Check with peers to get a sense of their forecast strength. If their forecasts are looking weak, ask why, and ask about their assessment of the market. The key is to be specific. Don doesn't want to look like a blind squirrel searching for an acorn. For example: "Bert, is last month's press announcement by competitor *A* causing your customers to delay decisions?" or "Bert, are you finding your prospects waiting for the trade show before buying?"

Gather the salespeople's comments regarding the state of the market and why business has gone bad. The key to getting honest-as-can-be answers is to ask second-level questions, for example, after Thurman tells Don that XYZ has scrapped their budget: "Thurman, when will XYZ reinstate the budget for their purchase? Who told you that?" Don has to do this only once or twice before the salespeople get the idea.

Consider personal contact, in the company of your salespeople, with several key customers or sales partners for a market assessment. For example: "Frances, we've noticed a significant slowdown in business at this end. Do you have any views on what may be happening in the industry?" This is doubly effective because the salespeople can use Don's model questions at a later time.

One of the things Don will want to determine is if this is a one-time hiccup or a major change in the market.

What Happened Inside?

This is the harder part. Don needs to critically review everything that feeds his forecast process.

- Do I have a new business-development plan, and are we implementing it?
- Do I have a way to regularly gather and catalog market and competitive information?
- Am I tracking key sales-generating activities, such as proposals, the way I should?
- Do I adequately understand the timing and activities associated with our sales cycle?
- Do I have a pipeline process, and am I holding my people accountable for its content?
- Do I have a clear criteria for moving an opportunity from the pipeline to the forecast?
- Am I treating forecasting as a continuous process or as a once-a-month administration event?
- Am I giving this the priority it deserves, setting a good example in the process?

- Am I asking the salespeople to prepare and submit relevant and sufficient info?
- Do my people understand my specific expectations regarding forecasting?
- Do I measure my salespeople on the accuracy and content of *their* forecasts?
- Is the forecast application in our SFA software understood, utilized, and effective?
- Am I rigorous enough with the forecast-related questions I ask my people?
- Have I adequately defined key numbers and terms? For example, 75 percent probability of closing a deal means _____. For example, a customer's commitment means _____.

A consistent and rigorous forecast-management process is imperative. Consistency leads salespeople to have confidence in the process and will lead Don's manager to have confidence in his forecast. Rigor eliminates surprises and reinforces confidence. In the end, it's a virtual certainty that Don will admit to himself that there is room to tighten up his process.

What Happened in the Past?

Examine forecasting history, especially those months that were weak. Search for sources of the weakness, review what actions were taken, and study ultimate performance. Stop to think if there is anything to be learned from prior experience.

Don should execute the preceding three-part analysis with R. Buckminster Fuller's advice in mind: "A problem adequately stated is a problem well on its way to being solved."

Start with a Clean Sheet

The best forecast processes and forecasts at times like these are often based on new and expanded formats because it forces you to dig further, think differently, and keep you from letting this happen again. Use everything that came out of the analysis. Consider the following:

- Reconfirm with your boss and other managers what forecast information they need to make decisions at their level. The answers will be pleasantly revealing and clarifying.
- Challenge your existing format. Create one that permits easy additions and changes throughout the period. Make it an easy read, a simple structure, heavy on bullets, and as short as can be on prose. This exercise will make you proud of your final product.
- Effective forecasts are penetrating. Highlight hard numbers, dates, percentages, probabilities, ranges, and facts. The minutiae will heighten your confidence and may even cause you to relish challenges to your forecast.
- Include references to customers or partners you've queried for opinions or data. Research in a forecast implies depth and thoroughness. Research offers proof without the asking.
- All great forecasts (weak or strong) are commitments. Your people should commit to you, and you should commit for your sales unit. Consider establishing three levels of

commitments, a Bet Your Badge number (which is bottom line), a Most Likely number, and an Upside number.

- Great forecasts follow the Missouri State motto "Show Me." Show everyone when, what, where, why, and who will be employed to hit the forecast.

In his forecast revitalization process, Don could include an outsider who will question and challenge his assumptions, thinking, and process. Someone from marketing or finance, with good analytical skills, can often suggest ideas to strengthen the effort. This person's business understanding and different perspectives are assets.

Time to Huddle

First, Don must meet with and coach his team on his revitalized forecasting process. He should then talk to all his people individually to obtain and review their forecasts.

Second, Don will want to talk to his team to plan everyone's short-term fill-the-gap plan. Fill-the-gap plans associated with weak forecasts should ooze teamwork. Other performance Problems in this book, such as 6–2, 6–5, and 6–6, can help with this critical attachment.

Write the Forecast

Outline the rationale for the forecast. Fill in all the numbers. Answer the "How did this happen?" question. Highlight the fill-the-gap strategies.

- Attach amplifying information that supports the forecast, such as copies of competitive promotional items, competitive prices, interest- and exchange-rate fluctuations, copies of correspondence from customers, newspaper and trade-journal articles, and customer-inventory levels. Collateral attachments help answer the "How did this happen?" question.
- Attach your fill-the-gap recovery plan, which answers the "What are you going to do about it?" question.
- Attach an outline of your revised forecasting process and state simply how it will eliminate future forecast surprises. Your initiative may help other sales managers.
- Anticipate penetrating questions from Vito, such as, "What do we need to do to get business from X account?" "Where do you need my help?" "What are your top five priorities?" "Why aren't you going after ABC Corp.?" And so on.
- Personally present the forecast to Vito, especially if it is not normal practice.

Fill the Gap

Execute the plan the sales unit developed to meet its final forecast commitment.

Note the plan's productiveness at the end of the period, consider how to strengthen it the next time, and share its effectiveness with the boss so that others may benefit.

LESSONS

Your candor and thoroughness will make you feel good. You'll also set a good example.

One of the major lessons of this problem is to challenge your pipeline-and-forecast process. Another major lesson is that you don't have a process to track market dynamics. A third lesson is that it teaches you to track key sales activities and understand your sales cycle. The pipeline and key activity levels are harbingers of future business. A weak forecast should never be a surprise.

Raise the red flag whenever you see customer and market indicators going against the company. Encourage early warnings from your people. Make it clear that such news is eagerly sought, not news to be disparaged or hidden.

Forecasting methodology should not be static. At a minimum, redesign it annually.

4-7 THE PROBLEM:

Reports are late and incomplete.

THE STORY

Caroline's boss, Bob, the region sales director, holds a conference call with Caroline and the other area sales managers once a month. Bob is always interested in the ASM's forecast, pipeline, key wins, losses, and competitive actions. In preparation for the call and as part of Caroline's normal business discipline, Caroline asks her sales reps for monthly reports.

Recently, Caroline has been receiving these reports late, and the reports have not been complete. Typically, she's received the forecast spreadsheet and the pipeline, but beyond that, the input has been spotty. And that's being polite. Garbage is more like it.

As a result, Caroline has been increasingly unprepared for Bob's calls.

TEMPTATIONS

When the sales unit halfheartedly responds to a task that has implications up the line, it doesn't take long for mushy temptations to kick-in.

Plead

"Hey guys, please, c'mon, I really need your inputs. My calls are not going well."

Give up

"I'll just scale back my requests. That way, everyone will be able to comply."

Boldly threaten

"Cut the bull. The next person who's late or incomplete will be sent packing."

The first sales manager at the dawn of history experienced this problem. It's still with us, and the solution is the same.

WHAT HAPPENED HERE . . . ?

It seems Caroline's people weren't being held accountable. And now Caroline is frustrated, embarrassed, and a little angry at her reps.

It could be the old report format that Caroline uses has lost effectiveness. It's gone stale and may no longer relate to the realities of the market or the reps' work.

Maybe Caroline has just instituted a new report format and her people are either not used to it, are confused by it, or they haven't been trained on it.

Caroline's sales reps may not understand the importance and impact of their reports and therefore do not take them seriously.

Maybe Caroline has gotten in a rut and has been superficially reviewing the rep's inputs, not challenging them. Her actions amount to signaling the reps that they can back off, in which case, Caroline has forgotten two historic sales-management truths.

EXPECT what you INSPECT.

and

INSPECT what you EXPECT.

And finally, sales reps (and sales managers) will try to do as little administrative work as possible.

OPTIONS

Some of Caroline's options include:

1. She could forget about the reports and gather the information another way, dodging a sticky issue.
2. She could simply demand that the sales unit comply with her request and back it up with a harsh consequence—similar to one of the temptations.
3. Caroline could conduct a conference call similar to her boss's, but that could easily degenerate into a BSing session.
4. She could revise her process and put renewed focus on the report.

    Her choice, first and foremost, should be in the context of benefit to the business.

POSSIBLE ACTIONS

The following process would be appropriate if Caroline is developing a reporting process for the first time or is revising and updating her present process.

The premise that Caroline should base the process on is:

- Keep it simple.
- Ask only for what you really need to know, not what's nice to know.
- Tell your people how you intend to use their inputs.
- Tell your people how their inputs benefited the business.

Determine Your Needs

What do you need to know? Be careful not to wear kid gloves and ask for too little in an attempt to appease your people by keeping the report short. You'll end up only having to poll your reps individually for missing information.

On the other hand, do not ask for too much. Experience will teach you balance. Some suggestions as to what might be included in regular reports are:

- Current forecast
- Current pipeline
- Key wins, and against whom
- Key losses, and to whom
- Competitive strategies, pricing, promotions, merchandising, new products, and organization

- Market conditions, obstacles, or trends
- Strategic- major-, or key-account updates
- Customer and sales partner needs and priorities
- Major proposal, RFQ, or bid status
- Issues, reactions, and feedback regarding your products and services

You surely have many other things you could add to this list. Remember, however, to always ask yourself, *Why* do I need this information? and *How* am I going to use it?

Then pull your sales unit together.

Describe Why Each Need Is Important

For example:

CURRENT FORECAST. "This information will be rolled up with that of your peers and presented to manufacturing so that components can be sourced, costs minimized, your special requests integrated, staffing levels confirmed, production plans drawn up, and *delivery schedules and availability fed back to us* to communicate to our customers."

PRODUCT INPUTS. "Your list of product strengths and weaknesses is presented to engineering by the vice president of sales. Your inputs are one of the factors that guide the company's basic research, product development, product redesign, quality programs, testing programs, competitive benchmarking, and *updated specifications that are fed back to us* in order to make our sales efforts easier."

The more specific you are, the better. People always do a better job when they know who is going to benefit and how they personally are going to benefit. If you can get the managers and staff who receive and utilize your salespeople's inputs to actually provide feedback of your people's inputs eyeball-to-eyeball, it really drives the point home.

Communicate When the Information Is Needed

Whether the information is for a quarterly meeting you attend, or a monthly conference call with your boss, clearly state when you need the reports and why you need them *at that time*. Advise them of the implications of tardiness and also spell out their personal consequences of tardiness.

Teamwork Works

Jointly design the report that will provide you with what you need. Your people's participation adds relevancy and fresh ideas and also facilitates buy-in.

- Discuss and agree on format options.
- Determine how reports will be submitted (personally, mail, E-mail, fax, computer network.) Obviously, if you have to revise or collate the inputs in any way, you may want to suggest a methodology that will simplify this process for you.
- Although it is usually best to have your report show up as one document, it could be delivered subject by subject in different formats. For example:
  - *Forecasts and pipelines* need to be massaged once you receive them. Therefore, you may request that they be sent on electronic spreadsheets and in a standardized format.
  - *Key wins and losses* could follow a standardized form and be faxed to you.
  - *Market conditions* could be typed, per a predetermined outline, and mailed in.
- Determine when the reports will be delivered to you. *Forecast and pipelines* may be personally discussed weekly according to a fixed schedule, comfortably prior to your submission date to your boss. On the other hand, *key wins and losses* could be sent in when they occur, and *market conditions* could be sent monthly. Other inputs that do not change rapidly do not need to be provided at a specific time. However, making the process easier and flexible for your team will require *you* to be more disciplined. This balance is important to consider.

Gain Their Commitment

Now that your team knows exactly what you need, why you need it, and when you need it and has developed the format and process to get it to you, look them in the eye and ask them for their commitment to provide their inputs complete and on time.

Distribution

You are probably the key person to whom the reports are to be sent. There may be others that could benefit from the information. For example, everybody on your team may benefit from the inputs of their peers. Maybe the marketing department or your sales-support team would also benefit. You could even decide to have your sales unit send their reports directly to your boss—to use as backup for his conference call.

The benefits of wider distribution includes more people getting useful inputs to aid their work. Frankly, your reps will probably do a better job in preparing their reports given that they are going unedited to a wide distribution.

On the downside, information from and about your team is going unfiltered to many people in the company. This can make some sales managers a little uneasy, but it's a statement of your confidence, empowerment, and style.

Go through this entire process at least annually to prevent slippage.

Spurious Requests

Do your best to screen, challenge, or eliminate requests for information that are sent to your team by other departments.

It seems *everybody* wants the salesperson's view or input on a pet project. Unfortunately, they usually need this input quickly and often do not provide enough context for your people to do a good job.

Many of these requests take up a lot of time and produce marginal results. Try to have all such requests come to you directly. Most managers will grant you that courtesy without your asking. You can then confirm that the request makes sense, ensuring that the inputs of your sales unit will be of maximum value to the requester. This approach gives you some control over the demands made on your people.

Reps' response to a manager's interdiction often results in better quality and timeliness because they know it must be important if the boss let it through her "screen." They feel respected and protected and will likely protect you in turn with their effort on all reports.

Feedback

It is important that your people know that their inputs are being used by you and upper management to improve the way your company does business. Tell them what happened.

"Bob really appreciates your hard work and aggressive forecast," or "Someone in engineering will be calling you to follow up on your product suggestions," or "The credit manager found it helpful to know that your customer has cash-flow problems."

Specific feedback sets the stage for even better contribution to the next request.

LESSONS

Understand *exactly* what information and reports you need, ask for what you need, use what you ask for, show your people how it was used, and thank people for their inputs. It is a simple formula that is often forgotten.

Personally challenge your report processes on a regular basis to keep them relevant.

Make reporting a team effort, not a top-down dictate.

4–8 THE PROBLEM:
Your expenses are over budget.

THE STORY

As Max was preparing for a trip to visit his East Coast dealers, the VP of finance called and informed him he was 17 percent over budget with operating expenses year-to-date. Max admitted that expenses were "up a bit" but that he was doing everything he could to pep up anemic sales.

Ten minutes later, while still in the midst of his packing, his boss stuck her head in the door and said, "Max, I'm not sure what you're doing, but you certainly have the people in finance unhappy with you—along with me. I just got a call from Leroy, who just pulled last month's financials. He's hot!"

Max slumped in his chair.

TEMPTATIONS

Getting an out-of-control expense budget back on track while sales are behind plan is not an easy task. This ugly two-edged sword easily gives birth to these nasty temptations.

Confuse the issue

"They're not *my* expenses. Those thieving people in Marketing must be using the wrong charge numbers again. Besides, these reports have never been reliable."

Whine

"For cryin' out loud, I was given a pittance of a budget to start with. You expect me to run a sales department on a hope and a dream, do you? Give me some slack."

Plead ignorance

"Holy cow, I had absolutely no idea. Just look at that. Oh my . . . how in the world . . . ?"

If you think and act as a business manager rather than as a sales manager, this problem can almost disappear.

WHAT HAPPENED HERE...?

It looks as if no one was minding the cash register.

Every sales manager lives in one of the following four quadrants from time to time. Max is in the worst possible quadrant right now.

Worst case: Expenses over budget—Sales under plan This is a disaster. If you find yourself in the worst-case quadrant, you should be reading Problem 6–5 along with this one. You need to build sales while spending virtually nothing.	*Bad case:* Expenses over budget—Sales over plan This is playing with fire. If you find yourself in the bad-case quadrant, euphoria with your sales results may be clouding your management judgment. You need to start closely controlling your expenses
Depressing case: Expenses under budget—Sales under plan This is serious trouble. If you find yourself in the depressing-case quadrant, it looks as if you haven't been doing your job—or don't know how to apply your resources.	*Best case:* Expenses under budget—Sales over plan This is sales-manager heaven. If you find yourself in the best-case quadrant, keep doing what you're doing—and consider taking the rest of the day off.

This sounds like a case where Max simply was not watching expenses. Perhaps he hasn't been reading the reports thoroughly. He could have assumed that he was unassailable because of sales results. And expense tracking and analysis is not considered fun work by most managers.

Max may have had a major expenditure in the last reporting period, and it has just hit the books. (His budget should have mirrored that fact, if that was the case.)

It could be that Max's business culture has not been a control culture, but a new finance executive is in the process of changing everyone's mentality. The screw is being tightened.

Does Max have a couple of Diamond Jim Bradys in the sales unit that he is letting get away with larceny? Maybe Max is a big spender himself.

Perhaps Max's people have not been submitting their expense reports on time, and then Max got a sudden tidal wave of reports to approve, which ended up as a big jolt to finance.

OPTIONS

You have four options in this case, and you may choose to use more than one of the options between now and the end of the fiscal period.

1. You can put a freeze or moratorium on certain expenses, such as hiring and travel, for a specific period of time, while protecting other expenses from the knife.
2. You can get your expense budget adjusted upward (using business or market conditions as the rationale) to reflect the reality of sales activity and market conditions. (This is sometimes called a dream option. Not a likely outcome, but perhaps worth a try.)
3. You can get specified expenses transferred into your boss's budget or another department's budget. (It's a little late for this, but maybe worth a try as well.)
4. You can put together a comprehensive expense-recovery plan that contains a multitude of restraints for all line items to bring things back in control by the end of the fiscal period.

And don't forget that while bringing expenses back in control you've also got to drive sales.

POSSIBLE ACTIONS

Strap yourself down and attack this problem in spite of your desire to focus on sales.

Analyze

Study the latest expense results and build an understanding of *exactly* what happened. You can't take a single corrective step until you see what has contributed to the problem. Identifying the primary expense culprits (line items or people) will enable you to focus your response.

Look at each line item and ask yourself, If I stopped spending on X, what happens? Look for expenses that were not budgeted and find out what happened.

Look for Help

Is there another colleague who has a great reputation as a cost-control manager whom you can talk to as a mentor? Can your boss provide some tips? See if you can get someone to share ideas and offer guidance. It is not easy to think clearly when you're under this kind of pressure.

Challenge Yourself

Start by looking for places where you can achieve some big savings, rather than nickle-and-diming.

Can you renegotiate office rents or leases, sublet some of your space, or move to more economical quarters?

Can you defer certain training or perform training yourself? (Look at Problem 7–10 for do-it-yourself ideas.)

Can you change your long-distance provider?

Can you consolidate the purchase of your office supplies and put together a contract with an office-supply superstore, or can you have your headquarters office send you office supplies?

Can you reduce the size or frequency of your ads?

Can you encourage some employees to work part-time, or fill open positions with part-timers instead of full-timers?

Can you share the costs of certain trade shows or field days with your dealers?

Can you postpone the big upcoming sales meeting or cancel participation in certain exhibitions? (Be very careful of this one because of a potential negative effect on morale.)

Can you recruit through newspaper ads and networking rather than through employment agencies and search firms?

Can you cut your sales coverage by having fewer people cover the same territories, or totally cease coverage in territories or markets where the investment has not paid off?

You may be able to answer a resounding yes to one or more of those questions. None of them are easy. Adopting a position that everything is fair game helps. Cutting or changing a heavy expense, or an item perceived as untouchable, sends a good message to all concerned.

Plan of Attack

Use your analysis and answers to the aforementioned challenges in conjunction with these six elements to build a good expense-recovery plan.

1. Get your sales unit together and make them a part of the process. Fully disclose the problem so that they will contribute to the problem-solving and buy-into solutions and implementation.

2. Establish new expense goals. Let everyone know that expenses will be reduced by X percent, assign a specific goal to everyone, *including yourself*, and hold everyone accountable for the new goal.

3. Keep compensation separate from other expenses so that it doesn't cloud other controllables.

4. Keep expenses that create heat or have a lot of emotion attached to them (entertainment being a good example) under a very, tight lid, or eliminate it.

5. Capitol budgets are usually separate from operating budgets, but shelving any ideas of capital expenditures in the short term may also help.

6. Be ruthless in terms of getting expense reports in on time.

Expense-Management Tactics

Many of the following tactics may be worthwhile to have in your plan.

- Ask several travel agencies to bid on your business and propose how they can help you better manage your travel expenses. Book flights 30+ days in advance.
- Ask for objectives and itineraries for every trip. If the objectives don't sound substantive, deny the trip request. (This is a good idea at all times.)
- Give every salesperson a small per-diem rate and let them manage their expenditures themselves.
- Standardize on less expensive car-rental companies and hotels to get reduced corporate rates.
- Use your own facilities rather than expensive hotels or conference centers for meetings.
- Eliminate outside trainers or consultants and stop spending on other outside services.
- Do not reorder sales-collateral materials. Use up all the old stuff in car trunks and closets.
- Have your people request approval for every expense above a certain figure.
- Cut out subscriptions.
- Ask the people in accounts payable to alert you to any invoice over a certain amount.
- Set a personal example of frugality by using inexpensive restaurants, hotels, and auto-rental companies when you're traveling with your people. Nothing gets the message across faster than the boss being willing to stay at a $39.00-a-night hotel with a big spender in tow. The key is to do these things matter-of-factly, not for show. Your actions need no words of explanation.

The dollars and nickels will add up if you chip away at everything, and you'll create some good sustaining disciplines in the process.

Now for the Second Half of the Problem

Revise your sales strategy. *Treat this problem as a profitability problem—not just a sales-expense-management problem.* You can enhance your image and keep your star in ascendancy during these tough periods by keeping expenses down *and* helping meet profitability objectives.

Look for ways to raise selected prices, discount less, provide fewer freebies, and negotiate harder. Sell higher-margin products and services in greater quantity, staying away from lower-margin products to the best of your ability.

Implement Low-cost/No-cost Sales Actions

With your sales unit's help, brainstorm for sales tactics that cost little or nothing. The team approach should identify several innovative ideas.

Here are some examples:

- Conduct inexpensive seminars that pull many prospects together in one place.
- Conduct a personal-letter (*not* form-letter) campaign to targeted prospects.
- Hire part-time help (if you can scrape up some cash) to provide inside administrative assistance so your salespeople can spend all their time face to face with customers.
- Ask certain executives in your firm to call specific customers as a thank-you or customer-service gesture. Those calls often raise additional opportunities.
- Spend 100 percent of your time in the field. Do your paperwork at night and on the weekends.
- Mail postcards announcing product specials.
- Use mailings of journal articles or copies of ads as a tool to remind people of your capabilities.
- Look for opportunities to use your phone and E-mail in lieu of travel.
- Issue a series of press releases to spur awareness in your company and its services.
- Conduct refresher training for all your sales and customer-contact people on a key product or service.
- Use a mail survey as a tool to get customers and prospects thinking about you.
- Invite customers and prospects to visit you at your offices and factories rather than the reverse.
- Volunteer to be a speaker at trade events or community events to heighten awareness of your firm.
- Keep your website refreshed.

You will find that customers will respect your frugal approach and respect a company that is not wasteful.

LESSONS

This problem takes discipline and creativity to resolve.

The problem will teach you that good expense management starts with thorough and thoughtful budgeting. Sales managers who give their budgets a lot of time and carefully consider needs, potential contingencies, and timing have a head start on expense control. A good budgeter will build in what-ifs (not fat) to cover potential hard times. Expense budgeting is an art form and is an ideal subject to explore with your boss and peers.

Start each fiscal year with a miser mentality, putting yourself in a favorable position from the start so that when tough times come you have dollars available to help you out of a rut. Finish each fiscal year with an investment mentality, spending on those activities that will have a multiplier effect on sales in the next period.

A sales manager who is viewed as consistently trying to control expenses and aid profitability is more apt to get some slack or incremental budget when he or she needs it and is more apt to be respected as a solid businessperson.

4–9 THE PROBLEM:

You must rule on a complex order credit and compensation award.

THE STORY

The two sales managers strode purposively into Harris's office. Maria started in by claiming that her rep on the East Coast had done most of the work at the customer's regional offices and deserved the lion's share of the commission. Bart interrupted, claiming that his rep's key relationships with the local office had enabled the firm to win the contract.

A major system, the first of a kind the company had sold, had precipitated this confrontation, and there was no formal compensation precedent to provide guidance.

"That's very interesting," Harris said, "and I also have a letter here from our country manager in the Netherlands who indicates that his account manager clinched this deal at the firm's corporate offices in Amsterdam, and he's asking for advice on compensation."

"Why am I hearing this now?" Harris asked, upset at the reactive nature of the problem.

TEMPTATIONS

Internal compensation contention is a challenge to manage and tests a sales manager's role as an objective peacemaker. The stickiness of the problem can lead to evasive-action temptations.

Give away the farm
"Pay everybody what they would get if they had handled it all by themselves."

Procrastinate
"Let's talk about it at the staff meeting."

Call a "jump ball"
"Hell, I don't know. Why don't the two of you just figure it out and come back with a proposal."

Order credit and compensation demand rigorous thought and impeccable action.

What Happened Here . . . ?

Both the reps and the sales managers feel that they are about to be abused. They feel threatened and are sure that there will be a winner and a loser in this effort.

The salespeople and sales managers were charging ahead to secure the business as they should, and no one stopped to think about credit and compensation, assuming they'd be taken care of. There could have been erroneous messages based on hearsay or previous situations.

Maria, Bart, or both of the sales managers could have done a don't-worry-I'll-take-care-of-you number on their salespeople. Many sales managers are known to take that tack.

All of the players could have assumed that there was a formal policy to cover the situation, or if they knew there wasn't a policy they could be playing the old I'm-entitled-to-something game by sticking unwanted or unnecessary fingers into the action, then staking a claim to all or part of the business.

There may have been no formal joint planning of the sales opportunity. Planning associated with complex sales should always raise compensation questions.

Perhaps the compensation plan in Harris's company is poorly defined, has no central ownership, and has been always reactionary in its response to these types of questions.

Options

You have two options with this problem, and they are both time and resources related.

1. Make a short-term, pacifying type of decision if this is an exceptional situation not likely to be repeated.
2. Make a judgment based on a very thorough study because of the size, scope, nature, and future potential for this type business. This option essentially amends the comp plan.

Your final judgment will be influenced by many things, including existing policies, the current comp plan, precedents, management's attitude about sales incentives, HR's stature, and the cost-control environment in your firm.

Possible Actions

Let the sales managers know you intend to be scrupulously thorough with this question and that you expect their objective cooperation. Get on it right now.

Objective

Your objective is to turn this into a winning solution, a win for each of the stakeholders involved, and to lay the groundwork with guidelines should this happen again.

Who Are the Stakeholders and What Is at Stake in This Situation?

A good place for Harris to start is to lead a comprehensive review of people and functions who have a stake in the outcome of the decision. All of the following stakeholders have differing interests, and they must all be considered and satisfied.

Harris, with help from managers in and outside the sales department, must think about both the tangibles and intangibles that are on the line. Some are obvious, but many are subtle.

The Stakeholders	What's at Stake?
The sales reps or account managers who actually pursued and won the transaction	• Commission payments and/or end-of-year bonus • Order, booking, and/or sales credit against budgets • Rankings within the sales-unit and product-sales rankings • Recognition. There may be end-of-year incentive awards or incentive trips or prizes at stake. • Morale • Continuity—the rep's motivation to support and sustain this type of opportunity, and continue to contribute to this particular customer relationship
Other sales reps in the same or in other sales units who are awaiting the decision with keen interest	• Your decision sends a message about what kind of opportunities to pursue and what to stay away from. Compensation provides sales direction.
National account managers who may have facilitated the business at account headquarters	• Bonus payments • Account performance measurements
Sales agency rep that bird-dogged the opportunity or used his local relationships to help win the business	• Commission payments
Telemarketers	• Inside-sales support may be on an incentive plan and they may have had a role in qualifying the prospect.

First-level sales management that coached and guided the reps and account managers involved

- Commission payments and/or end-of-year bonus

- Order, booking, and/or sales credit against budgets
- Rankings within the sales unit and product sales rankings
- Recognition—incentive awards, trips, or prizes
- The manager's credibility. The managers must look as if they had their respective rep's interest at heart and fought the good fight to get their people everything they deserve.
- A voice. These managers have a need to be heard.

Other sales-unit managers awaiting the decision because they have similar transactions underway in their sales units

- These people will be watching the decision closely because it helps them define the direction to give to their people.

Product sales specialists who provided technical, strategy, or presentation assistance during the sales process

- Specialists in all locales could have been supporting the sales effort and likely have bonuses, performance objectives, recognition, and unofficial bragging rights at stake.

Top-level sales management

- The top sales executive is concerned about the coherence of the compensation plan and its impact on the sales department's culture. He or she has a long-term perspective and doesn't want to make a shambles of the plan for the sake of one transaction. The solution must fit and be logical.
- The process. Top management will be very concerned about the players involved and the process to reach agreement.

Product-marketing managers whose products and services were sold

- Product marketing often, but not always, funds the comp plan, so they have short- and long-term money on the table.

	• Marketing also doesn't want to see the sales force turned off to a particular product, type of transaction, type of customer, or market segment.
The human-resources department	• HR often, but not always, "owns" the company's compensation plans. They are concerned about corporate-wide compensation balance, the coherence of the sales department's compensation plan, and precedent setting. They also are concerned about administration- and compensation-planning issues.
Order entry, customer service, MIS, accounting, and payroll	• The organizations and people who must process the transactions and maintain records and databases to support both employees and customers must understand the decision and be able to administer it within the constraints of existing systems, or be given the resources to modify their systems as needed.
Executive management	• Top management must feel comfortable with the fact that its compensation programs are being managed with integrity, a sensitivity to costs, and a mindfulness of the expectations of its employees.
The company	• The company itself has a stake because compensation helps to define its culture and the relative stature of the sales function within the whole organization.
Customers	• Customers have a stake through the follow-up, service, and cooperation they expect to receive from satisfied, motivated supplier employees.

This list could be more or less expansive depending on the firm, the products and services involved, and the specific transaction. The value of creating this list lies in the fact that you'll be thorough from the beginning, it sends a strong message of rigor across the organization, and it establishes a basis for future compensation-issue solutions.

Look at the Transaction Cycle

What happened? Break the cycle, from presale through post-sale, down into key activities. Harris's cycle and sales process is likely to be consistent and easily identifiable. Breaking the cycle and process down into the smallest possible pieces will enable him to determine who did what. The objective is not to compensate for every little piece but to build understanding of the transaction and be able to counter groundless generalizations or claims by participants. Understanding will enable him to quantify his response and help justify his final solution.

Additional Considerations

There are other questions and concerns that may have an influence on Harris's thinking.

- His decision sets a precedent. Will he be comfortable taking the same decision if the situation occurs several times in the near future?
- Consider both the physical efforts and the intellectual activities involved in these transactions. The time and effort spent on the initiative in identifying the opportunity, the elegance of the strategy, the inventiveness of the planning, the innovation of proposals and presentations, and negotiating creativity have great value along with the physical time and effort selling and building relationships.
- Do the rewards compensate for risks taken?
- Who will own the account after the sale? And if there are multiple owners, what will be the continuing specific roles of each owner in each location? Will your internal support and service staffs be comfortable with that arrangement?
- How will after-sale parts, supplies, and service revenues be compensated and recognized?
- What rep or manager will get the complaint and support calls down the road?
- What do the base salaries of the participants cover? Are there elements of this transaction that is intended to be covered by salary? If so, break them out to eliminate redundancies.
- Who led and who executed the activities that really made the difference in this situation?
- If you take the personalities out of the equation and plug in jobs or titles on a flow chart do you come out with the same answers? Personalities can skew these decisions.

These questions can help you organize your thoughts. What additional thoughts did these points stir up? Discuss these points, and others you generate, as you move toward resolution.

What Messages Do You Want to Send?

You send several obvious and subtle messages to your sales, marketing, and support organizations with these decisions. Factor them into your decision. Some examples include:

Personal values. You send a message about how much you value cooperation, team-work, innovation, and transaction-quality management.

Harvest-versus-investment mentality. You send a message that you are interested only in quick hits or a message that you value long-sales-cycle business.

Sales focus. You send a message of what sales and marketing behaviors you encourage, such as new-market development, new-application development, or strategic-account pursuit.

Opportunity pursuit. You send a message to go after similar opportunities for strategic or profit reasons, or a message to shy away from these opportunities because they are low margin or consume scarce resources.

The solution *itself* should carry the bulk of these messages, not accompanying explanations.

Resources to consider

These are complex decisions that deserve the contribution of experts as well as the stakeholders. The best way to achieve an equitable solution is to take full advantage of the knowledge and experience of people in and out of the organization who may be able to add insights to this problem. You are not expected to be a compensation expert, although you may have significant compensation experience.

- Human-resource executives and staff members usually have expert knowledge and experience on these situations. Their guidance can be invaluable.
- The top sales executives in large firms and presidents of smaller firms should always be consulted on these matters.
- An outside compensation specialist or consultant can add experience and insights that you could never imagine.

Compensation is a subject on which there has been a great deal studied and written. The subject is too important not to network and investigate the availability of resources.

How Should This Be Done?

Take a team approach to addressing this problem. Gather inputs and recommendations from all the stakeholders.

Many companies have a compensation committee composed of sales and marketing management, human resources, and payroll/accounting to handle these situations. In smaller companies, presidents and other top managers participate. These committees are most effective when they have a firm charter, meet on a regular basis, and are held accountable by a top executive. The team should make its decisions and document the circumstances quickly. Delayed answers and implementation sends a bad message to the participants.

Translate the decision into a written policy and explain it to the stakeholders.

Possible Judgments

There are many approaches to consider. Some common responses include the following:

- The commission and order credit can be split right down the middle—50/50—or since there were three parties involved in our story, 33/33/33. A set percentage can be given to the order taker, a set percentage to the order-receiver, and another percentage to a third-party-location participant. For example, a 60/30/10.
- Pay double. Give both the order taker and the order receiver their normal commission, and then split the order credit down the middle.
- Take a special course of action with the pay and then turn the customer into a house account or turn the entire class of customers into national accounts and give the customer's corporate-headquarters responsibility to a national account manager.
- If the nature of your company's business is all complex-sales situations, consider eliminating commissions and going to a base-salary–yearly-bonus type of plan

Implementation

Let all parties see you attacking the problem with vigor. Nothing upsets salespeople more than dilly-dallying with compensation issues. Vigor doesn't mean recklessness. It means integrity, swiftness, and keeping everyone informed. Put other things aside until you solve this.

You should have seen this problem coming if you have been tracking the changes in your customers and markets. What are some other compensation/credit potentialities you see? Ask your sales managers this same over-the-horizon question. Begin to discuss the scenarios *before* they occur. A side benefit of the question is that it gets your sales managers thinking about how they might cooperate in ways they never considered. It could result in incremental business.

LESSONS

Don't play with people's compensation. Compensation is a *very* emotional and personal issue. Better to err on the side of the salespeople and sales managers rather than disrupt an entire sales organization. Address these problems with dispatch.

Someone needs to own and be held accountable for the sales-compensation plan. That may be HR, senior staff, executive-sales management, marketing management, or the president of a small firm. These problems must be solved by a team, and the team must consider the implications on a wide array of people.

A single problem of this nature is reason enough to review your entire sales-compensation plan and administration of that plan.

4–10 THE PROBLEM:
You must make an exception to the compensation plan.

THE STORY

Paul, one of Sonny's top account reps, has informed him that a key account had just been acquired by another company and that all purchasing decisions would be made by the new parent. Paul was obviously concerned since his compensation was tied to the acquired company.

"I've got relationships there," Paul wailed. "They were going to be my meal ticket this year—I was going to ride them to the Chairman's Club trip—they were going to help me get promoted—that's where my kids' tuition was coming from . . ." And on it went.

The histrionics were not lost on Sonny. He loved it when his people came in craftily laying a tale of woe on his desk, pleading for deliverance. But this was a real issue.

"Give me 24 hours to think about it," Sonny said, as Paul dragged himself out.

TEMPTATIONS

Compensation gymnastics can drive any sales manager crazy. They are not fun issues to work on. They are so easy to stall, slough off, dodge, or minimize.

Stonewall

> "Paul, we've all got commitments. Some years up—some years down. *C'est la vie.*"

Throw some crumbs

> "Hey, I've some accounts downtown no one can crack. They're all yours!"

Unload it

> "Talk to Human Resources. They control the pay plans and influence those decisions."

Effective handling of comp issues are one of the best ways for a sales manager to demonstrate leadership. Speed is of the essence with compensation problems. Never let an account manager stew over a compensation issue.

WHAT HAPPENED HERE . . . ?

Paul's sales quota was set at the beginning of the year using the facts that were available at that time. Things change, stuff happens, and good sales managers have to adjust their plans in order to protect their people, maximize performance, and maintain the integrity of compensation plans.

There are both uncontrollable and controllable reasons to make exceptions to a compensation plan.

- In Paul's case no business will be transacted at the account location in Paul's territory.
- Another account in Paul's territory could move, go bankrupt, or simply shut their doors.
- One or more of Paul's peers could have assisted in a major sale, and now the rewards need to be equitably split.
- Sonny may have hired a new account rep, and she needs time to establish herself in an undeveloped territory.
- Sonny may want to trailblaze a new market, pioneer some major competitive accounts, or invest in a new-product campaign. In many of those cases Sonny will not have enough information to set an equitable quota.
- Sonny may want an account rep to take on a special short-term assignment that does not lend itself to his established compensation plan.
- A huge once-in-a-lifetime deal could have surprised everyone. A sales rep's dream.

For these and other reasons, it is necessary for Sonny to adjust his comp plan to be fair to his people. All reps need to believe that if they perform they will be rewarded accordingly.

OPTIONS

You could take a hard line and never change *or* you could realize that the only way to make your plan is to have every one of your people driving hard toward the common finish line. Here are four options that could keep Paul driving.

1. Change the makeup of Paul's assignment providing attractive opportunities while maintaining his sales quota.
2. Pay double for transactions from the affected account for the remainder of the period. His relationships can be vital during the account's period of integration by a new parent.
3. Split commissions for the remainder of the period, while adjusting Paul's sales quota.
4. Adjust Paul's sales quota, ensuring he stays financially whole against the new quota . . . which is the approach Sonny will take.

POSSIBLE ACTIONS

First of all, Sonny needs to make sure that everybody understands that exceptions are few and far between. Many uncontrollable events will transpire in a territory that do not demand changes or exceptions to the compensation plan. There is a threshold, or should be a threshold, at which point management must take action. If there is not a threshold, Paul would call time-out for every little hiccup in his territory, and Sonny doesn't have time for more theatrics. A threshold, or criteria, for management consideration must exist and be well understood by all. Those criteria could be the size of a transaction, in dollars or in a percentage of the total sales quota. Sonny's management team must develop and agree on its own criteria. The criteria should demand an extraordinary set of circumstances to exist before initiating any changes. *But,* at the same time, management must be flexible enough to look at unique and reasonable cases.

Work With Human Resources

Sonny should make it a policy to always involve HR when he decides to make an exception to the established compensation plan. They can help him understand the ramifications of his intended actions. Typically, the situation Sonny is encountering is also being dealt with by other managers. Precedence may already have been set and Sonny's solution may already be known.

HR is also a good independent and unemotional sounding board. Listen to what they have to say. Ultimately the decision will be Sonny's. But, occasionally, it will be HR's.

There Are Two Distinct Types of Compensation Exceptions

1. Sonny needs to reduce a rep's quota due to a significant *change in initial assumptions*.
2. Sonny wants to give a rep *a special assignment* that does not lend itself to his comp plan.

1. Change in Initial Assumptions

Here are the words:

Here are the numbers:

Assume that you have decided that a quota reduction is required. Sonny first needs to clearly understand what has changed since he originally set Paul's sales quota (1).

(1) Original sales quota $5,000,00

Then Sonny must assess the dollar magnitude of this change as well as the time implication. Using Paul's situation: One of his accounts has been acquired by another company, so Sonny needs to examine his original expectations for that account. How much did Sonny expect Paul to book from that account (2) and how much time (3) did he expect Paul to spend selling to that account? The calculated reduction in quota (5) should be equal to the account expectation (2) *factored* by the time remaining (4) in the compensation year.

(2) Account expectation	$2,000,000
(3) Time expected selling	12 months
Time elapsed	3 months
(4) Time remaining	9 months
(5) Calculated reduction	$1,500,000
(9 months, or 3/4 of 2,000,000 = 1,500,000)	

The next step is to determine how much business Paul can book from other accounts since he now has more time to devote to them. This number (6) needs to be added to the reduced quota to determine Paul's new net quota. (7)

Caution: Generally speaking, the new net quota will be significantly smaller than the original, so it is wise to normalize the year-to-date performance. If you do not do this, Paul's performance to date may dominate the full year's performance. Normalizing the year-to-date performance is accomplished by identifying Paul's performance to date (8) and calculating his performance % (9) against the original sales quota (1).

(1) Original sales quota	$5,000,000
(5) Calculated reduction	-$1,500,000
Remaining sales quota	$3,500,000
(6) Other accounts	+ $100,000
(7) New net quota	$3,600,000

(8) Performance to date $1,000,000
(9) Performance % equals performance to date (8), or 1,000,000 divided by (1) 5,000,000 equals   20%

Then the normalized performance (10) is calculated by multiplying the new net quota (7) times the performance percentage (9). Now Sonny has recast Paul's performance (10) into a number that relates to his new net quota (7). All performance actuals from now on should be added to Paul's normalized performance, 720,000 (10).

(10) Normalized performance equals new net quota, 3,600,000 (7) times performance percent, 20% (9) equals $720,000

In summary, Sonny is crediting Paul with $720,000 year to date, against his new net quota of $3,600,000, which means he needs to sell $2,880,000 more in order to finish the year at 100 percent. ($720,000 plus $2,880,000 equals $3,600,000.) Easy process? No, it takes a little effort, but absolutely the right and equitable thing to do.

2. Special Assignment

These are times when you want to assign a sales rep to a special job. Examples of this include:

- Crack a large account that you have had no experience with in the past.
- Open a new industry in your territory.
- Champion the sale of a new or recently announced product.

Typical compensation plans do not lend themselves to these types of assignments.

A. CLEARLY DEFINE THE JOB.   Your first step is to clearly define the work you want done. Be as specific as possible. You need to ensure that there is no expectation gap between you and your sales rep.

B. DEFINE THE MEASUREMENTS.   Be very clear. On what will you measure your rep in this assignment? Where are the data going to come from to support this measurement? How are these data going to be interpreted? Who will do the interpretation? Will the measurements be both qualitative and quantitative?

C. DETERMINE ACCEPTABLE PERFORMANCE.   Now that you know what the job is and what will be measured, it is important that you and your rep agree to unacceptable, acceptable, and exceptional levels of performance.

D. NETWORK.   Talk to your peers. They may have tried similar tactics. Do not get hung up on who has a "good comp idea." It was once said that new ideas are just history you have not yet learned.

E. INVOLVE HUMAN RESOURCES.   They can be very helpful in this process. Share your intent and plans with them. HR can help ensure thoroughness and fairness. They may even have information on how others have approached similar situations in other sales units.

F. ESTABLISH THE COMPENSATION PLAN.   Now comes the fun part. Firm up a compensation plan that appropriately measures your rep in his special assignment. Some options include straight salary, salary plus incentives against distinct objectives, salary plus bonus, salary plus commission plus bonus, and others.

Let HR be your guide. The bottom line is, keep it simple and focused on the objectives. A rep that witnesses your thoroughness in this process is more apt to approach the special assignment with confidence and enthusiasm. You have essentially helped engineer success.

G. TIME FRAME.   Establish a start date and an end date for the special assignment. Have the reps post-assignment job and comp identified *before* the special assignment starts. Uncertainty about what's coming next breeds anxiety, and you don't need that at the start of a special assignment.

LESSONS

Understand the rationale behind your current incentive plan and how it fits into the corporate compensation scheme so that when approached by your people you can thoroughly explain its workings and the implications of modifications.

The compensation change you make becomes well known and becomes the new threshold or precedent. Expect that someone will challenge it at some time, but don't wait to be challenged. Take the initiative when you see inequities or opportunities. Your sales unit will respect you for your leadership.

Make as few changes as possible to your compensation plan, but when you do, use good judgment and document the modification thoroughly.

Utilize the special knowledge and experience of human resources and senior managers in addressing this type of problem.

part five

TROUBLESHOOTING INDIVIDUAL PERFORMANCE PROBLEMS

5–1 THE PROBLEM:

*An experienced salesperson is setting a bad example
for junior people.*

THE STORY

Gene, one of Christian's most experienced reps, has just informed him that he does not intend to go to the training session on which Christian worked so hard to make available for the team.

"I've been a successful salesman for many years, and I don't need or want this New-Age stuff confusing the issue," Gene bluntly stated.

Gene had reacted in a similar way when the company decided to train all salespeople on the newly distributed laptop system. (Ultimately, he half-heartedly attended that session.)

The real problem is that Gene has not been quiet about his feelings. He has been open, and some of the newer people are beginning to question the value of the upcoming training.

TEMPTATIONS

When people you hold to higher expectations and expect to be positive peer leaders come up short, the disappointment is greater, and overreaction comes more easily.

Embarrass him

"Looks like you do need the training, Gene. You didn't do such a good job on those last two deals, did you, hotshot?"

Force him

"Gene, this training is not optional. Be there! End of discussion!"

Laugh at him

"You're right Gene, we couldn't teach an old dog new tricks anyway!"

These are always difficult situations. Handle them with care. One of your top people, not to mention the rest of your team, could be in the balance, since Gene is a peer leader.

WHAT HAPPENED HERE . . . ?

Gene has a problem. It manifests itself as a negative attitude, which is impacting the rest of Christian's team. The bottom line is that Gene's current actions are disruptive.

Maybe Gene is upset that Christian did not ask for his advice regarding the design of the program. Gene may perceive Christian's slight as a lack of recognition and respect.

Maybe Gene is in a rut. The challenge could be gone from Gene's work. Christian may have taken this experienced rep for granted.

Some insensitive, "Hey, Gramps, get with the program," type of remarks from other reps may have set him off. Needling could be causing him to withdraw.

Possibly Gene fell short once again in his quest to become a manager. He might feel that he has reached the end of his career road and does not like that.

It may be as simple as Gene being nervous that he cannot learn the new technologies and techniques, and he is acting like this to protect his ego.

There may be something in his personal life bothering him.

There are endless possibilities as to what might be happening. This is like the tip of an iceberg, as Christian has seen only a couple of the symptoms.

OPTIONS

Christian has both the immediate training problem and the longer-term negative-attitude problem facing him. He should be able to solve them together. He has two options.

1. *Overlook the situation.* The newer reps will figure it out on their own, especially if Gene is a habitual grouser and complainer. This may be normal barking. If there's no reaction from Christian, he can hope Gene will simmer down and attend the training.
2. *Put a stake in the ground* and address the issue head-on with Gene. This is appropriate if the symptoms are judged to be serious and represent a change in Gene's behavior.

Christian also has a couple of execution options that are relationship dependent. The stronger the relationship, the more open he can be.

One, if the relationship is strong and close, he can be informal, direct, and quick. For example, "Gene, what's bugging you? You're messing around with everyone's head. Let's cut the bull. Talk to me."

Two, if the relationship is anything less, Christian will probably need to be more formal and measured. Possible actions follows this track.

POSSIBLE ACTIONS

First of all, Gene has not forgotten what has made him a good rep. He still has the skill, but something has turned him negative. Find out what that is, help him rectify it, and Christian will have a productive rep again—and one who should willingly attend the training session.

Get Your Thoughts Together

Before Christian talks to Gene, he should make some notes to himself, clearly and specifically defining the issues he wants to discuss.

- Identify the inappropriate behaviors.
- Note specific examples when, where, and with whom Gene exhibited those behaviors.
- Catalog the impact and implications of Gene's actions on others.

Size the Problem

Is this a minor problem that Christian wants to bring to Gene's attention before it gets out of hand, or is it an ongoing issue that has become pervasive?

The size and magnitude of the problem will guide Christian's approach. If it's minor, his approach can be more informal. If it's serious, which it appears to be in our story, Christian needs to be more precise and thorough.

Time to Talk

Christian needs to make sure Gene understands that he is concerned about the welfare of *both* Gene and the team.

Ask Gene why he is acting the way he is. Why is he negative? He will probably deny that he has been acting this way; a natural reaction.

Cite some examples to illustrate the point. Be careful not to argue about his negativism in the examples you choose. Instead, move quickly to the impact of his actions in regard to the rest of the team. Gene may be able to defend his actions ("I said that because . . ."), but he cannot rationalize away the impact of his actions.

Christian needs to make sure that Gene understands that he cares as much about helping him as Christian does about eliminating the negative feelings he is causing.

If Gene shares what is bothering him, immediately begin to develop an action plan to help rectify *his* problem. Work together on the plan. Meet as often as necessary to assess your combined progress. Christian should dedicate himself to Gene's well-being.

The result will be that the negativism will stop, Christian will get a good rep back on track, and Gene will be committed to Christian's success as never before.

If Gene does not open up (which is the more likely scenario in the first meeting), make sure he realizes two things:

1. An expectation that the negativism must cease immediately, or more severe actions will be taken.
2. A desire on his manager's part to continue to work with him to determine what the root cause is. Gene needs to see that Christian is going to persevere.

The fact is, Gene might not even know what is causing his problem. Therefore, both Gene and Christian may have to give it some time and meet on a regular basis. Both of them may or may not ever get to the point of identifying the root causes, but *the process of trying* may be enough to turn Gene's attitude around.

However, during this time, the symptoms of the problem (the negativism) must be monitored and controlled.

Watch Your Attitude

Too often when a manager is working a problem-resolution with a salesperson, he sees only the bad because that is what is being examined. This can cause the rep to completely lose confidence, which exacerbates the problem. You can eliminate this possibility by being just as quick to catch and comment on the rep doing something good.

Closure

Christian needs closure on attendance at the training session and on the longer-term negative-attitude problem. Dialogue in a final meeting could go something like this:

"Gene, thanks for sharing what's been on your mind. I know we're both pleased that we have a game plan in place. I would appreciate it if you would go public in your own way about your planned attendance at the training session. I'll leave the execution to you. Just let me know what you've said or done. Can you do that? Thank you.

"Finally, I need your commitment that if you ever have a personal issue or an issue with a sales-unit activity that you'll come to me first to share your feelings. In return, I'll commit to listen hard, work with you, and integrate your ideas and experience to the extent that I can. Have I got your commitment? Thanks."

Christian can't leave the final meeting without closure. Closure is the stake in the ground that defines the new relationship and is the point of return if the problem arises again.

Review Progress

Christian should set up progress-review sessions with Gene. Initially schedule them close together, no longer than a week apart. As Christian sees progress, he can lengthen the time between sessions until they can be eliminated completely. However, Christian should immediately call attention to any reoccurrence of the symptoms (negativism) and not wait for a scheduled session to discuss it.

For the Future

A great way to help an experienced rep become more positive about his job, sales unit, and company is to ask him to mentor a new sales rep. Generally, salespeople take the role of mentoring very seriously. They lead by example and present a positive picture about the job and the company. Mentoring is recommended only if you can be certain that the rep will set a professional example.

When Christian is confident that Gene's negativism has stopped, mentoring could be a positive next step to bolster Gene's confidence and feeling of self-worth.

LESSONS

Sales is a very demanding profession made up of people with large egos. When a rep's confidence is shaken, strange things can happen. Always keep your eyes and ears open for small changes in your people and address them immediately. The more time you spend with your people, the more apt you will be to notice these subtle changes and nip them in the bud before they escalate into serious problems.

When salespeople see their manager providing complementary feedback, not focusing only on the negatives, they are more apt to open up and share their feelings and frustration during times of stress.

Keep your senior, experienced people engaged and challenged at a higher level than others.

5–2 THE PROBLEM:

A salesperson is in the process of losing a strategic customer.

THE STORY

"I have some bad news for you," Cindy delicately said to Marc, her sales manager. "NMR Corporation is planning to place their next order with our biggest competitor."

Cindy is one of Marc's better salespeople, and NMR is one of their largest customers.

"Oh, for cryin' out loud, now everyone will be down on our head. How did this happen? Who knows about this? Who at NMR told you?" Marc asked.

"Their director of finance," she answered. "He said they just feel as if it is time to give someone else a chance to solve their problems. I haven't told anyone else yet."

Marc was stunned by the news.

TEMPTATIONS

Highly visible losses frequently bring down that ominous, deep-toned, rumbling question from above, "What are you going to do about it?" The standard temptations are legendary.

Blame

"Corporate fouled this one up from the get-go," or "You must have taken your eye off the ball, Cindy." or "I knew their director of finance couldn't be trusted."

Paranoia

"I'll alert marketing to change all our pricing immediately before we lose everything."

Take over

"All right, Cindy, I'll take it from here. Gimme the file."

Calm, thoughtful responses are essential in times of major threats.

What Happened Here . . . ?

You were surprised, and surprises are an anathema to sales managers. There are four sides to this problem.

First, Cindy may have sensed some problems early-on and failed to bring them to Marc's attention because of overconfidence, fear, or other emotions. Poor account management and/or the lack of an open relationship with her manager could be contributing factors.

Second, surprises can result from a lack of management processes such as the following:

- Marc may not execute pipeline reviews or have a forecast system.
- He may not track the activities of the top competitors in his area.
- Marc may not spend enough time in the field coaching Cindy and the other reps.
- He may not have a formal major or strategic-account-relationship program and plan.
- Marc may have failed to stay personally involved with his strategic customers.
- He may have had a flawed sales-unit strategy, focusing his people's time and effort on finding new customers while they neglected the old ones.

Marc should get ready for more surprises of this type unless he puts the proper processes and strategies in place.

Third, surprises can arise from customer changes, initiatives, or dissatisfaction.

- The customer may have perceived product or service deficiencies.
- The customer may be aggravated by a lack of consistent support.
- The customer could have new influencers and decision makers in place.
- The customer's requirements could have changed, or a requirement ceased to exist.
- The customer may perceive arrogance, apathy, or passivity on the company's part.
- The customer could have had a change in acquisition policies.

Fourth, surprises can spring from aggressive, innovative action by a competitor that has captured the customer's imagination. Marc's firm could have been outsold.

It was once said about Harley Davidson (paraphrased), "Just because your customers tattoo your name on their chests, do not assume they will be loyal forever!" Marc may be guilty.

OPTIONS

Win the customer back. Now! As Henry Kissinger once said, "The absence of alternatives clears the mind marvelously."

POSSIBLE ACTIONS

Salespeople are in the business of solving problems and providing sound solutions for customers. Those that do it best, sell the most.

A sound solution is made up of three parts:

1. The approach, or strategy, for solving the customer's problem.
2. The execution of the strategy.
3. How well the salesperson and the company solve follow-on problems when they occur.

A breakdown in any one or all of these areas creates an unsatisfied customer, and unsatisfied customers look for alternatives. Marc and Cindy must review these three parts, reliving every aspect of their firm's relationship with NMR.

NMR is not yet lost. Marc and Cindy must do everything in their power to save NMR, and to do that they must first determine why the customer is considering leaving them. *Cindy will be looking for leadership, coaching, and involvement from Marc. Marc should be expecting ownership, candor, innovation, and perseverance from Cindy in return.*

1. Approach or strategy: Marc and Cindy must ask themselves the following questions and must answer from the customer's point of view, *in the context of today's requirements.*
   - Was the initial sales, support, and service strategy correct?
   - Has the strategy been adapted to the changing needs of the customer?
   - Was the strategy reviewed and confirmed by the customer?
   - Is the competition aware of their strategy?

2. Execution: Again, from the customer's point of view, did they execute satisfactorily?
   - Was their company's execution of the strategy timely and appropriate?
   - Was the execution seamless, or did Marc and Cindy's company have difficulty obtaining and focusing the necessary resources on the customer?
   - Was execution consistent with customer priorities?

3. Problem-resolution process: And again, from the customer's point of view, they must answer these questions.
   - Did their process to resolve issues take too long?

- Did the process appear seamless, or was the customer aware of internal machinations?
- Were issues usually resolved, but the process always painful?
- Was there any proactive digging on Cindy's part to uncover problems?
- Was their company perceived as committed to continuous process improvement?
- Were Cindy and Marc both involved in problem resolution? Who else was or wasn't?
- Assuming the customer has experience, is the competition's problem-resolution process better than theirs?

Expand the questions in all three areas to meet your needs and situation.

Build a Plan

The answers to the questions in those three parts will help Marc and Cindy build a plan to reengage the customer. Cindy must lead in these steps while Marc coaches. Since this is a strategic customer, other people should be pulled into the process as necessary. They must dig deeper into their own organization chart. The plan should be put together with more diligence and creativity than offensive sales plans because they are trying to overcome negative momentum. The plan must leapfrog competition, not just meet it. *Everything must be on the table.* For example:

- Reestablish the buying influences, needs, and requirements.
- Reconfirm the customer's criteria for choosing vendors.
- Review who the key players and decision makers are.
- Reconsider who should be a part of sales calls and presentations.

Speed is of the essence, but Marc and Cindy must be exceedingly thorough.

Meet with the Customer

Make a decision as to whom to call on, going to the highest level possible. That may mean stepping over a previous contact, but at times like this, the rules change. It is much easier to walk down the stairs than up the stairs, especially since you may be walking out the door.

Clearly state your intent. Be objective, honest, and specific. Let the customer know that you realize that your company failed to meet their expectations. It is imperative that the customer know that Cindy and Marc did their homework. They must use facts for illumination not, as drunkards use a lamppost, for support.

They must be careful with their words and attitude. On the one hand they don't want to fall on their own sword in a guilt trip, and on the other hand they don't want to imply that the customer caused all the problems and that their poor company is doing its best to fix the mess.

Cindy should clearly lay out her company's plan to fix the problems, or meet the customer's new needs, and then ask for time to execute her company's plan. If her company can't salvage all the business, they should try to maintain some of it.

It's Too Far Gone

Sometimes these situations are over the hill. The customer has emotionally moved away from your company to another. Your words and actions, immediately after realizing that you cannot hold onto this customer, will determine if you will ever have the opportunity to do business with them again. Take the high road. Help the customer through the transition. This is a counter-intuitive strategy, but it can work to save some of the business or position you for a return.

LESSONS

Relationships with customers must transcend the people involved. They must be company to company if you expect them to be long lasting.

Always treat your customers like prospects, constantly wooing them, because your competition can grow only by taking market share from you.

Value is determined by the customer, not by you. Never underestimate the value of value. Be committed to continuous value-assessments and value-delivery improvements.

Sometimes the change of a supplier is mandated. Make sure you are calling high so that you have access in times-of-change decrees.

Effective management processes can keep small issues from becoming major threats.

Reward salespeople who bring these problems forward. Shooting the messenger keeps customer problems buried and increases the potential for the loss of any customer.

5–3 THE PROBLEM:

You have a prima donna soaking up undue attention and resources.

THE STORY

John, the head of the sales-support group has been complaining about one of Archie's best salespeople, Miguel. "I know he brings in a lot of business, but is it worth it? He uses twice as much sales support as any of your other reps, and to make it worse, he never gives any credit to anybody but himself," John complained.

"Miguel says, 'You know, I closed this one,' when in fact, it was my people who put together the winning solutions," John fumed.

John continued, "I refuse to deal with him any more, Archie. He's on his own."

"John, please, calm down," Archie responded . "I assure you I'll deal with this."

TEMPTATIONS

When one your top guns gets into a mess it's easy to overreact to protect him.

Push back

"John, you're not doing such a great job yourself. Just look at these loss reports."
or

"John, this is one of my best reps. Learn to deal with him. You got that? See you later."

Ho-hum

"We should be so lucky to have a dozen other Miguels. What else is new? Relax."

Insulate

"Miguel, lay low with the sales-support group. Let me run interference next time."

A sales team is made up of many personalities. Your job is like an orchestra leader. You need to be able to create an environment so that everyone can make beautiful music together.

WHAT HAPPENED HERE . . . ?

Sounds as if Miguel is a classical prima donna. Don't panic! This is not all bad.

A prima donna is defined as

1. The principal female singer in an opera.
2. An extremely sensitive, vain, or undisciplined person.

Miguel is probably not a principal female singer, but he probably is somewhat sensitive, vain, and undisciplined. He probably has more in common with a principal female singer than is immediately obvious.

They likely both possess these characteristics:

- Highly skilled
- Very independent
- Extravagant
- Not afraid to tell you how good he is

- Difficult to deal with
- Accustomed to getting their way
- Obsessed with being the best
- Love playing to an audience

In the case of Miguel, all these things and more make him a great salesperson. Selling is a difficult job. Great salespeople must be supremely confident. Unfortunately, this supreme confidence can be derived from self-centeredness, or egotism, in some reps, thus, the negative aura of a prima donna.

It is rare that you will ever manage a team of reps that does not contain at least one prima donna. Your job, as a sales manager, is to deal with your prima donnas in a way that allows them to succeed without disrupting the rest of the sales-unit and support infrastructure.

OPTIONS

Archie has three options with this situation.

1. Change Miguel to be like the others. (Good luck!)
2. Leave Miguel alone. Work around him, and try to minimize his negative impact.
3. Set some boundaries that both Archie and Miguel can live with, and that will allow Miguel to excel without antagonizing the rest of the world.

POSSIBLE ACTIONS

Too often in today's corporate world, management focuses on the weaknesses of its employees instead of their strengths. Management creates detailed action plans to overcome these weaknesses and assumes the strengths will prevail.

It may be better to focus on taking advantage of an individual's strengths and neutralizing any debilitating weaknesses. This approach allows both management and employee to concentrate on what the employee does well. It is a significantly more positive approach.

Schedule a Couple of One-on-ones

Archie must ask Miguel to meet with him, asking him to prepare a list of his strengths, both personal and business oriented, to bring to the meeting. Nothing more needs to be said. In preparing for the first meeting, Archie should also compile a list of Miguel's strengths.

Archie should schedule a second meeting with Miguel at the same time—for the day following the first meeting.

The First Meeting—Defining the Strengths

At the start of the meeting Archie should state his intent, and that is to tell Miguel that he is one of the best reps on the team but that he has a tendency to rub people around him the wrong way. Archie must be clear and concise. Archie must make sure that Miguel understands that although Archie values Miguel's skills and the business he brings in, he needs to improve his interface with others.

Miguel's immediate reaction is likely to be push-back.

- "I don't have time for these office politics."
- "Which crybaby complained this time?"
- "What these guys need to understand is that I make their paycheck possible."

Archie must let Miguel vent, but not argue or debate with him. Let it go.

Archie must then switch the conversation to Miguel's strengths, a subject he will be more comfortable with. *Archie must make it clear that his intent in these two meetings is to help Miguel maximize his strengths and minimize his Achilles heel, his interactions with others.*

First, using the list Miguel compiled, Archie should write on the board all the strengths that he agrees with. Archie should be as liberal as possible without compromising his overall view. Then Archie should add any additional strengths to the board that he has on his own list.

Archie should then lead a discussion on how to make sure Miguel makes full application of the strengths. Archie should cite instances where he observed Miguel utilizing those strengths in recent sales calls or team meetings, and where he could have utilized them even more.

Miguel *must* leave the meeting feeling that he has gained some ideas, that he has the sincere commitment of his boss to make him even stronger, and that this isn't a setup.

Before adjourning, Archie should reiterate how he values Miguel's strengths and his concerns regarding interpersonal skills. Last, Archie should ask Miguel to compile a short list (three to five items) of weaknesses, or areas that need improvement, for the meeting on the next day.

Preparation for the Second Meeting

In preparing for the second meeting, Archie should also compile a list of Miguel's weaknesses, trying to keep the list short. Archie should also prepare his perception of how Miguel's weaknesses impact Miguel's performance. *This is the most critical element of the exercise.*

For example, the following perception could be a part of Archie's preparation:

Weakness: Miguel treats the sales-support organization with very little respect.

Impact: Sales support is reluctant to work with Miguel on future deals, or not provide him with the full measure of their creativity and effort. Subsequently, Miguel's workload will increase, his win rate will decrease, and his income will be impacted.

The Second Meeting—Define the Weaknesses

Archie should begin the meeting by asking Miguel to list his weaknesses on the board, trying his hardest not to agree with all of them. Once Miguel's list is completed, Archie can add his own.

They can discuss the list for a while, then together pick out the one weakness that they both feel has the biggest impact on Miguel and develop a plan to neutralize that weakness.

For example, in the area of sales support, suggest that Miguel get sales support involved early in a campaign, possibly letting them help with the strategy. Explain how this would make sales support feel more worthwhile and would make them even more committed to the result. Share your previously developed impact statement and together expand upon it. *Focus on the impact to Miguel*, not on the impact on others. Archie should use his coaching skills to suggest a more appropriate approach.

Remember, the goal is to neutralize weaknesses, not transform Miguel into an angel.

Once Archie and Miguel have a plan, they should set up a schedule for additional follow-up meetings, no more than one week apart.

Follow-Up Meetings

Archie should note any instances where he observed Miguel trying to change his approach and note instances where he might have slipped backwards. Archie should talk to people Miguel interfaces with, such as sales support, and ask them how they feel things are going.

Remember, change in an area of weakness is difficult for anyone. A prima donna finds it even more difficult because he may not completely buy into the fact that he has a weakness.

Start follow-up meetings by asking Miguel how he thinks things are going with the plan. Agree with him as often as you can, especially when he feels things are going well.

Share your observations with Miguel, again focusing on the impact to his success. After a few sessions like this, Archie should begin to see some improvement with the first weakness, and he must point out the improvement to Miguel and compliment him on it.

If Archie does not see any progress being made, he should share his disappointment, telling Miguel that he is surprised a talented person cannot make progress on such a simple plan. Archie should keep at it, understanding that some measure of success will occur over time.

Choose Another Weakness

When Archie feels Miguel has shown that he can consistently overcome the first weakness, they should both go back to the list and pick out another weakness as they did before, again building a plan together and scheduling follow-up meetings.

This is an iterative process. Do not try to do too much at once. Be patient. Miguel will get stronger. Warning: Do not expect perfection, but be happy with continuous improvement.

For the Future

Archie should periodically ask Miguel for his inputs on difficult problems Archie is personally experiencing such as a sales-force alignment issue, a need to strategize against a major competitor, or other heavy matters. (Don't ever go to a prima donna with fluffy questions.)

Archie will get some good ideas, and he will make Miguel feel more valued.

Even More Involvement

If Miguel enjoys the increased participation, Archie should try to give him more. For example:

- Present him with the problem of the month and have him discuss it at a regularly scheduled monthly breakfast.
- Let Miguel do a presentation on his favorite sales topic at the next sales meeting.
- Let Miguel help other salespeople strategize their sales campaigns.

Involvement with others is not the natural tendency of a prima donna. Therefore, do not be surprised if Miguel does not leap at opportunities. But keep working at it.

LESSONS

The fact is, the *stuff* that makes a salesperson great is the same *stuff* that can make him or her somewhat difficult to manage. Addressing this problem helps you develop a much deeper understanding of your key people and helps them maximize their talents. Approaching these problems from a strength viewpoint is likely to yield better results. Your effort also has a positive impact on the rest of your sales unit and other business functions and embellishes your reputation throughout the company as an effective leader and manager of people.

The lessons drawn from handling what can arguably be one of the most difficult performance problems is that it can make other performance problems easier to address.

Do not expect all your people to act the same. Instead, blend their talents together in such a way as to make beautiful music.

5-4 THE PROBLEM:

A rogue sales rep is creating havoc.

THE STORY

Steve's administrative assistant walked into his office and handing him some documents said, "I just noticed, in going through the order files that the signatures on the credit applications and the order forms don't match. I looked at some of Blair's other client packages and noted several other discrepancies."

"Blair, again?" Steve boomed back. "Last month he didn't show up for the big corporate dinner and instead took some clients out drinking."

This is it—he's "toast," Steve thought to himself.

TEMPTATIONS

Situations that on the surface seem abundantly clear in terms of options and necessary actions can become clouded by personal motivations, a mushy management style, or extenuating circumstances in the environment.

Only one more

"This is positively, absolutely, unconditionally the last time. Do you hear me, Blair?"

So what?

"What's the problem? It's a dog-eat-dog world out there. He's not hurting any-one."

Procrastination

"As soon as this end-of-year rush is over, I'm going to have a heart-to-heart with Blair."

Anything other than quick decisive action exacerbates these problems.

WHAT HAPPENED HERE . . . ?

Rogues are salespeople or sales managers who flaunt rules and expectations.

Rogues are not the easiest people to lead because they often have big egos; are often talented, but misguided; are often highly creative, but devious; are often self-reliant, but loners; and are very competitive, but often don't play by the rules.

Rogues can reveal confidential information to customers and prospects, ignore feedback, or make off-color comments about others.

Rogues often treat colleagues with disdain, or they treat them with kid gloves so they won't blow the whistle, even to the point of sharing commissions.

They are people who operate beyond the boundaries of propriety, good judgment, or legality. Rogues are simply difficult people.

And finally, a rogue colors and contaminates his immediate manager by his behavior and continued presence.

Some people have a hard time taking instruction and working in groups and teams. They can't tolerate not being able to do the job within limits. Blair may fit that mold.

Blair may have a chip on the shoulder, feel that he has been deprived or shunned, or feel that he's been abused in some way. His actions amount to retaliation.

Blair may give in and yield to pressure easily and quickly because he wants to be everyone's friend.

Blair has no qualms about doing anything that he feels like doing. He's a free spirit, feeling no shame or apprehension. His moral code is likely out of whack.

Previous managers may have looked the other way and tolerated the behavior, providing tacit approval. He probably has never been called out vigorously for behavior infractions.

Some people act this way because they believe that senior management values the behavior, or someone from senior management once made an offhanded comment that reinforced Blair's predispositions.

OPTIONS

There are only three options, your choice depending on *the nature of the infraction*.

1. Keep Blair, counseling and reprimanding him in the process.
2. Probation.
3. Termination.

Everyone will be watching how you handle this. People will be looking to see if you compromise yourself or your processes. There are no secrets in sales units.

POSSIBLE ACTIONS

The sooner Steve *thoroughly investigates* and reacts to this behavior the better for everyone.

Assessment

Think this through.

- Was Blair's activity just bad judgment, in conflict with company policies, or illegal?
- Have you unwittingly contributed to the behavior through deficient training in sales skills, product knowledge, negotiations, administration, or other skills or policies?
- What consequences, if any, were laid down from previous infractions? Those consequences must be implemented, or your credibility is destroyed.
- How much risk can you and the company continue to tolerate, if any?
- Would any reasonable person make the same mistake, or was there enough premeditation to indicate clear intent to deceive someone or violate policies?

If this was a first infraction, how tolerant can you be and is Blair salvageable and is he a valuable asset and performer? With a second or third infraction, this question becomes moot.

Talk to Others

Take the issue to your manager and to human resources, make them aware of your intended disciplinary action, gain concurrence, and integrate their counsel if any is offered.

Human resources (if you have that function in your business) *must be* a key player in this process. The nature of the infraction may also mandate a conversation with the firm's attorney. Have all of their suggested actions put in writing.

Expectations

Steel yourself for creativity and push-back in these confrontations.

- Rogues will try to get you to yield on your values when they are found out.
- Rogues will poke at your hot buttons and personal motivations to get you to compromise.
- Rogues prefer to deal emotionally in order to have you deviate from the facts.
- Rogues are always prepared to deliver solid, plausible stories to account for their actions.

Be prepared to hold your ground.

It's Time to Talk

Confront the issues—not the personality or the rep's performance—in order to keep the emphasis where it belongs. Rogues respond best to candor and focus.

Advise Blair of the impropriety of his behavior, of your assessment, and of the price he may have to pay for his actions. Always *document* as you proceed. Have HR and the attorneys review the documentation before you put it in the file.

Dig Deeper

Find out if there are any factors in or outside the job that fueled the problem. For example, "Blair, what led you to believe you should do this, or could get away with this?" This is a critical question because the answer may signal leadership, communications, or direction flaws on your part or the company's part. The answer should not minimize your resolve, but rather help you understand the motivation and the facts.

Find out why the rep insists on playing by his own rules and what about your policies he can't tolerate. The answers could help guide you with others, as well as help formulate his penalty. You must be precise in these situations.

Make a Decision

Stay or go. Confirm your decision with other managers, and gain confirmation that the implementation of your decision is consistent with company policies.

Lay It on the Line

Inform Blair of your decision.

If it's termination, do it in accordance with company policy. Isolate Blair from company assets and documents and arrange his departure as soon as possible.

If the situation is such that you are not going to terminate Blair

- Execute an official reprimand and document it.
- Counsel in the context of continuance of employment, compensation, and career development.
- Reiterate your expectations of behaviors, and all of Blair's goals and objectives.
- Tell Blair what specific behaviors need to be changed and inform him verbally and in writing what the consequences of the next violation will be.
- Set a series of future dates to meet to assess progress.

Small steps and changes in roguish behavior, over time, *can* be a big victory for all parties.

Tips for the Future

The following actions can lessen the temptation of roguish behavior in Blair and others.

- Communicate standards, boundaries, and consequences to your sales unit by using stories and what-if scenarios as a way to set examples of destructive behavior.
- Utilize corporate employee-assistance programs if they are appropriate and available. Human resources will be your best guide.
- Regularly let your people know how they are perceived by you and others. Sometimes their self-view distorts reality.

LESSONS

Sales units are a microcosm of society. Don't be surprised if your sales unit contains a representation of some of society's worst problems. These problems demand the immediate notification and involvement of top management, human resources, and the firm's legal counsel.

Speed and frank communications will be your best weapons in combating initial hints of roguish behavior. Lack of follow-up or the failure to administer consequences will destroy your credibility and make it difficult to take any further corrective actions. Thorough documentation throughout is critical in these situations. Other members of your sales unit will draw huge lessons, observing your actions from the sidelines.

5–5 THE PROBLEM:

A salesperson surprises you with a big, marginally profitable order.

THE STORY

Gong! Gong! Somebody was ringing the order bell outside Ellen's office.

It was one of her newer salespeople, Margaret. Margaret had gathered virtually everybody together for the event, as well she should. This was not only her first substantial order, it looked as if it was the largest order of the year for Ellen's sales team.

The problem was, Ellen did not know Margaret was working on this opportunity, and after a quick glance at the purchase order, Ellen knew that the company would make an infinitesimal amount of money the way the deal was structured. Ellen smiled weakly, gave Margaret a "high five," and wondered what she was going to do next.

TEMPTATIONS

It's tough not to be able to join a party with the level of enthusiasm that you would like. You could fill a book with crazy temptations on this one.

False congratulations

"Great job, Margaret, tell me all about it. This is *so wonderful.* I am *so proud.*"

Protect her

"Let's rustle up some protective documentation, like copies of competitor's quotes." or

"Hmmm, let's say, the customer guarantees future business at 5 percent higher prices. Okay?"

Give her "the needle"

"Great order, Margaret. Did you also give away your company car?"

Be careful, because a manager's reaction to a big win is one of the great rewards for a salesperson, and the reaction is enduring.

What Happened Here . . . ?

It is often easy to blame a sales rep for a situation like this. Many times the rep is at fault. Just as often, however, management and the environment in which the rep is working deserve just as much blame.

It could be that there was stiff competition, and the only way she knew how to get the order was to give a steep discount. Perhaps there was never any negotiating-skills training.

In the same vein, maybe Margaret does not know how to differentiate the company's products and therefore was left to competing only with price.

Maybe Margaret had an opportunity to pick up the order at that price, and no selling was needed. Her thought might have been, take the order and run and work out the details later.

It could be that Margaret, Ellen, and the whole sales organization are measured only on revenue, rather than on profit and other qualitative measures.

There could have been a very smart and crafty buying team on the other side of the table who took full advantage of this rookie rep when they saw her salivate over this opportunity.

Maybe Margaret made an honest mistake. Simple mathematics. It happens.

Ellen's company probably does not have a large order-review process or an established discount-and-allowance policy, or if it does, they are not strictly adhered to.

Insufficient training and coaching may have permitted Margaret to get into this situation.

Options

There are really only three options, any of which can only be executed after careful scrutiny of events that led to the order.

1. Reject the order.
2. Accept the order as is.
3. Renegotiate any and all aspects of the order with the customer.

Possible Actions

These are difficult decisions because there is so much in the balance. The best Ellen can do is gather the facts and then make the best business decision she can. This is not a Lone Ranger task. There are probably a wide range of suggestions and alternatives that other managers in other parts of the company can offer. Those opinions must be sought. Also, don't let Margaret hide while all this is going on. She helped create the situation—she must be a part of the solution. It's a great learning experience.

Focus on the Customer

This problem is not about saving anyone's reputation or stroking anyone's ego. Shelve the emotion, embarrassment, and aggravation. Ellen must keep *the customer* and the long-range relationship with *the customer* in mind as she goes forward. Counseling can come later.

The Facts

Talk to Margaret. Find out exactly what happened. Specifically, who said what and why, and who committed what and why. Ellen must let Margaret know that it is important that she be factual because Ellen will probably end up talking to the customer personally. And Margaret has a longer range relationship at stake. There's no room for stories.

Has the order been accepted? In most firms an order is not an order until it has been reviewed, accepted, and acknowledged. Ellen needs to check with her people, and possibly with the firm's attorney, to get a ruling on acceptance. This may just be soft paper at this time.

The Company Situation

There is an old sales manager saying that goes, "Where you *stand* is where you *sit*." That means the "stand" you take on an issue really depends on your company's current needs, or where it "sits."

- Does the company need revenue badly?
- What is the profitability picture in the company at this time?
- Are the company's warehouses full of product? Is the factory loaded or not?
- Does the company have hard-and-fast policies and procedures that govern situations like this, or is it flexible?
- How much resource will this deal soak up, resources that could be used elsewhere?

These and other factors like them will help Ellen decide the proper course of actions. This is another reason that it is imperative that Ellen talk to other people in the firm.

The Implications

It is important to assess the implications of accepting or rejecting this order, still another reason to get the opinions of others.

- Are you jeopardizing your abilities to sell to the government at your currently negotiated contracts or GSA (General Services Administration) schedule? Will this transaction withstand a GSA audit?
- How will your sales partners react to your team selling at such a low price, assuming they find out?

- Have you said no to other, similar deals brought in by other salespeople?
- Are the Terms and Conditions clean, or are there severe penalty clauses?
- Will this deal set a precedent with the customer? Are there other divisions or departments of the customer that will expect similar pricing and considerations?
- Is this the first order from this customer, and what is the likely long-range forecast?

Ellen and Margaret must consider all of these implications, and more.

The Decision

You can gather only so many facts and talk to so many people. Sometimes the answer is so obvious that it jumps out at you. Sometimes it does not. Decide what is the absolute best you can do with this deal. In the end, is it accept, renegotiate, or reject? Make the decision. The next step is common to either of the three decisions.

Talk to the Customer

If it's accept, do you want to set a precedent? If not, explain that this is the last deal you can accept at these prices and terms and conditions, and tell the customer why. Setting expectations at this point eliminates perceived gamesmanship and surprises in the future. Make it clear you intend to work hard to earn their continuing business.

If it's renegotiate, tell the customer that you made a mistake and need their help to rectify it. Ellen and Margaret should walk in with their facts, be prepared for a negotiation, and understand at what point the company wants them to walk. Most customers will strive to reach a true *win-win* solution with them. A few prefer and enjoy I-win-you-lose scenarios, in which case the two of them will likely walk.

Reject implies that the gap is perceived to be too great to negotiate. They should explain the reasons for the rejection, but still be prepared for a negotiation. When the customer sees how much they have to concede they may simply say, "No thank you." Ellen should apologize and make it clear her firm intends to continue to try to earn the customer's business.

Revisit Your Decision

The customer visit may have shed new light on the situation. Keep in mind that occasionally a negative decision (reject the order) and ensuing customer visit will bring out *all* the facts. Ellen should be open to bringing new facts to everyone's attention and revisiting her position if the new facts are compelling.

Work the process

Now that Ellen and Margaret have dealt with the issue, Ellen must try to fix the process that got both of them into the problem in the first place.

- Put a large-order review process in place.

- Establish a discount-and-allowance policy.
- Train her people on value-based selling versus price-oriented selling and on negotiating.
- Enforce the use of the pipeline process. (It is an excellent early-warning device.)

Fix all the processes, and you will eventually eliminate the problem.

LESSONS

Have clear and concise pricing guidelines, regular negotiating-skills training, and opportunity-review processes in place and stick to them.

Salespeople must be trained and coached so that they are smart enough and have guts enough to walk away from a bad deal. It is better if salespeople lose early and lose often so that they can concentrate on profitable business.

Sales managers must be involved in major opportunities.

The compensation plan, more than anything else, will drive selling behavior. Make sure your plan incentivizes your salespeople as the company desires.

5–6 THE PROBLEM:

A superstar's performance has suddenly slipped.

THE STORY

Pete, Yuki's best salesperson, left a disturbing message on Yuki's voice mail late last night.

"Well, boss, I just lost another one. Maybe you should put me out to pasture."

Yuki has tried all day to reach Pete, but to no avail. And he hasn't called in yet for messages, highly unlike him.

"Pete is on a heck of a losing streak. As a matter of fact, he has not won a deal in a long time," Yuki said to herself as she paged through her tracking log.

"Damn, I'm not used to dealing with people who don't have the kind of track record that Pete has. I'm not sure how to handle a situation with a top performer," Yuki thought to herself.

TEMPTATIONS

Anxiety is a sales manager's biggest problem when it comes to a superstar's performance because a disproportionate amount of production is expected from that person.

Pump him

"Come on, Pete, hang in there. It'll happen. Go get 'em baby. Reel 'em in slow."

Trite humor

"Pete, you're too young to retire . . . and you've already had your vacation this year."

Send him back to school

"There is a good sales-skills refresher course next week. I'll enroll you."

It's tough to stay calm with these situations, but that's exactly what's needed, and it's exactly what Pete needs to see from his boss.

WHAT HAPPENED HERE . . . ?

Selling is a difficult and lonely job. Salespeople usually talk to only strangers, or at best, acquaintances. Their conversations are usually guarded and almost always business oriented. They stay in hotels and eat alone. Most of all, they do not often have the opportunity to discuss their day with their peers.

Salespeople are usually staring failure right in the face. This is a major turn-on for most good salespeople, until they get on a nasty losing streak. When a salesperson begins to doubt his ability, or loses confidence, the position becomes a "job," and a death spiral can ensue.

While Pete has slumped, everyone else is rolling normally.

Maybe Pete is wrestling with a painful personal problem, such as his marriage going through difficulty, or his spouse being ill, or maybe he has a substance-abuse problem.

It could be that Pete's success is catching up with him. Maybe he has not kept up with the new products or the new selling techniques.

Possibly his old-reliable customers are not buying as much as they used to, or his old-reliable contacts have moved on, or Pete has not spent enough time finding new customers.

Pete also may have hit the wall. He's burned out, tired, exhausted, suddenly bored, or has suddenly reached the realization that it's time to do something else.

Pete is mired in a deep slump. Just like a baseball player, a slump for a salesperson can be a killer. In the beginning, things are not that bad. But if the slump continues, it plays on the salesperson's mind. He begins to wonder if he will ever get another hit or P.O. Just like a ball player, a salesperson needs a few hits in a row to break out of a slump.

Perhaps this is a brand-new experience for Pete. People who have an abundance of talent and lifelong success who have never experienced defeat often have the hardest time managing a losing streak when it comes along. It devastates them. They don't know what to do.

OPTIONS

Yuki has three options.

1. Take a soft line. Let it ride. Assume that Pete will be able to fix this one on his own; after all, he certainly has the skills. He's proven that.
2. Take a hard line. Put Pete on notice and manage his performance up close and personal. Yuki may not want others to feel that Pete gets special attention.
3. Take a consultative line. Help him work through his slump.

    *   If Pete has a personal problem, and he will share it with you, be a good listener. Give him the time and the help he needs to rectify his problem. Many companies have a confidential employee-assistance program (EAP) that might be just what Pete needs. If not, suggest he seek outside help.
    *   If Pete has a professional problem, be a good coach. Coaching a superstar is the ultimate test for a sales manager. Assistance for Yuki, in the form of some coaching counseling from Yuki's boss, may be prudent in this case.

It is obviously best to work with a good rep like Pete. Top people are very hard to find. If Yuki can help Pete through his problem, Pete will be committed to Yuki's success as never before.

The relationships between superstars and sales managers are most often warm and open, but they are also relationships that have never been tested by fire. On the one hand it would seem that problem resolution would be easy, but there is an element of unpredictability because this is new ground.

POSSIBLE ACTIONS

Loosen up. A tight ballplayer or salesman doesn't need a tight manager.

Play Back the Tape

In spite of the title of this problem, there is no such thing as sudden slippage. Yuki must go back to the time just prior to the start of the losing streak and think about the things that Pete was doing or not doing that were different from his normal patterns. Yuki must think about Pete's market and customer base and what was going on. Yuki must think about product, pricing, and support changes that were going on. To the best of Yuki's knowledge, she must think about what was going on in Pete's personal life. Yuki needs to look for and catalog signals that may seem faint and insignificant on the surface. Everything is fair game. Yuki may or may not discover anything that potentially contributed to the start of the streak, but she must turn over all the rocks.

What's the Difference

There *is* a difference in coaching a superstar and coaching anyone else. Yuki must get straight what her coaching approach should be. Coaching superstars has common threads.

Yuki must think about these threads, plus Pete's idiosyncrasies, and weave them into her coaching plan.

- The superstar will have already tried numerous home remedies to fix his own problem.

- The superstar will be an eager listener, but very selective, quickly discarding poorly perceived ideas.

- The superstar will quickly grow impatient with long-winded ideas. He wants useful hard bullets.

- The superstar will greatly appreciate, not fight off, thoughtful coaching as others may.

- The superstar's ego may get in the way, so treating him as an equal is helpful.

- The superstar will probably be overanalyzing and overthinking the problem. Therefore, be simple.

- The superstar will be tighter than any other rep, so you must discipline yourself to be looser.

- Superstars' pride tend to make them withdraw, thus, getting up close and personal may be a challenge.

Move Him Up

Yuki must change her field-travel schedule immediately and get out with Pete as soon as possible. Remember, Pete's self-confidence needs a boost. Try to catch him doing things well.

If Yuki sees some sales skills that need modifying, she should handle them carefully, as noted here. However, don't skirt the issue, just be as constructive as possible.

Yuki must use the opportunity to discuss things that came to her mind when she played back the tape. She should ask Pete to play back his own tape. *The two should trade and discuss recollections and suggestions calmly, like two consultants, as they go from customer to customer.*

Numbers Game

Selling is a numbers game. The more calls you make on good prospects, the more business you will bring in. Help Pete organize his day. One of Yuki's goals should be to help Pete get in front of as many good prospects as possible. Go through the leads and customer list together.

You have to be lucky in sales to be successful. However, it is amazing how lucky you get when you work hard. It was once said that good things come to those who wait, but only the leftovers of those who hustle. *Make sure Pete keeps his head up and hustles.* Thomas Edison said it best. "Everything comes to him who hustles while he waits."

Be Smart

A baseball player in a slump will begin to press. He will be so anxious to get a hit he will swing at bad pitches. Salespeople are no different. They will call on anybody who will see them. They will lose their selectivity. This will cause them only to lose more often.

One way to help Pete through this is to define his *A*, *B*, and *C* customers.

- *A* customers are those that have the potential to bring in 60 percent of Pete's business.
- *B* customers, 30 percent.
- *C* customers, 10 percent.

When you help Pete up his call volume, make sure that he is making most of his calls on the *A* customers, some on *B* customers, and very few on *C* customers. Also, make sure that he spends some of his sales time looking for *new customers*.

Back to the Numbers

Every business has a *dominant* sales activity, such as a demonstration, a proposal, a factory visit, or something else that fuels orders better than anything else. The more of these activities a rep executes with *A* prospects, the more business he will bring in. Yuki should help Pete plan as many of these dominant activities as he can, coaching him in the process.

Keep in Touch

More numbers. Pete will need Yuki's support until he breaks out of his slump. Yuki must call Pete at the end of the day two or three times a week to chat about how the day went, offer assistance, and answer any questions he might have. Yuki also needs to schedule additional time in the field with Pete. One effort is not enough.

Get Him Involved

Isolation fuels slumps. Integration mitigates them. Yuki should ask Pete to lead a training session at her next sales-unit meeting. Pete will feel good that he was asked, and just by preparing, he will remind himself of the techniques that have made him successful all along.

Be Patient

Don't lose it, or you may lose a good rep. Yuki must stay the course. If Pete is working hard and smart as Yuki has directed, he will break out of his slump.

LESSONS

Don't assume that your top people can care for themselves. Everyone, no matter how good, or at what level, has his or her soft spots or is susceptible to outside forces that can get him or her offtrack.

Always test morale by looking for opportunities to look all of your people in the eye and ask how they are doing. A sales manager must be a keen observer of events and attitudes, and you must constantly listen and watch for signals that can forecast a problem from *any* of your people.

Stay close to *all* of your people, not only those you are naturally comfortable with, or the problem performers, or the middle-of-the-roaders. Catch slumps early, and you will be better able to pull any of your salespeople out of them more quickly. Turning around the slump of a superstar takes more tact and creativity than normal. The exercise will push the boundaries of your coaching. It's like going to coaching school.

5–7 THE PROBLEM:

You have an employee not interested or willing to excel.

THE STORY

"Is *that* the best you can do?" Suzanne asked one of her account managers. Jane was such a bright, capable manager, but was again forecasting that she would be a little shy of her plan and could do no more. Jane's attitude was that she was trying as hard as she could.

Suzanne was frustrated because Jane was a gifted person. Suzanne had witnessed the skills. Jane was not a performance problem, she was just a middle-of-the-roader.

Suzanne's problem was that she wanted to make her division a big winner, and one of her account managers was holding her back. Suzanne had a difficult time accepting performance that reflected less than the capability of her people.

TEMPTATIONS

For a sales manager focused hard on excellence, it is often difficult to work with competent people who don't share your drive. It makes you want to jump up and down.

Turn up the heat
   "What's the matter with you, are you lazy? Are you sick? Are you sandbagging?"

Pawn her off
   "I think I'll go and talk to George. He has an open slot in his group. And he's gullible."

Cajole her
   "Come on Jane . . . you're pulling my leg, right? You just want to surprise me, right?"

Patient building of understanding is the better answer.

What Happened Here . . . ?

Suzanne has a competent, bright employee who is not fully engaged. Incompatibility of goals is a regular and complex sales-management problem. Two people with different personal agendas who have to work together invite sparks.

Someone may have told Jane that sales is easy and that she could make a ton of money.

Jane may find that sales offers great personal freedom that facilitates extra-curricular interests during the day. Jane may want to stay buried in the middle of the pack where she can safely hide and do her own thing. It may be useful to find out how she's spending her time.

Jane may have underestimated the work required. She could have seen someone working four-hour days making a decent living and felt that matched her personal style.

Jane may feel comfortably in control of herself. I don't need the heat may be her feeling. The achievement of balance in her life may be her big driver. Jane may have seen others burn themselves out or cause harm to others and doesn't want to repeat the mistakes.

Maybe the environment or the product line isn't stimulating, maybe the work itself isn't challenging.

Her husband may be a professional person who makes *beaucoup* bucks, and therefore she doesn't really need this income. The job fills social and personal needs.

Jane may be close to retirement and sees no need to break her back for some ambitious young hotshot out to make a name for herself. She just wants to be left alone.

She may not like Suzanne or her style and may have trouble supporting someone with whom she doesn't share values and interests.

Options

The company has chartered Suzanne to do a certain job—to lead a sales unit and surpass her goals. In light of that charter Suzanne must make decisions to support and exceed it. She is being held accountable for certain results and knows that her employer would be very pleased if she exceeded expectations. She is aware that she should respect her people and their motivations, but she also has a job to do. It can be a tug of war.

She's got three options.

1. Back off. Jane is making plan or coming close. Suzanne could devote her attention to other people who are more interested in improving their performance and help them to become even more successful. Fully support and coach Jane, but stop pressing her. You're essentially giving up on her if you do this, but circumstances may demand it.

2. If there are unique personal considerations Suzanne could modify Jane's job to fit her personal situation, or move her to another job that satisfies all parties.

3. Coach and motivate Jane to perform at a level she can—and the level Suzanne expects.

Motivating middle-of-the-roaders can be tough. Suzanne's objective is twofold: to get everyone utilizing their talents for the benefit of the enterprise and to open up new vistas of possibilities for her employees.

POSSIBLE ACTIONS

You need to settle in for a long trust- and relationship-building campaign. Be patient.

Understand Your Employee

Talk to Jane frequently and at length without fully sharing your opinion of her. There are so many potential causes that this situation will take time to explore. Suzanne needs to get to know Jane much better, and this could take weeks or months.

Talk about her plans and yours. Talk about her personal activities and interests and yours. Talk about the business in a casual sort of way, sharing observations and opinions. Ask for her opinion about what the division can do to strengthen itself. Talk about her level of job satisfaction. Always ask if there is any help you can provide. Ask if she would like another job or to work in another division. Keep the dialogue going. Be aware, though, that regardless of your effort, some people will not let you get close. If that's the case, you may want to get help from another manager to try to build understanding.

Without obvious probing, listen closely to how Jane's peers refer to her. Talk to your boss and to human resources to get their opinions and suggestions.

Try to find out what motivates her, sharing your motivations in the process. Managers who open themselves up first are more apt to get reciprocal responses. The understanding you develop through all these conversations will help suggest effective actions.

During this relationship-building campaign keep your eyes open for signs of avoidance, absenteeism, and excuses and then explore them.

Look at Yourself

Maybe you need to change *your* style with Jane. You may need to be more flexible, soft selling your ideas and your goals, or you may learn that she expects firmer leadership and direction. The current approach certainly hasn't been effective and is possibly counterproductive.

Pushback

Sometimes in these situations the rep will tactfully try to get a manager to change her goals so as to take the heat off herself. The rep may present arguments to get the manager off her back. If this occurs be receptive and thoughtful, and be ready to accept obvious gems of truth in the employee's arguments, but at the same time don't let yourself be duped.

Share Your View

Now it's time to share your opinion that Jane is not working up to the level of her talents. The relationship building and introspection will enable you to better word your comments. The strengthened relationship permits more productive dialogue than if Suzanne had broached the subject earlier. The subject becomes less intimidating and the exchange less confrontational.

Face Reality

It is a false belief that all salespeople place high expectations on themselves. Many sales executives feel that if someone came into sales in the first place, he or she understands the culture and the accompanying high expectations. The truth is that the person could have come into sales for a variety of reasons.

The reality is that you can't surround yourself completely with like-minded people. You can change some people to your way of thinking, but some you can't. Everyone has different potential, talents, and drives. Championship teams also require people who can play special roles and fill special needs.

Invest Your Support

You can find out if your people truly have the potential to achieve excellence by taking an activist role. Here are four steps that can nudge them along.

1. Engineer activities that fuel excellence.
    - Pick the one thing that Jane does the best and have her share the skill or activity with the rest of the sales unit. The effort creates confidence.
    - Ask for her opinions and help on matters that are outside her responsibility. Your request and her responses will make it obvious that she has something more to contribute than she previously thought.
    - Introduce her to another manager with whom you believe the compatibility and friendship can have a motivating effect.
    - Have her participate in a major company social function. It can be energizing.
    - Mastermind a mentor relationship with a senior person in your organization.
    - Team Jane up on a two-person sales-unit project with a top performer.
    - Maneuver her to participate on a special team or in a special meeting with people from other business functions to give her exposure.

    Engineered activities lead to engineered successes. Use good judgment so that your moves aren't perceived as intrusive prodding or pressure.

2. Perhaps Jane hasn't tasted the fruits of winning BIG. Personally help her close a *big* opportunity. Participate and help all the way, from identification of the prospect, to strategy development, to presentations, to closing. Big wins have a way of catapulting a middle-of-the-roader into a superstar. The experience opens up a whole new vista. The encounter also adds a big dose of confidence in you, as her manager.

3. Whet her appetite. In order to whet her appetite, expose Jane to some of the perks that accompany excellence. Look hard for accomplishments, however small, that

warrant such treatment. The spotlight and attention may cause her to say, "Hey, wow, I kind of like this!" More than one sales professional has been affected that way.

- Ask her to accompany you to a meeting in the CEO's office.
- Finagle participation in a high-visibility trade show, dealer meeting, or buyers' conference.
- Wangle a word of praise from a customer or sales partner.
- Have a note of congratulations come from someone high up on your corporate staff.
- Give a small gift as a token for a thoughtful action or special result.
- Mention an accomplishment at a staff meeting.
- Provide a small bonus or management award for something special.
- Have her picture appear in a company periodical.

4. Consider giving Jane some collateral assignments whose content take advantage of her interests and special talents. Nothing opens up the floodgates of creativity and commitment more than doing something for which you have a passion.

Suzanne should be willing to accept continuing small steps, over time, as big wins. Patience and perseverance may be the best strategy. Then one day something will happen—the light may go on—Jane's needs and desires may change or constraints may fall away and she'll be off and running at full speed. It can be a thrill to watch.

Lessons

This problem highlights the need to get to know all your employees well. Salespeople respect a manager who expresses more than a superficial interest in them. You always learn a lot about the motivations and desires of your people in this type of situation.

When you have obvious talent in your organization, you can't go wrong by making every possible effort to develop it. It is worth the struggle to invest every bit of your managerial and leadership skills and energy. The personal rewards that accompany taking your people to a level of performance that they never thought possible for themselves are priceless. The employee will never forget your investment and persistence to open new vistas.

But be prepared to accept the fact, as the old story goes, that not every horse that you lead to water will drink.

5–8 The Problem:

A productive rep is creating a huge "wake" in the office.

The Story

Looking down at the documents, Rajeev slowly walked down the hall, shaking his head.

"Molly, I'd like a word with you," he said, as he stuck his head into Molly's cubicle.

"Rajeev, baby, did you hear I got the BIG ONE," she retorted?

"Yeah, and the waves you are causing are just as big," was Rajeev's steely-eyed response. "Look at this mess. Order entry just stuck this garbage under my nose. No credit check, the order form is incomplete, data are missing, the delivery date is a Sunday. This is a disaster."

"Yes, I know, I'm sorry—but I nailed it—NAILED IT, Rajeev—neat, huh?"

"We'll talk about neat. This has gone on for too long."

Temptations

It is hard to reconcile joy and anger. You feel caught between a rock and a hard place and irrational responses spill out easily.

Tear up the paperwork
> "This is intolerable, appalling, and reprehensible! Start all over again, Molly."

Go get me another one
> "You bring 'em in and we'll clean 'em up—don't worry about it."

Sarcasm
> "Oh, Molly, I'm so very sorry to bother you, but could you pleeeeeeze help us?"

The behaviors you tolerate sends messages about your values. Many people will be watching your reactions.

What Happened Here . . . ?

You have a loose cannon that's hitting the target. And you're being taken advantage of.

This problem occurs because a seemingly innocuous habit was permitted to go unchecked a long time ago. A lack of discipline and accountability let the habit fester and grow. It sets a bad example for the rest of the sales unit and makes Rajeev look incompetent.

Molly may not understand the impact of her errors, or she *does* understand but couldn't care less. Maybe she wasn't trained properly, or she is a naturally sloppy, careless person who needs to get organized.

She probably sees herself above the little people and these mundane tasks. She may be living in a fantasy world as a warrior princess with a legion of serfs to clean up after her.

She may be interested only in getting the order, picking the tasty morsels out of the job description. Cherry picking is a sign of a self-centered, immature salesperson.

Molly is consciously cutting corners, just looking for more sales time and doesn't like administrative work. A dislike of paperwork is an old sales cop-out.

Molly may intimidate Rajeev or have him wrapped around her little finger. He may be afraid to rankle a good performer. And Rajeev may be uncomfortable handling conflict.

OPTIONS

Answer two questions first.

1. What kind of reputation as a leader and manager do you want to achieve? How do you want to be known?
2. Do you have personal standards? What are they? Do you establish them or do other people establish them for you?

The answers seem obvious, but how strongly do you believe in the answers, and how badly do you want to clean this problem up? This problem has a lot to do with personal resolve.

There is only one option. You have to put a stop to the "wake." However, you have a range of approaches that can vary between the following, depending on the rep.

1. The shape-up-or-ship-out approach: In the short term you clean this problem up with firm counseling. In the long term you keep it clean with scrutiny and harsh consequences.
2. The pamper option: This is a soft approach. The state of your business, the rep's attitude and cooperative spirit, and other circumstances may cause you to be more indulgent.

POSSIBLE ACTIONS

Take a deep breath. You're about to wade in and clean up a mess.

Put a Stake in the Ground

None of Rajeev's haranguing or pleading has worked in the past, so, first things first.

Display some management courage. Courage is defined as the attitude or response of facing and dealing with anything recognized as dangerous, difficult, or painful, instead of withdrawing from it. In simple terms, get a backbone.

It is sometimes difficult not to coddle productive people, especially in today's free-agency environment. The exceptional few that take unfair advantage of their good performance will continue to push the boundaries until you stop them. It is your choice.

Gather Your Facts

Talk to the people in order entry and wherever else the "wake" problem is apparent. Make sure you have a complete grasp of the issue, how things are supposed to get done, and what you are trying to correct. When you talk to Molly she will be alert to the slightest error on your part. Her gloating will be unstoppable if you don't know what you're talking about.

Get some sample documents—good and bad—to use as coaching samples.

Counsel

Don't even *think* about delegating this counseling session to someone in order entry.

Starting from square one sends a message. Ask Molly to explain the order-entry process to check her understanding of how it works, then go through the process yourself step by step, reviewing resources, and where and how to get questions answered. If there are any reference materials that the reps must use have her explain how she uses them.

Demonstrate to Molly her impact on the firm's quality programs, her impact on other people's measurements, and the ultimate impact on customers.

Show her what good documents should look like.

Molly's probable reaction to this baby-step coaching? "Rajeev, *please*, I *know* all this. I get your point." Rajeev's response? "Then, why don't you do it?"

Steel Yourself for a Snow Job

Rajeev will get a running string of excuses and rationalizations for every single transgression. Rajeev should know Molly pretty well, so he should know what to expect. He can prepare himself. Here is a short list of possible objections and answers.

Rep Objections	Sales-Manager Answers
"But you wanted the orders in quickly, remember, it was at the end of the month?"	"I wanted the orders in accurately. Inaccurate orders aren't orders—they're waste paper."
"Do you want a salesperson or a secretary?	"I want a professional salesperson."
"They get paid to do that work. I get paid to sell."	"You get paid to do a complete job."
"Do you want fewer orders?"	"I want more orders, and I would like them entered flawlessly, thank you."
"I was in a hurry."	"Slow down."

"I was solving the big Acme problem at the time, do you remember?"

"I remember you were the one who caused the big Acme problem."

"I'm not paid to do that stuff. I'm paid to sell."

"Do you like your salary? You're paid to do that stuff."

"Can't we hire someone to take care of that stuff?"

"We did. It's you."

"But that order was very profitable."

"Everything you made for us out there was lost in here."

"I thought you wanted me to help *you* win the contest?"

"I want *you* to win the approval of your co-workers."

"I need the money."

"Order entry needs peace of mind."

"Simplify the processes."

"Simplify the lives of the people in order entry."

"My laptop was in the shop."

"This is a pencil. Do you remember how to use it?"

"The people in order entry don't like me because I bring in a lot of orders."

"The people in order entry don't *respect* you because you bring in a lot of problems."

"Our price book is out of date."

"You are out of control."

"I have an idea to improve our process so we don't have to deal with this stuff."

"I'd be happy to hear your ideas as soon as you prove you can handle the current process."

"I was working away on that presentation *for you*."

"I'm tired of explaining away mistakes *for you*."

"I ran out of forms."

"You've run out of excuses."

This list can go on and on, but the publisher has limits. You get the idea. Your responses can be as hard or soft as your business culture demands and your understanding of the rep suggests.

Here are some objections to practice on.

Objection: "The customer didn't give me the information." Answer: _____.

Objection: "I ran out of time." Answer: _____.

Objection: "I didn't want anyone ahead of this order in the queue." Answer: _____.

Potential Corrective Actions

Here are some techniques to help Molly and everyone else at the same time. A few are gentle reminders, some are firm measures, and some are consequences. There must be consequences.

- Have Molly present every order to you for review prior to submitting it.
- Instruct order entry to return *everything* that isn't squeaky clean. Don't let order entry be accommodating of the slightest infraction.
- Ensure that Molly corrects every error herself, not letting her pawn off work on unsuspecting junior clerks.
- If customers call to complain about delays tell them the truth—that Molly is in the process of "making some corrections" and that she will personally explain her error.
- Hold commission payments (if you pay on the order) until you are satisfied that the orders are clean.
- Have Molly work for a day or a week in customer service so she can understand what it's like being on the receiving end of the line.
- Ask Molly to review order entry procedures for your entire sales unit at the next staff meeting.
- Have Molly teach order-entry procedures to new reps—and audit her teaching.
- Ask order entry to track errors for your sales unit for a period of time. Make the results public. The visible embarrassment could cure the problem quickly.
- Put a letter of reprimand in Molly's personal file.
- Document the problem in Molly's annual appraisal.

Stay Alert

Be prepared for continuing tests and probes to test your resolve. Stalwartness is your best response with "wake" makers.

Where There Are Waves There Is Erosion

Look closely at other aspects of Molly's work. What other responsibilities are being shortchanged? How accurate are the expense reports? Perhaps it would be prudent to review them more carefully from now on.

How valid are those forecasts? Perhaps it would be judicious to probe deeper.

How realistic are activity reports? Perhaps you should challenge the content further.

How many commitments are being made to customers without your knowledge? Perhaps you need to spend more time traveling with Molly.

When Molly finally gets it right, make sure you thank and encourage her and urge order entry to do the same thing. Ultimately, this may be your most effective action.

LESSONS

You'll feel better about yourself for having stood up to unacceptable behavior. You'll discover that you can, in fact, alter a productive performer's behavior for the benefit of the enterprise. The experience will make you more comfortable counseling similar problems in the future.

The rest of the company will respect you for your discipline and management.

The rest of the sales unit, having enjoyed watching a loose cannon being taken down a peg, will feel that you have leveled the playing field and that you are consistent with the application of your standards and expectations. All of your people will hold you in higher esteem for your example of professionalism.

part six

TROUBLESHOOTING SALES-UNIT PERFORMANCE PROBLEMS

6–1 THE PROBLEM:

Your people are not selling what the company wants sold.

THE STORY

"Nolan, could you please step into my office for a minute," said Jeff, the national sales manager, over the phone. Oh, for cryin' out loud . . . I know what this is about, Nolan thought, as he hauled himself down the hall.

"What the heck is going on, Nolan?" Jeff solemnly asked. "I'm looking at last month's sales figures and see that only 12 percent of your sales unit's transactions included our new service-contract offerings. That's way, way off the target. Young man, you're in trouble!" Jeff continued.

"This stuff is more trouble than . . .," Nolan started.

"Nolan, are you listening? How are you going to turn it around?" Jeff finished.

TEMPTATIONS

Talk about being caught between a rock and a hard place. When your heart is not in a task on which you're being pressed there is a tendency to look for escape hatches.

Concentrate on the hard stuff

"I'll nail the other product lines big-time. No way they'll give me any heat then."

Kill it with arrogant neglect

"We should never have gotten into that business. I can outlive it. I'm untouchable."

Belittle the people in charge

"Jeff, the people who designed these contracts must be from another planet."

The reality of sales and marketing today is that product and service offerings will proliferate or quickly change because of technology, competitive actions, and margin pressures. Sales forces must quickly buy into and become comfortable with new offerings.

WHAT HAPPENED HERE . . . ?

It appears this service initiative is basically nonexistent in Nolan's sales unit. Nolan's sales unit probably never had a specific strategy or plan for the services. It does take time for sales units to spin up to speed with new offerings, but it looks as if Nolan's unit may have spun out rather than spun up.

Sales managers watch for top-executive participation in new initiatives. Participation translates to *real* commitment. Nolan and his people may not have seen or heard any so far.

Nolan's reps may not understand why customers would want or need the services. Their training in this regard, or with everything associated with the services, could have been superficial. Additionally, salespeople are very sensitive to having perceived marginal offerings mess up their good relationships and taint other sales opportunities.

Nolan's compensation plan could be telling the sales staff that the service contracts are not worth their time. Comp plans speak louder than any executive ever could.

The service contracts probably need to be sold to new contacts in different departments, Nolan's sales unit may not have relationships with those people, and they probably don't understand the special jargon used in those departments. Nolan may not feel comfortable himself. Therefore his coaching is superficial. Salespeople pick up those signals *real* fast.

The firm's service offerings may not be competitive in the market. Competitors may have turned out to be stronger and more entrenched than anticipated.

The sales story may not be valid. The messages and collaterals may not fit reality.

Nolan probably learned a lesson a long time ago that cleaning up the problems after a new-product or service introduction is a huge waste of time. Perhaps he'd rather not be the point of a marketing spear again.

OPTIONS

You have many options with this problem.

1. Nolan could opt to play wait-and-see, to determine if this service-contract stuff is for real or if it will go away as quietly as it came.
2. Nolan can opt to execute a personal test, traveling with one or two of his people, hitting the contracts real hard to get a sense of reality and what is achievable. A personal foray can frame the next step.
3. Nolan could opt for a selective strategy, asking his top guns to hit the innovators, those few customers who always latch onto new offerings, shielding the bulk of his salespeople and customer base until the kinks are out of the program.
4. Nolan could opt to engage his entire sales unit, doing *just enough* of a job so that Jeff can't really zing him.
5. Nolan can decide to get onboard vigorously and attack this contract task with his entire sales unit.

   Is Nolan going to lead, follow, or get out of the way?

POSSIBLE ACTIONS

Make this a top priority, because it is Jeff's and the firm's top priority. Nolan must identify the personal issues that have been standing in the way of getting excited about service contracts and put them behind him.

Up Periscope

Nolan must listen, look, and feel what's happening all around him and above Jeff. What are the other *committed and top* sales managers doing about this? He should reread the materials associated with the original launch program.

There is one key to success to ensure that you are selling what the company wants sold: *your personal commitment*. There are five proven steps to build and sustain the commitment: (1) Find the champion; (2) build understanding; (3) construct a creative and aggressive sales-unit sales plan; (4) train your people fanatically; (5) manage sales of the product or service.

1. Find the champion: Somewhere, deep in the bowels of Nolan's company is the person (or the people) who birthed these service contracts. The champion is so into what he has created, so committed, so knowledgeable, and so eager, that Nolan *must* get to know him and get him in front of his sales unit as quickly as possible. And do it over and over again. And get the champion into the field with his people, over and over again. Whatever the champion possesses and whatever he knows must rub off on Nolan and his sales unit. The champion possesses ownership, and ownership implies energy and commitment.

In large corporations this may be difficult, *but* creative and persistent sales managers can get to this person, or someone on the champion's staff. And champions love it.

2. Build understanding: Meet with the champion. Have a cup of coffee or lunch. Again, if Nolan doesn't have access to the champion he must go to people who work for or with the champion to get some answers.

Nolan must internalize the strategy associated with the service contracts. He must understand why service contracts were introduced in the first place. He must understand how they fit into the overall marketing and sales strategy, if this is the start of a continuing product-line effort, and if this is a prelude to a whole new business direction.

It's helpful if Nolan understands the bodies, dollars, and resources that were poured into an effort like this. Nolan needs to understand what the corporate marketing plan is, including all the key concepts, facts, and messages that his sales unit should incorporate into its own sales messages. Nolan must air all his concerns, compensation as an example, and gain whatever commitment he possibly can that the concerns will be answered or rectified.

If Nolan is not aware of, or comfortable with, the corporate sales plan associated with these contracts, he needs to get clarification from Jeff. Jeff should have developed a corporate sales strategy as well.

Nolan must possess all this understanding if he is to communicate it to his people.

3. Construct a creative and aggressive sales-unit sales plan: Get the sales unit together. Nolan's major task is to pass on all he has absorbed. He doesn't have to do that all by himself. This is where the relationship with the champion and the champion's staff comes in handy. A sales planning effort, led by Nolan and created by the whole sales unit, will usually be thorough and devoid of fluff. The key themes must be *creative and aggressive*. If Nolan shares the ideas developed in Problem 2–4 about sales-unit strategies and in Problem 2–5 about sales plans, he's likely to find himself in pretty good shape.

If Nolan knows his people as he should, he understands their concerns and can use this opportunity to get their concerns on the table at this meeting. With the champion or staffer present, many of the concerns can probably be handled real-time.

A key element of this meeting *may* be compensation. Lay it out and make sure it's clear. If Nolan is really persuasive, he should have been able to negotiate some perks from the champion prior to the meeting. Letting the champion indulge the troops with some goodies as a meeting-closer is a great move.

4. Train fanatically: Nolan should ensure than an *intensive* training session for all comes quickly. His leadership and participation is mandatory. Jeff's attendance is highly desirable. It seems obvious, but ensure that the training is executed in the context of what the customer is buying, not what the company is selling.

Nolan should be alert in not trying to force-fit this offering into his sales process. Highly differentiated offerings *may* demand a modified sales process and the training that goes with it.

Refresher training classes, with the champion or the champion's staff in attendance, on a monthly or quarterly basis, is a very effective tactic.

5. Manage the business: Nolan needs to get out in the field to coach, to reinforce the sales messages, and reinforce the training. It communicates his personal commitment.

Inviting the champion or people on the champion's staff to help sell and close the first few deals also works well. The idea is to create an environment for his people seeing the product sold effectively. The initial wins should be highly publicized, and lessons learned should be spread around the sales unit.

Finally, it is important that all service contract opportunities should be in his pipeline.

Harsh Reality

Reality #1: There is some stuff that no self-respecting sales manager or rep wants to touch. No one wants to embarrass himself. In truth, companies sometimes come out with products or services that fall into this category. Say so! Step forward. Offer reasons, proof, or customers' comments, ensuring that you're objective, not emotional.

Reality #2: It takes proportionally more leadership and management force to start, accelerate, and maintain small value-added services or products in motion than core products.

Reality #3: The amount and extent of training associated with ancillary, value-added products and services *must* be in far greater proportion and effort than core products and services.

Reality #4: The salesperson's effort-benefit relationship is critical. If benefits don't equal or outweigh efforts in a rep's eyes, mind, and bank account you can effectively say good-bye to your new product or service.

Reality #5: Don't try to con the sales force. Don't make any new products and services out to be more than they are. Your credibility will go out the window.

LESSONS

This problem is a lesson in leadership and personal commitment.

It's tough to lead an effort that you have a hard time getting personally excited about, but that is exactly what you have to do. A key is the identification of resources, relationship building with those resources, and their integration into a sales unit's efforts.

Services and products outside the mainstream are a special challenge. They require a level of teamwork, training, and management-process above the norm.

Solving this problem demonstrates the power of a sales manager's strong example.

6–2 THE PROBLEM:

The productivity of the sales unit must be increased.

THE STORY

"Kristy, you've got to get sales up fast, but I can't give you more money to do it," said Mario, the VP of sales and marketing, pointing to an ominous figure on his sales manager's goal chart.

"And you can't get any more people. And don't plan on sending anyone else to corporate this year for training. The till is almost dry. You have to figure a way to get more out of the resources you've got—productivity has got to go up. Squeeze 'em and pleeze 'em.

"Now, are there any questions?" finished Mario.

"Yes, where is the stardust to make all this happen?" Kristy tweaked back.

TEMPTATIONS

Getting more with less is the reality of sales management today. It leads some managers to react in ways that are superficial or counterproductive.

Exhortation

"I think it's time to give one of my patented, compelling motivational talks."

Fire the laggards

"Now I've got the excuse I need to unload some deadwood."

Get a bigger whip

"It's time to put the leather to these people. Now we'll see who can handle the heat."

The task to sell more is a big enough problem. The task to sell more with the same or less resource is a whole different problem. This has ceased to be a sporadic issue. Productivity is a part of sales culture everywhere.

WHAT HAPPENED HERE . . . ?

Sounds as if there was an edict that came down from on-high. Kristy's firm may have found itself suddenly squeezed. Lofty performance goals and accompanying shortfalls are probably driving this.

Kristy and Mario may never have measured productivity or made it an issue before now. Orders or bookings may have been robust for some time, and they never looked at anything but the total sales number. Healthy economies and markets, and getting more business than you can handle, can cause sales management to take their collective eye off the productivity ball.

OPTIONS

Productivity is accomplishing more with the same or less resources. Productivity is an attitude that must pervade a sales manager's every thought. It's a common thread that should run through every action. Kristy's options are to begin to treat productivity in that manner, not as a sporadic event or program as some sales managers still do.

POSSIBLE ACTIONS

Productivity is viewed by many as complex and mysterious. It's not. The best way to prove that point is with an analogy.

Let's Play Tennis

Let's say Kristy, who is a doubles specialist, wanted to improve her tennis game to where she could win 80 percent of her matches this year, rather than the measly 30 to 40 percent she is currently winning. And let's say all she had was $200 to buy either a new racket or a pair of shoes, or invest in a couple of lessons. She'd probably look at her existing racket and shoes to see which are in worse shape. Let's say she spends $100 on shoes. *The same is true with sales productivity. You need a goal, and you must look at your sales tools and decide which ones to replace or refurbish.*

Then she may go to a pro and say, "I have only $100. I'm not sure what part of my game needs the most help." The pro will say, "Let's hit the ball for a few minutes," after which he'll say, "Let's spend an hour on your backhand, it looks like the weakest part of your game." *The same is true with sales productivity. As the "pro," you must look at your people and decide what skills need to be improved. As the manager, you must look at yourself and get a pro, like your own manager, to get help with leadership- and management-process improvements.*

Then it may occur to Kristy and her partner that their strategy has been flawed. Doubles is a very strategic game. Positioning, poaching, signals, who serves first, the score situation, attacking the other side's weaknesses, the wind, the sun all are a part of strategy. *Sales-productivity improvement also requires a sales-unit strategy.*

Then it may occur to Kristy that her doubles partner is the reason many of the matches are being lost. She could decide to find a new partner or to help the partner improve—acting as a coach herself. If she valued her relationship with the partner she may bend over backwards to help. A breakup may be difficult, but if she really wanted to win 80 percent of the time, she'd do it. *Sales productivity is the same. If your salespeople or sales partners aren't carrying the load, you have to make a decision to work with them or go your separate ways.*

Then Kristy may decide to find additional time to play. Something would have to give, because her schedule is full. So she may say to yourself, "I'll sacrifice one hour of sleep a night so I can play every morning for an hour. I'm a morning person and that gives me an advantage." *Sales productivity is the same way. Extra work and timing of your activities can carry the day.*

It may also occur to Kristy that if she started watching matches on TV and reading tennis and sports magazines and buying a couple of tennis books, she may be able to pick up a couple of tips. *Sales productivity is the same. There are many self-help resources out there, but many don't invest in them, and far less put into practice what they have to offer.*

Then Kristy may decide that the high-school courts aren't the best place to play because they are in bad shape, and the balls take a lot of funny bounces. So she may go find some first-class courts. *Sales productivity is similar. You may be playing in the wrong markets, accounts, and prospects.* (Kristy's game is starting to pick up by now, as you might imagine.)

Then it may occur to Kristy to find opponents that she felt she could beat 80 percent of the time. If she got clobbered by an *A* player the first time out she'd probably back off and look for easier pickings. *Sales productivity is the same way. Understanding what competitors are located where, embedded or barely hanging on, can help the win ratio go up.*

In time Kristy's win percentage will improve. Maybe she's winning 80 percent of her matches, maybe not. If she isn't, she may have rat-holed another $200 and decide to go and get a new racquet. Or, she may make another trade-off, cut-down on her dining-out habit and use that money for lessons. Let's say Kristy invests it on lessons to improve her serve. A booming serve could then became a fearsome weapon. *Sales productivity is comparable.*

You can shift some of your resources to where you would like them, and turn one of your sales activities into a fearsome weapon.

Finally, once Kristy starts winning 80 percent of her matches she may feel that 90 percent is a more reasonable target, and she may also want to find tougher opponents. *Sales productivity is like that. You'll want to start going after the big competitive accounts after you have beat up on everyone else and your confidence is soaring.*

Sales productivity is just like tennis. The key variables are analogous.

- The 80-percent win goal = your productivity target
- Racquet and shoes = your sales aids, collaterals, and computers
- The doubles partner = your sales unit and your sales partners
- The pro = your manager, mentor, trainers, or other expert resources
- The tennis courts = your markets, market conditions, customer segments, and customers
- Doubles strategy = your sales unit, major account, and customer retention strategies
- TV and magazines = your books, tapes, videos, and seminars
- The opponents = your competition
- Big serve = an overpowering sales activity or dominant sales skill
- The rat hole = your budget and potential trade-offs
- Kristy's final achievement and search for more challenge = your new and higher productivity target and search for new and bigger customers

And the cycle must continue.

This list of variables amounts to the who, what, where, when, why, how, and how much of sales-productivity management (the 5Ws and 2Hs). Astute management of the variables is what productivity is all about.

Let's Get Back to Productivity

What is the best sequence of actions? Why did Kristy first think of her racquets and shoes as the weak link rather than her partner or her choice of opponents or the courts they were playing on? Did Kristy start in the right place? Something caused her to start there. We'll never know.

Where would you start if you were looking at all the productivity variables in your sales unit? What do you believe is the basis or foundation of productivity? We believe it's people (the reps and the sales partner). If we had been in Kristy's shoes we would have talked to our partner first and decided what "we" as a team should do to get to 80 percent. What would be your sequence of productivity-enhancing actions to improve your game? It's never the same.

Analysis

Perhaps it would be a good idea to identify and look at the relative condition and importance of all the variables in your business and in your sales unit. You could look at how your top performers and peers are doing. You could go back and review a respectable sample of your wins and losses to get some clues of what's working and what's not. You could ask your marketing colleagues where you could find the "best courts" to play on.

You could pull your sales unit together and get their suggestions on the 5Ws and 2Hs.

It is important to give analysis a good effort because you have limited resources and you don't want to do any backtracking or unnecessary jumping around. If productivity is a corporate issue, this is a good subject for all the sales managers to discuss together.

What's the Target?

Kristy needs to identify her productivity target and the time required to hit it. That may be Mario's job, but the two of them must agree on it—just as in doubles. Kristy's target could be stair-stepped over a period of a year, or it may be a new plateau to attain in 90 days. Time frames must be a part of productivity goals.

Your Measure of Productivity

Productivity is a ratio. It is a measure of result, X per unit of Y, or a measure of X within a period of Y. It is doing more with the same or less resources. There are many ways to measure productivity. Here are some examples:

- *Order $s per sales rep.* For example, $1,000,000 in orders each year by each sales rep, or $1,000,000-to-1. The productivity goal per rep for next year could be $1,100,000-to-1.

- *Bookings $s per dollar of sales cost.* For example, $10 in bookings per each dollar of sales expense, a 10 percent selling cost. A 10-to-1 ratio. You may want to raise it to 11–1.

- *Average size of a transaction.* For example, raising the average transaction from $125 to $160. $160-per-sale is a productivity goal you may want to achieve this month.

- *Number of transactions in a given time period.* For example, 10 sales a week instead of 7, 10-to-1.

- *New customers.* For example, raising the number of new customers per month from 100 to 110. 110-to-1 is the productivity goal.

- *Account retention.* For example, losing only 5 percent of the customer base next year rather than the current 7 percent. The 2 percent is a customer-retention-productivity goal.

These measurements are a yardstick of your effectiveness, just as Kristy keeps score in tennis. And just as they keep score a point at a time, you need to keep score a sale at a time.

Kristy and Mario should take a look at the key measurements that corporate and their marketing colleagues use. To the best of their ability, they should try to be consistent or supportive of these measurements. Then everyone will benefit. They should also make sure that they can measure their productivity target(s) easily. And they should try to tie the productivity targets to compensation and recognition so everyone is pulling in the same direction.

Return on Investment

There is a quantitative side of productivity improvement that can't be overemphasized. How does Kristy know that investing in X is better than investing in Y? The nature of her sales unit and her responsibilities may be such that she has numerous financial- and sales-program options. She must sit down in front of her PC and create some investment pro-formas, a matrix of all her productivity variables, associated costs, and probable pay-offs. *Documentation* of her investment analysis is imperative. This investment matrix is a decision-making tool.

The Optimal Mix of Actions

What's the right mix of productivity actions for Kristy to employ? How do the tennis pros know? They combine their personal judgments and results analysis with the inputs of their coaches. Kristy should follow the same formula, blending in her investment matrix.

"Match Point"

The right salespeople, employing the right strategy, going to the right places, talking to the right people, asking the right questions, delivering the right message, using the right sales tools, engaging in the right activities, negotiating the best prices, providing the right follow-up, and being led and managed by the right processes can improve sales productivity.

LESSONS

Sales productivity growth is the chief means of measuring your performance and effectiveness as a sales manager. Sales is not a game of raw numbers. The name of the sales game is getting the biggest possible numbers in the most efficient and profitable way.

Productivity is an attitude that must permeate sales organizations. The winners will move on to the next round. The losers will be blown off the court.

6–3 THE PROBLEM:

Your customer retention rate is poor.

THE STORY

Dominic was meeting with Cecilia, the firm's director of support services, who handled all information systems, order entry, and customer service.

As the national sales manager, he was disturbed by the sales reports that Cecilia had sent over the previous day. The company had more than 14,000 customers, virtually all of whom were small retailers, and here it was May and more than half who had purchased last year had not ordered in the current year.

"What in the world has happened to all those people?" he asked.

"That's what I'd like to know," was Cecilia's response. "This is crazy!"

TEMPTATIONS

Customers can't be taken for granted in any sector. They are every enterprise's #1 asset. Trying to stop the churning of the customer base sometimes begins with these common temptations.

Blame product development

"I knew that the delays with the new lines would cause people to jump ship."

Blame competition

"Those devious foreign firms have a cost of sales that we just can't match."

Blame the price increases

"We warned marketing. It's all their fault. Those people are dense."

It costs much more to get a new customer than to maintain an existing customer. This problem has no room for blaming anyone or anything. It takes teamwork to solve it.

WHAT HAPPENED HERE ... ?

Dominic was surprised. There were obviously no formal systems in place to flag this problem.

Customer retention may not have been a historic priority in Dominic's business. Like many sales managers, Dominic may have been trained to focus exclusively on new-customer acquisition, and not on retentive sales measures.

Perhaps Dominic was looking at the wrong information or not studying anything of what has been consistently placed in his in-basket or E-mail. That's understandable considering what most sales managers' in-baskets, and E-mails, look like.

Dominic may have been in the habit of just watching total sales figures and wasn't digging into the numbers, or was focused on personnel problems or operational bombshells.

At times like this he can't help but ask himself, What *could* revenues and profitability have looked like if we had lost only *half as many customers?*

OPTIONS

Dominic has three options with this situation.

1. Get more new business—filling the bucket faster than it leaks. This option amounts to staying on the same track, accepting that this is a business or industry norm.
2. Dump this problem back on Cecilia. After all, customer service is her job.
3. Put together a corporate-wide customer-retention plan, or reclamation plan in this case, and execute it with vigor.

POSSIBLE ACTIONS

This is BIG! As a first step, Dominic and Cecilia could draft an outline of a plan, alert top management, get any needed approvals, and then proceed.

Dig

Dominic needs to go into a data-gathering mode.

- He must get out in the field. Call on a sampling of those old customers to gain some insights. What do they say are the reasons they left? Some will not want to see him, some will just be polite, but some will be candid.
- He should talk to his sales force and sales partners to get their opinions, looking closely at how they support and follow up with customers.
- He should look at his pricing and discount practices, comparing them to competition.
- He must look for trends. Find out exactly *who* has been deserting his firm and why. Once he can characterize or describe the customers who have been leaving, the better able he'll be able to focus on customers at risk with new retention efforts.
- If he has used any satisfaction surveys in the past they may also be helpful to use again.
- He must take an objective look at competitive marketing and sales actions in greater detail. They must be doing something right, or doing something that's appealing to customers.
- He should try to build an understanding of his *customer's customers*. Helping his customers satisfy their customers benefits everyone. Regardless of where your company is in the sales channel, working as a team with your sales partners makes sense.

Dig into Buyer Behavior and Expectations

Buyers are not only price oriented, although many salespeople see only that side of them.

Determine what is of value to your customers and put potential customer-retention actions in the context of *buyer expectations*, not seller actions. For example: Prompt delivery is a *supplier* promise and action. *Easy availability* is a buyer need and expectation. Use your buyers' expectations, needs, and sensitivities when designing customer-retention activities. Here are some examples of two different ways the two parties look at the same subject.

Seller words and actions	Buyer expectations
We offer prompt delivery.	I want availability in *my* storeroom when *I* want it.
We're a market leader.	I want *confidence* in my supplier.
We have a fair price.	I want top *value* for our money.
We sell a quality product.	I expect *no* returns and *no* service calls.
We are responsive.	I expect a person with the authority and the ability to help me with a question when *I* call.
Fast service.	I want you to fix it *now*.
We provide courteous service.	I want respect, civility, and calling me by name.

What else could you add to both sides of the chart that relates to your business? What variables are involved with a customer's decision to choose you as a supplier in the first place? A buyer is not interested in the left-column buzzwords. Design your customer-retention actions to match the right side of the chart. *Talk and act in the context of the buyer.*

Another good approach to understanding buyers is for all customer-contact people to document questions they repeatedly get and issues that continue to surface. Repetitive questions and issues are a loud signal that there is an opportunity to change something for the benefit of all.

You can also talk to the people who have purchasing responsibility in your own company. Ask them to share their expectations and observations of selling actions that they respect and those that turn them off. Perhaps there are some useful lessons close to home.

Dig into Your Own Buying Experience

Think back over all the times you were a buyer and recall how seller actions made an impression on you—good or bad. Think about everything from fast-food restaurants to department stores to automobile dealerships to banks to home-improvement centers. Any place that you lay out your hard-earned cash is a place to learn something about customer retention. Why do you keep going back to the same old places to buy? What causes you to change establishments you frequented for so long? Consider how you can apply those lessons in your own retention planning.

Dig into Your Transaction Processes

Another key to customer retention is transaction-cycle analysis. Your sales cycle includes all steps in which a salesperson is involved, from initial sales contact to closing the order. The transaction cycle includes all other activities involving customer contact by others within your company.

Identify every little step in your transaction cycle and place your handling of each step under the microscope. Steps on the front end of the transaction cycle could include handling of phone inquiries and lead qualification. Transaction steps on the back end could include installation work, technical service, service hotlines, customer service, and credit management. The entire transaction cycle is fertile ground for customer-retention opportunities.

Dig into Your Current-Sales Practices

Sales and marketing managers have a tendency to focus on *creating* reasons for customers to stay as customers. Those reasons usually cost money, they're relatively easy to do, and suppliers are skilled at it.

Eliminating reasons for customers to leave is often much cheaper, but the reasons are are often hard to identify, are harder to clean up, and often not as much fun. Concentrate on identifying and eliminating the practices that cause customers to leave.

Creating reasons to stay	*Eliminating* reasons to leave
Cut the price	"My calls are returned too late."
A 2-for-1 special deal	"I only hear from you when you want to sell me something."
Coupons	"You always take a long time to solve a problem."
A free starter kit of supplies	"It was dirty when I took it out of the box."

It's fun to focus on creating practices to improve retention; thus you often see retention efforts as listed on the left side of the chart. However, it's often somber work to correct the practices on the right. A buyer appreciates all the practices on the left but the nasty realities on the right often still remain as burrs under the buyer's saddle and when someone else comes along—good-bye.

Changing customer-service routines and developing new sales procedures to eliminate the nasty practices on the right is a must. It takes leadership to root out and admit to those practices.

Dig into Your Relationships

Scrutinize your relationship-building activities. These activities include entertainment, joint membership in associations, joint-product development with customers, distributor and rep councils, sales meetings with sales partners, executive involvement with customers, and other possibilities. Can you utilize any of those relationship activities to get a better sense of what's causing the retention problem? Or, heaven forbid, maybe you've forgotten to even engage in these relationship-building activities in the first place.

Dig into Your Customer-contact Behaviors

Here is a representative list of sales and customer-contact behaviors that affect customer retention. The list is obvious, but obviousness never meant execution should be assumed. Reinforce the retention-causing behaviors and eliminate the defection-causing behaviors.

Retention-causing behavior	*Defection-causing* behaviors
• Understanding the customer's business thoroughly	• Making only a superficial attempt to understand their business
• Working hard and fast to solve problems	• Making a superficial effort to relate to the customer
• Being long-term relationship driven	• Talking constantly about yourself and your staff
• Possessing outstanding product and applications knowledge	• Being short-term transaction driven
• Being on a first-name basis with customers	• Possessing a gun-and-run mentality
• Offering exceptional personal service	• Overpromising and overcommitting to requests
• Regularly delivering more than expected	• Providing minimally acceptable support
• Being a great listener	• Bouncing the customer around the organization to many different and insensitive contacts
• Exhibiting patience during times of stress	• Reacting to issues rather than searching for potential issues
• Exhibiting a consistent high level of civility	
• Always acting with urgency and with eye contact	

What else would you add to either side of the chart that relates to your business? A good sales-unit exercise is to ask your people to contribute to the lists. The good news is that all the retention-causing behaviors are trainable, and defection-causing behaviors can be laundered out.

Summarize All Your Digging and Process Analysis

Gather everything you've uncovered and ask yourself two final questions before creating a customer-retention plan.

If *you* were to attack your own customer base, how would you do it? Where are the soft spots, the warts, and the vulnerabilities? Those answers help tell you where to make changes.

If *you* could prioritize the three keys to establishing a customer retention *culture* in your business, what would they be? Go ahead, write them here in the book.
1._____, 2._____, and
3._____.

Build a Formal Customer-Retention Plan

The following plan elements will ensure that your effort is long-lived and effective.

- Identify a team and a leader responsible for customer retention and accountable to executive management. Customer-retention plans will almost always involve collaborative efforts with other departments within the company.
- Establish quantitative customer-retention targets and measures in *every* business function that touches the customer.
- Consider customizing your retention efforts for different customer classes and market segments. Start with pilot programs, react, and then expand.
- Build and manage a simple process that monitors and collects buyer feedback and expectations from such sources as sales calls, customer service, technical service, executive calls, surveys, conferences, trade associations, focus groups, and outside research.
- Create a simple retention strategy that is consistent with your overall sales and marketing strategies. Build the strategy around a key buyer expectation, such as availability. For example: product in your storeroom 24 hours after order! (Double-check Problem 2–4.)
- Identify and utilize retention tactics such as executive visits, anonymous buying, user bulletins, satisfaction questionnaires, outbound teleservices, putting your people inside a customer's location as virtual employees, and frequent application seminars.
- Work together with your sales partners to identify and implement actions that are mutually supportive up and down the channel.
- Build, maintain, and track a customer database. Put a system in place that reports new customers daily, flags customers who have not reordered in X days, or other key data.
- Design and implement a compensation-and-recognition system that has retention as a key ingredient.

When you're designing customer-retention efforts and plans remember that the road to winning a customer and keeping a customer is the same. It's not new advice. Heraclitus said, "The road uphill and the road downhill are one and the same" in 500 B.C.

LESSONS

You build and maintain a strong understanding of your markets and customers in the process of working on customer retention.

You learn that customer-retention efforts are collaborative efforts that include all the people and functions in your business that come in contact with customers.

You learn that for fiscal and strategic reasons the efforts associated with retention of customers should exceed the efforts associated with the acquisition of new customers.

The investments you make in customer retention will come back to you via referrals, continuing business, new and expanded business from the same accounts, increased loyalty in times of stress—and then even more business.

6–4 THE PROBLEM:
Your sales unit is in the midst of a prolonged losing streak.

THE STORY

Rayleen was excited about her promotion to sales manager and could not wait to put her mark on the team she inherited from John, the previous manager. Prior to John leaving, he gave Rayleen two sealed letters marked #1 and #2. He told her that if she had a bad first year to open letter #1 and follow the instructions, and similarly with letter #2, if the second year was also bad.

Well it turned out that managing her first team did not go as well as Rayleen had hoped. She missed her target by over 25 percent. Rayleen's boss, Stephanie, asked her to prepare a presentation describing what happened and what her plans were for next year. Rayleen was about to go to Stephanie's conference room to make her presentation when she came across John's two letters. Remembering what he said, she opened letter #1. It read:

> *Dear Rayleen,*
> BLAME ME! Sincerely, John

She did blame John, and the meeting went better than she could have hoped.

As it turned out, despite all her hard work, Rayleen's second year was worse than her first. She was beside herself and confused as to what direction to take. She remembered John's two letters and how well his instructions in letter #1 had worked. She found letter #2. It read:

> *Dear Rayleen,*
> Write two letters. Sincerely, John

TEMPTATIONS

There is nothing more frustrating than being a leader of a team on a losing streak. The anger and temptations come easy.

Throw in the towel
> "That's it. It's clear I can not manage. I need to find a new career. I'm a failure."

Blame your people
> "I inherited a sorry bunch that I had to train from the bottom up on everything."

Condemn top management
> "I am sick of trying to sell these antiquated products with the support of a stealth marketing group."

A better approach is to put a stake in the ground and lead the sales unit out of the woods.

WHAT HAPPENED HERE . . . ?

The simple equation that guides the performance of individuals and/or teams was not balanced.

Performance = Qualification + Preparation + Motivation

When things are not going well, there must be a breakdown in one or all of these areas.

Qualification: You are missing one or more of the basic requisites even to compete.

- Your products and services are not competitive.
- Your salespeople do not possess the basic attributes to succeed.
- You are not hired up to plan or properly deployed.
- Your marketing department or other support infrastructure is missing.
- Your team is not a team.
- The market has dried up or changed.

Preparation: You haven't executed one or more of the basics to get ready to compete.

- You are a new sales manager and are just learning the basics of pipeline management and coaching.
- Your salespeople are not trained on the products and services or need a refresher on selling techniques.

- Your sales unit does not understand the competition.
- Your marketing or product-development group do not understand the needs of customers and sales partners.
- You are not supporting, coaching, or communicating properly with your sales partners.

Motivation: You have an environment that's missing one or more intangible imperatives.

- Leadership is uninspiring.
- Morale is low. People are negative, apathetic, or have a defeatist attitude.
- Your people do not believe in you, your company, or your products.
- Your recognition and reward systems are noncompetitive.
- There is no opportunity for advancement.

When you are in the middle of a downward spiral, it is difficult to determine exactly what is causing the problem. The answer is always a complex combination of factors in the basic equation. Until you discover the root causes of the problem and eliminate them, you can never be completely successful. Experience and your boss's guidance makes the causes more visible.

OPTIONS

You always have these three options in this situation.

1. You could write two letters and resign.
2. You could ride the wave and see what happens.
3. You could dedicate yourself to leading your people back to the road of success.

POSSIBLE ACTIONS

A good approach is to begin to do as many things in the equation with as much excellence as possible. This will either help you identify the root cause or eliminate the cause without your really knowing it. There are many management actions that are required to pull a team out of a prolonged slump. *But,* do not get confused. In the end it will be Rayleen's leadership that will turn things around. Nothing else.

Leadership Is the Key

Some sales managers are *amplifiers.* They take the pressure from above, add to it, and drive it down to their people in the form of threats and ultimatums.

Successful sales leaders are *transformers.* They take the pressure and transform it into *energy,* energy to find a way to turn things around. And it takes more *focused energy* to reverse a prolonged losing streak than to keep a successful team sailing along.

Managers manage activity. Leaders lead people and teams. Rayleen always needs to be a blend of both, but in this situation, there needs to be a definite bias to leadership. Here are three leadership attributes that are requisites to solve this problem.

1. ARTICULATE YOUR PRINCIPLES.   List and share the principles, the fundamentals in which you deeply believe, by which you will lead, and by which you expect your people to act. Some examples of principles are

- Teamwork amongst ourselves and with our colleagues will be the key to our success.
- Creativity will get a warm reception in this sales unit—and will be recognized and rewarded.
- Customers and sales partners come first. This will be a relationship-driven sales unit.
- Do it now. If it doesn't work we'll try something else. This sales unit never stands still.
- Excellence in everything we do is an everyday expectation.

Rayleen can add to or modify the list. She must make sure that her team knows what her principles are and understands what she means by each of them. Once communicated, she can use the principles to guide her everyday activity. (Problem 3–1 is helpful in defining principles.)

2. DEVELOP A VISION.   Rayleen and her team need to know what success is. She should describe her picture of success in simple terms. The picture is the vision, and it is more than just a number. The picture could reflect the feelings, attitudes, or rewards that the team can expect to experience when the vision is realized. Everyone must understand what is over the horizon. For example:

- "I have a dream that we will all qualify for President's Club this year."
- "I see the VP calling all of us, as a team, up to the podium to receive Gold Key awards."
- "I can picture the president walking in next January with bonus-check envelopes for all."

Rayleen must talk about the vision constantly and work to have everyone embrace it.

3. EXECUTE WITH A PASSION.   Rayleen must physically and mentally get out—*and stay out*—in front. She must lead by example, by a level of energy that the sales team and others have never seen before. When Rayleen hears someone say, "What in the world has gotten into Rayleen?" she'll know she is there. She must keep adding energy until she hears similar-sounding exclamations.

Management Keeps You on Course

Next, Rayleen must invest additional energy in these key management activities.

CRAFT A STRATEGY.   The essence of a sales-team strategy is choosing to perform sales activities that are differentiated from competition, that dominate in the marketplace, and that meet customer demands. Sales-unit strategies are clear, easily understandable statements that focus a sales unit's efforts. (Problem 2–4 has several tips.)

BUILD A PLAN.   She must take the strategy and with her team develop a plan that will allow her and the team to achieve the vision. The plan should include such basics as deployment, customers to target, resources required, marketing support, customer service, technical-service support, sales tools, presentations, and other elements important to her business. She can refer to Problem 2–5, and remember, simple plans are best when it comes to stopping losing streaks.

PRIME THE PUMP.   Rayleen should identify several orders that are on the short-term forecast and give them as much focus and resource as necessary, pouring in her heart and soul to close them to build *momentum*. Each time her team closes one of these deals she should publicize it to the world because the growing positive impression on others in the company has a way of gaining incremental support. A little bit of momentum can go a long way to build a *can-do* and *can-win* attitude. Momentum feeds on itself.

EXHIBIT MANAGEMENT DISCIPLINE.   Rayleen must develop a *simple, consistent, and more frequent* process to ensure that the strategy and plan is being executed properly. Periodically (weekly, twice a month, and so on) she should review the pipeline, short-term committed orders, installed-account activities, new-account activities, or other measurements of her choice, with her people *as a team*. Doing this as a team, rather than on an individual basis, has the effect of energizing the team as they feed off each other's comments and activities. She should publicly praise those people who are focusing on the vision, executing the strategy and plan, and working by the principles.

TRAIN! TRAIN! TRAIN!   Rayleen can ultimately turn her sales team into the best in the industry if she makes training a major part of her turnaround plan. Training can help stop a losing streak and is an investment in the future. Rayleen must train her people for whatever she and the team feel a need. Training will help her people feel better about their abilities and develop a level of confidence that will help stop the losing streak and start a success streak.

The key to training during losing streaks is *consistent regularity*. Ad hoc approaches to training during losing streaks can hurt or delay recovery efforts. Whether it's one day a week, four hours at a monthly staff meeting, or one hour at a weekly breakfast meeting, Rayleen must be consistent. There must be unrelenting practice with key skills and activities.

STEP UP THE COACHING.   Rayleen should double (at least) the time she is spending coaching her people in the field. And she must provide an increased quantity of constructive suggestions. She can't let any of the little details slide, as she may have done in the past. Her people must perceive a higher and tighter level of feedback. The shopworn cliché "the devil is in the details" applies to losing streak-related coaching.

There is no magic in stopping a prolonged losing streak, just an awful lot of focused energy, hard work, strong leadership, and an attitude that reflects a Queen Victoria statement: "We are not interested in the possibilities of defeat."

Lessons

A couple decided to celebrate their wedding anniversary on a cruise. One night during dinner in the main dining room, a storm hit and the ship began to toss back and forth. People were falling down. The food was everywhere, and some of the passengers were beginning to be hysterical. The husband decided to go to the bridge and find out what was going on. He fought his way through the storm-tossed ship, holding on for dear life, until he finally reached the bridge. He then returned to the dining room where everybody was fearful, panic-stricken, and waiting for his return with word from the bridge. When he entered it was obvious that he was very calm and confident. Someone shouted, "What's going on, why are you so calm?"

He answered, "I just looked into the eyes of the captain."

LEADERSHIP IS THE KEY TO TURNAROUNDS.

6–5 The Problem:

You need to win a lot of business in a very short time.

The Story

President's Club was on the line. It was October 15.

Ed had never missed a President's Club in all his years as a sales manager, and this was the first year he had to struggle this late in the year. Several of his people were also pursuing the same goal. He had had a bad month in September, and October and November were looking bleak. A sales manager's nightmare.

To add to the tension, Ed's boss, the group VP, needed to make plan for the year and had made it *abundantly clear* to all that the division *will* make plan. Oh good, even more pressure.

Temptations

The temptations at times like this come down to playing by the rules or making up new rules. All the temptations are variants on the same theme.

Give it away

"Screw the margins, let's go for it! We'll argue later."

Overpromise

"No problem, we can get it there next week." or "Of course it'll fit in that space!"

> *Take some soft bookings*
> "I'm sure these will firm up in January, or February; after all, these are good customers."

All sales managers drift from the basics of their earlier successes. Reigniting bedrock energy, activities, and processes can be the key to getting you back on course.

What Happened Here . . . ?

Something in the environment has changed. The heat is on for Ed. There are two sets of circumstances that could have led to this problem.

The controllables: These problem roots could have been managed by Ed and others, and are all correctable for the future. Some of them may be able to be corrected for the short term.

- Perhaps there was weak prospecting or shoddy market development in previous periods.
- Several customers could have canceled their orders.
- There may have been insufficient or inadequate promotion and advertising.
- Maybe Ed did an inadequate job of managing his pipeline of prospects.
- Ed could have lost some key sales or staff people.
- Ed may have lost some strategic accounts.
- Maybe customer service or technical service has fallen below standards.
- Perhaps there are delivery or availability problems.

The uncontrollables: Some of these causes could have been identified early and been preempted or possibly minimized *if* Ed had been watching closely. Some could be surprises.

- Business commitments that were a lock fell through.
- A key customer changed his mind and left a huge hole in the forecast.
- The business was affected by a slowdown in another industry or business sector.
- The health of the economy had a negative effect on consumer spending.
- The announcement of a new technology impacted many of your current offerings.
- Competition made a sudden marketing move that caught you by surprise.
- Buyers who would normally purchase were drawn off by other internal distractions.
- The timing and content of government regulations worked against you.
- The politics associated with major contracts delayed decisions.
- Currency-exchange rates put you at a disadvantage.

Quick recognition of these and other signals combined with rapid reaction at the *first* whiff of one of these scenarios are the keys to preventing this problem from recurring.

OPTIONS

This problem has the potential to turn into a stimulating adventure or an embarrassment—depending on which of the four options Ed selects.

1. Admit to yourself that the ground you have to make up is too great. Throw in the towel.
2. Take a half-hearted stab at it, for show purposes, saying you're going to go for it but not really meaning it.
3. Compromise on a lesser target. There *can* be times when the pursuit of the bigger target is futile, a waste of resources, and reflects poor judgment. (Be careful this isn't a cop-out.)
4. Commit to the task at hand and invest every ounce of energy.

How badly do you want it? Are you willing to put in the time and the sweat to make it happen? How bad will the pain be if you don't go after it?

POSSIBLE ACTIONS

Don't panic. Let your competitive juices guide you. Let Martina Navratilova's famous quote cause you to dig in. "Whoever said, 'It's not whether you win or lose that counts, probably lost.'"

Envision an Approach

Formulate a vision, an outcome, and a general plan of attack in your mind. The key to remember at times like this is that you *can* manage efforts, but you cannot manage results. Your approach should be to manage the quality and quantity of specific sales-unit activities.

Communicate the Situation

Get the sales unit together ASAP, by phone or otherwise. Promptness signals severity. Tell the group, in a tone that communicates your commitment, what needs to be done. Structure your message as forward-looking to success, and not backward-looking for scapegoats.

Just as it was of value for you to envision an initial approach, give your people the opportunity for the same introspection. You may want to give out some preliminary action assignments before getting everyone to contribute to a plan. Also alert other sales-support and management elements of your predicament and likely need for extra help.

Plan

Get the sales unit together again to formally gather their ideas, review their preliminary action assignments, and outline a plan. Start the discussion with a refocus on your customers and prospects. Is everyone really comfortable that you all understand customer needs and expectations and that the sales unit is effectively addressing them? Don't scoff. It's a major reason sales plummet. The refresher benefits everyone.

Simplicity is the key to a short-term recovery. Adopt a strategy based on one or two key sales activities. What activity, or activities, within your sales cycle is the most productive, and if performed *with precision*, usually leads to a sale? Set short term goals around those activities.

Next, consider how you can focus your efforts on the markets or customer segments with the highest potential. Match your capabilities, resources, and activities to those opportunities.

There is no time here for any deep analysis, but take a quick look at your sales effectiveness. Are you being outsold? No one likes to admit to that, but if the sales unit takes an honest look at itself what does it see and what can be fixed real quick? Incorporate the answer in your plan. Train to correct the deficiencies.

Can you use this challenge to try some new approaches, such as experimenting with new presentations, using new sales tools, or using new sales techniques? Newness is invigorating.

Can any of the aforementioned controllables noted in What Happened Here . . . be quickly turned around?

To add a little sizzle and visibility, think about adopting a creative catch phrase to your plan, such as "60K in 60 days." It can help the team focus.

Management thoughts to mull over in your planning.

Can you turn this tough task to additional advantage, using the challenge as a vehicle to achieve other personal goals? For example, team building, heightening the usage of information systems, integrating previously nonutilized staffers, probing deeper inside existing customers, stimulating creativity, using adversity to expand the boundaries of your people, attacking competitive strongholds, and raising the sales unit's performance bar.

If you guide this crisis to a successful conclusion it demonstrates your leadership and management strength. If you're not successful you'll learn a lot in the process about yourself and your people and gain the respect that goes with an all-out effort. Either way, you can't lose.

Measurements and Feedback

Set up a system that tracks the key sales activities you identified in your plan and tracks interim results. Use your management-information systems to the fullest.

Break your sales-reporting period down into *much smaller* increments than you normally use. If you have a monthly budget, give your sales unit weekly or daily budgets. If you have weekly targets, give yourself daily, hourly, or by-the-minute targets if the nature of your product and sales activity permits. Keeping up with the smallest increments possible offers early warning to problems and keeps little shortfalls from getting to be huge deficits.

Conduct frequent and prescheduled meetings or briefings to give everyone updates on progress and feedback on common questions, what's working, and what's not working. Effective sharing has a multiplier effect.

The Players

In time of sales war, everyone should be eligible for the draft. People resources are the most overlooked element of sales crisis planning and execution.

A short-term crisis role can be exciting for office or headquarters staff—a welcome change of pace. Job titles and job descriptions can go out the window in times of sales crises. For a short period of time get people out of the warehouse, office, or lab, onto the floor, on the phone, or in the field. Company and departmental leadership that rolls up its sleeves and takes part at times like this has the same mobilizing effect as a general leading a cavalry charge.

Assign roles and train the newcomers. Let everyone know *exactly* what he or she has to do.

Technology

Use a customer or prospect database to help focus your efforts. If you don't have one, talk to marketing or MIS (Manager of Information Systems) to see if they can help. There are also firms that sell databases that you may be able to incorporate into your crisis sales plan.

Can you enhance the laptop sales presentations you already have? Technology does not close sales—but it creates interest and adds other implicit messages that strengthens your firm's image as a business leader.

Develop some promotional material using your in-house computer graphics and color printers or copiers. Look for places to put all of your in-house technology to good use and outsource what you don't have.

Tactics

Here is a listing of possible maneuvers to incorporate into your plan.

• Look for some high-probability big hits, but don't dwell on a home-run mentality because home-run hitters also strike out a lot.

• Conduct a sale on various items or your complete line.

• Modify your terms of sale, or credit policy, for a short period.

• Put together a package of components to sell as a system or kit.

• Offer a special on a particular product.

• Offer additional operator or user training as an incentive.

• Offer to install your product for nothing or at a reduced rate.

• Empower your people to negotiate above and beyond the current policy for a short period.

• Place some inventory into certain customers on consignment.

• Institute an inventory-rotation program to stir up new-product orders.

• Squeeze your national accounts for longer-term business.

• Put together special leasing or finance packages to induce sales.

• Include point-of-purchase displays or other marketing tools at no cost with certain-size orders.

• Make a special introductory offer with a new product.

• Look for pull-ins, opportunities to accelerate future business, but remember to refill the bucket.

• Consider selected price reductions.

• Put on a series of seminars.

• Target specific competitive customers with special inducements.

• Execute teaming sales calls so as to tell a more complete story and answer more questions on the spot.

• Put together a special promotion on certain supply items.

• Update your website with new information or special offers.

• Offer quantity discounts on certain products.

• Offer long-term delivery contracts.

• Ask all existing customers for x percent more on their next order.

• Send blanket, standardized proposals to certain prospect groups.

• Decrease the size of minimum orders for a short period.

• Offer older-product, B level inventory, or quality rejects at a special price.

• Cut delivery times with new modes of transportation or absorb some delivery cost for a short period.

- Revamp your demo rooms and show-rooms.

- Offer short-term trials that can be turned into sales before the end of the critical reporting period.

- Roll out a strong print-advertising campaign in targeted newspapers.

- Create a value-added program that enhances products with new services.

- Look for ways to beef up the order backlog with add-ons or accessories.

- Create and execute a quick-targeted direct-mail campaign.

- Accelerate negotiations on big projects with revamped proposals.

- Roll out a market-specific radio-advertising campaign.

- Off-load inquiries and after-sales support on the telemarketers to free the outside sales staff.

What else can your team come up with? Kick off your recovery effort with a conference call, video-conference, or personal meetings. Make it a strong mix of substance and motivation.

The Clock

Be careful *when* you start and *when* you finish the management of a sales crisis.

Start immediately when the early-warning indicators relevant to your business sound the alarm. Tolerating any let's-see-what-happens wishful thinking invites disaster. It is far better to have a false start than a late start.

Don't come out of your crisis mode prematurely. A dangerous tendency is to halt the extra effort at the first signs of a turnaround because people are tired. Nothing could be worse. Maintain your momentum until *well after* the crisis has passed. A side benefit is that your continuing pressure will further debilitate competition, and the new momentum you've created has a better chance of becoming self-sustaining.

Understand, that in spite of everything, you may not hit your goal. If that's the case, communicate an understanding of why you lost to your sales unit, and thank them *profusely* for their efforts. Cope with the loss, help your people to cope with it, and lead on with vigor.

LESSONS

A sales manager who operates in a state of constant vigilance to the changing environment will be able to minimize a problem of this nature. This problem also teaches that lapses of attention to the basics or drifting away from success formulas can come back and bite you.

You learn a lot about your own motivations and the strength of your sales unit at times like this. The power of teams and teamwork becomes evident at times of crisis. There is nothing like adversity to show the true colors and capabilities of a sales manager and sales unit.

You discover some tactics that work well that can be made a part of your continuing sales-and-marketing arsenal. Share these best practices with peers and with your manager.

This experience may also be a veiled lesson. Perhaps the bottom line is that your customers have been trying to tell you to sell and service them differently and you haven't been listening.

6–6 THE PROBLEM:

Your national account managers and field sales force are not cooperating.

THE STORY

As the vice president of sales, Doug's national account marketing unit reports directly to him, along with field sales management, so it was easy to spot the growing undercurrent of tension and nit-picking about the national account marketing program.

It seems the national account manager's (NAM's) have been asking for info on local decisions and problems and haven't been getting it, and the sales force needs to forecast but can't get info from the NAM's. The sales force feels left out of the loop on big opportunities, and the sales force feels a loss of control. And the list goes on.

Additionally, Doug can read the commitment level of his area managers, and it's clear that they are only diplomatically endorsing, not enthusiastically supporting, the program. Doug knows the situation is not what it should be and that this simmering can turn into a boil.

TEMPTATIONS

Whenever you get a large number of sales professionals trying to work together you'll always get sparks and noise. The limit of your patience lets foolish temptations rear their ugly heads.

Knee jerk to the whining

"Okay, that's it, I want all of you managers in my office on Monday."

Look for scapegoats

"It's time I pulled those uppity national-account people back in line."

Dump the program

"I knew this national account idea wouldn't work at this firm. We gave it a fair try, but I think it's time to give it the old heave-ho."

Question your management processes rather than bow to any temptations.

What Happened Here . . . ?

Most companies have major customers they regard as more important than others, and those customers are usually singled out for special handling because of size, revenue, multilocation management, splintered decision making, organizational complexities, and the need for coordination. They are a major challenge to manage. Coordination problems and counterproductive competition between local sales offices and the national account managers is one of the main reasons programs get dropped.

Top management, Doug included, may not completely understand national-account marketing. There may not be sufficient integration of the program into the company's overall strategy, interdepartment support for the concept may be lacking, or the communication processes that were established at the outset of the program may have become obsolete.

Perhaps the sales force doesn't understand the concept or the advantages of a NAM program. National-account marketing can reduce the need for some local selling, and it subjects sensitive local sales-rep egos to directions from perceived prima donna national-account executives. Some salespeople also have trouble with the fact that NAM delivers special treatment beyond their personal authorization levels.

Sometimes it is not the local reps that have the problem, but their managers. The local managers worry about loss of control and turf. Field managers can be behind-the-scenes agitators. National-account marketing is a natural enemy of fiefdoms.

It could be that both sides in this skirmish don't understand their respective roles. Programs can be harmed when roles are not defined, and then both sides end up at odds with each other. Neither side wants to play a gopher role in this program, either.

And finally, understanding and commitment on the part of the *account* is critical at all of its locations. Perhaps account headquarters is committed, but outlying facilities are not. There can't be infighting on the account's side. This may be an account cooperation problem as well.

Options

This is one of those problems that doesn't have multiple options, other than to address it or not. If you're committed to national-account marketing, there is only one choice. Your options have more to do with corrective steps. The inter and intra departmental nature of national-account marketing makes virtually all NAM problems political.

Possible Actions

Tread softly but resolutely.

Listen Carefully to the Bickering

Document the facts and the feelings from the managers, reps, and NAMs. Whether Doug does this himself or through others, he must make sure he turns over all the rocks.

Launch a Bridge-building Mission

Get the sales management team together. Doug has a complex issue on his hands.

If he has an audit procedure for sales-department matters, it is a good idea to use this opportunity to execute a national-account-marketing audit. *All* major sales programs benefit from periodic audits. If he doesn't have a NAM-audit procedure he should ask the top national-account executive, in cooperation with other sales managers, to create one. Doug can also contact the National-Account Management Association to take advantage of their resources to provide audit formats. Even though the issue of cooperation may be self-evident, an audit may shed light on additional contributing factors. One outline for a national-account-marketing audit follows and should be executed at least annually.

1. *The markets:* Confirm that your market is characterized by the need for a national-account marketing program. Are the forces and needs in play today the same as they were at the program's inception? Review and document how they may have changed.

2. *The company:* Meet with all relevant business departments and divisions to confirm understanding about the goals and expected gains of the program. Ensure that there are formal program linkages with those departments and divisions. Check that you are a seamless enterprise in regard to national-account marketing.

3. *National-account program mission:* Review the mission statement to ensure it is still valid, not in conflict with the balance of the sales department, and that it is consistent with corporate vision and direction. Also confirm that you are comfortable with the program's expectations and measurements.

4. *Organization:* Take a look at structure, staffing, national-account-executive position requirements and profile, company view of the national-account career path, NAM support staff, NAM compensation, potential compensation conflicts with the balance of the sales department, and reporting relationships of all NAM staff.

5. *Management:* Review the NAM business plan, with emphasis on major goals and objectives, budgets, expenses, compensation, forecasting, controls, processes, measurements, data gathering, information systems, and the content, timing, and destination of reports.

6. *Operations:* In this segment, review your internal- and external-communications protocols, communications-technology applications, field-support activities, sales aids and sales tools, contracts and agreements, NAM training, NA training for the balance of the sales department, policies, procedures, authorizations, and other activities to integrate NAM with the company.

7. *Account Management:* Review the formal account plans of each Account, including their goals, objectives, strategies, issues, current situation, risks, opportunities, trends,

results against plan, and your account-management processes. Also review your National-Account selection criteria to make sure the Accounts fit your profile. This is a common cause of conflict that sneaks up on you, because Accounts change over time.

Doug must outline the breadth and depth of the audit. It can be as comprehensive or focused as he desires.

NAM business plan.

A component of the audit may be a thorough review of the national-account marketing business plan. The outline of a thorough audit and the outline of your NAM business plan will likely be mirror images of each other. It is imperative that the business plan contain an extensive section on communications. Communications build understanding, which enables cooperation. Doug may choose to focus his audit on this section.

National account marketing communications plans.

A communications plan is the roadmap that creates an atmosphere of mutual respect conducive to integrated business growth. Lack of a communications plan, or a poorly conceived plan, can feed management and sales force frustration, as well as hurt the company's image with accounts. *Disciplined execution of the plan improves cooperation.*

The communications plan should have three levels of emphasis: a sales-department component, a national-account-marketing-unit component, and individual-national-account-manager components. The following suggested matrix format is a simple guide that can identify program elements, your rationale for including that element, the audience it is intended for, the person responsible for designing and delivering the element, how often the element will be executed, and the expected results. Costs must also be noted. The format can be consistent for all three levels of emphasis.

Communication Program Elements	Rationale	Audience	Responsibility	Timing	Expected Results
Element A					
Element B					
Etc.					

1. Sales-department National-Account Marketing Communications Plan

Potential sales department communications-plan elements may include:

A. Personally communicate the mission of the program if you are the top sales executive. If not, get that executive to explain it to the balance of management.

B. Restate the rationale and goals of the national-account program at every national or international sales meeting. Again, the top sales executive needs to lead this.

C. Create and facilitate a forum for various departments and divisions to ensure that all elements of the company that interface with and have a stake in NAM are familiar with the program's mission, objectives, and activities. Repeat it as often as necessary.

D. Explain to senior headquarters and field management how the NAM concept is consistent with TQM, JIT, BPR (Total quality management, Just-in-time, Business Process Reengineering) and other hot management methods to which your firm is committed.

E. Endorse and fund the use of communications and computer technologies because national-account programs are a fertile environment for their application. It is the best place to start with their implementation if you haven't already adopted sales-force automation.

F. Establish a NAM conflict-resolution process at the field-level-manager and the highest-sales-executive level.

2. National Account-Marketing-Unit Communications Plan

Potential national-account-marketing-unit elements can include:

A. Train sales-department headquarters, and regional and local offices on the national-account-marketing concept and describe your corporate program. This is worthwhile to repeat every year because of account and program changes and new personnel.

B. Provide summary briefings to all business departments and divisions on the NAM concept and the status and progress of the corporate effort.

C. Define the role of the national-account managers and executives and communicate what the balance of the sales force can expect from the NAM unit and what the NAM unit expects from the balance of the sales force. Let the sales force know that the account managers' and executives' roles may vary from account to account because of the unique relationships and agreements your firm has with each account.

D. Communicate the national-account managers' and executives' objectives to the sales force.

E. Provide monthly or quarterly reports on the NAM program. Review the reports personally with key field and headquarters managers.

F. Communicate the company's definition of a national account and the criteria the firm used to denote NA status. Identify all the current national accounts and, with discretion, forewarn them of potential changes.

G. Attend regional and district sales meetings to provide brief overviews and to answer questions. Ask for ideas that can strengthen the program and improve mutual results.

H. Invite top executives from the accounts to address major meetings and to address certain headquarters business departments.

I. Have the top level national-account executive speak at national- and international-level sales meetings.

J. Consider a recognition program to honor special contributions by field and headquarters personnel to the national-account-marketing program.

3. Individual National-Account-Manager Communications Plan

Account-manager communications plan elements can include:

A. Share formal account plans with stakeholder management in the balance of the company.

B. Plan and execute joint calls at account headquarters with field and headquarters managers.

C. Invite selected field reps to account headquarters on major opportunities.

D. Issue a brief account newsletter or E-mail to field and headquarters people who integrate with national accounts.

E. Volunteer to speak at regional; district; or area-office sales meetings.

F. Invite key purchasing contacts from the account's headquarters and outlying facilities to address the sales department or local offices at special meetings.

G. Communicate the highlights of major meetings that you have with account management.

H. Establish and live by a policy to answer phone, voice-mail, E-mail, fax, and written inquiries from the field within a specified period of time.

I. Copy your monthly forecasts and reports to field management. Get it in their hands several days before their own reports are due. Ensure that the quality and detail of your information is impeccable.

J. Communicate the strategic highlights and the operating details of contracts. Provide advice on where and how to take full advantage of the contracts.

K. Maintain a project- or order-opportunity-status log that you can share with the field on a moments notice.

L. Participate in trade shows, conferences, and exhibitions, working shoulder to shoulder with the field sales organization. Introduce each other to local- and national-level account contacts.

M. Distribute success stories to the field sales organization and to relevant headquarters managers.

These communications efforts amount to internal selling and common courtesy. For the national-account-management team, these communications efforts should be their highest priority, for without them, account sales efforts and the overall health of the program will suffer. Watch cooperation and respect reach surprisingly high levels when these communications tactics are planned and consistently employed.

LESSONS

The biggest factor in national-account-marketing success is meticulous integration of the program into the company culture, cemented by *intense* communications based on a formal communications plan.

National accounts are the company's jewels. Their size and scope demand a higher level of scrutiny. Account business opportunities, strategic and operating issues, plus national-account-executive initiatives can ripple worldwide, necessitating highly coordinated responses.

Success can be enhanced when you put people into national-account-manager and executive positions who are highly respected, are strategic in outlook, and who have *the highest level of teamwork and communications skills.*

part seven

TROUBLESHOOTING COACHING AND TRAINING PROBLEMS

7–1 The Problem:
Your coaching skills are questionable.

The Story

Maribeth had joined Josh's sales group from the marketing department about two months ago. It was obvious that she had the potential to be a top salesperson in a short time.

At the end of Josh's last coaching session with her, Maribeth asked if it would be all right if she asked Derrick, one of Josh's more senior salespeople, to accompany her on a few calls and give her some pointers. Maribeth's comment was, "I need somebody *really good* with some real-world experience."

Josh agreed to her working with Derrick and committed to call Derrick on Maribeth's behalf.

When she left, Josh sat back and wondered why Maribeth felt the need for another coach.

Temptations

When you've just been stung it's easy to say something foolish.

Get defensive
  "What's the matter, I'm not good enough? Huh?"

Shallow humor
  "I must have bad breath. Right?"

Take a shot in return
  "I understand. *I need* people *really good* who can sell."

Making calls with your people and helping them with their sales techniques and customer strategies is one of the most important things a sales manager does. There is no room for emotional temptations.

What Happened Here . . . ?

Something is on Maribeth's mind. Josh passed up an opportunity to find out. The implication in the story is that Maribeth is not satisfied with Josh's coaching.

Possibly Josh's coaching style intimidates her, or he may have been overly harsh with his past coaching.

Maybe Maribeth just wants inputs from another source. Maybe she just is not learning enough from Josh. She's hungry for more.

Maribeth may have a lack of confidence and may get nervous making calls with her boss.

There is also a subtlety here that needs pursuit. Maribeth's comment to Josh could be perceived by many managers as insensitive. It raises the question: What other insensitive statements is she making to customers and internal staff? The statement suggests that Josh should be alert to how Maribeth speaks to others and should coach her communications style.

On the plus side, it is not a bad thing to have your experienced people work with and coach your junior people. In fact, these mentoring relationships benefit both parties.

OPTIONS

Coaching is so important, your only option is to get good at it.

POSSIBLE ACTIONS

Let the stinger wear off.

First thing Josh should do is go back to Maribeth and ask, "Exactly what kind of real-world experience are you looking for? I may be able to direct you to additional resources." Her answer could help Josh suggest other options and help Josh prepare for his own next steps.

Commit Yourself

The first step to becoming a good coach is a commitment to the process. It is much too easy to let other issues monopolize your time. The fact is, there are few tasks more important than coaching your people.

Therefore, get your calendar and mark off every Monday and Tuesday *for the rest of the year*. Two days per week is not too much time to spend on your most important task. (Three days is better, and some sales managers work four days in the field.) We have chosen Mondays and Tuesdays because all too often the pressures of the business build up over the course of the week, and the temptation to cancel coaching appointments may become too great.

Communicate Your Intentions

Let your team know that you will be calling them to schedule customer visits. Tell them that you want to help them with their sales techniques and customer strategies as well as to answer any questions they may have about the business or the company.

Make sure they know that you will want a schedule and a complete briefing package from them at least one week prior to the scheduled visits.

Set the Schedule

Figure out a suitable rep rotation and place the names in your PC or on your calendar (in *ink*). Then publish the schedule. Spend two consecutive days with the same rep. This may allow you to have dinner with your rep and discuss a wide range of topics. She will relax over time and give you invaluable feedback on the programs you and the company are putting in place. Two days also allows you to see a wide range of customers, not just the few that the rep can control.

The Coaching Process

This simple three-step process, if used religiously, will improve your performance as a coach and your salespeople's performance on sales calls.

1. Watch and listen to your reps perform.
2. Compare performance to an *agreed-to standard.*
3. Discuss deviations from the standard.

The second step is often overlooked, which then raises contention during the third step.

Define the Standard

Ascertaining the standard is best done as a team. Together with your salespeople, develop the profile of the quintessential sales call, including its preparation. Once completed, you will have a standard with which your sales team agrees and is committed to execute.

This standard could include any or all of the following:

- Effective, trust-building, opening statements.
- Fact-finding about the buyer's situation.

- Needs and concerns identification questions.
- Reaching situational understanding and agreement.
- Determination of buying criteria.

- Influencing statements
- Delivering recommendations and solutions.
- Answering questions.
- Effective objection handling.

- Closing techniques.

Tailor your standard to your needs and refresh it periodically. The key point is to *be consistent in your use and interpretation of your standard.*

Many companies have acquired or have developed their own sales process, sales model, or selling methodology. There are many effective ones in use today. They are 'standards'. They must be integrated into your sales-call model and used religiously.

Prepare Yourself

Always remember that although your primary purpose for being there is to coach your people, you are visiting a customer. Get familiar with the customer's history, issues, and the business transacted with your company. And be prepared to contribute to the dialogue.

The Sales Call

Most sales managers have a strong background in sales, and many are tempted to jump into the middle of the conversation and take over the entire call. This, of course, does no one any good. The best way to guard against this is to consider yourself as working *for* your rep. Let her call the shots, manage the call, and cue you when appropriate.

Above all, avoid jumping in when your rep seemingly stumbles. She might have a reason for handling the situation the way she did. You will never find out if you start talking.

Discuss the Deviations

Remember, your goal is to help your rep grow. *Do not criticize!* Be constructive.

Oftentimes, asking open-ended questions can get you to a point without antagonizing your rep. For example; "How do you think the call went?" "How do you feel you handled the customer's objection about product quality?" "How might you have positioned our ISO 9000 efforts?"

It is imperative to use your standard in your discussion. Point out those areas that you think your rep executed well. Do not dwell just on those areas that need improvement. Be clear and direct.

Avoid the proverbial bologna sandwich. That is, two thick pieces of bread with a thin slice of meat in the middle. It sounds something like this:

(Bread) "Maribeth, what a great call! You opened extremely well and you asked great probing questions."

(Meat) "Your criteria setting needs some work but . . . it was . . . okay."

(Bread) "What a great presentation you gave. You also handled some tough objections and performed a beautiful trial close. I'm sure we'll see you at the 100 percent club in August."

Do you think Maribeth walked away from this discussion understanding that she needed to improve her criteria-setting skills? Probably not.

Also avoid the legendary Dagwood Bumstead sandwich. That is, two thin, perfunctory pieces of bread grossly overloaded with meat. It's the exact opposite of the Bologna sandwich.

The best approach is to provide balanced feedback, not letting your rep miss the important points that need development.

Receiving criticism, even if it is given in a constructive way, is difficult. Open-ended questions makes it easier and can also help you avoid dummy statements, that is, any statement you make to which you could append the word dummy and it sounds okay. For example, "Boy you really missed a clear buying signal in there (*dummy*)." Statements such as this will only cause your rep to get defensive. You cannot coach a defensive rep.

Attributes of a Great Sales Coach

Good coaches in sales, sports, or other fields share many other common attributes, aside from being able to provide constructive criticism. Here are several attributes we suggest you consider adding to your coaching repertoire.

- Has outstanding sales, product, and company knowledge. Continues to develop to stay ahead of the curve.

- Knows when and how to be either hard or soft in his or her approach.

- Has played the selling game in the past. Understands the game inside out.

- Is conscious of coaching with actions and attitudes, as well as with words.

- Is sensitive to the differences and motivations of his or her salespeople.

- Has a great peripheral sense of impact. Knows that when speaking to one, he or she is speaking to all.

- Has a great sense of timing—knows when and where to speak and when and where to be quiet.

- Stands up and fights hard for the interests of his or her people.

- Is a sharp observer and recorder of details.

- Can exhibit as much or as little patience as required.

- Challenges his or her people in the coaching process.

- Has the ability to "act" to get a point across.

- Projects charisma, confidence, and leadership.

- Is a rich storyteller who can make lessons memorable.

- Treats coaching conversation as sharing, not telling.

- Is an outstanding listener who can listen between the lines.

- Matches coaching to salespeople's learning style—visual, auditory, or kinesthetic.

- Can be inspirational or analytical or go ballistic as the situation demands.

Integrate these attributes into your coaching style. Watch your acceptance grow. The next time you get together with your peers expand this list to be consistent across your firm.

Be Coached

Give your rep an opportunity to coach you. Ask her how she felt you did in the call. Unfortunately, reps are reluctant to give negative feedback to their boss, especially during budget-setting and salary review times. So, be specific if you really want the input. "Did I talk too much?" "Did I dominate the call?" "Did you think my answer on our company's financial stability was effective?"

Listen attentively and thank your rep for her inputs.

You must think of coaching as a relationship that grows over time, not discrete feedback exchanges. Aside from a willingness to be coached, this list of attributes represents the goal you should be working toward and characterizes strong sales-coach–salesperson relationships.

- Candid, open communications are the norm.
- There is a conscious effort to understand how the other person feels—hard listening is going on.
- The salesperson uses the manager's suggestions and has the courtesy to feed back the results.

- There is sincere respect that can border on affection.
- One party seeks out the other for advice. Coaching is not just a one-way reaction to events.
- There is a wink, a nod, or a word of thanks to express gratitude.

Talk about these expectations when you talk about standards with your sales unit. Also ask your manager what he or she believes makes for a good coaching relationship. We'll guarantee enlightening discussions.

Follow Up

Document your two days of joint calls with notes to the rep's file and a summary letter of points discussed to the rep.

Watch for Subtleties

There are many small things that go on prior to and during a sales call that give you a better understanding of your salespeople's effectiveness and need to be coached. For example:

- You can get an indication of your rep's work ethic by noticing how early and how late appointments were made, and if you were picked up on time.
- Did she know the way to the account, or did she have to get directions?
- Did the customer's receptionist, secretaries, and other employees know her?
- Did the conversation with the customer indicate a strong personal and professional relationship?

Subtleties such as these can help you complete your picture of your rep and help you be a better, more effective coach.

LESSONS

Coaching is one of your most important managerial tasks. Get good at it.

You must set regular time aside to be with your people, and you need to compare their performance against a standard. Then you must coach them in a constructive way.

Coaching is integral to your overall training effort. There are significant fringe benefits.

Because you are working directly with your reps, you can sense their morale, answer their questions, and ensure that your operating philosophies are understood and adopted.

Because you will see most of your customers frequently, you will be able to sense industry trends and get a firsthand view of how your products and services are perceived.

Because you will see your reps at work, you will see them present your products and services, set buying criteria, ask opportunity-assessment questions, handle objections, and close. You will be able to pick out the best techniques and share them with the rest of your team.

Coaching is hard but gratifying work. It is the essence of sales management.

7–2 THE PROBLEM:

You don't have a ready answer to a sales question.

THE STORY

Newt and his district sales manager, Bill, had just left a lengthy, challenging presentation. Both had been well prepared, but so was the prospective client. The order wasn't theirs yet, but they were agonizingly close, and they were talking about the situation as they got on the elevator.

"Bill," Newt asked, "in this sales situation, how can we integrate the client's values and our values to strengthen our message and at the same time unlock their creativity to aid in building the solution to their problem?"

Bill, who was usually pretty glib, said, "Wow, I never thought of that."

I wish this guy would ask me simple questions, like how to close the order, Bill thought to himself, as the elevator descended. What am I going to do with that one?

TEMPTATIONS

Sales managers are expected to be fountains of knowledge. And when the fountain runs dry there is often the temptation to dance.

Twist the question and answer to your own liking

"Close this order by offering a 90-day free trial. Don't worry about that mushy stuff."

Belittle

"Boy, that's a fluffy, fanciful question, Newt. We've just got to close harder."

Toss it back.

"That is a *great* question, Newt. What do *you* think the answer is?"

The best answers are honest answers.

WHAT HAPPENED HERE . . . ?

You don't have a ready reply to a seemingly relevant question. It is as simple as that.

Sales situations continue to grow more complex, reps are getting smarter, and the questions are getting tougher.

Some sales calls turn out to be very stimulating interchanges because of the interest, needs, and preparation of the prospect. Those types of calls are energizing and often push salespeople to a higher level of inquisitiveness and creativity.

Newt may be a resourceful thinker, and Bill may be a practical street fighter. Newt may have a higher level of intellectual curiosity and be more adept at conceptual problem solving.

Salespeople, rightly or wrongly, judge their managers by their ability to answer questions. In the heat of competition they often want and expect quick fix pills to win the business.

But, as W. H. Auden, the English poet, once wrote, "To ask the hard question is simple." Hmmm. Hard questions don't expose the questioner. Answers to hard questions expose the answerer. Is Newt playing games? Maybe yes, maybe no.

OPTIONS

There are four options with this problem.

1. You can say that you don't know and let it go. As irresponsible as that sounds, some managers do that for reasons known only to themselves.
2. Offer a partial answer, on the spot, to the best of your ability.
3. Say "I don't know" and suggest that both of you try to develop the answer together.
4. Say "I don't know" and ask for time to develop a full answer.

Options #3 and #4 are obviously the most responsible coaching approaches.

POSSIBLE ACTIONS

Be happy. You *want* your people to ask questions. The tougher the better.

Questions are a sign of engaged salespeople. A lack of questions from any of your direct reports is a danger signal. No salesperson or staff member is so well trained, informed, or led that he or she does not have questions.

A manager answering questions from his employees sends multiple messages about leadership, coaching, teamwork, and respect for his staff. If you make the questioner feel comfortable and satisfied he is more likely to return with other questions. Questions are revealing, help you understand your staff, and open the door for continuing dialogue.

Question the Question

Just as when a customer puts a tough question or objection to you, go back for clarification.

"Why do you ask, Newt?" or "Newt, what occurred in the meeting that stimulated that thought?"—or—"What customer comment triggered this?"—or—"What perceived feelings gave you that idea?"

Clarification builds understanding, which will better enable Bill to answer the question.

Where Did the Question Come from?

"Where did you pick up the idea for your question, Newt?"

The stimulus for a question is important because it helps you to know what sales concept is being used, what information is causing your people to think, and what material you need to reference to develop an answer.

Did the question have its basis in:

- Your corporate-training programs?
- Seminars that you haven't personally attended?
- Books, magazines, or newsletter articles that the sales rep read?

A question may signal that there is a hole in your training that needs filling.

Seize the Question

Let Newt see you do something with the question, such as write it down. Your act emphasizes the value of the inquiry. Say something that emphasizes that point, such as "You're right, that is an important point."—or—"I can see how that could be a factor in . . ." —or—"Let me think about it . . . I'll get back to you tomorrow."

No questions should ever be considered inconsequential or insignificant. And don't drag your feet getting the answer. It is disrespectful and demotivating.

Dig

Don't be so proud as not to ask a peer, your manager, or another account manager if he or she has any thoughts on the subject. Follow Will Rogers' observation, which was, "Everyone is ignorant, only on different subjects." Do some research. You set a terrific example by aggressively pursuing answers. If you treat the search for an answer as off-the-cuff, Newt may assume that the question was shallow or trivial. When you treat the inquiry with respect Newt will think, "Ah, that must have been a good question." It makes Newt feel valued and encourages continued thinking and creativity, and it stimulates problem solving.

Answering the Question Speaks Volumes

Don't delegate the answer. If there is another individual who has expert knowledge and is better positioned to answer the question, use him or her as a resource but make sure you are present when the question gets answered. A lack of presence will be interpreted negatively.

Provide more information than was asked for. That does not mean that if someone asks the time you tell them how to build a watch. It means to enliven your answer with more than was expected.

Answer the question in the format that matches Newt's learning style or preferences. Every sales manager should make it a point to understand his or her people's preferred learning style.

- If the salesperson learns visually, draw it out on the chalk board or chart pad.
- If he learns primarily by hearing, tell him.
- If he learns by doing, roll play the situation with him.
- If it takes all three approaches, use all three.

Get assurance that the answer was understood. Whether the answer is totally bought is not the issue. It is your responsibility to coach. Newt's responsibility is to seize your answer with the same vigor that you seized his question and integrate it into his style.

Follow-up Items

Make your office look and feel like a place where answers can be obtained.

Maintain a library of professional books, including sales, sales-management, marketing, and general-business books. Subscribe to sales magazines or newsletters and business dailies. Offer to lend out your materials, but don't make the search for an answer punitive by saying, "Here, look it up," or you'll never get another question. Q&A should be a rewarding learning experience.

Hold court informally from time to time in your office with one or more of your people, encouraging discussions on sales and management techniques.

Keep a sales-resource database in your PC. Point out resources for additional information on sales and account-management matters.

Bring the rep's question up for discussion at the next sales meeting. "Newt asked me this question last week. It stumped me, and it's a good question. I thought we could all benefit by it. Here's what I said . . . What do you think?"

Log the question and send a note to your sales training providers and ask them to include the question and alternative answers in their training material.

LESSONS

Your reactions to questions emphasize that you and your people are partners in continuous learning, and your reactions reinforce your image as a top-notch leader, coach, and manager. Let your people see you as intellectually curious. It's a great example to set.

Don't ever lose sight of your own self-development and the need to maintain a level of expertise so that you can effectively support your sales unit. Keep pushing the edge of your knowledge envelope.

7–3 THE PROBLEM:

Your coaching creates confrontation.

THE STORY

They were sitting over a cup of coffee after coming out of a big presentation. It had been tense.

"Perhaps you could have held off getting into the pricing until after we had reviewed the service elements of our proposal," Winnie, the sales manager, said. "It might have given . . ."

"They weren't interested in that," Cecil fired back. "Didn't you see the intensity with which they wanted to discuss pricing?"

"What I saw was . . . ," Winnie started.

"I can't do these things your way, Winnie. I've got to go with what I see and feel. I don't agree with that style of presentation at all."

Here we go again, Winnie thought to herself. Every time I make a suggestion or try to give some feedback he gets defensive.

TEMPTATIONS

When you are trying your best to do your job, and your own employee isn't buying into your coaching, these unsavory temptations can bubble-up to the top.

Let him fail
"Think I'll let this one self-destruct. I don't have time for any more word games."

Yell
"When are you going to learn that pricing questions aren't objections? Maybe that's why you are only 93 percent of plan, Cecil."

Lick your wounded ego
"I'll work with those who appreciate my expertise. Cecil doesn't recognize my wisdom."

Coaching is a sales-management art that takes sensitivity and flexibility as well as subject expertise.

What Happened Here . . . ?

You have an emotional rep who is pushing back rather aggressively. It sounds like one of these cases where you can tell him anything, but you can't tell him much.

Cecil may not see the reasons or value in doing things the way Winnie suggests because something is getting in the way. He may see himself as more competent than she is.

Cecil may be older, and not about to take any direction from this young whipper-snapper. Conversely, he may see Winnie as a good ol' girl, not really interested in a young man succeeding and competing with her.

Cecil may be very bright and considers himself the intellectual superior because he is college educated and Winnie is not. Different formal-education levels sometimes get in the way.

Maybe Winnie was promoted to manager primarily because of other skills and achievements, and her coaching capability is not one of her strengths.

Is Cecil a pompous superstar who isn't about to take any direction from anyone, someone who just doesn't like to be told what to do? He may be a very proud person—or high-strung and super-sensitive—or a rep who always has something to prove.

Cecil could be absolutely correct in his assessment of the sales situation because of his previous experience. Winnie's suggestions may be off the mark.

Perhaps Winnie has a track record of abrupt, insensitive coaching that turns Cecil off.

Options

You have one option. You are responsible for leading and managing Cecil. He is responsible for his performance. You are his coach. It is up to you to find a way—*some way*—to help him meet his objectives while working to meet your sales unit's and company goals.

Possible Actions

This is a middle-of-the-road performer who sounds as if he needs help. Stop where you are. Don't push it. There will be another time for which you can be better prepared.

Listen

What is Cecil saying to you? What is feeding this reaction? Is this situational, or does it happen all the time? Is this simple frustration because you didn't close the order? Is this a rep who is always tense around management?

Is Cecil still mentally in front of the customer? When some salespeople come out of a call they are too keyed-up to have a reflective discussion. A cool-down before feedback can be beneficial and helps foster thoughtful analysis.

Is he mad at himself? Some reps hold themselves to such high standards that they feel they can never do anything right. Don't be confrontational in return, unless of course he gets to be abusive, and then you need to stop the discussion cold.

What are you *really hearing* from Cecil?

Why Not Ask Him?

A simple request to ask why he feels so strongly may get the issue on the table. If it does, answer it and go on. If it doesn't to your satisfaction, listen a little more.

Time for More Introspection

You cannot be everything to everyone. You will click better with some of your people than with others. Have you received the same reaction from other reps?

How would you describe your coaching style? Are you happy with it? Do you need to modify your coaching approach?

Do your reps come to you on a regular basis? If you are never or rarely approached, it's a dead giveaway that you have a coaching problem.

Motivation

What drives this particular rep? The best coaching is often delivered in the context of the rep's drivers and motivators.

For example:

"Cecil, I've got three easy $50 ideas and one big $2,000 suggestion for you today . . .

"Cecil, here is a suggestion that will keep your name on the top of the . . .

"Cecil, these techniques can be your plane ticket to Maui next . . .

Sensitivity to what is important to your rep will always help. This does not mean that every coaching statement must be made in that context. Your own judgment will tell you when to push these buttons.

Has your manager ever said anything to you about your coaching ability or style? Perhaps your boss will share his or her philosophy on coaching confrontation.

Listen to peers or other managers when they give directions, instructions, or feedback. Some managers are very smooth when giving advice and are more successful at having their suggestions accepted. Adopt their style, to the extent you're comfortable with it.

Practical Tactics

Here are some general suggestions to help reduce confrontation during coaching.

- Establish roles for each other before going into a presentation. Roles rather than personalities then becomes the basis of sales-call debriefing and reduces confrontation.
- Announce when and where you'll debrief after a sales call. The early warning sets an expectation and makes for an easier transition to coaching after the call.
- Tell your rep that you expect the two of you to treat each other as partners when you are in front of the customer. Let the titles drop away. The egalitarian approach fosters better critiques as well as results. The customer should never perceive the slightest friction.
- Ask Cecil his opinions about the call before providing any personal input. Ask him to focus on what he saw, felt, and heard, rather than on what he did or said. The focus on the customer reduces defensiveness.
- Offer a sincere compliment or recognize progress since the last time you worked together.
- Beg off a rep's question for clarification with "Let me think about it" if you don't have a clear, concise response. Fumbled responses during coaching exacerbate confrontation.
- Be respectful and watch your language. Stay away from emotionally charged words such as "weak," "gross," "bad," "dumb," and the like. You get the idea.
- Deliver your critique in the third person. Say, "A salesperson could benefit from . . .", instead of "You could benefit from . . ."
- Ask what-if questions. "What if we had done this instead of that?" "What ifs spur thinking and are nonjudgmental.
- Provide a thorough explanation of why you are making a suggestion. A lack of rationale colors your comments as emotional and subjective, rather than as objective.
- Coach in the context of your firm's sales process. It adds legitimacy.
- Find alternative ways to get your message across such as films, books, newsletter articles, trade magazines, chalk-talks, and existing training materials. Coaching that is always verbal is not responsive to the different learning styles of your people.

Tips to Dodge Some Common Confrontation Bullets

The following sample reactions and suggested responses will stir your own creativity.

Rep reaction	Possible sales-manager responses
"You don't understand the customer. *I* understand the customer."	• "I expect you to understand the customer better than I do. I provide another set of eyes and ears to help you understand your customer *even better*. I am a resource to help *build* your understanding even further." • "My inputs come from experience in similar situations. I am sharing what I have seen as effective elsewhere."
"I can't do that. It is beyond me."	• "You have demonstrated that you can do *many things* well. Your array of sales skills has grown ever since you have been in this sales unit. I expect it will continue to grow. I would be happy to send you to a seminar to acquire this particular skill." • "Talk to your peer, X, to learn how she has incorporated that skill." • "Let's try that skill on our next call. You can prove it to yourself." • "I will demonstrate that skill on our next call. Then you try it. Okay?"
"That is someone else's idea. I like to use my own ideas."	• "You can modify the idea to fit your personal selling style. All sales ideas are someone else's ideas. It is up to each sales professional to adapt ideas to their style. As an example, you used the X approach to begin the presentation. That idea was published by Y several years ago. Many people have developed it further since then." • "It is important to use your own ideas. I encourage you to be creative, but that doesn't mean you should discard proven ideas."
"I don't feel *the need* for that approach. I accomplish the same thing by doing X."	• "Customers often don't feel their needs either, do they? And don't *you* try to point out those needs and how *you* can meet them? My suggestions are given in the same spirit."

"Your idea simply does not work. I tried it before."

- "It is true that there are certain sales approaches that work better for some people than they do for others. It takes practice to really hone a sales skill, doesn't it? Will you try it again?"
- "Isn't it true that when a customer buys our product their understanding and appreciation of it grows as they use it?"
- "It is not my idea. It is an approach I saw one of your peers use with great success last week."

"The suggestion doesn't grab me. I have to be excited about something in order to use it."

- "I understand that we all would like to find the BIG idea. Like you, I am always looking for magic pills and gems that can make our lives easier. I have learned that most good sales ideas are small, and the secret to success is the *consistent execution* of all those small ideas."
- "I understand that sometimes sales ideas don't sound effective, or they don't stir our imaginations. No self-respecting salesperson wants to use ideas that are not grabbers or do not represent him or her well. However, remember that the sales idea must grab the *customer*, not you."

"I won't look good using that particular approach. It's not me."

- "I can see that. I like to leave a good, positive impression as well. Remember that it is our job to make our product and services look good and our company look good and the customer look good before thinking about ourselves. If we can accomplish those three things, you'll look good to everyone when you get the sale."

"I really wouldn't know how, when, or where to use that idea. I don't see the fit."

- "I understand. I will describe two situations where the idea would be helpful. Let me draw it out on my notepad . . ."
- "Let's role play one possible situation. Make believe you are the customer and you just said . . ."
- "I saw an article in a sales magazine that discussed this subject in detail. I will send the magazine to you."
- "At our next sales unit meeting I will discuss this in detail. May I use today's situation as an example? Will you help me get the message across to the rest of the sales unit?

"I once used that technique, and frankly I was embarrassed. Besides, it had no discernible impact."	• "Yes, I've embarrassed myself as well. Let me tell you the story . . . I learned that different people respond to different presentations. I stuck with this technique because I wanted to find out what kinds of situations and what kinds of people responded to it. Then one day, voila! Let me tell you a second short story . . ."
"Your suggestion is a very old idea. These are young buyers."	• "Frankly, ancient is a better word to describe it. But the classics are still popular in all fields and professions, aren't they? Age is not a sufficient reason to discard a proven sales activity. Its effectiveness, or lack thereof, should be the only reason we discard sales activities. Besides, these buyers are so new they have very little experience. Old ideas delivered in current language and wrapped in current values can be very effective."
"I may try that when I'm in a rut someday, but I'm not in a rut now."	• "I don't think you're in a rut either. Other managers have said that the best time to try something new is when things are going well so that if the sales approach does not work there is no great loss. When we are in a rut the pressure often keeps us from being ourselves, relaxed enough to be creative, and relaxed enough to apply new techniques with skill." • "This sales technique can keep us both *out of* ruts. Think of the sales approach as preventive medicine."
"That sales process that the sales-training company sold to our firm has no credibility in our sales unit. None of us like it."	• "I have some trouble with the sales process myself, and I have heard similar feedback from others. But all sales processes or methodologies have gems within them. It is our responsibility to find and use the gems." • "I am in the process of evaluating other sales processes for the sales unit's use. Would you like to be a part of the evaluation team?"
"With all due respect, I think the suggestion is corny and phony."	• "In all honesty, I agree with you. It is an alternative. As sales professionals it is our responsibility to possess as broad an array of sales approaches as possible. Sometimes, what seems like an off-the-wall idea to us is accepted as highly creative and stimulating by the customer. Corny approaches can also differentiate us from the competition and make us more memorable."

"I think I'm a pretty competent persuader who doesn't need suggestions more appropriate for rookies."	• "You certainly are competent. You have proven that. However, think about the next level above competence, which is *excellence*. Excellence in any field or endeavor is always accompanied by mastery of the basics. Wouldn't you agree? Speaking of *mastery*, that is the next level of sales professionalism above *excellence*. And that is my destination—how about yours?"
"Your idea is conceptual, and I like to stick with practical sales ideas."	• "Different customers like and appreciate different approaches. Many, like you, prefer to focus on practical facts and data. But many executives also prefer to think about concepts and the big picture. Concepts, which are just broad ideas, permit them to mentally juggle and fit our products and services into the context of their own problems and agendas. Concepts also help them facilitate their own internal selling needs and approval processes. So, from our perspective, we help the customer by selling both practically and conceptually."

These sample responses should get you to think of additional replies. Your understanding of each salesperson will help you customize your contentious coaching dialogue even further.

Don't turn coaching into a competition. It is not your approach versus his approach. It is your combined approaches versus the prospect and the competition. Remind Cecil that you are both sitting on the same side of the table.

It Comes Down to Your Judgment

You know the salesperson best. You may have even hired him. You have to put the coaching in the context of where he's come from and where he is now.

Stick with It

Cecil will be sensitive to your perseverance. If you back off your field time with Cecil it weakens the relationship and your credibility.

Caution the Multiplier Effect

You can expect that Cecil may share your discussions with other salespeople in the sales unit. When you coach one salesperson, it's a good idea to assume that you are coaching all of them at the same time. Contention is more likely to be spread around the sales unit, maybe because it's human nature to gossip, revel in bad news, or take shots at the boss.

Conversely, you can expect that your good ideas will be closely guarded by Cecil because, after all, the salespeople have their own rankings to look out for. It is an unusual team player who spreads effective coaching tips amongst his peers.

It's Your Job

Your people must understand that coaching is a part of your job. Sometimes you need to remind them of that fact. Sharing your job description from time to time is always a good idea.

LESSONS

Keep the high ground when coaching. Be willing to admit to yourself that you may be a part of the problem. All coaches don't always click with all players.

Don't confuse sales-management processes with coaching approaches. You must use a consistent management process with *everybody*, but different salespeople require different coaching approaches. Managers can get in a coaching rut the same way salespeople get in a sales-style rut. Be flexible and creative.

Be sensitive to how *you* accept suggestions from your people. Your own responses serve as a model for their reactions to your coaching.

7–4 THE PROBLEM:

You must coach someone through a complex sale.

THE STORY

Ida, like many good sales managers, has an effective process in place to allow her to stay close to her business. Every Friday afternoon she reviews pipelines and forecasts with her team.

"I've got a new one on the line that feels like Moby Dick," Brian, one of the account managers, announced right off. "This is a monster," Brian shared, "and very honestly I'm a little lost."

"Let's talk," Ida offered, and Brian seized the opportunity.

"You bet! I'll fax a few things and drive in first thing Monday morning. They're asking me questions I never heard before. They're telling me things we need to do to get the business, and wow, this is *way, way* over my head. I don't even understand some of the words they're using," Brian enthused.

Just what I need, another time-sink, Ida thought to herself. But, who knows.

TEMPTATIONS

Every salesperson, at one time or another, needs some help with a complicated sales opportunity. These situations don't lack for numerous unhealthy temptations.

Take over

"Just give me the facts, Brian. I will take it from here. Out of my way. Let me show you how a master works."

Keep your hands clean

"Talk to Gordon, in marketing. He can get it started. Let them clean it, and we'll fry it."

Sour grapes

"Let's not bother with it, Brian. It's loaded with issues. Plus, we probably won't win."

Salespeople ask for help only when they really need it. And they ask only those they trust to help them.

WHAT HAPPENED HERE . . . ?

The good news is that the operational process worked. Brian has latched onto something new and different. The better news is that the account manager recognizes he needs help and is not afraid to get his manager involved.

What makes any sale complex? A departure from mainstream business. Also, complex sales are characterized by special customer requirements, penetration into a complex market, such as the government or international, the necessity for several vendors to collaborate, highly unusual contractual requirements, customization of products and services, geographical location of the opportunity, peculiar provisions for packaging and shipping, very long-term supply commitments, abnormal prototype or testing processes, unique financing arrangements, a strange mix of decision makers, a sales cycle that can be months or years long, or a combination of any and all of these factors. And more.

Maybe other corporate resources that Brian has already approached, such as product managers, have already backed off on this situation and encouraged him to take the opportunity up his chain of command. Ida's intervention could break a log jam.

This may be the first deal of this type that Brian, and maybe Ida, has ever seen.

In some industries and businesses *all sales* are complex, and no two situations are alike. In those environments this problem is not a problem, it's what they deal with day in and day out. (Maybe Ida can make some networking phone calls. Nothing ventured, nothing gained.)

OPTIONS

First, in regard to coaching, there are no options. Ida must step up and help Brian.

Second, this situation may be bigger than Ida. Complex sales are often like that. Now Ida has options. She can try to tackle this alone or she can elect to bring in additional resources. This could be a major team sell.

Third, there may need to be a go-no-go decision made at the division or corporate level whether even to pursue this opportunity. Ida should have the acumen to get the data together for an assessment by the management team. She'll hope the company has a process to make such decisions. Assuming the company is committed, and says go, Ida must now get back into her leadership and coaching mode with Brian.

POSSIBLE ACTIONS

Coaching an account manager through a complex sale is the ultimate. For a sales manager, it does not get much better than this.

The Difference

Complex sales require a depth of thinking, a level of planning, a breadth and frequency of internal communications, and precision of execution far above mainstream business.

- They are often *big* investments of people, dollars, and materials.
- They can take an inordinate amount of time to pursue.
- They take cross-functional teamwork.
- They take a tight cross-functional-management *process* to keep them under control and on track.
- They often require a close relationship with various outside service providers, such as banks.
- There are large numbers of sales, account, product, and service variables to consider.
- They often require building many new relationships with key-customer staff and strengthening relationships with current contacts.
- There is room for many new problems that must be anticipated, but in spite of that there always seem to be surprises.
- There will be subtleties and nuances of execution that are new to the participants.
- The return on investment to the company has the *potential* to be sizable.

Be Careful

Do not take over. Stay in the help mode. *Coach, do not play.* It is likely Ida will be coaching and coordinating more people than Brian on this sale. It should be assumed that during all the following steps participation will be broad and varied.

Ida's primary role is to keep her eye on the big picture and help her account manager and other resources find their way through the labyrinth.

Simplify

Many sales managers feel that complex deals require complex strategies and solutions. Although this is true occasionally, most of the time it is not. Again, a complex sale requires you to think of more variables and new variables. That's what makes it complex.

The fact is, if you make the strategy and solution too complicated, you will have difficulty explaining it to inside staff and the customer.

Have Brian reduce the strategy and solution to a single-page diagram. If he cannot get to that point, help him. Keep working it until he can put it on a single page. Simplicity aids focus, execution, and the probability of winning.

Power Coalitions

Help Brian determine how the customer generally makes decisions of this magnitude. Ask him to be specific. Do not let him take anything for granted.

Help Brian determine who the decision makers will be. Too often, account managers assume that there is *one* decision maker and all other people are rubber stamps, even in complex sales. While single decision makers occur in exceptional cases, it is more complicated than that.

Generally, decision makers fall into three categories, and in all three categories Ida and the rest of the selling team should expect to be facing buying teams of decision makers.

1. *Technical*: These people decide whether your company has the capability to solve their problem. These people can usually eliminate you from the competition but are rarely the final authority.
2. *Users*: These are the people who will be directly impacted by the solution you are proposing. Here again, they can eliminate you but probably do not have the final say.
3. *Financial*: These are the folks who determine the affordability of the solution and who negotiate. Most often they have the final say. Also, they are often considered the rubber stamp by account managers. This is a mistake.

Once Ida has helped Brian determine who the decision makers are, they should try to identify some inside salespeople. These are people who are employed by the customer (or are contracted by the customer) and would like to see Ida and Brian's company win the deal. Inside salespeople will help them position their solution in the most favorable way. They will give Brian insight as to the needs and desires of the decision makers. And they will let Brian know how he is doing relative to the competition.

Know Your Enemies

Help Brian determine which of his competitors are involved and what their strategies or solutions are likely to be. The inside salespeople are invaluable in this exercise. Once

Brian knows who the enemies are and what their probable strategies will be, help him differentiate the company's solution vis-à-vis the competition's.

Buying Criteria

In many complex sales the criteria and the decision-making process are provided to the vendor in writing, in exhaustive detail. These criteria can be influenced in many cases if the vendor has a close relationship with the customer. In some cases the customer will give all potential bidders the opportunity to influence the criteria.

If none of that happens, Ida must help Brian determine the criteria by which the customer will choose a vendor. Occasionally, the customer will not know what criteria they will use. So help them. Develop a list of criteria that, if used, Brian will be the chosen vendor. Most of the list will be obvious. The key is to add a few criteria that only Brian's company can completely satisfy. The work Brian did to differentiate his solution from those of the competition will help in this step.

Determine the Resources

Help the selling team determine what other corporate resources will be required to both sell and deliver the proposed solution. Also help them determine how these resources could be effectively used or demonstrated during the sales cycle. Finally, help Brian and the rest of the selling team secure those resources.

Prepare the Story

Ida will need to help the selling team develop a *compelling* presentation that everyone in her company believes. Let's face it, if the selling team does not have total faith and commitment in its solution and story, how can they ever sell it to the customer?

Ida will also need to help them prepare a flawless, creative *compelling* proposal.

Review the Materials

Make sure the selling team reviews and rehearses each and every key presentation prior to presenting to the customer. Pull in a few other people for the rehearsal. Have them role-play the customer's staff that will be in attendance. Ask them to be as difficult as possible.

It is always best to prepare for the worst. Then surprises are only positive.

Put together a "red" team to go through the proposal with red pens and nit-pick it until it is absolutely perfect.

Anticipate Objections and Roadblocks

Ida can help the selling team by being as difficult as possible during this exercise.

Here again, pull some additional staff into the process. For example, get a couple of finance-department managers to role-play the customer's financial people. Have them fire tough questions left and right. Assist the selling team in handling each challenge. Record the best answers for future study.

These can be tedious sessions. Try livening them up by giving prizes to the toughest objections and the best responses.

Finally

Help the selling team come up with action plans for the following scenarios.

1. We lose the order.
2. We win the order.
3. The customer delays the decision.

What will we do in each case? It is best to know up front so you do not waste any time.

LESSONS

These opportunities teach you to help, not take over.

Your biggest contribution may be bringing what you learned in one of these coaching sessions with you to the next one. Coaching a complex sale also makes the coaching of mainstream opportunities much stronger. Your leadership and facilitation skills get sharper, and you push the edges of your coaching envelope.

It reinforces how you feel about teamwork, and it gives you the opportunity to showcase your teamwork skills and management principles in front of your people real-time.

You build a good understanding of your own business, you create awareness in your people of the priorities in other parts of your company, and you build a sensitivity to your colleagues.

Finally, the word gets out to others in your sales unit about your capabilities in these matters. Expect the phone to ring quickly.

7–5 THE PROBLEM:
A salesperson escalates a major customer roadblock for assistance.

THE STORY

"Sorry, boss!" Saul said to Lin. "I know I promised that PO this week but the customer came up with a serious demand. This is a tough one."

"What now?" Lin asked, with disgust in her voice. "We've caved in on everything else."

"They want a six-year contract with no more than a 2 percent-per-year price-escalation cap. Can you believe it? They said if we can do that they're ready to sign tomorrow," Saul added.

Lin shuddered, "Wow! Never in all my years as a sales manager have I heard of that."

"I know, I know, the company has never done more than a one-year deal before," Saul said. What should I do? Whaddaya think, can we do it?"

That's incredible. They'll laugh at me if I take this up the line, Lin thought to herself.

TEMPTATIONS

These kinds of situations can be deflating. You see a monster obstacle and you feel, no way. You start thinking if you really want the business. The temptations are easy ways out.

Push back

"Saul, are you listening? It's time to start selling. Now go get the order!"

Take over

"Let me take a crack at closing it, Saul. Make an appointment for tomorrow."

Give up

"It's absurd, Saul. Let it go. Let's not waste our time."—or—"Sooner or later we need to say no. Now is as good a time as any."

On the one hand, these are often high-visibility projects of strategic interest that can be profitable. Your mind bounces back and forth. The better answer is leadership and coaching.

WHAT HAPPENED HERE . . . ?

An avalanche is blocking the road to this order. Roadblocks are not objections, they are simply highly unusual needs or demands that you don't know if you can handle or how to deal with. You simply can't proceed. Some roadblocks are avalanches that have completely obliterated the road to the order, others are simply a few boulders that cause you to step over or around them.

Sometimes you can get around these roadblocks, and sometimes you can't. They are untypical requests that must be dealt with in an untypical, or nonstandard way.

The problem is that major roadblocks call for customized coaching and problem solving, but there is usually no precedent and few, if any, guidelines. Both the account manager and the sales manager are in the dark.

Customer scenarios that could cause this roadblock include the following:

- First of all, the customer may really need what he or she is asking for. It may be essential to the success of their business.

- The customer may be overstating their need, knowing that compromise will get them to where they want to be.

- Maybe the customer has not heard a loud enough "no" as yet. Some customers will continue to ask for more and more until the vendor puts a stop to it.

- It could be that Saul did not handle an initial question or objection effectively, and it has snowballed into what it is now.

- Possibly one of Lin's competitors has done a good job of setting the customer's buying criteria and has included something that Lin's company does not do well.

There are also some scenarios on Lin's side to consider. It is important for Lin to understand the circumstances surrounding Saul coming to her. It puts the upcoming coaching in perspective.

Saul could be just plain stumped. He may have tried everything. He may have beat his head against the wall. His efforts to date may have been exemplary. He simply wants help.

Saul may respect Lin's wisdom and experience in regard to pricing and contractual issues. Saul may simply want to strategize and consider moves and then go and solve this himself. He may want to use Lin as a backboard to test ideas and concepts.

This could also be a strategic and politically sensitive order, and Saul just wants the boss in the boat with him—just in case.

Is Saul just unloading a monkey? Maybe he's too lazy and doesn't want to think about this. Going to Lin is an easy way out. Lin should understand his track record.

Does Saul want confirmation of the futility of this situation? Saul may be presenting futility as a way to get Lin to tell him to back off so that he can work on other stuff.

The good news is that a roadblock means that the customer is still talking to you and that you are still in the running for the business.

Options

From a coaching perspective, you have two simple options.

1. Try and handle the roadblock yourself. Lack of resources may be a factor. You may feel comfortable with the subject. Personal pride also comes into play. There's a risk here.

2. Get help. Coach and solve this as a team. You'll get many more ideas. There are no guarantees that the outcome will be better. Inputs from others can both help and hurt.

   There are three subsets to "team" with this option. One definition of team is the people in your sales unit. Having them assist is a good team-building exercise. They gain satisfaction from learning something new, helping a peer, and they will realize that similar support is available to them if they ever have a major roadblock. The second definition of team is your own boss, plus selected managers and specialists from other departments in the company. The third definition of team is a combination of both.

From the business perspective, your best option is to follow Aristotle's advice, "Probable impossibilities are to be preferred to impossible impossibilities."

1. Say no. Sometimes it is just not worth it to take on an impossible job. The risks are often high, and the profits can be very low. Plus, they're tough to implement and manage.

2. Negotiate. Come up with a compromise, a mutually agreeable solution.

3. Agree to the request and put the appropriate infrastructure and processes in place to support the nonstandard solution.

Possible Actions

Assuming the team approach, raise the flag and identify your team. The team may include subject-matter experts required to craft the solution, as well as technical service, legal, marketing, and executive management. Expect that team membership will change as you go forward.

What's the Difference

There are some key points about coaching a major roadblock as opposed to coaching other situations. Keep these in mind.

- Admit to Saul this is new ground. Setting false expectations doesn't do anyone any good.
- Lin is learning new subject matter on the fly. Let Saul see that you value the new knowledge and suggest how the knowledge will be useful in the future.

- Lin must keep her poise. Saul will be looking her in the eye constantly to check her resolve as the situation moves forward. This is leadership.
- Lin must take her time and keep her eyes and ears open. There will be many unforeseen subtleties and nuances with the solution. Let Saul witness the alertness.
- Crave ideas. Lin must demonstrate to Saul that she is hungry for inputs and is listening closely to others. She mustn't be overly judgmental. A good lesson for Saul.
- She should document her actions and all the discussions. The lessons may be helpful for the next major roadblock that comes along. It's also a management lesson to Saul.
- Birth a process. The first major roadblock Lin coaches and manages will essentially establish a process model for future situations. Track the process as it unfolds. This is also a lesson to Saul that Lin values processes.
- Lin must let Saul see her being coached by others. It's another great lesson.

Tell Me What's Happening

The first thing Lin needs to do is ask Saul to fill her in on what's happened throughout the sales process to date. This sets the stage for coaching. Ask Saul to lead a chalk-talk just for her.

- What has occurred, what's been said, and what's been done before the roadblock appeared?
- What is the size, scope, and strategic value of this opportunity?
- Who is involved, whom do we need to prepare for, who is sitting in their back room that we can count on or that we should be apprehensive about? How do they all feel about our firm and our products?
- Why has the customer asked for this?
- What are the obvious agendas, and do you suspect any hidden agendas?
- Finally, diagnose this roadblock together.

Saul is anxious to spill out what is on his mind, but doesn't want to appear stupid. Lin must be patient and ask second-level questions—and maybe send him back for more facts.

This update must be followed by asking for Saul's recommendations. (He really should have done this on his own in the first place. If he didn't, Lin is guilty for not asking her people to bring a solution or two when they present a problem. Maybe Lin initially cut Saul off and didn't give him the opportunity. It's a good tactic to maintain silence after a salesperson presents a roadblock. It encourages a further outpouring of ideas.)

Decision Time

Gather the management team. Nonstandard solutions to major roadblocks usually require people in your company to do nonstandard things. It is always best to have the team involved right up front. Have Saul lead the presentation, using the information and coaching from the previous step. Chip in as necessary.

Do you want this? *The team* must decide whether or not they want to provide the customer the requested nonstandard solution, or a modification thereof. If they do, then the team will need to commit to putting the appropriate steps in motion and infrastructure in place to provide and support that solution.

Remember, this is a coaching problem, at the same time that you are trying to win the business. Lin must think carefully about what tasks she is leading and executing and at what points Saul should lead and execute and she should coach. It is better to err on the side of having Saul do as many things as possible. Every situation will be different. The tendency is to take your eye off the coaching and focus solely on the business. Saul doesn't learn much that way.

As the process unfolds Lin and Saul should meet one-on-one regularly, such as before and after every session with the team and the customer, to discuss Saul's plans, activities, and lessons learned. She should also ask for feedback from Saul regarding her participation.

Some coaching sessions will include other team members, with either Lin or Saul facilitating. Those sessions are more appropriately called "debriefs" or "assessments," but the facilitating and sharing amounts to coaching and learning.

Go Back to the Customer

Both Lin and Saul should sit down with the customer and try to further understand exactly what they need. The devil is in the details. Lin and Saul must bring a subject-matter expert with them if they feel the discussion may range outside their sphere of knowledge.

They should try to capture the must-haves and weed out the nice-to-haves.

Once they have finished the requirement discussion and the request seems to be in line with the company's willingness to pursue the business, they should ask the closing question:

"If we commit to doing this, will you commit to the contract?"

Assuming they are the only vendor involved, they must stay in the meeting as long as it takes to get a yes to that question. They should be reluctant to proceed in the development of the nonstandard solution without a yes. If the customer says yes to the question, write it down in a letter of understanding. If the customer says, "Well, we have to see your proposal first," they then must make a judgment call whether to proceed.

Even if there are other vendors involved it doesn't hurt to ask the same question, but expect that the customer will say, "There are other firms to whom we are presenting the same requirement, so we can't commit without looking at everyone's final offer."

Pull the Team Together Again

Now come up with the best solution. As a team define exactly how you plan to solve the problem to the customer's specifications. Put together a clear and complete statement of work (SOW). Share the SOW with the customer. Confirm that what you intend to do is what the customer really wants.

Create an Execution Plan

Once the strategy and solution is set, your team needs to determine how they will execute. Be specific and thorough with the tasks to be performed and who is responsible to perform them. Think the implementation through all the way to the end.

Design a Process to Fix Problems

Nonstandard solutions by their nature create nonstandard follow-up problems.

Lin's company probably has a process to deal with customer problems that arise from the use of standard products, services, or contracts. Lin's team will need to augment this process to accommodate problems that may arise from the nonstandard solution. She and Saul must be prepared to adapt the process on the fly because it is difficult to anticipate all the potential problems that may arise when they provide a customer with a nonstandard solution.

Win, lose, or no-decision, Lin must finish the attempt to solve the major road-block with a final coaching session. By this point there should really be some healthy give-and-take between the two. Thank Saul for his efforts, complement him where deserved it, reiterate constructive criticism made throughout the process, and take his feedback to heart.

Conclude the coaching by having him share the assault on the roadblock at your next sales-unit meeting. It's good training, and it closes the coaching loop.

LESSONS

The major lesson of this problem is that it takes your coaching capabilities to its limits. You find yourself coaching ideas and processes you never coached before. You build a relationship with your account manager far beyond what you could do in mainstream coaching scenarios.

You learn a lot about yourself and your leadership and management predispositions, because the major roadblock is stressful.

The exercise enables you to see your salespeople's creativity and problem-solving skills as you've never seen them before. Of course, the reverse is also true.

On the business side, you also learn a lot about your business and everyone on your team. Handling of major roadblocks expands the firm's frontiers of probabilities, as well as your frontiers of coaching.

7–6 THE PROBLEM:

*Your suggestions for improvement don't match
your salespeople's style.*

THE STORY

"I don't think that works for me," Lorraine said, as she and her district manager got back in the car. "Vic," she continued, "you keep telling me to ask for commitments, but that's not me.""And another thing," she went on, "I didn't forget that application. I knew it wasn't important. If I'm going to be successful I have to sell my way, not yours," she concluded.

Vic knew that the call had not gone well, and there was little likelihood they would win the business. It seemed that every time he and Lorraine worked together there were these philosophical battles. His suggestions were taken as an affront or a challenge.

As they drove away, Lorraine continued, "If we don't get this order, it's because our price was too high." With that, Vic's eyes rolled.

Drumming his notebook he thought to himself, what am I going to do.

TEMPTATIONS

One key to effective coaching is in the way sales managers deal with conflict, but those conflicts will often stretch your limits and breed foolhardy temptations.

Scream

"What's the matter with you, for cryin' out loud. What are you so darn defensive about? Lighten up and listen. I'm only trying to help lift you out of mediocrity."

Threat

"Just remember this lost order when it comes time for your appraisal and salary review."

Withdraw

"That's it! I've had it. She can grapple on her own. It's the last suggestion I'll make."

It's easy to get frustrated when you can't seem to connect with an employee, especially one who impresses you with her potential.

What Happened Here . . . ?

Lorraine and Vic are two different people, seemingly incompatible. Either or both may also be obstinate.

Disagreements between sales managers and reps can stem from differences in opinions about techniques, about selling philosophy, about the customer situation, about the market, about what works, about values, depth of training, experience, age, sex, background, education, and on and on. Differences are to be expected.

Lorraine may have a hard time accepting suggestions. She may be super-touchy. Some people are like that. Some salespeople are not as open to ideas as others.

Lorraine may have been unduly influenced by something she read in a book or a magazine, heard at a seminar, or heard from a peer or close friend with sales experience.

Vic's suggestions could be inappropriate, as much as he doesn't think so. Vic has to be man enough to recant his suggestions if he hears any arguments to the contrary. One sign of a good manager is flexibility in the face of employee suggestions and arguments.

Perhaps Vic threw up someone else's name as a point of comparison, a person for which Lorraine has little or no respect.

Vic may not meet the image of what Lorraine expects in a sales manager. Maybe she doesn't respect Vic because of his minimal experience, skills, knowledge, or approach. She may have worked for a dynamite coach in the past, and Vic doesn't measure up.

Sales is a very style-oriented profession. Salespeople are simultaneously entrepreneurial and proud and comfortable with their largely self-developed sales approaches. Introducing new ideas is almost always a challenge.

When differences are not resolved they often fester and lead to performance degradation and further tension and strife. Vic's got to leap on this.

Options

The first question you have to answer is, is Lorraine worth the effort? It sounds as if she is. If she was a poor performer, she has little right to argue, and this becomes a very different problem.

Vic has only one option, and that is to find a way to impart ideas and strengthen Lorraine's performance.

As Lorraine's manager he has to figure out if this is an employee with whom he has a chemistry problem, one who is plain stubborn, or one who is touchy. Vic needs to take the same steps and that is to find creative ways to get his suggestions for improvement across.

Possible Actions

Step back a minute from this coaching confrontation rather than continuing to frustrate yourself.

You have a responsibility to develop Lorraine, and she has a responsibility to listen and to develop herself. You may have to help her understand that basic fact as you go forward.

Explore

Have a talk with Lorraine's previous manager, if he or she is available, to gain insights into Lorraine's style and behaviors. Look at her relationships with other people and see if you can discern a preference for certain types of relationships or communications. Observe how she reacts to advice from other people.

Look for other signs of distress or problems that may be spilling over into work activities. Her reactions to suggestions and coaching could stem from other issues. Your understanding and sensitivity will be appreciated.

Consider how Lorraine reacted to change with other matters in the business, or obtain impressions from her training instructors. Look for lessons anywhere you can.

Look in the Mirror

There are two sides to every story, so it's worthwhile to investigate your own propensities. How do you measure up with these managing and coaching questions?

- How have *you* reacted to suggestions from other employees, from Lorraine, and from your boss? Do *you* get defensive yourself?
- What is your reputation within the sales unit as a coach? Do other people come to you?
- Do you value creativity, diversity, and change, and do your people know that?
- How do you present ideas and corrective action to your other employees? Are you creative and adaptable, or dull and repetitive?
- Do you have a tendency to take over in sales calls, making your people feel worthless?
- Do you have a reputation for overcontrolling every detail of the sales unit's activities?
- Are you trying to clone yourself?
- Are your coaching priorities with Lorraine in order? Are you attacking the biggest and most important issues, or are you unnecessarily nit-picking details?
- Are you inconsistent, counseling on a point at one time and neglecting it at other times?
- Do you compliment and recognize your people for things they do correctly?

If you're guilty of any shortcomings, you might want to correct yourself before launching into a counseling session with Lorraine.

Coaching is like making a sales call. Just as you try to juxtapose and modify your sales style to fit a customer's style and situation, you need to juxtapose and modify your coaching to fit your employee's style. You have to balance the fact that you're the coach who you are with the need to be flexible. Loosen up and bend a little without sacrificing the message.

Time to talk

Schedule a one-on-one to talk about what you perceive as an unhealthy coach-sales rep relationship. Make it clear this discussion is purely for Lorraine's benefit. Reinforce what your role is. She may be perceiving you as a policeman rather than a coach. You may want to share some of your thoughts on coaching or selling philosophy just as a way to get the conversation going. Your own admission of difficulty in accepting new ideas is another way to help this discussion.

You may want to start by asking Lorraine to identify her style. Don't be surprised if the response is thin and you need to probe. Ask Lorraine to share how she feels. It's not likely she will unload all her thoughts in this first meeting. Expect that you'll have to come back to this a second or third time. Ask her if there is a better way for you to get ideas across, a way that would be more helpful to her. Confirm your understanding of her comments.

Ask Lorraine to share any other reasons she has trouble with suggestions. Ask if it's you or the suggestions. Her performance is not at a level that warrants being argumentative. *She knows that, so don't rub it in.* These conflicts can be minimized if you take an approach that uses logic and facts, instead of personalities, emotion, and needles.

Accepting suggestions is sometimes painful because it causes people to change closely held opinions. Determining what is closely held may not be easy to identify by Lorraine's initial responses. Give it time. Share some things that you closely hold to help open the door.

In the end, describe to each other how you agree to give and receive suggestions. Travel with Lorraine as soon as you can after your discussion. It reinforces your role and the fact that you mean business.

Experiment with These Suggestion-giving Nuances

Modifying your context and language can provide huge dividends. Since suggestions most often come across as criticism, putting your suggestions in the context of one or more of these 21 techniques can strengthen your coaching.

1. *Suggestions from others*: "The company would suggest that you . . ."
2. *Reference the sales profession*: "Everything you read in the literature points to a . . . approach."
3. *Fear*: "I would caution . . . based on what I've seen in similar situations."
4. *Alternatives*: "I would recommend . . . or . . . in that type of situation."
5. *Humility*: "I know I couldn't pull . . . off, but perhaps you can."
6. *Cause thinking*: "What other approaches did you think about before you did . . . ?"

7. *Emotion*: "How do you think the prospect <u>felt</u> when you said . . . ?"

8. *Power*: "If our president had been there, what do you think <u>he would</u> have said in response to . . . ?"

9. *Training*: "Did they show you the movie on . . . <u>at sales school</u> last year?"

10. *Paint a picture*: "What would the situation <u>look like</u> if you had tried . . ."

11. *Challenge*: "How could <u>you</u> modify the . . . concept to fit your style for this call?"

12. *Prove it to yourself*: "<u>Experiment</u> with . . . in a few situations and see how it fits your style."

13. *Ask for permission*: "<u>May I</u> share a technique I saw used at . . . with good result?"

14. *Play a game*: "Would you like <u>a hint</u> that you might find beneficial?"

15. *Blend*: "Why don't you <u>tie</u> . . . to . . . which you already do very well?"

16. *Fact*: "Marketing <u>research data</u> shows that 55 percent of people prefer . . . approach."

17. *Authorship*: " . . . is a new approach that <u>someone in our unit</u> needs to lead and refine. Would you like to write it up?"

18. *Reference*: "I once saw <u>a star salesperson</u> named . . . do . . . , and it was very effective."

19. *Credible source*: "I heard . . . at <u>a Miller Heiman seminar</u> that works well."

20. *Mystery*: "If you did . . . , <u>I wonder</u> what would happen?"

21. *Knock-out*: "Competition <u>wouldn't be able</u> to respond to . . . if you . . ."

The next time you get together with your sales-manager peers, see if you can add to this suggestion-giving list. It's a good bet you will.

Execution

Consider *when* you make suggestions and *where* you make suggestions. The sooner after the sales effort the better, but sometimes a brief cool-down to get settled works best. It depends on the rep and the situation. A place that permits you both to concentrate, take notes, and go eyeball-to-eyeball usually works best. And again, come at the coaching with facts, not emotion.

Support Lorraine's own style and give her credit when her approaches work.

Look for other ways, such as diagrams or role-playing, to get your suggestions across besides simply trying to talk things out.

Always ask Lorraine if she understands the suggestions. Understanding is critical. If so, move forward. If not, explore it. Don't ask if she is comfortable with suggestions. Comfort is impossible and invites contention. Comfort comes only after repeated usage of a technique.

Offer to send Lorraine to a seminar or school, suggest she work with other reps, share some articles or a book, or direct her to someone else who can help her. A manager who makes these alternate suggestions exhibits self-confidence in himself and confidence in his employee.

LESSONS

Spend as much time with your people as possible, getting to know them personally and letting them get to know you personally. Mutual understanding helps take the edge off coaching.

Where there are shared values there is more apt to be listening on matters of coaching and counseling. Find something shared with which to connect. The more connections you can create with your people the easier it is to coach.

Differences of opinion should be constructive in coaching situations. You don't want to be unyielding and neither do you want to be a wimp, but your job *is* to coach in the face of differences of opinion. Balance and judgment come into play.

Respect the differences and diversity of your staff's approach to their work, always pressing for improvement within the context of their approaches and natural inclinations. People will change and grow if they sense esteem for their ideas and sales style. Your relationship with your employees will grow, and the sales unit's performance will improve.

7–7 THE PROBLEM:

You witness an unsatisfactory presentation.

THE STORY

Vern was sitting in the back of the conference room while one of his salespeople, Nelson, was engrossed in giving a computer-based presentation. Vern's fists were clenched and his stomach was beginning to churn because of what he was seeing and hearing.

This is not good, he thought to himself. It doesn't feel good.

The attendees were throwing curves at Nelson, and they were starting to flash ominous glances at each other. The atmosphere in the room was just not right. Vern felt as if he were watching a 1957 B movie.

Damn, he thought to himself as it continued, this is getting out of control. I've got to do something.

TEMPTATIONS

When you are in the middle of a sales event and it is going poorly there is no shortage of foolish temptations.

Grit your teeth
"Wait till I get a hold of this guy when this is over. He's performing like a donkey."

Trivial chatter

"I'm going to get another coffee. Anyone else want one? How about a donut? A bagel?"

Save yourself

"Thank you, Nelson. Why don't I take it from here. You'll have to excuse Nelson, ladies and gentlemen. I assure you that I can answer your questions."

Remember that Robert Louis Stevenson said, "Politics is the only profession for which no preparation is thought necessary." In spite of the enormous amount written and preached on effective presentations and necessary preparation, it is amazing how many salespeople still think of themselves as silver-tongued politicians.

WHAT HAPPENED HERE . . . ?

Your sales effort is self-destructing, and you are exasperated.

Nelson may have assumed that the deal was a "slam dunk" and didn't put everything into this presentation that should have been put into it. Maybe he didn't even practice it.

Both Nelson and Vern could have been surprised with new people in the meeting on the customer's side, and the unexpected people asked some unexpected questions.

Competition may have briefed their allies at this company on what questions to ask, and both Nelson and Vern were insidiously ambushed.

Nelson possibly doesn't understand the audience. He may not have done sufficient homework in building understanding of the customer's needs, motivations, worries, concerns, and priorities, and therefore did not anticipate questions and issues.

There likely was no confirmation or review of the agenda with the customer prior to the presentation.

Nelson may be disorganized in his delivery. Nothing will turn an audience off quicker than poor structure and execution.

Perhaps Vern didn't help Nelson get ready for this presentation, or review it, because he begged off with other work. If so, he has himself to blame for this predicament.

The customer could have minimized the scope of the meeting and told Nelson it was a casual meeting or not to worry about it. As it turned out, the meeting was more important and comprehensive than Nelson was told it would be. It happens all the time.

OPTIONS

In reality, Vern may have two problems here, the presentation situation and his sales rep's performance. His first priority is the audience. He can deal with Nelson later.

He has three obvious options with the presentation.

1. *Call time out.* Interrupt, reassess the audience, and take a drastically different tack assuming you have the information and materials to present.
2. *Stop it cold.* Vern could ask for another shot and fall back and regroup if it is mutually agreed that the discussion is clearly beyond what they came prepared to discuss and the audience is sincerely interested in the offerings.
3. *Correct and coach on the fly.* This happens in all presentations, but there are good and bad ways to execute.

POSSIBLE ACTIONS

The customer is the first to know that a presentation is not going well. Customers have seen good presentations and bad ones. The customer also understands their own problem—the one you are trying to solve—and can sense more quickly than anyone if your response is on track.

The rep is likely the second party in the room that knows the situation is not going well, because he knows the people. But in the rep's case, knowing and doing something about it in front of the boss can be frightening. There is probably a tug-of-war going on in Nelson's mind.

By the time Vern picks up the vibes, the negative dynamics are already underway.

Look Out for Your Own Behavior

Act as a leader. The customer will be conscious of how you treat your rep and the situation. That treatment sends a message about you and your company. If you are perceived as a professional, that perception alone can help the customer overlook the gaffes of the presentation.

When and if the time comes, take the blame for what is happening. You help your personal credibility, your company's credibility, and you protect Nelson, with this admission.

Reality

All presentations have high points and low points. Don't prematurely rush to stop or correct a situation that will correct itself. Your own experience with the personnel on your presentation team, other presentations in which you have participated, the perceived strength of your products and services, and the relationship with this particular audience will be your best guide.

Where Are You?

When during the presentation did you get the impression that things were unsatisfactory? Timing is everything. *Speed of response sends a strong message that you're listening and that you understand the audience, but not so fast that you appear to lack confidence in your rep.* In general, the closer your interjections are to the beginning, the more positive impact you can have on the presenter and the audience. A good rule of thumb is to be quick and soft at the beginning, so as not to be disruptive; but deliberately slower and more direct the further you go. Slow deliberation communicates thoughtfulness. Directness implies your comprehension.

What Is Unsatisfactory About This Presentation?

Think about what is wrong. Don't leap to conclusions. What *you* perceive as unsatisfactory may not be unsatisfactory to the customer.

- Is it Nelson's delivery and presentation skills? If it is, you can coach on the fly to some extent. Shifts in media usage, from the laptop to chartpads, or from the chalkboard to statistics in the proposal, from lecture to interaction, or from overheads to handouts, is a way to reignite interest.

- Is it content, the concepts, and your solutions? If it is, your extensive knowledge of your products and services should enable you to correct on the fly.

- Is it the presentation materials? If it is, you'll probably never know it, unless you get feedback from the audience at the end. However, comments about the difficulty to see or read, or numerous questions seeking amplifying information are signals. Correction is difficult or impossible.

- Is it the lack of vigorous give-and-take and participation? If it is, you can ask questions, take a survey, seek opinions, share a philosophy, or query about attitudes.

- Is it the atmosphere—the comfort and chemistry? If it is, encouraging conversation, acting less formal, using anecdotes and stories, injecting humor, and providing physical movement can liven things up.

- Is it a combination of all these factors? This is the most likely scenario, and you'll need bits and pieces of all the previous suggestions and your own ability to think on your feet.

Decision Time

OPTION 1: CALL TIME OUT.   This is a bold option. Interrupt."Excuse me, but I feel a little as if I am watching a B movie here."Establish why you feel that way and why you feel your message is not coming across. Expand on why and what you feel. The customer will respect your candor.

Probe for consensus. If the audience, either politely or firmly, concurs with your feelings say again that you sensed the same thing and *offer a solution that relates to what is unsatisfactory*. If the audience does not concur with your feelings, their feedback will provide Nelson and yourself with renewed direction. Watch the body language of the audience, look them in the eye, and measure their words to get a sense of the sincerity of the feedback.

Be careful of your timing, because you can use this option effectively only *once*.

OPTION 2: STOP IT COLD.   This is highly unusual and is reasonable only when you have a very long and strong relationship characterized by patience and understanding. For this option to be viable, both parties understand that they intend to work together but don't want to waste any more time.

Call it off and ask for the privilege to reconvene.

OPTION 3: CORRECT AND COACH ON THE FLY.   One aspect of this option begins with taking the measure of the audience from time to time by asking for feedback. The place to ask the first question is right at the beginning after you review the agenda. For example, "Does this accurately reflect our previous discussions?"

Ask again after reviewing the audiences situation. "Are we on track?" or "Have we nailed it?"

Ask again after presenting your alternatives and solution. "What do you think?" or "Are we headed in the right direction?"

Ask again after reviewing your benefits. "Everybody comfortable with this so far?"

Ask again after showing how you will work with the customer to ensure a smooth transition to your product or services. "Do we agree on the solution?" or "On target?"

The technique creates respect. This progressive testing also serves to set the stage to ask for the audience's commitment and business.

The second aspect of this option is correcting and coaching based on your own observations. You do this with *subtle* participation.

- Ask Nelson if you can personally emphasize a point. Use your comment as an *entrée to set the stage* for the rep for the next item on the agenda.
- Execute one small element, or answer one question *in textbook fashion* as an example, hoping that Nelson picks up on your illustration.
- Transfer attention from the presentation to the customer by *expansive probing for understanding*. Their answers will provide renewed direction.
- Suggest *mutual* follow-up actions as the presentation proceeds. The audience's concurrence or deference will confirm that they are with you or against you.
- Make a *camouflaged statement* to the rep that reminds him of something from your presentation practice session. Nelson should quickly pick up on your tip.
- Make a suggestion to the rep to do something or review something. For example, "Nelson, could you please go back and review point A?"
- Play customer by asking leading questions that prompt the sales rep to provide information that is helpful to the customer. For example, say, "Nelson, if the customer wanted to perform their own service, how would they do that?"
- Ask another member of your team to pinch-hit on a specific presentation point. For example, say, "Flo, can you address the next point?" Then, turning to the audience, add, "Flo is our systems engineer who designed this element."
- Change the subject to what *the customer* wants it to be. Letting the customer take control at key junctures can help the presentation flow.

Correcting and coaching on the fly *can* get intrusive. However, if you let the audience know from the beginning that several people on your team will be participating, they will never know what is going on.

Caution

At some point Vern's participation can turn this presentation into *his* presentation rather than Nelson's presentation or the company's presentation. Don't do it.

After-the-fact Counseling

Execute a constructive debriefing with Nelson and the rest of your presentation team. Put policies into place that minimize the potential of this problem ever happening again.

LESSONS

Planning and preparation will always be the foundation of successful presentations. Put worst-case scenarios and potential objections in your planning and practice sessions and include role definition, deciding on who will do what if something goes awry. And make sure everyone understands what outcome you want from the presentation.

Start every presentation with a review of the agenda, ensuring that the customer's requirements and expectations are being addressed and asking if there are other items that need to be covered.

Astute handling of unsatisfactory situations will be perceived by customers as an expression of your adaptability, confidence, and professionalism. You set an outstanding example for your people in the process.

7–8 THE PROBLEM:

Transitioning your salespeople from direct sales work to supporting sales partners is proving to be difficult.

THE STORY

Chet's company recently decided to sell after-market parts and services through wholesale distributors and independent sales agencies. The expense of maintaining a sales force, and of maintaining sales offices, had become burdensome.

Several people in Chet's downsized sales force had been chosen to manage and support the new sales-partner network. A few big accounts were being handled directly. As the national sales manager, Chet assigned salespeople who were his best performers into the sales-partner field-support group. Two of them, George and Stan, have been having trouble with the transition.

What Chet was hearing included, "These people aren't giving any attention to our products," "They are not recommending the right items," "They won't take me on sales calls," "The won't give me a forecast," and "They don't want me to know what they're doing."

This had been going on for a couple of months, and Chet was getting exasperated.

TEMPTATIONS

Sales-channel transitions are not easy. With careful planning and implementation you won't have to face these temptations.

Cajole them

"Come on, guys, I know you two heavy-hitters can do it. Go get 'em for ol' Chet."

Yell and scream

"For cryin' out loud . . . quit bellyaching, and get out there and do your job, you turkeys!"

Buy in

"You know, I think you guys may be right. I'll take this issue upstairs."

A few lines from an old Irving Berlin song, "Must you dance every dance with the same fortunate man? You have danced with him since the music began. Won't you change partners and dance with me?" is a better refrain to adopt.

WHAT HAPPENED HERE . . . ?

Two successful salesmen have given you several good years of selling. And your company, like many, has decided to change its sales channels in an attempt to reduce costs, maintain market share, penetrate new markets, take advantage of new technologies, and do a better job of satisfying its customers. At the same time, many industrial buyers and consumers now prefer buying through local dealers, sales agencies, warehouse clubs, by direct mail, by phone, on-line, or through a host of other innovative formats. Sales channels are proliferating, and many sales professionals are being caught by surprise with the shifts. Personal selling is becoming more targeted and niche-driven.

Sales partners, which include wholesale distributors, dealers, value-added resellers, retailers, mass merchandisers, independent sales agencies, brokers, and others are *not* customers. Nor are they hired guns. A sales partner is a *partner* in the sense of the two enterprises working in a highly collaborative relationship to *jointly* satisfy end-user customers, and both grow and profit in the process. It demands teamwork. It's certainly different from selling direct.

George and Stan—or maybe Chet—may not understand the difference between customers and sales partners.

Perhaps Chet, George, and Stan do not understand the different needs of partners and the roles that different sales-channel members require of one another. The three of them may be doing the wrong things. Not all salespeople and managers can make the shift and do it well. Chet may have a couple of salesmen whose motivation and skills may not match what the job requires. Are the wrong people in this slot or is it time for them to learn a new dance?

OPTIONS

First, you need an answer to these two questions:

Can George and Stan *do* this work?

Do they *want* to do the work? If the answer to both questions is yes, then your only option is to train George and Stan to work with your distributors and reps.

If the answer to either or both of those questions is no, then you have these three options.

1. Place George and Stan (providing there are slots and relocation is not an issue) back in a direct-sales role servicing some of those major accounts.
2. Move both of them into other sales or marketing positions if there is a capabilities match.
3. Finally, you may be faced with the option of terminating George and Stan.

POSSIBLE ACTIONS

The Specs for the Job

There are three specs to think about when addressing the option questions. Do your people have the *innate motivation* to work with partners, are they *coaches*, and do they possess in-depth business *knowledge*?

THE MOTIVATION.   Salespeople who are intense competitors, who must experience the thrill of winning, who are focused on themselves, or who must beat other people will be frustrated if they have to stand and watch sales partners experience those thrills. Some salespeople have trouble dealing with the loss of control, loss of recognition, loss of direct customer contact, loss of conquest, loss of customer ownership, and loss of direct customer relationships.

Salespeople who are motivated by service to others, problem solving, and relationship and partnership building, are usually best suited to sales partner support. Such salespeople are often characterized as "farmers" because they like to stay close to their buyers and watch them grow. These people take the time to find answers and solutions, are constantly alert to ideas for the partner's benefit, and follow up on everything. Salespeople who are motivated by personal accomplishment are also good at supporting sales partners because they enjoy seeing other people succeed. These people are comfortable coaching and providing advice.

THE COACHING ROLE. A salesperson who calls on a sales partner is a *coach*, first and foremost. Just as in sports, your salesperson is meant to be on the sidelines supporting, teaching, prompting, providing feedback, encouraging, yelling, whatever else, to help that sales partner do the best possible job. Coaching also implies the ability to sell ideas and counsel business processes at the highest level of the sales partner. Selling is the *sales partner's* prime responsibility—that's why you have him or her in the first place. The sales partner is the *player*. If you and your people can visualize, internalize, and execute the coach/player analogy, you are all a long way toward working well with sales partners. The best relationships between a coach and a player (or a supplier and a sales partner) are characterized by candor, a willingness to listen, mutual respect, and a commitment to each other. Chet must make an assessment. Can George and Stan be coaches? Just as great players don't necessarily make great coaches, great salespeople don't necessarily make great sales-partner managers.

THE KNOWLEDGE AND SKILLS. The final requisite is the highest level of product, service, and technical knowledge, sales and marketing acumen, general business knowledge, and the ability to communicate that knowledge. Your sales-partner managers need to be businesspeople first, not just simple messengers of marketing and sales tips and product specs.

There is certainly a sales component to working with sales partners, but the service and support component of the job most often outweigh it. Sales managers and salespeople who understand these three key differences and adapt their dance style will succeed.

Coach the Front Office

Even though this problem deals with Chet's salespeople, it is important to recognize that everyone in Chet's firm who will be dealing with the sales partners must be trained to work with partners. For example, credit and customer service. There are two key parts to that training.

One, Chet must build an understanding in the inside staff of how partners work and what they value. He can perform that training himself, or he can have a couple of the partners come in and help him.

Two, Chet should provide a refresher in products, services, manufacturing processes, technologies, applications, and other matters that are important to the partners. Partners want crisper, quicker, more thorough answers when they deal with inside staff.

Coach the Coaches

Start with some basic business training on finance, marketing, and business management so your people can appreciate the partners' business and priorities. Sales partners are businesspeople.

Partners often work in a different way from the way Chet's salespeople did it, so no one should expect them to do it "our way." Partners will not act like employees. George and Stan must understand that.

YOUR EXPECTATIONS.   Here's what Chet, George, Stan, and the rest of Chet's team should expect from sales partners:

- Detailed knowledge of markets, customers, and contacts.
- Guidance and suggestions on how to improve their joint marketing and sales efforts.
- Maintenance of jointly agreed upon inventory levels.
- Adding value and services to products, if that is part of the partners' business.
- Responses to legitimate inquiries for information, but not the reporting bureaucracy to which the old direct sales organization was accustomed.
- A fair share of sales and marketing time commensurate with the partners' other principals.
- Execution of special promotions.
- Assistance in collection and administrative problems, if appropriate.
- Relationships that are often closer and more informal than that with customers.
- A well-managed business with which they can be proud to be associated.

THE SALES PARTNER'S EXPECTATIONS.   It goes without saying that partners demand quality products and services offering fair commissions or margins.

Chet's sales-support programs should not stop because partners still need contact and help, but they may need it in other forms and formats. George and Stan shouldn't be surprised if there is a request for increased support in certain areas because partners are highly focused marketers. Expectations will vary slightly, but here are some priorities:

- First, partners expect integrity of word and action and professionalism in all matters from Chet, George, Stan, and the rest of the staff.
- They expect that Chet will do a superb marketing job with promotion and advertising to help pull the product through the sales channel.
- They expect that George and Stan will work hard to build an understanding of the partner's business, goals, and strategies.
- Training on products, services, and technology is a major expectation. Partners need to understand offerings in great depth because the partner's customers expect it. They also need competitive insights and information.

- Partners expect Chet to make an investment in marketing and sales-communications technology in order to improve efficiencies and cut costs.

- Many could use and would appreciate George's and Stan's marketing- and sales-planning expertise.

- Partners are interested in ideas to improve their own sales productivity and thus would have an open ear to George's and Stan's suggestions.

- Partners are interested in actions that both firms can take, independently or together, to improve responsiveness to end-user customers.

- The communications flow is expected to be clear, timely, simplified, and documented.

- Partners expect a great attitude, willing backup sales support, an ear for their ideas and criticism, decisive steps to solve problems, and a spirit of partnership.

Both Chet and his partners are likely to have additional expectations, all of which must be regularly communicated and evaluated. This point cannot be overemphasized.

BEST PRACTICES.   Best practices are proven winners, activities that guarantee mutual success. They vary from industry to industry. Chet and his people must establish a best-practices model for their use and the partners' use. Some possible practices include the following:

- George and Stan must provide ideas and suggest successful strategies that other partners are using, including application tips, selling and negotiating suggestions, and answers to objections. (Assuming a noncompetitive relationship between partners.)

- George and Stan could help the partners' sales forces design prospecting and retention programs.

- They should jointly discuss how value-added services may help differentiate both parties.

- Chet's staff must be responsive to a fault. They should fall all over themselves getting information and answers to partners.

- Chet should conduct regular surveys of his partners to make sure he understands their needs.

- They should jointly look for ways to improve the to-market processes up and down the sales channel.

- Chet must take advantage of the partners' detailed understanding of the customer base by building a database for their joint marketing benefit.

- Chet should ensure that he has an early-warning process of industry and economic conditions that he can pass on to the partners.

- Both parties should participate in industry associations. The learning and relationships can be invaluable. Taking an active role provides a bigger return on investment.

- Chet should ask his sales partners to come and speak to his sales organization and other supporting business functions. Most are happy to discuss their business and their roles.

- Chet should consider modifying George and Stan's compensation plans to more adequately reflect their work. A higher percentage of salary, combined with both short- and long-range incentives based on business measurements, not just sales revenue, can work well.

Be Careful

Redundancies occur when suppliers consciously or unconsciously do the same work as the sales partner. Redundancies are wasted costs that Chet should work hard to identify and eliminate.

Some sales partners are large, very sophisticated enterprises who are quite competent on their own and may not take kindly to George and Stan coaching them on how to do everything. Their own good judgment and open dialogue will tell them how to best work together.

LESSONS

Sales-partner managers, or those who sell to and support sales partners, must be able to get their psychic rewards through the results of others.

If you're going through any channel changes think about the knowledge and skills required of your people before you launch the program. Factor your people's training needs into your implementation plans. Don't assume that everyone can easily learn the new dance steps.

When hiring people for this job, look for those who have a strong motivation to coach, to solve problems, and to provide service. Relationship skills are critical.

Remember that compensation packages may need to be different for sales-partner managers.

7–9 THE PROBLEM:

Training for your international salespeople and sales partners is inadequate.

THE STORY

"Fix it, Brady," Jake, the VP of sales and marketing sternly said.

The "it" that Jake was referring to was last quarter's international sales results and the evaluations of the recently concluded training program for the Europe-Africa region.

Brady was the director of sales and had led the recently concluded three-day training meeting that included country managers, sales engineers, and independent reps from the region.

"We've been in the global arena only a couple years, and it *is* better . . .", Brady started.

"Brady, I don't care. We're an international business now," Jake continued. "The Asia-Pacific region meeting is six months away. I'd like to know how you plan to improve this."

"We'll definitely improve," Brady said as he walked out, not really knowing how.

TEMPTATIONS

It always seems as if it's someone else's fault in these situations. A stiff neck and a wounded ego can be obstacles.

Self-satisfaction

"Frankly, I thought it was a great session considering what I had to work with."

Contempt

"Our stuff is complex, and I don't know if those people will ever catch on. I guess we'll really have to dumb-it-down for the next crowd."

Find scapegoats

"The product managers did a terrible job. They screwed up the whole meeting."

Training cross-cultural sales teams is becoming the norm. It's been a global market for years, and the trend will accelerate.

WHAT HAPPENED HERE . . . ?

The results of training sessions are binary. You either hit a home run, or you strike out. Brady went down swinging. (A bad idiom to use, since we're talking about international audiences.)

The typical training bugaboos of poor planning, poor preparation, and insufficient practice may have been compounded by using speakers and instructors not cut out for training this audience.

The expectations may not be aligned. Brady may have focused on his agenda, an inside-out approach, rather than concerning himself with the participants' needs, an outside-in approach.

Brady may have simply carbon copied the program he uses for U.S. audiences believing naively that it would be sufficient.

Brady's program may have been shallow and filled with sizzle and hype, not containing the meat that his offshore colleagues demand.

And while he may not admit it, Brady may be new to international sales and marketing and may have been a little intimidated.

OPTIONS

Brady has two options to resolve this problem.

1. He can patch up his current training program. Other priorities and limited resources may not permit anything else.
2. He can start with a clean slate to build a world-class training program. It takes time, but is worth the effort.

On the execution side, he also has two options.

1. He could decide not to bother anyone else, try to be a super-hero, and show Jake he can pull it off.
2. He can take advantage of the feedback and additional input of people from the recent session. He can then get key players from sales, marketing, and other functions involved and make the next session a team effort.

POSSIBLE ACTIONS

Attitude is the starting point to solving this problem. Brady must have a deep desire to serve, be flexible, and be responsive because he has a cross-cultural audience.

When you are training your international reps and sales partners—either home or abroad—you are a linguistic host, a culture host, and a subject-matter host. Brady's reps and partners are linguistic guests, culture guests, and subject-matter guests. The attitude, common sense, and respect that accompany host-guest relationships is the best guide.

What to Expect

Understanding the expectations of your colleagues from abroad and sharing them with your training team will help make preparation easier and more thorough.

- Get ready for a diverse group, in terms of background, language capability, and job responsibilities. In spite of your urgings, the people who ultimately come to the meeting may not be the right ones. The people being taught may not be the ones using the information directly. You may be training the trainers in some cases. It's okay.
- Expect to be tested on a wide variety of subjects—not just product and sales—because they tend to be very business-oriented and are intellectually curious.
- Expect a broader spectrum of questions—very high level to basic level—because the group will not be as homogenous as a typical American audience.
- Expect to allocate more time because your delivery will be necessarily slower, and the audience will ask more questions.

- Expect less grousing and barbs. International audiences tend to be more civil. Be prepared to be pulled aside after hours for sensitive feedback or personal questions.
- Expect a work ethic beyond what is usual. Education is more rigorous in many other countries of the world. They are accustomed to more structure and longer hours. They know they are not attending for a holiday.
- Expect a more serious, sophisticated audience. Many will be more worldly then Brady is used to. They don't expect fluff.
- Expect that when the training day is over the same level of intensity may be devoted to after-hours socializing. Rest up.
- And finally, expect that world-class training sessions take a little cash.

Preparation

Query attendees well in advance, asking them about issues that they would like on the agenda and issues they would like to discuss with you personally. (Always cite samples when you make these requests.) Do this two or three times in advance of your session, maybe first by memo, then by phone, and then face-to-face if the opportunity arises.

Be careful not to schedule training that conflicts with their local holidays.

Send a memo well in advance of the training, detailing how the training will be executed. Inform them how they can prepare and on what subjects they will be asked to comment and contribute. Emphasize that last point to avoid embarrassment. Offer your preparation assistance.

A good rule with international-training preparation is to double the usual preparation time allocation.

Characteristics of Successful Global Trainers and Coaches

This is like finding needles in a haystack. When you boil it down to absolutely the barest minimums there are two absolute requisites: a culturally adaptive style and functional competence at the highest level.

When you look inside those two requisites you should find the following:

1. *Culturally adaptive style:* This is a person motivated to work cross-culturally, who is patient, able to mirror behaviors, and skilled in reading cross-cultural cues. The person possesses a "rubbery" mind, that is, not tradition-bound or a zealot. The trainer or speaker has a sense of humor, a strong imagination, and is able to open him or herself up. A person with an ethnic thread, that is, a bridge such as being a recent immigrant, able to speak a second language, from an ethnic neighborhood, being a second- or third-generation American, or someone who was a student or served as a volunteer overseas can better feel the audience. Historically conscious people with a track record working with diversity, sensitive to cultural differences, and sensitive to the values of every person make a good fit.

2. *Functional competence at high levels:* These are people held in high esteem and recognized as experts in your company. Their competence can relate to engineering, market-

ing, sales, finance, or whatever disciplines are priorities in your business. Microcompetence is especially valued. They should also be able to nurture relationships after the training is over.

If you have or can find more people who fit this dual-requisite mold, hold on to them dearly. They are more precious than gold.

Communication Skills

Possessing competence and communicating it are two different matters.

Trainers and speakers who are sensitive to their delivery are respected and can get away with errors, but communicators who are not sensitive will have their shortfalls greatly magnified. Here are an even-dozen guidelines that will help generate even-handed applause.

1. *Speed—slow:* Follow the excellent example of many TV newscasters.
2. *Vocabulary—simplify: Try saying "make worse" rather than "exacerbate," or say "take" rather than "confiscate."*
3. Degree of difficulty—simple, not simplistic: Use a model such as the style of *USA Today.*
4. *Enunciate—clearly:* It is amazing how opening your mouth and savoring each word makes a difference.
5. *Idioms—avoid:* Forget about "home runs" and "touchdowns."
6. *Jargon—minimize:* Even though you're in the same business, the special business jargon you use at home may not be used over there. At least explain it.
7. *Acronyms—avoid:* Acronyms in English are not the same as they are in another language.
8. *Complex sentences—avoid.* Use short sentences containing single thoughts, such as this one.
9. *Pauses—frequent:* Pauses give participants time to absorb what they see and hear and translate in their mind. As a result, chunky-style deliveries are best.
10. *Eye contact—almost constant:* Your eyes and facial expressions also convey the message, plus your lips are being watched. Don't engage in conversations with your flip charts.
11. *Expression—varied:* Frequent changes in tone, volume, inflection, and pace help keep attention and act to emphasize points.
12. *Gestures—absolutely:* Use appropriate nonverbals to make your point.

Have you ever stood in a line or been in a crowd and listened to a couple of people converse in another language? It sounds machine-gun fast, doesn't it? Bottle that feeling of helplessness and confusion and remember it the next time you're standing in front of a group of your international salespeople or sales partners.

Training Materials

Overemphasize the graphic element of presentations. Always use overheads, flip charts, chalkboards, or computer-aided presentations.

If the audience shares the same language, you may want to have your presentation materials translated, while speaking in English. The availability of foreign-language-software fonts for your PC remaps your keyboard and makes the task easy. Take-away copies in the home language will permit the materials to be more easily shared back home.

Execution

Think of the training session as a journey, letting the audience know where you are taking them. Understanding your destination will help them frame everything else you present. Advising participants of everyone's role and your rules of conduct are also important for an international audience.

- Create a comfortable, hospitable environment. Hospitality is a high priority in many other cultures.
- Don't ask the group for their expectations at the beginning of a session. They expect you to have done your homework to find out.
- Confirm understanding frequently. Ask questions in a preprogrammed fashion, going around the room in the same order, not at random. Randomness creates anxiety.
- Q & A sessions are good. Make sure you repeat and paraphrase their questions to ensure that you have understood the inquiry.
- Role-plays are not a good idea. The technique could lead some participants to lose face, and in many cultures that is bad.
- Brainstorming is not a good idea. It can be threatening to people from hierarchical cultures.
- Balance group and individual exercises. Some cultures are group oriented, others are not.
- Execute minisummaries frequently throughout the course of the training. It prevents losing participants. Also allow plenty of time for summaries at the end of each day.
- Get multiple layers of your management to participate. Titles, power, and authority are respected and valued in many cultures.
- Be consistent and predictable with your pace and flow. The audience appreciates a rhythm. International audiences don't react well to being jerked around.
- Alternate from leading to following. This action sends a message that you value their participation and home-grown techniques and that they are a part of the team. Feeling a part of the team is *very important* when you work 8,000 miles from headquarters.

- Be highly interactive. They didn't travel 8,000 miles to sit through a lecture.
- Create memories. The audience is not likely to be back for training for some time.

Keep the Lights on

Losing visual touch with an international audience is a no-no. Since nonverbal cues make up much of communication, avoid slide presentations, videos, movies, and any other media that don't let the audience see you or you see them.

Keep Things Moving

Pack your agenda with hands-on activities, demonstrations, games and contests, and tours of the factory floor, labs, and shops. Practice assembling your product and running software programs.

Keep Everyone Involved

The world is intellectually rich beyond imagination. Your audience is loaded with excellent ideas. It's your job to get them out. People everywhere are proud of their accomplishments and anxious to share local practices and techniques. Make *sharing* a major part of your international training culture. None of this off-handed, "Hey, has anyone got an idea" approach. Rather, put firm time on the agenda to discuss specifics.

Ask participants to come to your training sessions prepared to share stories, anecdotes, and techniques about specific items. Ask them to bring samples of their sales aids and collateral materials. Execute a show-and-tell as a part of training.

There is a wealth of creativity out there that is absolutely awesome.

LESSONS

Cultural competence is essential in international business. Cross-cultural and multilingual knowledge will be among the most highly valued sales management assets in the future.

Work cultures have their basis in social cultures. If you want to understand how your people work, start with experiencing their social cultures. Bring those lessons home and integrate them into your training.

7–10 THE PROBLEM:
Your expense budget for training was slashed.

THE STORY

It seems that it happens every year. The same wrenching edict comes down to cut training activities. The year is half over and the business is behind its revenue and profit projections. It's been a tough year to date. Everyone in the company has been hustling, but the results are not there. Ramon, a branch sales manager, has seen this before, and he hates to lose the training resources because he understands their value. No amount of arguing has changed corporate's position in the past, and his hunger for fighting this issue is just about gone.

"[Expletive], now what do I do," Ramon cursed to himself.

TEMPTATIONS

Training is like religion in sales. In spite of all the high and mighty homilies in regard to the value of training, it's just talk with many executives. The cutbacks are always frustrating.

Accept the decree docilely
"Oh, geez. That's too bad." or "Hmmm. I guess we'll have to do without."

Whine
"Aw, come on, reduce the cut a little. We can't sell if we don't train these folks. How do you expect me to keep my people? We're behind budget as it is. Hey, this is unfair. Are you listening?"

Use the decree to rationalize poor results
"Well, there is no way now that I can make plan this year either."

What often comes after these cost-reducing actions? More bad scenarios. It usually gets worse, doesn't it? It behooves Ramon to get busy.

What Happened Here ... ?

Business is bad and costs are cut. Everyone has been through it. Training is an historic target for the budget-cutter's knife. Ramon probably saw this coming. If he didn't, he has a more serious problem. Such decrees are seldom surprises.

There may have been other spending needs viewed as more critical. For example, funds for new product development, a big ad campaign, a trade show, or completion of a management-information system may have been voted as more important to the health of the business.

The top sales executive may have buckled under pressure and chose to save other expense alternatives.

Sales training may be perceived as boondoggles by management. Trips to exotic conference centers and use of overpriced training firms and consultants may have tainted executive viewpoints. Training dollars may have been used ineffectively or with poor controls. Maybe there isn't, and never was, a well-articulated training plan.

There may have been poor evaluations of past sales-training efforts.

Top management may have witnessed some past sales-training endeavors and not been impressed, or the decision makers may never have been involved in Ramon's training programs.

The human-resources function in Ramon's firm responsible for corporate-level training may be held in low esteem, be politically insignificant, or be led by a weak manager. The net effect could be a disparaging cloud over all training.

Options

The training budget was slashed, not eliminated. A very small percentage is left. At least Ramon has *something* to work with.

Understanding the health of the business, Ramon has four options.

1. He could make do with what he has left, prioritizing it appropriately. What he has left may be so small as to really lack effectiveness. In those cases, it is sometimes best not to spend anything. It's a judgment call.

2. It may be possible to reallocate funds he has available for other expense items. If it doesn't rub management the wrong way, or seriously hurt another aspect of the business, he could then beef up the training-expense line.

3. If he had a big training event or training program planned, he could ask for X dollars for that single priority. It may be possible to salvage a single program. However, asking for flexibility at times like this can create an impression in some executives that Ramon doesn't understand the severity of the situation.

4. He can get creative and reach into his bag of training tricks and plow ahead.

Finally, he may be able to blend the four options. At times like this a manager's true colors regarding training and development are on full display. Your people are watching.

Possible Actions

Don't let this get you down.

Communicate

Inform your people of the new expense constraints. Let them know that, one way or another, the sales unit *will continue* to train and develop itself. It's a good leadership move.

An implicit message to salespeople in cutting training expenses is a lack of company commitment to people and their development. By gritting your teeth and coming across with a we'll-work-our-way-around-this attitude you send the opposite message.

Plan

1. You should have a good personal sense of your sales unit's training needs. Prioritize based on what you have seen and felt.

2. Ask your sales unit for advice and ideas on what's needed and what should be done. Blend the inputs into your own list.

3. From your viewpoint, identify what specific *activities* are critical to the success of your people and the sales unit. In reality, there is a small handful of key sales activities that drive business—presentations, for example. In your business it may be another activity. Focus on the key activity, or activities, that *must* be taught or reinforced, and leave the rest for later. In other words, do a *few important things* well, rather than trying to do everything and diluting your scarce-to-nonexistent resources.

4. Reevaluate and prioritize what training you had planned for the rest of the year. Consider focusing on product knowledge because customer surveys habitually show that salespeople are delinquent in this area. Also, consider focusing on negotiation skills because it behooves you to keep your prices high at times like this. Additionally, consider focusing on customer-service skills and relationship-building skills because customer retention is more critical during bad times.

5. Use your own salespeople to help train, picking ones who have mastered certain skills or product lines and make them subject-matter champions.

6. Evaluate your other internal resources. Can you bring in some sharp folks from engineering, marketing, manufacturing, or information services to help teach some subjects?

7. Look for people or applications where you can get a multiplier of your bootstrap efforts. Look for situations where you can "train one-impact many." For example, training your dealer-management team who can then coach dealer sales staffs, or training product specialists who travel with many salespeople.

8. Take a look at how you're spending your free time—Saturdays, evenings, whenever—and commit to building some training activities during those times. If you are really serious about improving the skills of your people and improving your results this won't cause you any pain at all. Your efforts will not be lost on management.

9. Determine when the budget will be reinstated, if at all, or determine what conditions have to exist before it will be reinstated. This will help frame the depth and detail of your bootstrap training plan.

10. Have an ROI mentality. Conduct training that will generate the biggest return on investment. Think about *both* the dollars and the time invested.

Outsource with a Small "o"

With Ramon's limited funds, he could go to an outside training supplier *for a small piece* of training help. Many will encourage Ramon to take their whole package, arguing that their ideas and concepts will be diluted if they don't deliver a complete program, but astute ones will recognize that a small piece of pie today will position them for bigger pieces in the future.

A second approach is to team with an outside training provider. Assume some of the workload yourself and give some to them. Jointly create a program.

Innovate

Stir up some activities and materials that you've never tried before. Get the whole sales unit involved in generating ideas. The focus should be on no-cost or low-cost items.

- Role-play sales calls at meetings, one-on-one in your office, or while traveling.
- Make your own training videos with your own personal video camera.
- Create your own audio tapes.
- Bring in pro bono guest speakers such as professors, graduate students, retired executives, community leaders, friends with a special expertise, or supplier's salespeople.
- Convince some customers and clients to share their expertise. Barter their lecture or training time, if necessary, with incremental product and services.
- Try monthly sales-tip or product-tip bulletins, E-mail, and bulletin-board postings.
- Utilize informal round-table or what's-working conference calls to have your own people share success stories.
- Visit your local bookstore and invest in a couple of skills-related books.
- Subscribe to sales- or industry-specific magazines and newsletters. Many are great.
- Create your own PC-based instructional newsletter. Ask an inside staffer to do it.
- Give product, technology, or services tests and quizzes at every sales meeting.

- Freshen manuals and other training materials with new computer graphics. Look in the closet, back rooms, and old file cabinets for old programs that can be revitalized.

All these ideas, and more, should be summarized in a bootstrap training plan.

Execute

Make it a sales-unit policy that some level of training will be a part of *every* meeting, or training will be a stand-alone event at regular intervals. Consistency is critical.

Make the first events you execute no-cost actions. Spending *anything* right after a budget-cutting decree can only aggravate management and bring down further wrath.

If the timing is good, spend money *you don't have* and execute the training at the end of a fiscal period and pay the bills at the beginning of the next fiscal period. (But get approval first.)

Document and evaluate your bootstrap efforts. Share your plan and results with management and track every nickel you spend. Let them see that the cut hasn't stopped you.

Thoughts for Tomorrow

Here are ten points to help your future efforts, some of which may minimize future slashing.

1. Always execute *quality* training. Build a reputation for benchmark training activities. It's difficult to cut stuff that is held in high regard.

2. Utilize your training-expense budget quickly. Depreciation of training budgets is straight-line, degenerating to zero at the end of a fiscal period. Training dollars spent the beginning of January have 12 months to work as opposed to training dollars spent at the end of September that work for only three months. Get your money's worth.

3. Always evaluate the impact of your training investment. Tout evidence of your efforts, but don't ever make the mistake of attributing increased sales solely to training. It is not a credible statement. There are too many other variables at play.

4. Get the fiscal decision makers involved up to their eyeballs in your training from the get-go. Management doesn't easily slash activities that they godfathered, endorsed, or in which they participated.

5. Share all that you are doing with management. Share your training plans, needs surveys, training materials, evaluations, sales-partner-training requests, and customer comments or complaints that suggest specific training.

6. Management admires enterprising creativity and spunk in the face of hurdles and obstacles. If things get worse, at least you raised the value of your personal stock.

7. The innovative training programs you execute could have application *across the business*. Your leadership could ultimately lead to incremental corporate-wide funding.

8. Bootstrap training programs have the effect of bringing sales units closer together and becoming more of a team. The adversity and creativity fosters togetherness.

9. Don't execute training as a switch that gets turned on and off. Training should be hardwired "on." When the switch is "off," training is not visible, and what's out of sight is out of mind. And what's out of mind doesn't need a budget.

10. Do not make a budgetary mistake by bundling training expenditures. Big budgetary line items draw attention. Unbundle. Put training expenditures under meetings, conferences, seminars, printing, consultants, supplies, sales aids, sales collaterals, and of course, training.

LESSONS

Successfully handling this problem will demonstrate to you that a proactive, creative attitude can work wonders and can be just as effective in other aspects of your responsibilities.

Your leadership example sends a strong message of commitment to your people, and the commitment itself, often more than the actual training, can motivate them to heights of improved performance.

You create an impression as an adaptable businessperson—an impression that is not lost on top management.

You will likely beat others in coming out of the hole, you'll be better positioned for the next fiscal period, and you will feel better about yourself.

part eight

TROUBLESHOOTING PERSONNEL PROBLEMS

8–1 THE PROBLEM:

You are about to lose a superstar performer to an executive search effort.

THE STORY

The calm of a productive sales week was shattered on a Friday afternoon when Amanda walked into Willis's office and announced that she had been offered a sales-executive position at another company and has decided to resign. Willis could see that she had some difficulty delivering the bad news, but his groaning "Ohhh, noooo" could probably be heard all over the office building. She sat down and explained to Willis that one of those big search firms in San Francisco contacted her two months ago with this opportunity and that it was very attractive. She said that she had been offered an account executive position.

Willis's mind raced because Amanda had been his most prolific producer for two years running, and she had literally carried his sales unit through thick and thin.

TEMPTATIONS

Get a hold of yourself. This stuff happens, especially in today's climate of reduced loyalty and increased mobility. Don't let yourself be pulled into one of these seducing traps.

Anger

"How can you leave after all I have done for you?"—or—"OK, if that is how you want it, pack up your desk and be gone by 4:00 P.M. today!"

Challenge

"Have you thought this impetuous move out? I can't believe you're leaving us for that cutthroat company."

Counter-offer

"If you stay I will give you a 25 percent bonus, and I'll promote you to a similar position."

It is difficult not to overreact when you are about to lose one of your best performers. Keep in mind, however, that quick actions or reactions that do not fit into an overall plan will only hurt you personally and complicate any effort to save Amanda.

What Happened Here . . . ?

Well, first of all, your number-one performer just resigned and *you were surprised.*

Willis must ask himself if he is spending enough time with *all* of his people. Sometimes managers focus on the poorer performers and let their best people run alone. Even a top performer needs to know that Willis appreciates her and all that she is doing for the company.

Does Willis have a formal performance-appraisal and career-development process in his company? The presence of either or both could have minimized or eliminated this problem.

Amanda may have felt stifled from a career perspective. Advancement was important to her, and maybe Willis never inquired.

Amanda was Willis's top performer and presumably made quite a bit of money over the past few years. Did Willis assume that his people were happy and content just because they were making a lot of money? People also need to feel that they are growing.

Did Amanda feel that Willis and the company were investing in her? Did she have the opportunity to periodically attend training? Was the training focused on improving her as a person or just her product knowledge? Once again, people need to feel that they are growing.

Did Willis periodically ask Amanda what would make her job more enjoyable? The answers can illuminate frustrations. It is important to create opportunities to look employees in the eye and ask them if they are happy.

Maybe the problem was the overall environment in Willis's group.

There are many factors that cause an employee to leave. Some can be controlled. Some cannot. Solid communication will always be the key to retaining your best people.

Options

As a manager, you need make only one decision. Do you want to let Amanda go, or do you want to try to keep her?

If you want to let her go, do it with class. Make it clear that you are disappointed that such a good employee is leaving, but that you respect her decision and wish her the best in her new assignment. If possible, notify her customers and execute account transitions in a professional manner. Identify issues that need quick attention and pending business that someone must quickly close. Have her help you source her replacement. Ask her for input on how to improve the environment in your group. Ask her to critique you as a manager. Often this will be the best input you can receive.

If you want to keep the person, get ready to execute a "save" campaign.

Remember that, in either case, if Amanda is planning to go to a competitor, you should immediately isolate her from the company's files and records, gather other company assets that have been in her control, and walk her to the door.

POSSIBLE ACTIONS

Stop the Bleeding

The bleeding could be that others in the group are contemplating a change. Willis must get to the informal leaders of his team. Find out how they feel about Amanda's decision. Try to determine if there are others who are looking to leave.

Talk to Amanda again, quickly. Often, when someone is leaving there is no limit to what they will share. Ask her if she is actually going to a new job or leaving her current one. The difference is subtle, but very important. If she is leaving, begin to determine why. Her issues may be shared by others.

Listen

Now for the save campaign. Remember, this conversation is like a sales call. It is important to understand that all decisions of this magnitude (career change) are backed by sound logic. Often, however, much of the logic and rationale was developed well after the decision was made. So even if you are successful in poking holes in the logic, you may not be touching the real issues.

Try to understand the issues that caused Amanda to start looking for a new opportunity. Every good salesperson is periodically approached by other companies. Most often they are flattered but do not listen or consider the offer. Amanda's head was turned. Was the offer so great, or was she just ready to leave?

Initially, ask as many nonthreatening open-ended questions as possible. For example:

"How do your friends and family feel about you taking another job?"

"What type of compensation plan will you have?"

"Did you set any criteria for choosing a new job?" "What were they?"

Your objective is to have a casual conversation with Amanda, putting her at ease, and collecting as much data as possible.

People enjoy talking about their new jobs. Let her tell you all about it. Listen carefully for areas of excitement and areas of concern. This will help you later in your discussion.

When the conversation slows down, ask her if there is anything you can do to personally help her through this *d i f f i c u l t* transition (stress difficult). Again, listen very carefully.

Now it is time to carry out the campaign.

Think

Consider everything you have heard to this point, begin to formulate a track for continuing dialogue, and visualize how you will facilitate this mutually thoughtful exchange.

- Focus on the position's unknowns, areas that are universally important to salespeople.

- Mentally get on Amanda's side of the table and into Amanda's values and motivations.
- Stay away from areas that were described with excitement.
- Get ready to dig deeper into areas that were described with concern.
- Do not create tension. Prepare to think and facilitate in a consultative manner.

Execute

Project Amanda into that new job by causing her to think about some key issues and the concerns previously noted. By inquiring into these elements of her new opportunity you are calling into question expectations that may not have been previously examined or explored.

"How easy will it be to develop new relationships within the new company?"

"Is the culture one that you will enjoy?"

"Why didn't they fill this position from within?"

"Is the portfolio robust?"

"Are your accounts rich in opportunity, or have they already been picked over by others?"

"Will the support be sufficient and consistent with the support with which you are familiar?"

"How strong is your current pipeline of opportunities?"

"How long is a sales cycle?"

"How strong is the new comp plan, and will they give you time to get up and running?"

"Are the goals reasonable?"

"Are the reimbursable expenses satisfactory, and is the expense budget acceptable?"

"Will the travel require long absences from home?"

"How long will it take to be considered for promotion?"

Build up the risks of leaving in Amanda's mind. If possible, help reduce her concerns in *one* of the risk areas. This will help her remain comfortable with you and the conversation. If you are successful at reducing some fears, ask her if she feels that she can develop a solid working relationship with her new boss.

Your style will dictate the best way for you to present and discuss these subjects. Do not treat the discussion as a competition between yourself and the other firm. The key is a consultative focus on the unknowns and risks. Such discussions often create new awareness.

In conclusion, ask her to think about your discussion and make it clear you are happy to discuss these matters further before she departs. Also offer her the opportunity to discuss any elements with other (prebriefed and like-minded) managers in your firm. Amanda must develop new decision logic and a rationale for staying. Give it time. Feed it. Nurture it.

Be prepared for a request from Amanda to match the compensation she was offered with the other firm or to increase her responsibilities. If the discussion turns into a power play for a raise, you are better off to let her go. Creating a way to give her more responsibility is another matter and may be the lever to alter compensation.

If Amanda reverses her decision and decides to stay, ensure that you understand why, reinforce the revised logic and rationale, maintain closer-than-normal collaboration for an appropriate period of time, and quickly execute any action items that came out of the discussions.

Lessons

Stay close to all your people at all times, treating them as you would treat your most valued customers.

You must have development and progression plans and activities in place to prevent these situations from occurring and don't try to unduly impose your personal career clock on your people.

This is a visible problem. Many will be watching. Ensure that others draw positive conclusions from your actions.

Employees who stay with you should be considered at risk, managed appropriately, and experience some change to the status quo.

Be ready to replace anyone on your team at a moment's notice. Open slots book very little business.

8–2 The Problem:
The turnover in your sales unit is excessive.

The Story

Wanda's secretary knocked quietly on her office door. "Bert is on the phone. He asked me to interrupt," she announced. Bert was the national sales manager, and Wanda's boss.

"Felicia, the HR director," Bert opened, "just came by to point out that you lost 38 percent of your people last year, and this year is not looking much better."

"Now, we both have known that you have a problem because we've talked about this before," Bert went on, "but why don't you plan on flying in on Monday and let's talk about what's going on, what you're doing about it, and how I can help."

"Yes, yes sir, I guess it is a good idea to talk," Wanda answered, as the conversation came to an end. Bert's call certainly helped Wanda prioritize the rest of her week.

Temptations

Calls like that always get your attention. Turnover can really get you down and angry about your personal situation. The depression and exasperation can create some bad temptations.

Protect yourself

"I hired those people, so it can't be me." or "These people aren't used to working for a manager like me that holds them accountable."

Lash out

"It's no wonder people leave this two-bit outfit considering the crummy support."

Jump ship

"I think my people have got it right. It's time to vacate this company."

Turnover can cause you to start buying into the reasons your people leave, and then you become part of the problem. The best approach is to look at the problem with calmness and determination.

WHAT HAPPENED HERE . . . ?

You have a revolving door. If it continues, Wanda will be history. What is worse is that it appears there is no plan to fix or slow down the problem. Turnover sneaks up on a sales manager and a company. It's not sudden, unless there has been a cataclysmic event at the corporate level.

The environment in which salespeople and sales managers work is extremely important to their success and retention. It is a simple equation:

If the *environment* is *bad*,
The *success* rate will be *low*,
And *attrition* will be *high*.

The five elements of environment, with some sample issues, include:

1. THE COMPANY.   If sales people feel instability or risk they will leave.

- The company may be in financial trouble or there may have been rumors about its sale.
- There may have been unflattering stories in the press. No one likes to play defense.
- Competition leap-frogged the firm's products. No one likes association with laggards.
- A key supportive department such as Marketing could be an embarrassment.

2. THE COMPENSATION PLAN.   If salespeople don't feel fairly rewarded they will leave.

- It may take unrealistic performance to make any real money.
- Incentive payments could be late, inconsistent, in error, and a hassle to correct.
- Incentive compensation may be charged back, or deducted, for unreasonable causes.
- There may be no safety net in the first three to six months. People starve out of the box.

3. THE ASSIGNMENT.   If the job content does not meet salespeople's expectations they will leave.

- The ability to make creative, substantive contributions and decisions may be blocked.
- Work content could be flawed. The amount of real selling time may be minimal.
- There may be a lack of support infrastructure, collateral materials, and automation.
- People may be asked to be hit-and-run artists, and that rubs them the wrong way.

4. THE FUTURE.   If salespeople don't see a future they will leave.

- There may not be a real career path for good people.
- Maybe Wanda's company may not value personal and professional development, or training is limited or nonexistent.

5. THE MANAGER'S STYLE.   If salespeople feel a lack of interest or a constant contentious atmosphere they will leave.

- There may be no teamwork, no camaraderie, and no team identity or spirit.
- Wanda could be very demanding, abusive, nit-picking, or overcontrolling.
- Maybe Wanda never lightens up, cuts loose, or celebrates.
- Coaching could be minimal or poorly administered. She may be a poor communicator.
- It may be that Wanda does not easily recognize or thank her people for a job well done.

The story implies that the turnover in Wanda's sales unit is much higher than elsewhere in the company. That may mean that style is the major culprit because the other four elements of environment are likely common in the other sales units. (The style of managers above Wanda can also be a part of the problem.) All this potential is for Wanda, Bert, and Felicia to sift out.

If an environment is negative or stagnant it is difficult to keep good people. Remember that sales environments are *relative*. What Wanda thinks is good may not stack-up so well with the sparkling reputations of other firms in the area, with previous employers of her salespeople, or with stories they read about other sales organizations.

There is also room for extenuating circumstances.

- It could be that Wanda's turnover rate last year was a result of her cleaning out the deadwood.
- It could have been that many salespeople were promoted or hired away by other divisions of the company because Wanda's hiring is the envy of other managers.
- Conversely, Wanda may be doing a sales job on candidates, falsely promising quick riches and painting an unrealistic picture of the nature of the work.
- Wanda's profile for salespeople may not match the job. She could be a poor recruiter trying to pound square pegs into round holes.

Some firms let the intense pressure of the environment act as a screen to eliminate folks who can't handle the mental, physical, and psychic pressure associated with the job. In other words, turnover by design, running an environment as a meatgrinder. These cases are exceptions. Could Wanda be trying this tactic?

How much turnover is excessive? It varies between businesses and industries. Top management, human-resource staff, and HR consultants should be able to share hard data. Establishing a turnover target to stay beneath is worthwhile in any sales organization.

OPTIONS

You have only two options.

1. Execute the last of your temptations and get a new job.
2. Fix the problem. Take a leadership role and make yourself a part of a team effort to transform the current environment to reduce turnover.

POSSIBLE ACTIONS

Turnover reduction actions fall into two broad categories.

1. Triage.
2. And long-term care.

Triage

The definition of triage is, "the sorting of, and allocation of, treatment to patients and especially disaster and battle victims, according to a system of priorities to maximize the number of survivors." That sounds as if it describes Wanda's situation to a T. The objective of triage is to keep the patient, or in this case the sales unit, alive.

Wanda must stop the bleeding. To do this she must determine the cause. Triage benefits from professional help in identifying causes, or priorities. Wanda is already getting all the help she needs thanks to the call from Bert. It's too bad *she* didn't initiate that call for assistance. (Lesson learned.) Together, with help from Felicia in HR, they must tear apart the environment. Bert may want to consider inviting other sales managers to contribute if the problem is systemic.

The triage process must examine the five key elements of the environment model: the company, the compensation plan, the assignment, the future, and the manager's style. The hardest priorities to identify and swallow as a problem is *management style*. This is where Bert and Felicia must be candid with Wanda, and Wanda must open herself to examination. Wanda must remember that this is *her* problem, and not shovel it off. Wanda must be viewed by her people as the most active fixer of the problem even if some of the elements are out of her direct control. She puts herself at grave risk if she doesn't exhibit leadership and openness.

Next, Wanda should talk to her people, asking them their opinion as to why so many people are leaving. She must listen carefully in spite of the fact that they may not tell her the whole truth, but they should provide some clues. She must talk to the peer leaders, who will usually be more informative. Peer leaders often take the position of, "Some of the reps feel . . ."

Through all of these discussions Wanda, Bert, and Felicia will identify and confirm the priorities. Some may demand the combined efforts of corporate management or sales management to cure, others may demand Wanda's personal style-changing actions, and some may require the combined effort of her sales unit.

The key to triage is to find the biggest reason for turnover, the #1 priority, and solve it. Or to put it another way, to find the biggest, most visible dragon and attack and slay it *in clear view* of all the salespeople. As an example, cure the sloppy administration of compensation, or have the customer-service manager totally revamp his department, or unload all the mundane nonsales stuff and give it to inside support staff. The impression left on the sales unit must be, "Wow, they're really serious about fixing this!"

Then, following the definition of triage, attack the next priority, or dragon, and slay it. And so on.

For those priorities that deal with Wanda's own management style, counseling time with Bert or discreet seminars or other training should be executed.

For those priorities that she must work with corporate to solve, she must keep herself in the middle of the fight.

For those priorities that she can cure with her team she should pull all of her people together and tell them that she is committed to lowering the attrition rate, values every one of them and will do everything possible to keep them onboard. Together they should build an environment-enhancement plan.

Wanda must frequently communicate her's and the company's progress to her people and continually ask them for feedback on how the environment is progressing.

Before launching into the long-term-care element of curing the environment, Wanda, Bert, and Felicia need to establish a target of what is acceptable turnover in the company. Long-term-care actions should be developed to keep turnover below that level. When turnover rises above that level it should serve as a signal to the entire sales-management team and HR to triage the bleeding again and reexamine their long-term-care program.

Long-term Care

Long-term care sets the environment. It should be built around the same five elements of the environment model: the company, the compensation plan, the assignment, the future, and the manager's style. The role that Wanda can play in each element of the model depends, of course, on her relative position in the company and the size of the firm. Top sales management, HR, and other managers should have an active role in long-term care.

The environment elements that Wanda, as a sales-unit manager, can influence the most is probably #3, *the assignment*, and #5, *management style*.

- *Communicate direction:* Tell people what is going on, always letting them know where she and the company are taking them.

- *Ask for input:* Salespeople appreciate being asked how they feel and being included in decisions.

- *Create plans:* Write a job plan that describes the work the salespeople are expected to perform and how that work fits the sales unit's goals. Formulate a performance plan that defines the specific sales goals and objectives of each salesperson. Devise a development plan that defines the personal-development needs and opportunities that will help all salespeople meet their performance plan.

- *Deploy everyone smartly:* Challenging assignments should match the talents of her people and should be consistent with sales and marketing strategies.

- *Communicate expectations:* Communicate what she expects from her people and what they can expect from her.

- *Create relationships:* Get to know her people and build trust levels.

- *Train:* Become a training zealot, helping her people gain all the skills and knowledge necessary to excel and grow.

- *Empower:* Authorize her people to act, let them run, and hold them accountable.

- *Monitor and coach:* Keep a close eye on how each salesperson is performing relative to plans. Give them real-time feedback and help them if they are running into problems.

- *Recognize:* Recognize those people who are working their plan and contributing to the success of the sales unit and the company.

In summary, if Wanda, with help from her colleagues, executes triage and the long-term care she will find that:

The *environment* will get *better,*
Her *success* rate will be *higher,*
And *attrition* will be *lower.*

LESSONS

This problem reminds you that while companies have high expectations of their sales staffs, sales staffs also have high expectations of their company.

Working hard to create an environment that will allow your people to succeed takes time and it takes discipline, but one of the benefits is that you'll have members of that winning team with you for a longer period of time.

Turnover sensitizes you to build a better understanding of people's values and motivations. Expect that you will also need to examine your own behavior and demeanor and be willing to make changes in your management style at times like this.

Salespeople will look at their manager more closely for reactions during times of excessive turnover because they expect leadership. Your people must see you stand up for their rights, values, and needs. They must see you as combative, working hard to help cure the priorities and keep the environment free from dragons. Even if you don't win all the battles, let your people see you coming back beat-up from the dragon wars.

8–3 THE PROBLEM:

A salesperson doesn't have the aptitude for sales work.

THE STORY

Gerry was a highly successful sales manager who had taken over a new sales unit a short time ago and has come to some conclusions about the strengths and weaknesses of his people. Aside from some minor counseling needs, he had discovered only one problem rep.

It was clear to Gerry when he traveled with Austin, who had been with the firm for about eight months, that Austin was trying hard but was not comfortable with what he was doing. Austin was not relaxed nor was he really enjoying himself. He just didn't seem natural. Austin had been to all the required training classes and had obtained a little business, but every order seemed to be a major struggle.

What in the world am I going to do with this one, Gerry thought to himself.

TEMPTATIONS

Pride and overconfidence are the enemies when strong sales managers feel they can pound round pegs into square holes. Temptations to soothe self-image are not the answer.

False encouragement

"Come on, Austin, you can do it."—or—"Stick with it—you'll make it."

Invest against your better judgment

"I'll send him to some skill seminars and to listen to some motivational speakers. I'm sure that will fire him up."

Preferential treatment

"I can turn *anyone* into a winner. I'll spend evenings and Saturdays with him if I must."

Candid assessments and quick, equitable decisions are the better answer.

WHAT HAPPENED HERE . . . ?

Someone gave Austin a sales job for some reason, and it doesn't seem to be working. Austin may have a great attitude and desire, but not everyone is cut out for selling.

Perhaps Austin is just a few years removed from college with limited work experience. Austin's initial or current image of what sales is about may be flawed or unrealistic.

Someone close to Austin may have convinced him that sales was where "the action" was, so he got himself a job in sales. All his friends may have gone into sales and the big-bucks stories and the peer pressure may have gotten to him.

Austin may have convinced the hiring manager. People in need of work can do that. The act of convincing, itself, could have led that manager to believe that Austin had what it takes.

The hiring manager may have been scrambling for bodies, or the hiring manager may have made a poor decision. There isn't a sales manager (or any leader) who ever lived that batted 1,000 when it comes to hiring.

Maybe Austin is just a slow starter, or a late bloomer. Many highly competent people in many fields came up to speed slowly.

People who do not have the aptitude and the potential for sales end up putting a questionable mark on their resumé. They often try to force this to work or are afraid to admit that they don't know what else to do.

OPTIONS

First, a big question. How is the sales unit doing? Do you have the luxury to work with Austin or not? If you have some slack, you might want to go the extra mile. But don't lie to yourself.

Without slack, or if it's clear Austin just can't cut it, you have two options.

1. Counsel Austin out of sales and attempt to place him in an appropriate position in your firm.
2. Counsel Austin out of sales and out of your company, aiding him to the extent that you can in finding another job.

POSSIBLE ACTIONS

Decide to be candid with both yourself and with Austin. It is your job to spot, confirm, and develop sales talent, and this situation represents a good test.

Time for an Objective Assessment

Pull together Austin's sales and training history since he has been in the job and add your own notes and observations. You are about to affect someone's career, so do it with facts and figures.

Treat this assessment as a new-hire situation. When you are considering hiring an individual you determine who, and who can't, in your judgment, be good at sales work in your company. What is the profile you use during those times? What knowledge, skills, and attributes do you look for in a person? What are the key make-or-break factors necessary for success in your sales unit, and in your company? Use the same criteria in this situation. Which of the factors are present or lacking in Austin's makeup? Which of all the skills, aptitudes, and factors can he realistically acquire?

Does he have the intellectual capacity and the psychological makeup to be successful *in your industry*? It's quite possible he could be a sales success elsewhere. That's not uncommon.

Is it possible that he can't be successful under your leadership and coaching? It is not unusual for experienced sales managers to admit and suggest that a certain person could make a better start working for another manager in another environment. Can Austin make it working for some other sales manager in your company? Is that option possible in your firm?

What about Austin's manner, style, or attributes convinced you of the fact that he doesn't have the aptitude for sales? You must be specific.

If Austin walked in your door today, cold off the street, would you hire him?

If you opened your own business tomorrow, would you hire him to represent you?

Would the other sales managers in your organization hire Austin? Do they covet him?

If you sent Austin to all the available skill seminars and schools, could he be a *top-level* performer? Do you want to encourage someone to stay in a position where they can be only mediocre, at best?

Has Austin been fully cognizant of your expectations and his own goals and objectives, or have you erroneously assumed that fact?

Answers to these questions will set the stage for your next steps.

Confer with Others

You are Austin's sales manager, and this is part of your job, but you're dealing with an existing employee, so this decision must take on a heightened level of diligence.

Talk to your manager, other sales managers or senior managers, and human resources to get their opinions. Also talk to your colleagues in other business functions to get their impressions of Austin. Managers in other departments can often provide fresh and objective assessments based on their contact with salespeople. Make your decision, draft a transition plan, and prepare for a one-on-one with the rep.

> If you feel *convinced* about your assessment and decision that Austin leave, plan to communicate it in a convincing fashion. If you feel even a little mushy, perhaps you better give Austin every chance to prove himself and *commit* your personal support to his continuing development.

Broach the Subject

Initiate a discussion with Austin. Share your observations and discuss hard examples of behavior to make your point. Don't dwell on results, but rather the aptitudes that you believe are missing or incompatible with sales. If you have been doing your coaching job, these points should not be a surprise to the employee.

The biggest problem in these types of situations is to convince the employee that a decision to move on does not imply weakness or failure. As a matter of fact, the opposite is true. People who have the courage to admit that they are in the wrong job will be better off for the realization in the long run. Tell Austin that there is life after (insert your company name).

Gerry needs to convince Austin that many capable people have tried sales at one time or another in their life and discovered it was not for them. There is no dishonor in that admission.

Deliver Your Decision

Inform Austin of your decision that you do not believe he was cut out for sales. Don't kid him or yourself by stringing him out or putting him on a phony development plan.

If . . . there are no other opportunities in your firm ask Austin to resign his position. It is unlikely that he will balk, but if he does, you must be prepared to terminate him.

Counsel him, to the extent of your knowledge and experience, to pursue a profession where he can be successful. Provide Austin with your assessment of what field you believe he is best suited for and encourage him to talk to other professionals in your firm and on the outside.

If your company can afford it, keep him on the payroll for a time to aid his transition, or engage an outplacement service for his benefit.

Provide suggestions on how and where to look for a job and furnish resumé counseling.

Give him an honest and enthusiastic reference for a new position.

If... there are opportunities in your firm, give Austin first crack at those positions and suggest to Austin that he speak to the appropriate managers quickly. Initiate the contacts and lay the groundwork on Austin's behalf. This alternative amounts to a sure thing. In other words, your efforts have basically set him up in another department. It is left to the hiring manager only to execute a courtesy interview, make an offer, and have Austin accept.

Give Me a Chance

Be ready for a plea. If you give in to the plea you are essentially compromising your beliefs and standards, delaying the inevitable, and hurting your productivity.

The Optics

These situations are always visible, and other sales reps likely had personal opinions about Austin that mirrored your own. Announce the decision in your sales unit as a positive and courageous outcome, which it is. Treat Austin's leaving the sales unit as a success, not a failure. The example will be a good lesson to others, for now or in the future. It may also cause others to examine their professional choice and admit their feelings.

LESSONS

Honest, fact-based feedback on a regular basis will help you if you must counsel an employee out of sales or out of your company. Always execute these actions with help from other managers and human resources.

Motivated employees are valuable employees. It is not unusual for a firm to have numerous talented and motivated individuals in the wrong slots. Their own reticence plus their manager's squeamishness to address reality often dooms them to depreciating their potential, gnawing dissatisfaction, or unnecessary stress. Your own honest and sensitive leadership is the best tool in these situations. Help all of your people to be as successful as they can, regardless of where that might be.

8–4 THE PROBLEM:
You must make a decision about a marginal performer.

THE STORY

Shaking her head, Catharine hung up the phone after talking to Lembert, one of her reps who had called to let her know that a contract had been awarded to a competitor. Lembert had been with the firm for a few years, and his performance had always been passable or borderline.

Catharine was trying to build a solid sales unit. Nonperformers had been terminated and Catharine's attention was now on marginal performers who had potential and were recoverable.

Catharine had put together a comprehensive development plan with Lembert 60 days ago and the corrective-action period was coming to an end. "What am I going to do with this guy," she said to herself. There were sparks of excellence, but more often he came up short. "He's got good intentions, but his execution often misses the mark. It's time to make a decision."

TEMPTATIONS

Marginal performers are tough people to deal with because they challenge your convictions about people's desire for excellence and threaten your desire to balance task and people management. The tug-of-war between compromise and firmness leads to these thoughts.

Drop the bar
  "Maybe I've just been expecting too much from Lembert."

Waffle
  "Well . . . I guess he'll do all right. His heart's in the right place . . . but I'll nail him if his performance drops a notch."

Ultimatum
  "One hundred ten percent or you're history, Bozo. You got that?"

Marginal or middle-of-the-road performers are a sales manager's biggest challenge.

WHAT HAPPENED HERE . . . ?

You've given Lembert an opportunity, and now it's time to make a decision. The problem here is *disposition*—what is Catharine going to do with Lembert?

Was the development plan designed poorly or executed badly? Understanding the length of the sales cycle and market potential, was the length of time sufficient to give Lembert ample opportunity to perform?

Did Catharine spend an appropriate amount of time with Lembert, and was it rigorous coaching or was much of it windshield time?

Does Lembert recognize that this isn't the job for him? Employees are the first to understand their native capabilities and talents and it's often the manager who tries to save a hopeless situation in order to salve her own ego.

Maybe Lembert's heart wasn't in the development plan. "Corrective action"—or—"development" can be a euphemism for "you're gone." Alert employees know that, and you can't kid them with a lot of fluffy talk. Legal departments are particularly sensitive that managers go through these corrective paces to protect the company from lawsuits. Many employees, when identified as marginal or in trouble, will simply go through the steps of a development plan while they simultaneously look for something else. They will attempt to stretch out the corrective action for as long as possible, giving themselves more search time.

OPTIONS

You have several options. But first, a question. Is Lembert salvageable? And by salvageable we mean does he have the "stuff" within him to become a contributor who regularly *exceeds* goals? No sales manager wants people to simply *make* their goals, unless you are happy being a mediocre or marginal sales manager yourself. The "stuff" is your hiring criteria. Would you hire Lembert today if you had an open slot and he came through the door? Be honest.

Two months ago you made a decision that Lembert had the stuff to be successful. Were you honest then? Do you still feel he's got it? If you do, then you have one course of action.

You must continue to train and develop Lembert if you're convinced he will benefit from it, *or* if you feel that you didn't execute the development program as you should have.

If you now believe that he *doesn't* have what it takes, then you have four options.

1. You can decide to tolerate the situation if upper management doesn't give you any choice. The reason you may have to hold the hand you've been dealt is for circumstances outside your control, such as a hiring freeze. (This is more of a default than an option.)

2. You could decide to move Lembert to a different position in the sales department or to another department that better fits his talents and skills.

3. You can counsel him out if you feel he just doesn't have what it takes. Let him resign since he's given it a solid try.

4. You can decide to terminate Lembert because you feel he isn't worth further time and effort, your efforts didn't yield desired improvement, and his attitude was wanting.

Speed of decision is critical. The demands on sales managers are too great to tolerate marginal performance. You are cutting your own throat by not acting promptly.

POSSIBLE ACTIONS

You want to make the right decision. These decisions are just as important as hiring decisions, and your leadership, management style, and values are on display.

First, what did the 60 days of corrective action confirm or deny? Was there quantifiable growth, change, or positive movement during the 60 days?

Next, answer the following questions in order to help make the best possible decision.

Think About Your Initial Assumption

Were you totally honest with Lembert from the beginning, or was this development plan a charade? If you were kidding yourself, let him make a graceful exit and hire someone else.

Does Lembert get you excited with his potential, or leave you feeling flat? Your *own emotion* is a good sign of whether this is a go or no-go. Don't deceive yourself.

Think About the Reality of Today's Business

Has the job content changed, leaving Lembert behind? Have the market and customers changed, leaving Lembert in the rear? Have technology, products, and services changed, leaving Lembert obsolete? Can he realistically catch up in areas of deficiency?

Was Lembert's assignment consistent with that of other staff members? Did he have equitable goals, considering his assignment? Should his assignment really have been redefined?

Think About Fit

Is the truth of the matter that Lembert shouldn't be in this particular job, but should be doing something else in the sales department?

Is the truth of the matter that Lembert shouldn't even be in sales, that he should be in marketing, operations, or service?

Specifically, what knowledge, skills, and attributes does Lembert possess, and are there any places in the business for those qualities?

Is work ethic the issue? Does Lembert have a tendency to be lazy or passive? If so, call it as it is. Lembert may have thought that sales was easy or that it was a golden egg.

Has your business culture changed to such an extent that Lembert doesn't fit anymore?

Think About the Employee's Motivations

What does the employee *really* like to do? With what elements of the job do you see bona-fide enjoyment, pleasure, or passion? What elements of the job does he execute *very well*?

The answers to these questions are usually dead giveaways of Lembert's true motivations and are signals of what type of work he should be doing.

Think About Your Personal Example

Marginal performance is the result of marginal activities, and marginal activities over time are partially the result of marginal management and marginal leadership.

- Are you truly committed to a culture of excellence?
- Do you execute your management processes thoroughly and consistently?
- Are you a proactive, committed coach?
- Are you both demanding and fair?
- Do you set high attainable expectations, exhibit trust, delegate, and empower?
- Do you set a good example with your own work and work ethic?
- Do you recognize and reward performance?
- Are you known to give people the opportunity to start clean with you?

If you're a part of the problem, it is only fair that you fix yourself while you're working on Lembert.

Test Your Development Plan

Confirm that your development plan was as thorough as it should have been.

- Did you *define* marginal performance so Lembert easily knows when he's crossed the line?
- Did you establish a *benchmark* for activities and results?
- Did it *measure* the quality and quantity of specific activities and specific results?
- Did you *meet* on a prescheduled basis and did you *document* your meetings?
- Did it hold Lembert accountable for *where* the activities would take place?
- Did it hold Lembert accountable for *whom* the activities were intended?
- Did it hold Lembert accountable for *when* the activities took place?
- Did you *recognize* things he did well to light his fire and create momentum?
- Would your development plan withstand the *scrutiny* of top management?
- Did you spend the planned *time* with him?

Self-test

If you had been in Lembert's position would you feel that you had been treated fairly and rigorously? When you've satisfied yourself with your introspection and self-test you're ready to talk to Lembert. Run your game plan past your manager and HR.

Test Your Decision

Talk to your boss and talk to the people in HR and possibly to your legal counsel. Go in with your assessment, facts, your decision, and an outline of next steps. Get their ideas and listen to their questions. Modify your plan based on those discussions.

Pull the Trigger

Announce your decision first and tell Lembert why that was your choice. Review the options you considered. Having another manager in the room with you to witness the message is a smart thing to do. Let HR be your guide.

Lembert's mind is going to be focusing on your decision, the rationale of your decision, and *his* options, but you must be prepared for a detailed discussion of the results of the development plan. That discussion must be frank. Focus on the quantity and quality of *activities* you had in the plan. If you focus on results, you open the door for bad-luck excuses.

IF THE DECISION IS TO CONTINUE TRAINING: Present *an already prepared* and more rigorous improvement plan with specific activity goals and result targets. The tone of your conversation and this plan must make it clear that *you want this person to succeed.* This is an investment strategy.

IF YOU HAVE TO TOLERATE LEMBERT'S CONTINUED PRESENCE: Tell him that the existing corrective action plan will be tightened until performance is at sustained levels of expectations. The employee will likely interpret this action as a real dead end and may resign, or the constraints that caused this decision will disappear and you'll be able to terminate him.

IF THE DECISION IS TO MOVE LEMBERT INTO ANOTHER POSITION: Describe the details of the new position and show him why the management team believes he can make an important contribution in that role. *Sell* the new job. If the job is outside your department have him talk to his new manager immediately. If he declines the position his alternative is to leave the company.

IF THE DECISION IS TO COUNSEL LEMBERT OUT OF THE BUSINESS: Be candid and tell Lembert why you believe he doesn't fit. Suggest that he start looking, while continuing to perform his work. Provide outplacement assistance if that is your policy, or give him an opportunity to resign with a severance package.

IF THE DECISION IS TO TERMINATE LEMBERT: Make the termination effective immediately and execute it in accordance with company policy. Escort him out of the building that day.

LESSONS

Candor is your best counseling tool with all employees.

These are complex decisions. Make sure you work with your manager and human resources.

Marginal employees can easily sense whether or not you are committed to them. Many will work hard to improve their performance if they perceive that the development plan reflects your sincere belief that they can succeed and that the plan contains a heavy investment of your time.

The longer marginal performance is tolerated the harder it is to correct.

Make sure your development plans are well conceived, focus on activities, are measurable, and are scrupulously managed.

When it comes time to make a decision, don't vacillate. Make it quickly and move on.

8–5 THE PROBLEM:

The performance of a salesperson nearing retirement has gone bad.

THE STORY

Blake, a district sales manager, and his boss, JM, were in the midst of their regular monthly one-on-one going over everyone in Blake's sales unit. Clyde's numbers stopped them cold, creating a mutual reflective pause.

"What are we going to do with this guy?" asked JM.

"He came up short again. Year to date he is performing poorly," Blake countered. "The guy has been with the company for 37 years for cryin' out loud. There were so many years of good performance, even great performance. I remember him on a couple of incentive trips."

"I just don't know," mused Blake.

"Well, you have to figure out something," concluded JM.

TEMPTATIONS

When a longtime performer falls on hard times, self-serving easy-outs can get mixed up with good business sense and responsible personnel management.

Shuttle him off

"I'll give him that worthless open territory on the west side of town. It'll keep him busy"

Squeeze out the last drop of blood

"I don't care if you retire tomorrow, bubba. I want a full effort all the way until the end."

Dump him on someone else

"Let's put him in the shipping department to label containers. I hear they're looking."

These are sensitive matters that demand intense thought and integrity of action.

WHAT HAPPENED HERE ...?

A veteran has stumbled. Perhaps he was taken for granted or forgotten.

Blake should have seen this coming but probably wasn't watching. He may have let himself slide into benign neglect because Clyde detracted from the aura or chemistry of the sales unit. Sales unit members who are different can make some sales managers uncomfortable.

Perhaps Blake has been carrying Clyde for some time because he feels queasy about getting tough or potentially pulling the trigger on a veteran sales rep.

Blake may not have been giving Clyde any attention because Clyde shunned perceived hand-holding. Many veteran salespeople are reluctant to adapt to changing markets, customers, and products because they don't want to look amateurish or incompetent in front of others.

Blake may have felt threatened by Clyde's vast experience and knowledge and therefore left him to his own devices for too long.

Clyde may have made a conscious decision to throttle back because he feels untouchable based on past performance, feels he's earned a more leisurely pace, is experiencing personal problems, or is bored.

Sometimes veterans feel out of place in training sessions. Blake may have made the assumption that Clyde didn't want any training or refresher sessions. Clyde could have balked at earlier training attempts because he may have wanted to display his competency in lieu of looking weak or deficient.

Old friends and buyers at many of Clyde's accounts could have retired and been replaced by people with whom he has little relationship, and Clyde may have exacerbated his problem by selling the same old solutions the same old way.

OPTIONS

You have five options with this problem.

1. Provide an early-retirement package that fairly compensates Clyde.
2. Ease Clyde out by giving him a series of "special assignments."
3. Modify Clyde's current assignment in response to identified legitimate circumstances.
4. Take Clyde out of his current assignment and give him a highly focused and responsible position that takes advantage of his capabilities and experience and also adds value to the company.
5. Counsel and support Clyde to get him back up to speed in his current assignment.

Respect, dignity, fairness, and his sales unit's goals should be the basis of Blake's choice.

The big question is, can Blake realistically light Clyde's fire again? It *is* possible to rejuvenate a former super-star. Does Blake *want* to do it is another big question.

POSSIBLE ACTIONS

Take your time on this one.

A Responsibility Review

Just because someone is near the end of his career is no reason for either manager or rep to back off or let up on the other. Blake has a responsibility to the employee and to the company to do the right thing, which is to coach and counsel Clyde, ensure that Clyde is in a position that takes full advantage of his skills, and to fulfill the sales unit's sales plan. Clyde has a responsibility to meet his manager's and employer's expectations and remain vigorously engaged all the way to the end of his assignment.

Think About the Situation

Look at this situation from three points of view.

1. *How do you candidly feel about this?*
   - Is your personal agenda clouding your judgment on how to deal with Clyde?
   - Do you have any personal roadblocks or biases that are getting in the way of executing your responsibilities with Clyde?
   - Are you anxious to boot Clyde out the door because you have a young hotshot in the wings? (Be careful here, this may be dangerous.)
   - Are you committed to Clyde with the same vigor that you are committed to your other people?

- Have you honestly contributed to this problem by not giving Clyde the attention that you know he deserved?
- Someday you will approach the end of your career. How do you want to be treated when you get there?
- If Clyde were your father or uncle how would you want him treated?

Honest answers to these questions should help frame your approach and solution.

2. *If you could put yourself in* Clyde's shoes *how do you think you would feel?*

Let's step inside Clyde's heart and mind to see what he might be saying to himself.

- "I really know how to sell, and how to deal with people. It's unfortunate these folks here haven't given me an opportunity lately to share all that."
- "It's funny. These people think that ideas or techniques from yesterday must be flawed."
- "I see Blake struggling with some stuff, and I know I could give him some ideas, but he doesn't seem to be comfortable with me."
- "No one seems to be interested in my territory, accounts, or me anymore."
- "This is a great company They have really taken good care of me, but I get their message loud and clear without them saying anything."
- "I know I'm really not as comfortable or competent with these computers as the young people. After all, they grew up with them."
- "The buyers used to be simpler. Some of their questions now are pretty complex."
- "Everyone wants everything done so much quicker nowadays, there is no time to get to know the people."
- "I don't know how much time I should put into learning all this new-product stuff. It really doesn't seem worth the effort."
- "I don't have the stamina and the energy I had 37 years ago, but I'd never admit it."
- "I don't believe they are interested in investing in me any more; why should they?"

If you articulated comments like these to Clyde, and invited responses, you'd probably open doors and spark a relationship that you never thought was possible.

3. *If you were in Clyde's* territory, *what does potential look like?*

A market-back view causes some questions and awareness, doesn't it?

- Odds are the history of business out of this territory has never been grand. True? This is probably a backwater assignment that doesn't have much potential, and people will rise or fall to meet the realities of their assignment. True?
- This territory is a dried-up raisin, not a plum. True?

- If you put one of your top people in here, would it really do much better? Odds are, no one worth his or her salt would want this assignment. True? Odds are this assignment would be better for a new trainee. True?

- Odds are someone made the assumption a few years ago that this would be a nice retirement assignment for Clyde. True?

Thoughtful analysis from these three viewpoints probably helped you figure out something. True? Don't jump to conclusions about an option just yet.

Go Get Some Advice

Talk to JM, other senior managers, and to human resources (if you have that function in your company). Have them help you firm up some options. Many probably know Clyde and can give you guidance.

Time to Talk

All the thoughts and answers that the previous introspection raised will make a candid discussion with Clyde much easier, even if you haven't had a candid discussion before. Start by sharing your thoughts and feelings. Share the deficiencies of all parties as you see them.

"Clyde, help me understand what's happening."

Then give Clyde the floor. Follow Clyde's comments with these questions, as needed.

- Ask Clyde what's wrong.
- Ask Clyde if he is slowing down on purpose or taking you for a ride.
- Ask if there are personal problems that are affecting his work.
- Ask if he would like you to shave back or change his assignment.
- Ask him where and how he feels he can contribute the most.
- Ask him if he would like to go back to a previous position or to a different position.
- Ask him if he would like to take an early retirement. (*If* you have a retirement plan.)
- Ask Clyde what skills sessions he would like to participate in and don't take "none" for an answer.
- Ask Clyde what you can do to help him, and don't take "nothing" for an answer.

If this is your first serious discussion with Clyde, don't expect full disclosure. It may take a second, third, or fourth meeting. Clyde will respect your perseverance.

An Appeal to Pride

Clyde possesses solid experience and many great lessons. Recognize his credentials and knowledge and challenge him to put that know-how to full use for the benefit of the sales unit.

Agree on an Option

Present the options as you *now* see them, and ask Clyde to share options as *he* sees them.

Agree on an option and jointly create an implementation plan that is satisfactory to both parties.

The Best Option

Blake's chosen option and its implementation should be able to withstand the scrutiny of management and the entire sales organization and make both Clyde and Blake feel that they have done the responsible thing. "Blake handled that first class and with consummate professionalism," and "They really took good care of Clyde and did the right thing by him" are the responses Blake wants from everyone.

Reengage

If Blake and Clyde agree to dig in, to relight the fire, and to turn things around and engineer an auspicious exit a year from now, stick to these points.

- Take the mutually agreed-upon coaching and training steps to eliminate deficiencies.
- Hold Clyde up as an example in the sales unit. He will relish the recognition. Smart old pros, with support from savvy managers, can motivate less experienced reps.
- Don't do anything false just to stroke Clyde's ego. Clyde will see through any gamesmanship quickly, and then trust and respect are gone forever.
- Listen intently to Clyde. Because many suggestions may be delivered in the context of past events, be prepared to ask second- and third-level questions for your understanding.
- Defer to the veteran's experience and give due process to his ideas. Adopt some of Clyde's ideas and let the sales unit know where the ideas came from. Give Clyde the courtesy of letting him know what ideas you will and you won't accept, and why.
- Be big enough to yield or submit to legitimate suggestions and criticism from Clyde.

A Tip for Engineering Success in the Future

Create a masters forum or masters-mentoring program that brings veterans and rookies together on a formal basis.

LESSONS

Veteran salespeople are a tremendous resource in any sales unit if fully engaged and managed, just like anyone else.

Learning is a lifetime experience and expectation. Help veteran sales reps adapt and never make assumptions about people's attitudes toward new initiatives or toward their motivations based on their ages.

Treat *all* your people with respect, dignity, and fairness. Hold them *all* accountable for agreed-upon objectives, and follow performance improvement policies and processes consistently with everyone.

8–6 THE PROBLEM:

You must present an unsatisfactory performance appraisal.

THE STORY

"Well, where are they?" Christopher asked Gabriella, an area sales manager, referring to long-overdue performance appraisals for two of her reps, Charlie and CJ.

As human-resource director, Christopher had put in place a schedule for the completion of performance appraisals for all of the company's employees. Gabriella had completed all of her appraisals on time, except she was dragging her feet on the last two. The fact was that both Charlie and CJ had finished slightly behind their quotas, and both had other deficiencies.

Gabriella was having a problem rustling up the courage to craft and deliver tough messages. "Yes, yes, I know. I've been very busy. I'll have them done by the end of next week," she responded.

Now what am I going to do, she thought, as she shooed Christopher out the door.

TEMPTATIONS

It is easy to deliver the positive messages. The negative ones cause a little more difficulty.

Rationalize

"Well, their numbers are close to target. That's all that really counts anyway. Right?"

Push back

"You know, you HR guys have no feel for the business. Here it is, the end of the quarter, and all you can think about is some arbitrary appraisal schedule you put together."

Play games

"Okay, I'll give you a choice, Chris—revenue or appraisals? You choose."

Salespeople are hungry for feedback, good, bad, or lukewarm. People want confirmation on how they are doing, and they want it when they know it is scheduled.

WHAT HAPPENED HERE . . . ?

Procrastination, plain and simple. The two salespeople have not performed very well. The salespeople's performance problems, whether it's an abrasive approach to co-workers, customers' complaining about them, or the fact that they show up for work only on days that begin with *B* is not important at this point. Gabriella is apprehensive and tardy, and that's the issue. Unfortunately, many sales managers are good cheerleaders, but when it comes time to deliver the difficult messages, they have a tough time.

Gabriella likely doesn't have a process that focuses on performance management. Without a formal process, most sales managers are left with just the numbers. Is a sales rep making his or her quota or not? That approach makes for a thin appraisal.

Gabriella may be concerned about anticipated push back from Charlie and CJ. Disputes during an appraisal are not uncommon. They usually occur when expectations, goals, and objectives haven't been sufficiently communicated and documented.

Gabriella may not have sufficient hard data and qualitative notes. Lack of preparedness and mushy documentation can make these tasks gruesome.

Gabriella may be new, and she may have high standards. Reviews by the previous manager may have been erroneously glowing and now she has to bring Charlie and CJ back down to reality. These reversals can be tough plays.

Gabriella may have a poor relationship with Charlie and CJ. The lack of chemistry makes it harder to deliver bad news.

It may be that Gabriella did not provide any feedback during the reporting period, so what she puts in the appraisals will amount to surprises, and she knows salespeople hate surprises.

Other senior managers and Christopher likely have a low opinion of Charlie and CJ and expect that Gabriella will give them an unsatisfactory appraisal. Even though she knows that those people are right, she may have been planning on fudging a little with the two appraisals. The planned disparity creates pressure.

Unsatisfactory appraisals are usually given for two basic reasons, "the numbers" and "other" reasons, which include severe process, work-practice, or relationship issues. Unsatisfactory appraisals based on bad numbers are not as hard to prepare and administer because they can be objective. It's the "other" category, such as in the case of Charlie and CJ, that are more subjective and therefore the toughest.

OPTIONS

In the short term, Gabriella must get busy. The apprehension in the story implies that Gabriella is not prepared. In spite of that, she must prepare and present the two appraisals as best she can.

Then . . . she has two options:

1. *Pull up* the following appraisal date by six or nine months and give a second appraisal, which would be more thoroughly documented by that time. That would mean that Charlie and CJ get two appraisals within a three- to six-month period.
2. Keep Charlie and CJ on the standard appraisal cycle.

In the longer term, Gabriella has some work to do. She must develop a sound performance-management process if she doesn't already have one, or she must strengthen her existing process. Either way, she'll be busy again.

POSSIBLE ACTIONS

Stop what you are doing. This is an important matter that needs immediate attention. People who are performing below expectations know it. They know where the warts are. Gabriella will not be saying anything that Charlie and CJ don't already understand or suspect. Relax.

Go and Get Some Help

This is the most important part of this problem. Christopher should have picked up on Gabriella's procrastination and suggested that he could provide some help, but he didn't. Gabriella is asking for trouble if she proceeds on her own. It is easy to envision a couple of bungled appraisals.

She should consider these actions:

- Gather all her notes and other performance data she collected throughout the performance cycle, including notes from coaching sessions. This may be skimpy, but she'll have to use what she has.

- She should go to her manager, armed with data and notes, admit that she is apprehensive, and ask for some guidance. She must be specific about what is bothering her. If it's a lack of documentation, say so. If it's because this is a first-time experience, say so.

- Alternatively, or in conjunction with talking to her manager, Gabriella should share the same concerns and documentation with Christopher. (In firms without a dedicated HR function, this may be a VP or other executive who is in charge of personnel matters.)

- Some sales managers will ask their people to draft out their own appraisals and then give the draft to the manager. That permits the employee's comments and perceptions, to the extent that they are viable, to be included in the final appraisal. If Gabriella has done that with other salespeople, and if her manager and Christopher agree, she should ask Charlie and CJ for drafts by a certain date. In lieu of drafts, Gabriella can ask Charlie and CJ to provide her with any data they want included in the review.

- She can inquire of Christopher if he can share a copy of one or more unsatisfactory appraisals from his file (identities scrupulously protected) or from his reference materials.

- Gabriella should roll over in her own mind how she felt about the other performance reviews she has given and reviews that her managers have given of her performance. There are likely some lessons, some good do's and don'ts that she can recall. She should use those lessons.

- It's probably too late for these two appraisals, but there are several good books on the basics of sales management that have sections on appraisals. If she doesn't have one, she should get one, or borrow other books from Christopher. This is a good way to pick up some fundamentals. (For a sales manager in a small firm without HR resources this may be the only source of ideas.) Additionally, she should inquire about seminars that her firm, or outside providers, offer on performance appraisals.

- She should draft the two appraisals in accordance with company policy and the guidance received to date. Like most companies, it appears that Christopher has developed a standard review form. Gabriella is already familiar with it. She should write what she means. Language should be short, simple, and unmistakable. The appraisal must be thorough—through and through. Don't slough off minor irritations. Nothing is minor, and don't minimize anything. Gabriella must put herself on the other side of the desk. If she were the person receiving what she is writing, what would be her reactions, questions, concerns, worries, and where would she want clarification and suggestions?

- Gabriella should present the drafts to her manager and to Christopher. Listen to their comments and questions and make any necessary alterations. The guidance from Christopher and her manager should also include how to present the appraisals, and how to prepare and present follow-on action plans.

- The next step is to dry-run, or practice, the appraisals as much as necessary with her manager or Christopher, or both.

Schedule the Reviews

Gabriella should schedule the reviews on different days, starting with what she believes will be the least contentious of the two. That will let her go to school, so to speak. It will also permit her to make any changes in delivery and alterations in format for the second appraisal.

It may be prudent to schedule Christopher or her manager to be in attendance as an *observer*—emphasis on observer—not to help present the appraisal. Gabriella's comfort level, the severity of the unsatisfactory performance, company policy, and the previous records of Charlie and CJ will be the best guide.

Conduct the Review

By this time, Gabriella should be feeling much more confident. She will have been coached thoroughly, and the appraisals will be as squeaky clean as they can be.

Her manager and Christopher have likely made the following points, and much more.

- Review your notes before the review. Be as familiar with the information as possible.
- Do not get into specifics early on. Start with an overall view of performance first. Remember to be as constructive as possible. Point out what Charlie and CJ do well.
- Focus on comparing Charlie and CJ's performance to the goals and plans that were developed with them at the beginning of the performance period.
- Be objective and direct. Use examples (which should be in your notes) to make your points. Without examples, don't bring up the subject. You're just asking for contention.
- Stick to the issues and don't get emotional.
- Communicate disappointment.
- Be very clear when discussing those areas that require improvement.
- Take notes of key points made by both herself and the sales rep during the appraisal.
- Anything mentioned as a performance problem must have a follow-on corrective action plan. Set precise follow-on objectives, not just having to do with sales figures, but with key sales activities and personal behaviors as you spell out action plans.
- Demonstrate via words and delivery that you want to help Charlie and CJ improve their performances.

Schedule follow-on performance review meetings every 30 days for the next six months, or for whatever time increments Christopher and Gabriella's manager counseled. These meetings are intended to ensure that Charlie and CJ are making progress and hitting objectives.

For Next Time

As Gabriella already knows, one of a sales manager's most important responsibilities is performance management. True performance management goes well beyond the numbers. It stretches into the methods and intangibles that in the long run allow salespeople to exceed their goals and achieve personal growth. *Performance appraisals are a major part of the performance-management process.* Many firms have their own well-defined process. Some key points include the following:

- Define an appropriate performance period. Many companies use one business year in order to have accurate performance data at the time of the review. A year is the longest acceptable period for salespeople and sales managers. Shorter periods are more desirable for sales, but that depends on company policy, your personal style, and your people's needs.
- Develop and set *both* business and personal goals for each salesperson.
- Develop a performance plan (or sales plan) for each salesperson. The sales plan should be focused on business goals, the numbers, and should cover the who, what, where, why, and how associated with bringing in the business.

- Create a development plan for each salesperson. The development plan should focus on personal improvement goals. Some personal goals will address becoming a better salesperson while other goals will address becoming a better person. Some sample elements of the plan could include attendance at corporate training sessions; other sales or product seminars or courses; skill sessions such as listening, computers, and proposal writing; or books to read and tapes to hear. The development plan must reinforce the sales plan.
- Monitor, coach, and give feedback continuously throughout the performance period.
- Execute monthly or quarterly interim performance reviews on a less formal, but a structured basis.
- Place notes, both good and bad, in everyone's personnel file as the year goes by. Record big and little observations and coaching notes. Date them.
- Start organizing and writing reviews at least a month in advance, simultaneously giving your people time to gather and prepare their own notes.

LESSONS

Giving an unsatisfactory appraisal is a challenge. Using your resources is a major lesson of this problem that will stay with you throughout your career.

Unsatisfactory appraisals should never be surprises. At the first inkling that a salesperson has done something subpar, a sales manager must coach or counsel. You respect managers who give you useful, quick feedback, don't you? When you screw up doesn't it feel better if someone tells you about it in a constructive manner right away? Appraisals then become a review of what everyone already knows.

The best performance appraisals are built comment by comment on an ongoing basis throughout the performance period. A good practice is to devote 15 to 30 minutes at the end of every week popping notes into everyone's personnel file. You will feel so good, so confident, so prepared, and so pleased with yourself that you may even look forward to future appraisals.

Performance appraisals are serious, complex matters. Search out further training on the subject.

8–7 THE PROBLEM:

A customer asks for removal and replacement of your sales rep.

THE STORY

Homer, the VP of purchasing at a major customer called one day and shouted, "Luke, if you don't get this guy out of here you can kiss all of our business good-bye."

"This guy" that Homer was referring to was Ralph, a longtime successful sales rep with Luke's firm who, like many salespeople, apparently had come across someone with whom he just didn't click. The phone call was not a complete surprise because Ralph had previously hinted at the coolness of the relationship. Luke had also witnessed that Homer was a demanding person with whom to work when he traveled with Ralph.

Homer's emotion overrode his explanation on the phone, and Luke couldn't get a clear explanation of the issues. The problem with Homer's opinion and emotion was that Homer was influential and had a lot to say about *who* got the business—and how *much* they got.

TEMPTATIONS

These situations are more likely to happen as professional buyers continue to face mounting pressure. The following emotional, defensive postures can come naturally.

Assert your dominance

"No one is going to tell *me* how to run *my* business! After all, I'm the sales manager."

Unequivocally follow Homer's lead

"I'll give Ralph a good verbal lashing . . . chew him out royally for screwing up a major customer. I'll yank Ralph off of the account immediately."

Protect your own

"It's time to remind Homer that he's lucky to have *my top guy* servicing him."

Don't be personally offended. This problem is not a challenge to your hiring and deployment judgment. This happens to all sales managers.

WHAT HAPPENED HERE . . . ?

You don't *really* know what happened. Not yet.

All Luke knows is that the chemistry may not have been the best, so the phone call should not have been a total surprise. These problems are seldom surprises.

Ralph may have been asking good, tough questions of Homer. The questions could have had the effect of exposing Homer's weaknesses or flawed order-award process.

Ralph could have done something to have a negative effect on Homer's personal performance measurements, or to cause Homer to catch some heat from his colleagues.

There could have been a piece of bad work on Ralph's part. A single event, at the worst possible time, may have gotten out of control.

It may be that one of Ralph's recent recommendations led to an operational or financial problem—and embarrassed Homer.

There could have been poor support from someone else in Luke's company, and the effect of that action was mistakenly or prematurely laid at Ralph's feet.

It could be that Ralph was not paying attention to changing expectations within the account. There may have been sudden pressures or changes at the customer site that neither Luke nor Ralph were aware of. Customer situations *are always changing,* and reps who have been servicing a customer for a long time often fail to monitor the dynamics.

Perhaps there has been a continuing, and unknown, repetition of a minor irritant. There may be a style issue here—something about Ralph's behavior, mannerisms, language, or habits that irritates Homer.

A competitor may have planted seeds of distrust because the competitor's rep wants Ralph out. Ralph could be getting *too much* business. As underhanded as it sounds, this stuff happens.

It could be that Homer has nothing personal against Ralph, Luke, or the company. He may just want someone stronger—with better skills and knowledge—to meet his needs.

Options

You have only two options here—Ralph stays or he goes. But you have several implementation alternatives.

Possible Actions

Remove the Emotion from the Situation

Tell Ralph to "lie in the weeds" if you think this can be handled quickly.

Ask others in your company (marketing, technical support, shipping, customer service, credit, and so on.) who are in regular contact with this customer to be especially sensitive and supportive of the account during the problem-solving period. Ensure that all open transactions will be serviced beyond reproach.

Alert your manager to the situation. Present an outline of your approach and inform her that you will keep her posted as the problem solving and implementation develop.

Do not broadcast the situation all over the firm. Do not let others read blame or hysteria into your words or actions. You don't need more fuel on this fire.

Listen

Go into a fact-gathering mode. Just remember—there are three sides to every story. Homer's story. Ralph's story. And the real story. Try to side with your rep as long as you can.

Call Homer back after a short time—after he has calmed down—and matter-of-factly ask Homer to share any additional details or issues. Let him know that you want to thoroughly understand the background and the situation. Let him know that you intend to work with him to solve the problem and, if necessary, advise him of any short-term or interim actions you are taking for account coverage.

Meet with Homer eyeball-to-eyeball (if distance permits). You're going to learn *a lot more* when you look him in the eye. The objective of this call is further information gathering. Prepare in great detail. Make it a two-person call, if possible, with someone who already knows Homer, so that there is someone else to absorb perceptions and comments. Be alert for both professional *and* personal issues or differences. Take notes.

Project yourself to Homer's side of the desk. What do *you* see? If you worked in Homer's job, what is *your* assessment? What would *you* like to see happen?

Pay particular attention to the adjectives—the descriptors—being used by Homer. The strength of those words will often make your decision for you.

Inquire if Homer has suggestions for a replacement. Having Homer help create the criteria (or nominate an individual) makes him a part of the process and implicitly requires him to support the new choice. There can be devious motivations at play here, so be careful with this question. Make it clear when asking the question that you will abide by his suggestion if at all possible. If you say no to his suggestions or recommendations you may become "0 and 2," not "0 and 1"—and you don't want a "strike three" at a major account.

Meet with other key contacts at the customer location by yourself, with the other person who accompanied you, or with Ralph.

Do an analysis of the situation with Ralph. The customer called for a reason. Meet with Ralph both before and after your Homer conversations and meetings. Dialogue in a non-accusatory fashion. Pay attention to Ralph's adjectives. Keep your cool and stay impartial. Don't let Ralph read you wrong, or read you as having already made up your mind. Ask Ralph for *his* recommendations and take notes.

Consider asking a former manager of Ralph's at your company if he or she has any ideas or observations based on his or her personal knowledge of Ralph.

Talk to support staff and other departments in your company that regularly have contact with Homer. Get the history. Look for signals and for those adjectives again. Don't indicate possible courses of action or any predisposition in those discussions.

Ask other reps who may have previously dealt with Homer what his propensities are and what their opinions are of Homer. Peers are less likely to be objective so as not to incriminate Ralph, so don't even ask their opinion about Ralph, but be ready for volunteered comments.

Study

Examine the most recent account transactions in great detail. Go through all the paperwork for the last several months. Separately, review all of Ralph's weekly, monthly, or trip reports.

Take a renewed look at Ralph's style, work habits, actions, and attitudes.

Find someone in your company who you know has the *best* relationship with the account. For example, the customer-service manager or a service supervisor. See if that person can help you develop the action plan and deliver the solution.

Think

Consider the implications of your actions and delivery. Take an account-first approach, keeping names and personalities in the background.

- Do not look for blame or place blame.
- Dwell on solutions and implementation, not causes.
- Watch how you frame the problem solving and the delivery of the solution. Make it "us against the problem," not "Ralph against Homer," or "us against Homer."
- Do not let anyone perceive that you are on a witch hunt.
- Don't make yourself the new rep, and don't let that happen accidentally.

Execute

Review your implementation plan with your boss and all affected parties before you execute the first step. You must all be singing out of the same hymnal. Practice your pitch. Let your manager and that aforementioned best-relationship person critique it. Keep Ralph in the loop throughout the whole process. You *need* Ralph.

IF THE DECISION IS RALPH STAYS: *Ask* Homer for a second chance. Don't just *tell* Homer that Ralph is staying. Counsel Ralph and have him modify his behavior. Tell Homer what actions you've taken with Ralph, and thank Homer for his continuing support. However, the level of Homer's displeasure may take away this option.

You could take a team-selling approach at the account. If practical, keep Ralph in the account but *out of that department*. Have someone else work with Homer. Since many major customers are now handled by teams, a realignment of people may be possible.

IF THE DECISION IS RALPH GOES: Put in a new rep whose credentials are *clearly* equal to or stronger than Ralph's.

Consider using a realignment-of-territories strategy as a cover to put in a new rep. That protects your role as manager, Ralph's ego, and Homer's position.

Consider turning the account into a house account, letting someone on the inside manage the business and the relationships.

Consider using the opportunity to elevate the account to national-account status because, as the story notes, this *is* a major customer.

- If time and distance allow, implement your plan and deliver your solution message personally to Homer. Do not delegate this task. If a personal visit is not practical, do it by way of a conference call with the new rep and other key players. Don't even *think* about doing this via letter or fax!
- Thank Homer for bringing the matter to your attention and for his continuing business. Limit the hand wringing. Get the conversation and the relationship back to business as usual as quickly as you can.

- Don't ask Homer if he is satisfied with the new rep, otherwise you may find yourself on a personnel merry-go-round. Homer's success at orchestrating this change could prompt him to repeat this little scenario if he is at all displeased with the new rep. It could happen in a heartbeat. Once a customer sees that he can manage you, it is not unusual to see repetitive behaviors with other business matters.
- Brief the boss as the implementation unfolds.

Stay personally involved with the account for a long period of time, and let Homer *see you* involved and concerned.

Watch the numbers like a hawk for an extended period of time. Watch the key sales activities, such as RFQ's (request for quotations), proposals, demonstrations, and visits, that lead to further business.

Execute more frequent account reviews with all parties concerned.

Follow up

Consider sharing this story with your other direct reports, *but leave that decision up to Ralph.* Show others on the sales team how the two of you turned the scenario into a win. If Ralph made any errors, let him admit it. Ralph's courage and forthrightness could set a good example for others to come forward with similar potential problems.

LESSONS

A problem such as this is the tip of an iceberg. You have more marginal or unsatisfactory account relationships out there than you realize. You must proactively search them out.

Travel with your salespeople on a regular basis and assess their skill sets, knowledge base, and customer and sales-partner relationships. This will always be the best way to expose these potential conflicts. When you see cool relationships like our story, leap on them before they leap on you.

Always ask your people where they think they are vulnerable, where the chemistry is poor, or where they are at risk for personal reasons. Don't accept "none" as an answer. No one is so lovable and professional that they do not have detractors in their territory. Proactive reassignments can generate incremental business.

Encourage your people to come to you first to be taken off an account, before a problem such as this descends on them. Of course, this action creates another problem. Your rep may be trying to unload a dog. Stay alert.

part nine

TROUBLESHOOTING SALES-PARTNER PROBLEMS

9–1 THE PROBLEM:
You are having trouble finding good, capable sales partners.

THE STORY

"Terese, you're not going to believe the fax I just got," Magdalena howled to her general-sales manager. "The sales manager and the marketing manager of our distributor in Brisbane both quit the company. It seems they had a big fight with the owner. We're dead! They were our key contacts. The owner doesn't know diddly about the business. We're going to have to find someone else immediately. They were our top distributor in Australia."

Magdalena, who was the Pacific-region sales manager was frantic. "What do I do?"

"Do we know anyone else who can fill those shoes?" Terese asked, feeling just as depressed.

"No, I don't have a clue," said Magdalena as she rushed out.

TEMPTATIONS

Attrition of key individuals can sabotage an existing sales-partner relationship and cause a supplier to scramble. Frustration can lead to some questionable temptations.

Hope and prayer
> "Let's maintain the current relationship and keep our fingers crossed. I have faith the owner will hire new people who are just as good."

Infinite arrogance
> "People down there will have heard about this. We are *so* well known and *so* respected, I'm sure we'll get a ton of calls and letters from folks asking to represent us."

Sales-partner roulette
> "Here's a name I heard at a cocktail party. Let's take a chance. I think he'll work out."

The best time to look for partners is when you don't need them. Sales managers must always keep their eyes and ears open. This is always a #1 priority.

WHAT HAPPENED HERE . . . ?

You lost your horses. Magdalena doesn't know the details, but she knows she's in hot water. She's really upset or, as they say in Australia, "mad as a cut snake." Other events that cause churning of sales partners include:

The world is opening up. Suppliers are venturing into new markets, and the demand for top sales partners has skyrocketed, causing some to drop one principal for another.

The unacceptable performance of a sales partner could be driving a supplier to consider a replacement.

Financial strength and working-capital requirements have gotten more important for partners. The resources needed are bigger than before. A partner could have closed the doors or scaled back as a result of the pressure.

Suppliers are changing their strategies, processes, and technologies, and that has an impact on partners' roles. More partners will be changed out because they haven't kept pace or can't keep pace with operational demands.

And finally, the shoe could also be on the other foot. A sales partner could fire a supplier for lack of performance, support, or the inducements of a competitive supplier.

OPTIONS

You will always have these four options with this type of problem.

1. Go to the file. (If Magdalena had been doing her job she would have a ready file of potential candidates.) How does your file look?
2. Redesign your sales channels in the affected market and reach customers in a whole different way. Sometimes adversity creates a fortuitous opportunity.
3. Decide to invest and set the two departed managers, or someone else, up in business opting for either a majority or minority stake. That option is becoming popular in some sectors and strategic markets.
4. Start the search process from scratch. (Part of the search process in the case of our story could be approaching dealers or major customers of the collapsed distributor.)

It is imperative to have the best possible partners out there.

Here is a supporting quote. "The choice and resulting performance of a specific partner or partners are, of course, the ultimate determinants of the success or failure of a marketing channel. All of the planning and analysis means absolutely nothing if the right partner cannot be found to execute it." (Stern and El-Ansary, *Marketing Channels*, Prentice-Hall.)

POSSIBLE ACTIONS

You need a search plan. That plan should include drawing up a search process, designing a profile, and identifying all potential sources of candidates. (In Magdalena's case, it may be a good idea to track down the two departed managers and ask for recommendations.)

Common Threads

Whether you are looking for an independent sales agent in Kansas, a retailer in Sweden, a value-added reseller in Brazil, or a distributor in Australia, the search process is the same. Whether the partner you're looking for is a big company or a mom and pop entrepreneur, the same due diligence is required. Whether you're selling frozen chickens, personal-care products, or engine components, the best approach is to put together a team of sales, marketing, finance, and executive players (and possibly human resources) and assign everyone a role in the search-and-interviewing process.

Draw up a Rigorous Process

Duplicate the rigor your firm would employ if it were searching for a top executive.

The selection process is a variable series of steps from initial contact to making the official appointment a grand ceremony. The process can include multiple interviews; presentation of your company and support program; visits to the candidates' offices, showrooms, and warehouses; customer visits; site or installation visits; credit checks and financial reviews; reference checks; reviewing draft sales and marketing plans; reviewing draft contracts; and obtaining sign offs for your ultimate choice. Create a process that meets *your* needs.

Thoroughness breeds good decisions.

The discipline of a meticulous process is not lost on a potential partner. It is a great way to send a message of professionalism and start a relationship on a high note.

Build It—and They Will Come

It's time to build a profile. Get your search team together. Your profile is a detailed description of the type of organization with which you want to work.

The first step in building the profile is to *identify the common denominators of success of your existing partners.* Make those common denominators the basis of your profile.

Think About the Future

Don't appoint sales partners only for today's business; appoint them for tomorrow. Your vision of the future is the next point in building your profile. Your future partners will likely and necessarily have capabilities different from the capabilities your current partners possess . . . but what kinds of capabilities?

What will be going on in your business and industry tomorrow? Characterize *anticipated changes* in product and services, end-user buyer demands and behaviors, and your business structure and strategies. Partners must meet the realities of tomorrow. Think about those realities as you build your profile.

Classical Competencies

Here are 20 common profile elements that research indicates many firms look for in their partners. They are not in any particular order because priorities vary by company.

1. *Reputation* in the market is critical. Their reputation becomes your reputation.

2. *Honesty and integrity* are imperative. These traits can minimize or eliminate all kinds of future problems and issues.

3. The *financial strength* of the potential partner is mandatory. You'll want people who can pay their bills and invest.

4. *A creditable track record* is key. The track record is a window into the future.

5. The candidate must have the *physical resources*—the plant, equipment, technologies, and facilities—to get the job done.

6. The candidate must have a *viable organization*. Without the depth and breadth of horses, don't expect the business.

7. Partners must have *services capability*. It's one thing to be able to sell products, but it is another thing to provide the needed front-end and back-end soft stuff. Buyers expect it.

8. Partners must be *knowledgeable* and committed to keep themselves smart. The capacity and hunger to engage in continuous learning is key.

9. Your business philosophy and the partners' business philosophy should be a mirror image. Look for that *reflection of values and beliefs*. It reduces future conflicts.

10. Partners must be good marketers, salespeople, and managers. One talent without the other is no good. You must find people who are able to manage their business.

11. *Chemistry* is a factor. When you have found a good and capable partner you'll also want to know in your gut that it feels right.

12. *Language* is important. The top management of international partners should speak English—or you or another key manager in your firm need to know their language.

13. *Positioning* as one of the top revenue producers in a partners' business helps guarantee results. You won't get much attention if you're an ant on the back of an elephant.

14. With many international partners today, *political competence* is just as important as product and market competence. It's whom you know, as much as what you know.

15. The partner must be *totally committed* to the job and be willing to spend big chunks of time and cash to build the business. Commitment means immersion by the top execs.

16. Flexibility and versatility assist speed of response in the market. Because business is always moving and popping, ensure you have a partner who *can handle change*.

17. The capacity for open, close working *relationships* is imperative. A partnering approach or family approach will help you to work together as a team and overcome obstacles.

18. Your products and services should *complement* other elements of the candidates' business. Commonality or linkage means your stuff will be pulled as well as pushed.

19. The candidate should be able to spell out *plans for growth and continuity*. You don't want to start looking again anytime soon.

20. Their *capacity to integrate you* is key. Make sure the partner can handle the load. Some candidates will honestly turn you down, but the greediness of others will cause you harm.

There are literally hundreds of other small, but critical, criteria that could be a part of your profile. Identify them to ensure the best possible fit. The better you can design and articulate your profile the more likely you'll satisfactorily fill it. Recognize that different markets may need slightly different profiles.

In the end, the management team should be able to look at the profile and look a candidate squarely in the eye, and say, "We're serious." "We mean it." "This is the kind of organization with which we want to have sales-and-marketing partnering relationships."

Profile Applications

Once the profile is together and on paper, it's time to put it to use. Some of the best uses are as a handout to inquirers, a trade-show handout to interested parties, an embassy leave-behind for the commercial attaché, an agent-distributor-search (ADS) guideline and a Gold-Key search guideline, a newspaper or trade-journal ad outline, and as an interview guide.

The profile is also a good reinforcing tool with existing partners. Share it.

Potential Sources of Sales Partners

Suppliers have found the following sources and techniques most effective in finding good, capable sales partners. The key is to explore them all.

- *Networking*—always at the top of anyone's list. Make it a practice to inquire of everyone you come in contact with.
- *Competitors partners.* Someone else's sales partner could be fed up with the treatment and ready to move up to a more compatible supplier.
- *Your suppliers.* Talk to the people who provide products to your firm.
- *Your service providers.* Talk to your banker, attorney, accountant, auditor, consultants, freight forwarder, customs broker, advertising agency, and public-relations firm to get names of their contacts in various markets.
- *Complementary suppliers.* Call your counterpart at firms whose products and services parallel your own.
- *Ads* in trade newspapers, journals, directories, association magazines, and local newspapers. The potential list is long. Your problem will be focus.
- *State-trade promotion organizations.* These organizations are anxious to improve the business health of companies in your state.
- *Associations.* Virtually everyone belongs to an association of some kind. Look in the Directory of National Trade and Professional Associations at your library.

- *Telephone directory Yellow Pages*, both overseas and domestic. These are available at libraries and many U.S. Export Assistance Center offices.
- *Trade show attendee lists.* These are available from show sponsors and organizers.
- *Existing partners in neighboring markets.* The network is tight, and the grapevine is usually hot.
- *Existing customers and clients.* If you appoint one of their recommendation, there is shared ownership and commitment to that new partner.
- *The U.S. Commerce Department.* Their trade shows, Gold Key Service, agent-distributor service (ADS), industry and country desk officers in Washington, trade missions, catalog shows, commercial attachés in overseas embassies, matchmaker missions, and ads in *Commercial News USA* are all outstanding sources. Contact your local Export Assistance Center of the Department of Commerce.
- *The Foreign Agricultural Service.* Agricultural suppliers can contact the Agriculture Department in Washington.
- *Direct inquiries from interested parties.* This is listed last because many will be a far cry from your profile . . . but every once in a while you'll find a gem.

Utilization of this list, and continuous networking, will lead to many additional sources.

Go!

Get out there and spend time in the markets talking to candidates. Look under the rocks. You can't expect to find good, capable partners by phone or fax from behind the desk.

When you go, prepare yourself well up front and execute your meetings and interviews in a professional manner. Spend an extensive amount of time with candidates. Investigate them thoroughly. These decisions are too important to be casual.

Sell Yourself During the Process

Sometimes the problem is not identifying good capable partners, but signing them up. Don't turn interviews into tests. Enthusiastically sell the candidate on your company, products, commitment, long-haul view, support programs, growth plans, values, and operating culture.

Reality Check

No one will fit your profile exactly. A profile is a guide, a map, and a standard. Don't get so wrapped up in the knots that you fail to see the value and beauty in the whole tapestry.

Go with what works for you and what local conditions dictate as customary.

Finally, profiles change because business conditions and environmental factors change. Revamp your profiles at least once a year.

Candidates Are Looking at You Just as Hard—if Not Harder

Sales partners are expecting more from their suppliers . . . more information, support, linkage, and perks. Partners around the world want long-term relationships.

Expect that both international and domestic candidates will come to discussions armed with an extensive list of probing questions about you and your business. Be ready.

Take Your Time

Time is enemy #1, the biggest part of the problem. Take the long view. Don't rush into a relationship. Think of the search-and-appointment effort as an investment.

LESSONS

Always keep your ear to the ground because you can never tell when there will be an emergency.

Part of your job of developing a good understanding of your markets is identifying and tracking all the possible sales partners in those markets. Build a database. Treat the process with the same intensity as the process you would use in looking for salespeople and sales managers.

The important thing is to take your time, clearly define who and what you are looking for, explore all possible sources, and make a decision as a team.

There is no need to compromise. There are capable sales partners all over the world.

9–2 THE PROBLEM:

Sales partners are not giving you a fair share of their efforts.

THE STORY

As the plane touched down in Caracas, Jerry, the director of Latin American sales, and his accompanying sales engineer were already tired from an extended South American swing.

Surprisingly, Luis, the distributor's sales manager, was not at the airport to meet them as they expected. Riding up to the city in a taxi, Jerry was wondering if this relationship had any future. Luis hadn't been at the last sales meeting, and it had been almost two years since Luis visited Jerry's offices in the United States. There didn't seem to be any enthusiasm for the business.

They were anxious to meet with Luis and also with the general manager and the new product manager, so they hustled over to the offices only to be told that everyone had been delayed at the warehouse outside the city. It sounded questionable.

Rosa made them feel at home with coffee, but now Jerry was seething.

TEMPTATIONS

It's difficult to handle disappointment in situations when people in which you had so much confidence, and in whom you rely heavily, come up short.

Fire them

"I'm tired of baby-sitting and trying to be nice. These guys are history."

Read the riot act

"Luis, this is [expletive]! If you want the stuff on back order, get your act together."

Challenge

"Okay Luis, how are you going to prove to me that you want to represent us? You've got three months to turn it around."

Effort is linked to relationships, and relationships are more than a business cliché. That's what must be challenged.

WHAT HAPPENED HERE . . . ?

You don't seem to be high on this distributor's agenda. The signals aren't good.

It may be that Jerry's company's style has been one of arrogance and bullying behavior. Jerry and his firm may not have been treating their distributors as independent business entities, as partners, and as a result distributors are avoiding him.

The distributor could be absorbed with internal structure, finance, or management problems. The firm may simply not have the resources—the people, money, or time. They may not be sharing their problems because they don't trust Jerry and fear that he'll terminate them.

Luis and his firm may not be competent marketers. They may be too proud to ask for help, don't know what to ask for, or are uncomfortable with Jerry's coaching.

The distributor may not be committed to Jerry's firm. It could be that Jerry's products are just being used to fill out their line card, or to keep Jerry from establishing a distributor relationship with one of the distributor's local competitors.

Other suppliers could be taking hold of the market, and a competitor may have begun to supply products to Luis. If we assume the lack of a written agreement, that fact possibly emboldened Luis to seek other sources.

Jerry may have given his products to a firm that already has too many lines, or Jerry's piece of this distributor's business is so small he's an inconsequential supplier. This may be the wrong partner and could point to Jerry's sales-partner selection process as being disjointed.

Perhaps Jerry doesn't understand what motivates his partner and hasn't been sensitive to reading and meeting those needs.

And finally, Jerry's firm may about to be terminated.

OPTIONS

Jerry has two options.

1. *Bail out.* If he bails out he has to deal with the local legal complexity, that in spite of no written agreement, Venezuelan law will treat this as a formal relationship that could keep him out of the market for years and may cost him compensation in the process.
2. *Dig in.* If he stays (assuming that the distributor wants him) he has to make a major investment in this relationship.

But first—determine if this is a keeper.
Before rebuilding and investing in this relationship, its time for a gut check. Is this salvageable? Do you *want* to salvage it? Does the distributor want it just as much?

- Ask yourself if this firm would meet your *current* sales-partner selection criteria.
- Is there a better alternative in the market, or would you hire these people today?
- Has something about their business changed since you established the relationship? For example, has a principle owner retired, has there been a major drain on cash, has there been a change in strategy? Have they decided to be in a different business?

It may be best to bite the termination bullet now, rather than later. If it's a keeper, then plow your energy into option #2, which may incidentally strengthen relationships with *all* other partners.

POSSIBLE ACTIONS

Scrap the original agenda. Bring out a clean sheet because it's time to go back to square one.

Think

Examine your actions. Have you contributed to this problem through your inaction, discombobulated processes, lack of support, lukewarm commitment, or arrogant style?

Would you feel excited and committed if *you* were on the other end of this relationship? Would you be thrilled if a principal with your track record were coming for a visit?

Does your product or service fit with the rest of their lines and with their business strategy? If the fit doesn't make sense to you, ask the partner to explain it.

The cultural aspect of overseas sales-partner work adds a level of complexity, *but the issues associated with sales-partner effort are the same all over the globe.*

Talk to Your Partner

Jerry should put the facts and figures aside for a while and spend some time on the relationship. It sounds as if both sides need a little time to get personal. Jerry might want to change his flight and spend an extra day or two in Caracas. Leave the papers in the hotel.

Slowly turn to discussing the situation in general terms, seeking to understand local conditions, the distributors' plans and priorities, and what steps the two of you can take together to build the business. Outline a game plan that identifies activities, timing, and responsibilities.

If the tone of the discussion is sour, ask the partner if he would like to terminate the relationship. By opening the door for a partner, it makes it easier for him to be honest and to save face. Be prepared for the same question in return, so don't ask the first question if you're not ready to offer an honest answer to the second.

If the tone is positive, arrange some visits to several current customers so you can gain firsthand information on your products from users. Thank the partner for his openness.

Go Home and Build a Model for Increasing Share of Effort

Design a four-element share-building model based on commitment, communications, support, and expectations management. These four elements are the basis for a mutually profitable partnering agenda. The objective of the model is to facilitate an overwhelming advantage for your partners in their markets.

1. COMMITMENT MEANS . . .   Commitment is executive-management involvement and active participation in the sales-partner network. It also means money, but there is no substitute for personal time invested in relationships and sales and marketing efforts—here or abroad. Executive commitment is a cornerstone that sends a strong message. Don't invest in the other three elements of the model without it. On the sales-partners side, commitment also means active executive involvement.

2. COMMUNICATIONS MEANS . . .   Communications is a comprehensive package of hooks that keep the partners together.

Communications is not simply heavy use of the phone, fax, or E-mail, but rather *how* information is supplied, *to* whom, *by* whom, in what forum, how it's packaged, how often, and how substantive it is. To that end Jerry should make sure that he has these nine sets of hooks, all of which are intended to improve the relationship. Here are some sample hooks.

1. *Key documents and publications.* Publish clear, useful policies and procedures, prepare a distributor manual to organize all important documentation, furnish a fair contract sensitive to the needs of both parties, regularly distribute a dedicated sales-partner newsletter, and provide a bidirectional key-contact directory to ease mutual access.

2. *Daily operating information.* Examine the user-friendliness and usefulness of regular documents and electronic transmissions such as order-status reports, lead-time reports, shipping notices, and technical bulletins. Consider how value can be added to this infor-

mation. Ensure that the partner knows how to use and take full advantage of the information. Don't take these operating documents for granted.

3. *Hospitality practices.* Take the time to be a warm host (or guest) to build relationships. First-class treatment and sensitivity to protocol can create enduring associations.

4. *Group relationship-building activities.* Execute top-quality regional, national, or global sales-partner meetings, institute a distributor, rep, or dealer council, encourage reciprocal office or factory guest visits, and suggest reciprocal guest speaking engagements.

5. *Technology.* Keep abreast of the rapid changes in presentation technologies, electronic data interchange (EDI), networks, communication devices, special-application software, and sales-force automation (SFA). Invest in technology when and where it offers mutual advantage.

6. *Business planning.* Share business, sales, and marketing plans and execute periodic formal business reviews on mutual action plans. Partners like to know where you're headed as much as you like to know their strategies.

7. *Recognition programs.* Institute informal and formal rewards and incentives. Public proclamations of appreciation and quiet personal thank yous both go a long way. Gratitude is a great relationship builder.

8. *Cultural considerations.* Since the global economy is a fact of life, include internal cultural-sensitivity training, language training, and bicultural staffing. Be sensitive to the content and style of written and verbal communications and read extensively to keep up with current events and business practices in your partner's markets.

9. *Reciprocal communications.* Show your partner what communications you would appreciate in return, such as forecasts, market and competitive information, and changes in the partner's business. Demonstrate how you will use that information to further strengthen your support.

All these hooks are effective in helping to build share of effort.

Which ones should you use? Only those that make sense to both partners, of course. Answers to the following questions will help define your communications plan. "Does the hook strengthen understanding?""Does the hook strengthen the relationship?" "Does the hook help my partner's business?" "Does the hook help our business?" "Do these techniques make it easier for them to do business with us?""And does the hook fit in our budget?"Be creative with your communications. Experiment, ask your partners for needs, maximize internal-staff contribution, and execute all the hooks with professionalism.

3. SUPPORT MEANS . . .   Support is a *comprehensive* toolbox of materials and programs. Support is more than tossing a few brochures, data sheets, and a cost list on the table. It is coaching and counseling, responding to exceptions, and bending a rule from time to time to add value to what's in the toolbox.

Jerry must build a three-point-support toolbox. Here are some sample contents.

1. *Sales and marketing materials.* Supply *quality* sales aids such as drawings, analyses, comparisons, testimonials, ad copies, trade journal articles, application abstracts, endorsements, test results, photos, overheads, videotapes, disks, slides, CDs, cutaways, and models. The key point with sales materials is to *share ideas* on when, where, and how to use those items.

Supply *quality* promotional materials, point-of-purchase displays, trade-show materials, posters and signage, literature, camera-ready art, and product manuals.

2. *Sales programs.* Sales programs are people and activities that can help spur local sales. Provide a liaison who is a solid businessperson as the key field contact; provide product, market development, and business-skills training as needed, service support, technical support, hotlines, help desks, a sales-operations guide, proposal assistance, quotations assistance, sales seminars, and open houses.

3. *Marketing programs.* Furnish an industry voice and visibility to the market, market development and research, product development, quality programs, corporate advertising, corporate trade shows, a quality lead-referral system, customer-survey assistance, local service or parts depots, inventory-management programs, competitive analyses, and most important, *acceptable margins, or commissions, as the case may be.*

Everything in your toolbox helps to build share of effort. Customize your toolbox contents. The objective should be quality and usefulness, not quantity.

Answers to the following questions will help define the contents of your toolbox. "Does the item meet a need?" "Does the program solve a problem?" "Does the tool help my partner's sales efforts?" "Does the investment help our business?" "Does the toolbox make it easier for them to do business with us?" "And does it all fit in our budget?" Jerry should be just as creative with his support efforts as he was with communications.

4. EXPECTATION MANAGEMENT MEANS . . .   Expectations management is a report card that identifies, measures, and shares mutual expectations. When partners share their mutual expectations and agree to specific performance criteria, they can measure and improve upon performance.

The analysis should take the form of each partner identifying and communicating expectations and then evaluating each other against those expectations. Everyone in the sales channel likes to know where he or she stands. If you have clear and measurable expectations between a supplier and its sales-partner network, and both parties act to meet and improve upon those expectations, the revenues and profitability of the partners should improve, and the level of partnering, dependency, and understanding will grow.

Management must be willing to open itself for examination, measurement, and critique to a greater extent than ever and in essence have its partners help manage the business. At the same time, management is also taking on the responsibility to help manage its partners. A company that practices expectations management must understand that it is effective only if it is practiced bidirectionally. The report card keeps everyone focused and on track.

Build a Bond with Your Partner

In summary, here is a top-ten list that Jerry can use to further strengthen the bonds.

1. Pick the right partners in the first place. Flawed selection processes are often culprits.
2. Make sure you keep working to understand your partners. The task never ends.
3. Treat your partners as partners, not as customers or hired guns.
4. Be out there! Regular, substantive, shoulder-to-shoulder contact is a great prescription.
5. Make sure your partner understands all that is available to him or her with your communication hooks and support toolbox and reinforce the message regularly.
6. View every partner relationship *individually.* Their differences in tenure, markets, organizations, competition, and other variables demand it.
7. Always look for ways to make it easier for the partner. The partner will then make it easier for you.
8. Don't let your partners live or die by the grapevine. Make sure *you're* the one announcing new products, organization changes, structural changes, operating problems, or other matters in which they have a vested interest.
9. Compile a best-practices model of all the top-notch activities and approaches you see utilized throughout your partner network and share it with other partners (to the extent that you are not compromising your partners' proprietary information).
10. A fair share of effort is built on the bedrock of trust and integrity of action.

A Concluding Credo

> If you give your partners an overwhelming advantage in their markets, they will give you an overwhelming share of their effort.

LESSONS

A major lesson of this problem is that it causes you to take a long, hard look at yourself and your practices. Where there is smoke, there is fire. When one partner is not giving you a fair share of their effort, others are probably doing likewise. This problem is most often systemic.

It takes a well-organized effort and investment to build and maintain a fair share of effort in sales partners. These attitudes don't develop overnight, and don't expect your corporate logo or brand names to carry the load. These dynamic relationships must be nurtured with sweat.

9–3 THE PROBLEM:
A reseller's performance is below expectations.

THE STORY

The two of them were quietly absorbed in the figures. The sales director, Ray, and one of his area managers, Woody, were looking over the bookings figures for the past month. Glastonbury Systems caught their eye.

"The year is half-gone, and sales are only 62 percent of where they were last year," Ray noted.

Glastonbury Systems was a value-added distributor. They took Ray's products, made some modifications, added some software, and included some services in their final package.

"The trend is not good. These people have been with us for seven years. I thought this was an anomaly two months ago," Ray somberly added.

"Yeah, so did I. Chuck and his team have sure gone soft," added Woody.

TEMPTATIONS

When a reseller's performance falls, the initial rush of responses is often a reflection of the relationship. If you're close, the temptation is utmost patience and unruffled coddling. If there's been a history of contention, temptations are likely to be wild hip-shots.

Take him behind the woodshed
  "If we ever catch you falling down again, you're 'toast'."

  or

What, me worry?
  "Hey, this guy is a rock. I have confidence in him. I'm sure he'll turn it around."

The right answer is a middle course. Emotion and predispositions are the chief enemies of performance improvement.

WHAT HAPPENED HERE . . . ?

It's tough to tell. We really don't know much.

There are two kinds of performance problems with resellers that are relationships based.

1. *Open problems*: Open problems are characterized by spontaneous disclosure, awareness, and understanding. There is often a lot of ranting and raving and mixing-it-up, but things are happening. They're not hard to handle.

2. *Closed problems*: Closed problems are characterized by stealth, uncertainty, or ignorance. People aren't communicating. Stuff is probably going on behind the scenes. They are much more difficult to address.

This appears to be the closed, or difficult variety of a reseller-performance problem. The troubles are usually in one or more of three major areas. All need exploration.

INTERNAL RESELLER ISSUES: Glastonbury Systems may be going through an internal upheaval. Priorities could be in flux, new lines may be in the process of being designed, cash may be limited, the organization may be churning, or they could be considering an exit from the business. The prospects are lengthy.

MARKET ISSUES: Market conditions for Glastonbury's products may have declined, competition may have become fearsome, major customers or major market segments may have dried up, or the market may have outrun Glastonbury's capabilities. The possibilities here are also lengthy.

SUPPLIER ISSUES: Ray's firm could have been providing lukewarm support and direction. Woody may have assumed that he could focus on other resellers because Glastonbury had a good track record. In some manner the supplier has dropped the ball. This is a common cause, but a most difficult one to 'fess up to. (There may be a "Woody problem" buried in here that Ray will have to address as well.)

OPTIONS

First, a couple of questions to frame possible options.

Is this a reseller that you would be happy to see go away, or is it a firm that you value, need, and want to improve?

How is the state of *your* business? If you are in good shape you may be able to afford a little more time and investment. If not, options may need to be quicker and harsher.

If you are Ray, you then have five options.

1. *Let it go*. Extenuating circumstances or other priorities in your business may mean letting it slide temporarily.

2. *Touch it lightly*. Resources or the relationship may warrant that you issue a gentle wake-up call, ratchet up your attention a bit, and give it time—the gentle-laxative approach.

3. *Jump on it*. Take a firm and serious approach to investigate, counsel, and help turn the situation around.

4. *Terminate the reseller*. If you have alternatives in the market and the relationship or circumstances lead you to believe that there is no hope, then end it. Delay hurts both parties.

5. *Put another reseller in the same market.* If the dynamics of your business, market needs, and the existing reseller's limited capabilities warrant, add another reseller or sales channel.

POSSIBLE ACTIONS

Ray needs to have a serious discussion with his area manager, Woody. Assuming they've decided on option #3, a detailed review of the reseller may shed some light on the situation.

Check the Signals

Both managers must think hard about what they had been, and currently are, seeing and feeling. Performance problems *should not* be sudden problems. You should be able to see performance problems *well in advance* and begin taking action when they are small and manageable.

There are common signals.

- Communications dry up. Calls or faxes are not returned as promptly, and conversations become shorter and cooler.
- Someone reports that the reseller's organization, staffing, financial situation, or other infrastructure-related element has changed.
- It becomes more difficult to get together. The reseller begs off on attendance at meetings because of other priorities.
- Reports or forecasts, normally on time, are now late or missing.
- The normal bitching and complaining dries up. Questions dry up. Arm-twisting for concessions dry up.
- The reseller stops squeezing you for literature, demo samples, and promo materials.
- Attendance at a hot show, conference, or exhibition is suddenly canceled.

What are other early warning signals in your business? Ask the people in your sales unit to identify and confirm your personal set of signals. The key point with these signals is that they are observable *before* there is a slowdown in orders or bookings, and the signals themselves *must* precipitate immediate action.

Additionally, *when* were the signals first picked up, and *what* was happening in your business and the markets at that time? The answers may offer some clues.

All of Ray's people should be trained to keep their eyes and ears open for the signals. Immediate reporting of signals should be the rule. No one should be afraid to cry wolf.

For Safety's Sake

Just to be sure, Ray needs to check *what* he is measuring. Are Ray and Chuck using the same performance ruler? Is Ray just measuring bookings, or is he measuring specific product performance, market-share growth, key market/account-development activities, or other items. Ray must be sure that Chuck understands on what he is being measured.

There are literally hundreds of different expectations that one firm could have of the other. Does each side know what the other side expects? Are the expectations between the two firms aligned? What communication took place between Ray's and Chuck's firms to ensure that expectations have been communicated? To what formal event, meeting, or document can Ray point? Does Ray have a process that ensures that goals, objectives, and expectations are communicated and embedded?

Self-assessment

Judgment on performance is a two-way street. Ray may have unwittingly contributed to the problem. Ray must ask himself: Have I failed to execute or provide something? Are my communications "hooks"and support "toolbox"as fresh, complete, and relevant as they could be? As a next step, Ray might want to consider asking Chuck if he, Woody, and the firm have been doing everything possible to meet Chuck's needs. He should expect "no" as an answer. Ray must then repair or remove legitimate issues that originated with him. That *could* make the problem disappear.

Time to Talk

Step #1 should always be to ask why. Sit down with the reseller and go over the business in detail. Listen closely to what the reseller says. Ask second- and third-level questions. In turn, share the facts as you see and know them. Don't *ever* show up at a performance meeting without opinions, without ideas, or empty-handed. Ask "How can we help?" "What did we miss?"

Find out what the problem is—the *real* problem—*if* the reseller will let you know. This is a big reason to have a good relationship with your resellers. Chuck must let you inside his business. The distributor will let you get involved in his business only if there is trust and a good relationship. You must be close enough to him to be able to creditably counsel and be listened to. If there is trust, help, get involved, and straighten the situation out quickly.

If there isn't trust (and there probably isn't since this is a closed problem) you'll have to convince Chuck to trust you first. It may take several trips, figuratively sitting on the same side of the table, poking at the problem, and slowly inching toward solutions.

It may help Ray and Woody in this process to visit Chuck's customers with Chuck's staff so they can see what's happening firsthand in order to make better recommendations.

Action Plan

Both parties must come out of the meeting (or meetings) with agreed-upon actions and time-tables. Sample actions could include:

- Reduce the territory or take away one or two product lines to take off some of the load.

- Joint creation of a short-term sales-and-marketing plan.
- Specific training for specific people at either Chuck's or Ray's location.
- Cooperate on a special program for a specific product.

Both sides must then vigorously implement the plan, after which it becomes a case of shape up or ship out. *Your next step, or consequence, must be a part of this action plan.*

Habits that Build a Performance-based Culture

Performance must be nurtured through creation and management of a culture defined by Ray. Ray should employ the following items that fit his circumstances and add more of his own. He should continuously churn his culture to keep it performance-focused.

• Performance criteria must be laid out clearly in your contract. Use them as a performance and evaluation tool.

• Measure performance one at a time. Resellers all have a different heritage, resources, and market conditions.

• In the process of handling performance problems, document everything.

• Use your regional and worldwide sales meetings to foster performance and team-building.

• Use your annual user conferences as a forum for an exchange of ideas, issues, and strategies.

• Bring all your resellers in and have them share their plans and activities with one another.

• Have the resellers work the booth or the platform with you at trade shows, exhibitions, and field days.

• Conduct formal quarterly, semi-annual, or annual performance reviews.

• You need market experience to evaluate performance. Make sure you know what you are talking about.

• Put and maintain a comprehensive toolbox of support programs in place. Freshen it regularly.

• Conduct thorough reviews of major systems' opportunities and execute tight reviews of losses.

• Initiate a rep, dealer, or distributor council.

• Put proposals together as a team.

• Coach and counsel on creative promotion and advertising techniques.

• Set mutually agreed goals. Talk about performance against goals regularly.

• At the *first sign* of trouble respond with everything and everyone you can.

• Ask for a market analysis on a regular basis. It can tell you if the reseller knows what's going on.

• Ask to see a formal marketing plan. Show yours. There is a correlation between plans and performance.

• Implement formal and informal recognition programs.

• Review the inventory whenever you visit the reseller, or do it at least quarterly or semi-annually.

• Ensure that you have top-quality area managers who are proficient coaches supporting the resellers.

• Make regular executive-level visits to the resellers to build relationships.

• Monitor market development and promotional activities—along with sales results.

• Reformat your inventory rotation and management practices, if required.

• Make use of your industry association for guidance on relationships, expectations, and performance.

• Link up your sales-force automation systems and employ electronic data interchange (EDI).

• Share your values and philosophies, what's going on in your business, and where you are going.

• Don't hurt yourself with your own pricing practices. Let the reseller make a buck.

Create and Share a Best-practices Model

It is likely that Ray has seen and heard numerous creative and effective reseller business practices, or common threads of reseller success. He must share those practices, a model of excellence, with the rest of his reseller network, respecting proprietary interests in the process.

LESSONS

Strong relationships are imperative to maintain and improve performance. Stay close. Get closer.

Leap on performance problems as soon as you pick up a signal. Problems are much easier to solve at an early stage. Make sure you aren't a part of the problem.

Build a performance culture and manage everyone on the basis of that culture.

Make every possible effort to try and cure performance problems. The cost of starting over is almost always higher.

Examine your reseller-selection processes. If you pick the right reseller in the first place, performance problems can shrink dramatically.

9–4 THE PROBLEM:
A distributor is having trouble getting support from a principal.

THE STORY

Jan is the sales manager for a specialty-wholesale distributor.

The company represents 21 manufacturers, one of which is a problem. The principals product is a good one, and Jan is glad he is handling it, but his performance would be better if he had better support. It seems the only time he hears from this principal is when they want an order. To date he has tolerated this principal because of their unique technology.

Jan has hardly heard from his counterpart, Todd, at the principal, except for last-minute price-change notices or other operating communications, which come across as admonitions or dictates. There is simply no substantial relationship.

TEMPTATIONS

Your frustration could easily lead to retaliatory conduct, which is most often self-destructive.

Withhold payment

"We'll hit them where it hurts. These turkeys can wait. Maybe it'll wake them up."

Second-shelf them

"It's time we gave them some competition. There are other suppliers out there."

Disregard their edicts

"We'll just forget about the forecasts."—or—"Screw the sales meeting."

It is often difficult to understand why firms whose livelihood depends on each other don't bend over backwards to build relationships.

WHAT HAPPENED HERE . . . ?

This is an old-fashioned Neanderthal alliance.

Each of the partners seemingly has a very different definition of support and a different set of expectations regarding the relationship. Todd's firm may be new to selling through alternate sales channels. They may think that they are doing exactly what they're supposed to do. Additionally, many principals erroneously think of distributors or dealers as customers rather than as sales partners. Todd may naively assume that Jan is a self-sufficient enterprise merrily plodding along.

Todd may be new in his job as well and doesn't understand his responsibilities or the myriad of options that he has available to support his sales partners. Management may have wrongly assumed that Todd knew what he was doing—a common explanation for this problem.

Todd's firm may be consumed with internal problems and priorities having to do with operations or other matters and has unconsciously let the sales partners slide to the back burner.

Other markets and sales partners could be more important. Maybe there are some squeaky wheels out there that are getting all the attention. Another issue could be the fact that Jan or his market is viewed as small potatoes by this manufacturer.

Todd's firm may be in financial difficulty, and as a result Todd has hardly any budget—or no budget—to support his sales partners. Some principals are also flat-out misers trying to unload *all* marketing costs on their sales partners.

On the scary side, Todd could be looking for another distributor, getting ready to terminate Jan, or is planning on adding another distributor in the region.

OPTIONS

Putting yourself in Jan's shoes, you have two big questions to answer.

One. Do you *really* want this line? Is it an important element of your long-term strategy? Would you be hurt badly if you didn't have it and someone else did? You have a business to run and a reputation to protect. If you're not successful, *you* are the one who will be blamed, not the principal. If you want the line, then you have to put together a support- and relationship-building campaign. If the line is not critical begin to look at other suppliers and terminate this principal.

Two. Who's got more muscle, or power, in this relationship? Power is the principal method of one sales partner to get another sales partner to do something. Power is built, and shifts through time, through the possession and control of resources that are valued by the other partner. These resources include such things as brand names, market knowledge, reputation, contacts, customer base, technologies, financial resources, the size of the firms, the presence or lack of alternatives, and other measures. If you have the bulk of the power you can be more aggressive demanding support. If the principal has more power a softer approach is called for.

POSSIBLE ACTIONS

Jan's goal is a renewed level of commitment, a partnering relationship, and solid support. He needs to remember that this may be a *long-term* process unless Todd catches on real quick.

Huddle

Jan needs to get his team together and discuss how to get and hold the attention of this principal's top sales and marketing executives.

Outline a Support Program

Using the following five menus of typical sales-and-marketing support items to draw from, Jan should draft a support package that contains *selected items* that meet his needs. Jan must be able to show Todd how the requested support will integrate with Jan's sales-and-marketing plan, *how* and *where* he will use the support, and how it will enhance their *mutual* results. Jan may think that all the items on the following five menus are self-evident, but many principals aren't aware of, or never thought of, many of these items.

SALES AIDS. Sales aids are items that Jan's salespeople will use to strengthen a sales call. Sales aids amount to something in the hand that can be left behind or used to emphasize a presentation point. Principals can easily and economically provide most of these items.

• Samples	• Trade-journal articles	• Product literature
• Drawings	• Newspaper articles	• Company-capability literature
• Analyses	• Technical data sheets	• Services brochures
• Comparisons	• Test results	• Oversize photos of products
• Testimonials	• Endorsements	• Photomicrographs
• Ad copies	• Reprints	• Overheads for presentations
• Cutaways of products	• Specialty software	• Videos for process descriptions
• Scale models	• Multimedia presentations	• Disks with presentations on them
• Sample-product components	• Application abstracts	• Slides for presentations

SALES PROGRAMS. Sales programs are supportive activities that Todd can develop and that Jan's business can apply to strengthen his sales-management and selling efforts.

- A dedicated sales manager from Todd's firm whose job it is to support Jan's business in daily operational matters
- Product, service, and installation training for Jan's staff at Todd's facilities and at Jan's location
- Dedicated customer-service and technical support from Todd's firm for quick resolution of issues
- A sales-operations guide that details proven sales techniques and recommended sales activities
- Proposal and quotations assistance on opportunities of joint effort or unusual size or complexity

- Engineering support for product modifications and customization
- Sales counseling and teaming on large or complex opportunities
- Demonstration support, demo protocols at dedicated sites, or adequate demonstration samples
- Corporate seminars for large groups of Jan's targeted prospects at industry events
- Formal open houses and factory visits for prospect groups or individual customers
- Effective communication on inventories, order status, lead times, delivery, receivables, and other hot daily info
- Regular national or international sales meetings to exchange ideas and issues
- Detailed communication of competitive information and counterselling strategies
- Contests for the sales, marketing, and service people and promotions and incentives for management

MARKETING AIDS.   Marketing aids are items that Todd can provide and that can be very useful to Jan's business to generate awareness and promote interest. It's likely that all of these aids already exist. The key here is to suggest to Todd how the marketing aids can be made even *more* effective or utilized to *greater* advantage in Jan's market.

- Promotional items to be left with customers and prospects
- Camera-ready artwork for Jan's own brochures
- Prepared advertising copy for Jan's own local efforts
- Point-of-purchase displays for Jan's sales counters, showrooms, or offices
- Trade-show materials and samples for Jan's own local shows
- Posters and signage for Jan's facilities, and for shows, exhibitions, or conferences

MARKETING PROGRAMS.   Marketing programs are activities that Todd can execute to strengthen local market development and promotional efforts.

- Executive leadership from Todd's firm, active in the marketplace and at special events
- A creative, regularly refreshed World Wide Web site
- An industry voice and visibility in industry forums, associations, and periodicals
- Broad market research that feeds Jan's understanding of trends and needs
- Corporate print, TV, radio, and special-event advertising to create awareness and help pull in prospects
- A cooperative advertising program to help local market development
- Direct-mail programs to spur customer interest
- Corporate leadership and sponsorship of selected trade shows
- A lead-referral system that gets *quality* (emphasis quality) leads to the field quickly

- Customer surveys to measure customer satisfaction and probe for needs and wants
- Expeditions physical-distribution programs or warehousing that provide a competitive advantage
- Price protection on outstanding business, early price-change notification, and flexibility for unusual situations

BUSINESS PROGRAMS.   Business programs are activities that Todd could provide and that could be useful to strengthen the management practices at Jan's firm.

- Business-skills training, such as planning, cash management, and personnel practices
- Inventory-management programs that minimize costs, prevent out-of-stock situations, and ensure hot-item access
- EDI or other automated information systems that cut costs and improve productivity
- Sharing of strategies, business plans, and marketing plans so that Jan's efforts are consistent with the principal's

Jan and his team should modify, scrub, and distill his five menus and present them fully or piecemeal. Principals sometimes create sales-and-marketing aids and programs in a vacuum and clog them with redundancies despite the best efforts of sales partners. *Offering to help with the design of support-program elements and offering to be a pilot user helps ensure support-program usefulness.*

Engage This Three-point Support-Building Strategy

1. ENCOURAGE A PARTNERING APPROACH.   The following 12 points characterize an understanding, supportive principal. Jan can use this guide to tactfully reinforce his expectations.

1. Management at all levels of the principal is committed to distribution and to a coherent systems structure. The principal understands wholesale distribution.
2. Top management at the principal is intimately involved in the relationship.
3. The principal makes a superior product and is committed to total quality management.
4. The principal is financially strong enough to keep investing in production technology and product development and works aggressively to keep costs down.
5. The principal has capable field management and headquarters staff people supporting you.
6. The principal provides a fair contract.
7. Communications are quick, candid, and substantive.

8. The principal responds to problems and contingencies with a "we" attitude.
9. Principal management won't desert you over a big order or go behind your back for business.
10. The principal's credit department exhibits a good balance of fairness, firmness, and creativity.
11. The principal works with you as a team in all planning matters.
12. The principal is committed to mutual profitability and mutual growth.

Jan could modify this list to suit his situation, and he should expect that Todd, as he grows to be a supportive principal, will reciprocate with a list of distributor expectations of his own.

Benefits of a solid partnering approach include mutual help in a crisis, exceptions to policies when needed, avoidance of wasteful efforts and investments, early information on subjects of mutual interest, and reciprocal preferential treatment in times of unusual demands.

2. CREATE INDISPUTABLE VALUE IN YOUR MARKET.   Jan must work to make his distributorship a more valuable asset to this principal. If he does some things such as create market-education programs, create and share a specialty sales tool, offer kits and systems, provide extracurricular reports on industry and market issues, provide enhanced forecasts, use the latest computer systems, maintain a good customer database, and certify himself to do testing, training or service, he is adding value. Jan adds more power to himself through his own initiatives, becoming more desirable and thus creating more leverage for further support requests.

3. SHOW-AND-TELL.   Show Todd your business and marketing plans, show him the other lines you sell, show him how you bring in the business and how you hold on to the business, show him how the market development, service, training, and maintenance you provide is enhancing the principal's image, show off several of your customers so he can hear from the horse's mouth, and show off the investment in your facilities.

Tell Todd about the problems that his misunderstandings of your efforts cause, tell him about the lost opportunities when his firm doesn't listen, tell him how the voice mail makes it difficult to talk to real people, tell him about the impact of his firm's extended lead times, tell him how lack of follow-up has cost you both business, tell him how inaccessible upper management makes it difficult to make plans, tell him how his unilateral decisions affect your commitment, tell him how not seeking your opinions is costly, and tell him how treating you as an outsider hurts both of you.

Simple Tactics to Complement Your Campaign

Here's a final list of minitechniques guaranteed to foster a supportive relationship.

- Invite Todd or his sales manager to sit in on as many of your meetings and training sessions as possible.

- When you talk about your customers, talk about "our" customers.
- Discuss and display the effective support practices of other noncompeting principals.
- Keep your prices high, and make sure Todd knows your focus is on profitability.
- Pay the principal's invoices on time.
- Visit the principal regularly, but only when you can meet with top management and you have a crisp, substantial agenda.
- Invite executives from the principal to visit you. Make the time spent a good blend of business and relaxation.
- Introduce Todd and all of his people to all your employees. Let Todd see the capability, depth, and enthusiasm of your team, no matter how small it is.
- Send Todd articles and advertisements about your firm from the local press.
- Ask Todd to have his sales manager in your place x times a year and establish expectations for that visit.
- Keep Todd and his colleagues posted of organizational changes and responsibility changes in your firm and ask him to reciprocate.

Now that you've got your campaign outlined, pick up the phone and schedule a meeting to launch a new beginning; then persevere until you've got the relationship where you want it.

LESSONS

You can't sit back and assume that all principals are of the same caliber and understand your role. You may have to take the lead in many situations. Sales-partner work is not as well-known as direct selling among many sales and marketing executives.

Setting the example and making mutually beneficial suggestions can position you for long-term advantage in the marketplace and gain security for your business.

Don't put all your eggs in one principal's basket. Diversify your lines and relationships so that if one pulls out or can't support you, you're not left high and dry.

This problem cuts both ways. Principals also expect solid performance in response to their support, so don't ring their bell unless you're ready and able to bring in the business.

9–5 THE PROBLEM:

A manufacturer's policies are violated by a distributor.

THE STORY

Michael took the call from his Argentine distributor. Antonio was upset because he had discovered that several of his dealers had been offered product, or obtained product, from another distributor at prices he could not afford to match.

"From Jearl, in New York, am I right?" offered Michael.

"Si, of course," Antonio responded.

Jearl was one of Michael's largest wholesale distributors and had a reputation as a wild card. Jearl had often not sent people to training, failed to submit requested point-of-sale reports, wasn't following up on leads, and sometimes tried to muscle returns outside of policy.

Michael's exasperation was at its limit. And he now wished he had a contract to fall back on.

TEMPTATIONS

When a sales partner blatantly disregards policies it is easy to yield to emotional temptations.

Neglect him

"We'll devote our time and support to other distributors in the area."

Isolate him

"I don't think I'll invite their people to the next sales meeting."

Punish him

"I'll divert the next shipment to the West Coast where they're screaming for product."

When you have these feelings, recall "Dear Abby's" advice. "People who fight fire with fire usually end up with ashes." Each member of the sales channel is part of a bigger organization, so remember that you are in effect managing yourself when you manage partners.

WHAT HAPPENED HERE . . . ?

A sales partner stepped out of line and upset the network. The fact that there is no written agreement exacerbates the problem.

Jearl may not respect Michael, his company, or his policies. He may see Michael's policies as burdensome or obsolete. The distributor may feel that Michael won't enforce the policies. Jearl may see Michael as weak and indecisive and that if he did try to enforce his policies, Jearl would simply go over his head. He may have even refused to sign a contract in the past.

Michael could be a new sales manager, and the old one had a whole different way of doing things and let the sales partners get away with virtually everything.

Michael's firm could have fuzzy boundaries to begin with, and Jearl may have heard from other distributors that Michael doesn't enforce primary areas of responsibility.

The distributor may be getting ready to dump Michael and buy from another supplier, so they are just unloading their inventory wherever they can.

Finally, maybe Jearl's play was just a dumb move—a mistake. Chalk it up as ineptness. It never dawned on Jearl or his staff to think about implications. Not likely, but it happens.

OPTIONS

If you're Michael you have three options with this problem:

1. *Do nothing.* Accept the situation because of circumstances out of your control or because of additional risks that action could create.
2. *Terminate the partner.* If the history, current performance, and existence of alternatives are such, you could elect to use these issues to end the relationship.
3. *Counsel the sales partner.* Take steps to stop the partner's violations, gain compliance, and bring the relationship back to standards—and get an agreement in place.

Before Michael picks an option he must consider who has the power, and how much. Possession and balance of power has a lot to do with what Michael can and can't do. Power is the ability of one partner to get the other partner to do something, in this case to enforce the policies.

- How large is his company compared to the distributor?
- Which partner needs the other most?
- Which partner has more or better alternatives?
- Which partner has the financial foundation to withstand a temporary setback?
- Which partner would be the big loser if the other went away?
- What resources does Michael have that are valued by the sales partner and vice versa?

- Is the power Michael possesses sufficient to motivate compliance with his policies?

Each partner has at least *some* power in the relationship. Power gives Michael the potential for creating persuasive messages and taking influencing actions. If you're Michael, it's time to look at the three options again.

POSSIBLE ACTIONS

Assuming that the balance of power is acceptable, settle down for a counseling campaign.

Get the sales, marketing, finance, and operations managers who have a stake in possible outcomes together. Provide everyone with a copy of your policies.

The Facts

Explain the situation to the team, including to the firm's attorney. Share all the facts concerning the questionable activities and transactions and the policy violations.

Review the policy infractions from two perspectives.

1. *Importance of the violations.* When you strip away the emotion, are these critical policies or policies of lesser importance? React appropriately.
2. *Frequency of the violations.* Has this been going on for a long time or are these initial infractions? React fittingly.

After looking at the size and scope of the problem, ask the team if it is willing to go to war over this or how far they are willing to go to gain compliance and get an agreement signed *and* what consequences they are willing to impose and live with if that doesn't happen.

Build Understanding

It is a challenge working with partners who look at things differently. Therefore, call upon *all* the people in your firm who have had contact with this partner and ask them to share their impressions and suggestions. There are gems out there. This is intelligence gathering.

The Message

The message is your simple statement of what you would like the partner to start or stop doing. A formal distribution agreement should be the vehicle. Craft it carefully. Legal assistance is imperative.

The Tools

There are five major approaches, or tools, from which your team can pick delivery tactics to make your message persuasive. Keep Abraham Maslow's wise counsel in the back of your mind: "If the only tool you have is a hammer, you tend to see every problem as a nail."

1. LEVERAGE TO CONSIDER.   When used with care, these levers can help bring your partner back in line.

A. *The carrot*—you can give something to your partner, such as special deals, allowances, assistance, or preferential considerations (within the realm of good judgment) if he complies with your policies. This lever is listed first because it is most likely to create cooperation.

B. *The asset*—you may have special capabilities, knowledge, brand names, contacts, technologies, or products that are of special value to the partner. If the partner lost this asset it could be devastating. This lever has the potential to create long-term loyalty *if* the asset continues to hold its value in the market.

C. *The group*—you may have a reputation of such magnitude and acclaim that the partner likes to be considered a part of your group and bandies around the fact that he is affiliated with you. You are a star and he is a groupie. This lever is sometimes fleeting because stars rise and stars fall.

D. *The entitlement*—you may feel that your history, reputation, and track record are so strong that you are entitled to deference from your sales partners—that you have the right to ask whatever is needed to protect the sales channel. This lever can yield results if you both feel that such a pecking order exists.

E. *The stick*—you can threaten to punish, withhold, or penalize a partner if he or she fails to comply or perform. Sticks are negative sanctions and usually lead to a continuing pattern of adversarial behavior. This lever is listed last because it is least likely to yield results.

F. A combination of two or more of the above.

These levers can be the foundation of your message-delivery strategy.

2. COMMUNICATIONS STYLES TO CONSIDER.   In increasing order of strength, here are six possible approaches to gain compliance. Start at the top or start anywhere in the middle. History and your current relationship will be your guide.

- *Suggest.* Suggestions are advisory statements and review reasons to observe the policies.
- *Request.* Requests are polite and respectful appeals to conform with the policies.
- *Recommend.* Recommendations are serious and official guidance to comply.
- *Instruct.* Formal communications that leave no room for misinterpretation.
- *Demand.* These are firm directives that spell out sanctions to follow.
- *Threat.* Implications and consequences of continued disregard of the policies are stated.

These nuances, when integrated with the levers, help shape the effectiveness of your communications strategy.

3. FRAMING TO CONSIDER. Put a teamwork slant on your tone and delivery. Framing emphasizes that you are both a part of a bigger whole.

- Try to understand motivations and causes, rather than placing blame.
- Talk about progress and moving forward, rather than about the status quo.
- Discuss mutual gains and upsides, rather than loses and downsides.
- Think outside the box and offer some innovations, rather than beating a dead horse.
- Talk about "our" solutions, rather than "my" problem and "your" problem.
- Converse about what could be, rather than what was.

4. PROCESS CONSIDERATIONS. Consider the steps through which you'd prefer to communicate, understanding the potential investment of time, money, and firepower. You can start at whatever point you choose, but anticipate second, third, or fourth steps, as required. Ask yourself what approach this partner will most likely respect, and consider how egregious the policy violations were.

1. A verbal notification by the sales manager
2. A higher-level manager's verbal request
3. A sales manager's personal visit
4. A formal letter of complaint
5. A higher-level manager's personal visit
6. Top executive verbal contact
7. Top executive personal meeting

5. CONSIDER WHO WILL BE THE MESSENGER. Titles, clout, and personal relationships have value. Don't be bound by your organization chart, but judge who is acceptable and will have impact. When considering messengers remember that lengthy parades of executives to halt violations are usually ineffective.

Your counseling campaign should now be ready to kick off.

The Delivery

There will likely be several contacts, but at some point you must lay the contract on the table. Throughout all the discussions:

Display concern for and interest in the partner's agenda. Push for building your own understanding of the partner's actions, trying to determine if the violations relate to poor management, short-term opportunism, or other factors. Don't accept superficial explanations.

Put the policy violations in the context of the entire relationship.

Demonstrate the benefits of the policies to the sales partner. Show how the policies are meant to assist everyone. Make detailed explanations of the policies, as needed.

Offer to help with policy implementation if there is uncertainty, misunderstanding, or limited resources. If there are local issues take a joint problem-solving approach. Don't just throw the policies on the table. Be as flexible as you think is proper.

Make promises of corrective action on your part, if warranted, to eliminate policy one-sidedness, abuses by other partners, or correct associated business practices of your own.

Reference how the policies have assisted other partners and how others comply without risk or loss.

Present the consequences of continued violation. You should have already formulated and accepted your willingness to employ consequences.

Make it clear you want to maintain the relationship.

Hand Jearl the pen.

The Hammer

Sometimes nothing works. Regardless of how much planning you do and how careful you are with your communications, there will be times when you need to take the hammer out of your management toolbox. Use it. Your own style, philosophy, and situation will be your guide.

The Future

A sales partner's willingness to continue to cooperate with you increases with many factors, all of which are under your control.

- *Reputation.* Keep your reputation in all operating areas squeaky clean and ensure that you always come across as a fair, high-integrity firm.
- *Understand your markets.* Conduct market research and surveys to ensure that you know what is out there and share that knowledge to strengthen the partner.
- *Pricing.* Reasonable prices should permit acceptable margins and keep the relationship mutually profitable.
- *Products.* Manage your product-replacement cycle to keep your lines fresh. Weak product causes the partner to look for other ways to make up for deficiencies.
- *Support.* Quality and quantity of support communicates commitment and value. Your support creates an implicit obligation for the partner to uphold your policies in return.
- *Communications.* The higher and broader the communications level, and the more relevant and timely the content, the more responsive both parties will be.
- *Similarity.* The greater the resemblance between the two partners in terms of goals and philosophies the more likely you will cooperate.
- *Training.* Train your own people how to work with partners and how to communicate policies. Poor explanations lead to beliefs that policies will not be enforced.

- *Coaching.* Coach your partner on sales-and-market development tactics and tools to improve productivity, market penetration, and profitability.
- *Joint work.* Get out in the field and listen, and see how and where the partners work in order to build your understanding.

Execution of these items leads to longevity of the relationship, and older relationships lead to even further cooperation.

LESSONS

Written agreements should be considered mandatory between sales partners.

There is a constant internal strain within sales partners. Part of their conscience tugs them toward autonomy, and part of their conscience tugs them toward cooperation. You can add weight to the side that tips the balance in your favor by consistently and proactively executing all the possible actions discussed.

Strong relationships and balanced power (to the extent it is possible) are the basis of enduring and cooperative sales partner arrangements.

9–6 THE PROBLEM:
You must terminate a sales partner.

THE STORY

"You know, boss" Seth said to Nancy, "I am tired of dealing with these guys." Seth was referring to Meriden Enterprises, one of their sales partners. "They sold to one of our customers in the city. They are not supposed to sell in the city. I know that. You know that. And they know that," Seth continued. "They didn't achieve their contracted purchases last year. And they're behind year to date. We've talked about this eventuality with Meriden for some time. We've given them a lot of support and performance counseling to help them turn it around, but it has been to no avail."

"Calm down," Nancy pleaded. "All right, all right, it's probably time to cut them loose."

Ugh, I'm not looking forward to a confrontation, Nancy thought to herself as Seth left.

TEMPTATIONS

Sales partners that do not play by the rules or miss commitments create a real problem for a sales manager. The specter of a termination creates some bad temptations.

Let someone else do it
"I'll be out of here in six months. Someone else can handle the dirty work."

Delay pulling the trigger
"Seth, maybe we should give them more time to recover. Let's hope, and hang in there."

Let them drift into the sunset
"Let's just not bother with them anymore. They'll go away on their own. No hassle."

What are you afraid of? Is it because of the extra work it will generate, because you may look bad, or because you may miss some sales for a short period? You must face up and admit to the reality of terminations. They are challenging, but sometimes it's best to prune the tree.

WHAT HAPPENED HERE . . . ?

A relationship failed. Maybe management, or leadership, on either or both sides, failed. Two parties can no longer meet each other's expectations.

Aside from missing sales commitments and selling outside their territory, there may be other reasons for a termination decision.

- Meriden could be selling without adding the value they contracted to provide.
- They could be doing a poor job of servicing their customers and giving Nancy's firm and its brand names a black eye.
- There could have been other repeated policy violations.
- Meriden may have altered its business or strategy to such an extent that Nancy's products now get minimal attention.
- Meriden may be unwilling or can't afford to invest in things that need to be done.
- Nancy's business may have changed dramatically, and the partner can't keep up.
- The partner may be letting their business run down. Meriden seems to have lost interest and commitment. Meriden could be thinking about closing or selling the business.
- Payments may also be far behind, their financial situation bad, and the outlook worse.

The list can go on. The reasons to terminate a partner can be as varied as the number of stars in the sky. No two potential termination situations are the same.

OPTIONS

Understanding that there is an intent to terminate, there are five major options.

1. Terminate the partner in accordance with policy and your contract. Cease the relationship completely.
2. Terminate the existing responsibilities, but initiate a new reduced-role relationship. For example, take away several product lines and leave the partner with one line.
3. Terminate the partner, but buy some or all of the assets and turn it into a captive distributor.
4. Ask the partner if they would like to terminate you. This is face-saving, relationship-preserving gesture that can be effective in many markets and countries. It is also much easier.
5. Terminate the sales partner but maintain a relationship (a) as a direct customer, (b) as an employee, or (c) in a different sales channel role, for example, having a distributor now act as an independent sales agency.

And there are probably twists and spins to put on these five possibilities.

POSSIBLE ACTIONS

Put yourself in Nancy's shoes and think a minute. What are you doing? You are dissolving a partnership. This is not to be taken lightly. It has fiscal, market, and image implications.

Legal Alert

It is imperative to consult with your in-house and/or your outside legal counsel prior to terminating a partner. The time to do this is at the first inkling that you have a performance problem, policy violations, or operating dispute, *not* when you're ready to pull the plug. Even if the problem gets resolved, it's far better for counsel to have started to review the contract and the circumstances surrounding your potential action. It doesn't matter if the partner is a distributor, dealer, independent rep, or anything else. The legal aspect of many relationships and situations can be extraordinarily complex and beyond your awareness. Whether or not there is a formal document that defines the relationship, this step must be taken. Expect that counsel will grimace noticeably when they find out there is no contract or letter of understanding.

Keep legal counsel apprised as operating actions, any corrective actions, and terminating steps go forward. Consult with counsel *first* so as not to exacerbate your situation. Document all discussions with counsel. Have counsel proof all letters and fax's before they are sent to the sales partner. Copy counsel on all written communication from the sales partner and provide a copy of notes of all conversations with the sales partner.

You should always assume that the sales partner will have alerted his own legal counsel when he first sensed he was in trouble. We live in a litigious society. It behooves you to protect yourself and your company.

The Contract

Nancy must read it and must share a copy with all other managers who will have a voice in the termination decision and process. Ask counsel to explain confusing elements. It's best to err on the side of thorough probing for understanding. Don't let your pride get in the way.

Sometimes the contract has languished in the file, and there is little correlation between what it says, your desires, and what the sales partner has done or not done. This is a hard lesson—to always keep your contracts freshened and relevant to today's business. Let legal counsel be your guide.

The Termination Team

Identify those managers and specialists in the firm that should have a say in this decision. Certainly, marketing management, credit or cash management, top sales executives, the president in smaller firms, sales channel managers, and the manager responsible for this particular partner should take part. The makeup will vary. Meaningful decision making is inversely proportional to the size of the team, but don't leave key stakeholders out.

What Is Your Plan?

Assuming the termination goes as planned, what are you going to do next? This will be one of top management's first questions. Nancy and Seth should probably start to look for, or keep eyes and ears open for, a potential replacement. However, do not commence this searching activity without checking with counsel. There may be implications. A change in sales partners should also be a signal to freshen the profile and process you use to find sales partners.

Perhaps you are thinking of changing sales channels, or modifying the existing channel, or installing a second channel. Keep marketing and product management involved, solicit their suggestions, and again, share your intent with counsel.

As you are terminating one sales partner, consider what you should be doing with the other partners. Terminations often shed light on supplier deficiencies. Correct them as you uncover them. A sales partner network also has an informal grapevine. This partner's problem is no one else's business. Don't air the laundry throughout the family.

Design a Process

Create a logical and thorough series of steps that you will take to conclude the termination. The process should identify who will do what, and when. If the firm has terminated other sales partners, Nancy should review how past events were handled for lessons learned. Some examples of process steps include the following:

- Contract review by all parties
- Review of the sales partner's business history with the firm, including all actions that have led to the termination decision

- Drafting and reviewing the notice of termination
- Decisions on handling of business in process, including transactions up to and including the termination date
- Decisions on communication of the termination to the sales partner's customers, other sales partners, and internally to all affected departments
- Disposition of inventory decisions
- Disposition of sales and marketing collateral materials
- Receivables handling, and agreement on any write-offs
- Decisions on payment of commissions or other compensation or benefits due
- Execution of the actual termination notification
- The transition business plan in the vacant market, including support of existing customers and how inquiries out of the market will be handled

The process will vary. Nancy and Seth should draft the process, trying to think of everything that should be done, and then have the team, including legal, edit it.

Execute

Carry out the termination, step by step, as planned. When it has been accomplished and memories are fresh, get the team together to document lessons learned for the next time.

A Model for the Future

Establish a procedure that represents a series of steps that you will execute in the event of future termination-inducing problems. Your reactions to an impending termination are extremely important. Subjectivity and inconsistency have no place in termination actions. For example, if you choose to terminate a sales partner for not making their contracted minimums, it is important that you terminate all partners that do not make their contracted minimums. If you do not, your actions could be looked upon as arbitrary in nature and there may be repercussions.

Another example: Chances are you have not been as operationally consistent as you should have been. Many companies have a tendency to overlook infractions when the violator is a good sales partner. This practice could cause a problem when you want to take a strong stance with other less favorable partners.

A suggested model:

Let all your partners know that, regardless of past practices, any breach of contract or policy could result in termination. Be precise with your language. Do not leave anything for interpretation. Have legal help craft your messages.

1. *First offense:* After the communication, if there is a contract violation or policy infraction, slap their hand—hard. Do it in a way that clearly states that you do not condone the actions and that a repeat of the actions could cause termination. Document it.

2. *Second offense:* If the partner ignores the first warning and there is another problem, you must take stronger actions. For example, if they bought product from you at a discount and then resold it to a customer they were not authorized, by contract, to sell to, you could bill them back for the discounted amount. Put the warning in writing again and reiterate that the next violation will cause termination.

3. *Third offense:* If the partner ignores the second warning, terminate them. Do it with all the aforementioned suggestions in this problem.

Customize the model to your liking. Make sure that legal is a part of its design and sign-off. The key point is that this will let you have a *consistent framework* within which you can customize specific words and steps associated with execution. Consistency has great value, but don't become its prisoner, in this or other sales-partner matters.

LESSONS

Terminations are almost never surprises. But, as with an employee, it is best to try and take every possible step to cure the infractions because the costs associated with replacement can be high. However, there comes a time when a termination call must be made. Unsatisfactory or marginal sales-partner relationships are a handicap to both parties. It is best to sever them.

This problem teaches you the value of good legal counsel and the value of good contracts that reflect your strategy and desires. Make sure your contracts are clear regarding termination.

This problem reinforces the necessity to document performance and policy issues so that if a termination is necessary the stage is set to handle it properly. You learn to act very objectively, precisely, businesslike, and in concert with your colleagues when faced with executing a termination. There isn't room for any other kind of behavior.

This problem also teaches you that everything you do today in regard to sales-partner management helps set the parameters for tomorrow's potential terminations.

part ten

TROUBLESHOOTING INTEGRITY AND JUDGMENT PROBLEMS

10–1 THE PROBLEM:
Your salespeople are providing questionable entertainment.

THE STORY

It was Monday morning, and Tom was reviewing expense accounts. "WHAT?" he bellowed as he bolted upright, simultaneously grabbing the phone, upon seeing the $657 receipt from the Flaming Promises on Jules's report.

"What in the world is the Flaming Promises?" he screamed into the mouthpiece.

"Hey, Tom, it's all right, it's that new topless restaurant. Great food, and they have all the new microbeers."

"Is that all they have?" Tom loudly responded.

"Hey, the ladies are okay, too," Jules admitted.

"Just "okay," for $657?"

Jules was a good, solid performer, and Tom wasn't naive about the entertainment options his people had.

TEMPTATIONS

Entertainment and the expenses associated with it are a timeless sales subject loaded with all kinds of emotions and tasteless temptations.

Ask to be included

"Whoa, this must be a *great* spot. Take me along the next time that client is in town."

Bury it

"Jules, break this up into little pieces and resubmit them over the next few months."

Results

"All I want to know is, did you get the order? For those bucks, you better bring it in."

Entertainment is awash with management challenges.

WHAT HAPPENED HERE . . . ?

One of Tom's boys looks as if he got a little carried away.

A box of donuts for a meeting, a cup of coffee, a lunch, a ball game, a fishing trip, or a dinner all have great sales value. Entertainment is fun and rewarding. It is one of the great perks of the sales profession. It is useful and it works. It is an element of a sales professional's bundle of tools, just like a sharp presentation. Entertainment can make the selling job easier and is a great way to build personal and professional relationships.

Jules's actions go beyond frequenting the topless bar. There is the question about the size of the expense, and then there is a larger question that deals with appropriate, timely, and cost-effective entertainment.

Did the customer spur this entertainment, saying, "Hey, Jules, it's Flaming Promises time." Maybe Jules is being used in the worst sense of the word "use."

Is the pressure on Jules so intense that he feels the need to spend $675 for lunch and lap dances? "I hope this helps me nail this contract, or I'm a goner."

Does Tom's firm have any guidelines in regard to entertainment, and were they ever discussed? Jules may have recently come onboard from another company where going to the Flaming Promises was sanctioned.

Jules's personal code may leave him feeling that there was nothing improper about the entertainment, and this was the right thing to do to satisfy this customer.

Does Jules feel that Tom is a pushover, and he can get away with anything he wants to do or spend? Jules may not be sensitive to expense control or sensitive to the impact on the women reps in the sales unit.

Like some salespeople, maybe Jules is basically lazy and has come to believe that this is an easy way to get the order.

OPTIONS

You've got to deal with the surprise of Jules's expenses and you've got to deal with the bigger question of entertainment practices.

You have two options with this situation.

1. Tolerate it. This entertainment is a growing fact of life. You may or may not like it, but you could quietly condone it and not promote it.
2. Get a message out on entertainment guidelines.

Beyond that, you need to have a counseling session with Jules, pending which option you choose.

POSSIBLE ACTIONS

Questions to Consider

These are personal and professional matters that demand careful thought and attention. Here are ten questions to stir your reflections about entertainment practices and policies.

1. Do you want to buy the business you gain, or do you want to sell to win it?
2. Do you want to be respected or liked by customers?
3. How do you want your firm, your people, and yourself to be known and viewed?
4. Will someone in your or the customer's organization be a loser because of your practices?
5. Does the nature and expense of the entertainment offered raise your level of anxiety?
6. Does it feel proper, suitable, appropriate, and befitting in the best sense of those words?
7. Is the entertainment you condone exemplary to hold up to your sales unit as a model?
8. Do you want to feed a customer's destructive habits or dependencies?
9. Are you aware that certain entertainment can open up possible sexual harassment cases?
10. Are you convinced that one of the paths to sales success is through good judgment?

Use Your Judgment

The issue with any entertainment *is* good judgment. Business pressures and social pressures cause sales professionals to face challenges to judgment every day.

Judgment is defined as "the process of examining facts and arguments to ascertain propriety and justice," or, "the process of examining the relations between one proposition and another." Some synonyms for judgment include discernment, discretion, wisdom, critical reasoning, prudence, and good old common sense. It would be nice to have your people and your company described with these kinds of phrases and words, wouldn't it?

Good judgment in entertainment spills over into good judgment in other matters such as negotiating, discounting, time on the job, and quality of work. Customers respect good judgment just as they respect integrity, creativity, and civility.

Good judgment in *all* matters is a weapon that can lock out the competition, and good judgment carries more weight the higher up the customer's chain of command you go.

You don't want to lose customers by denying their preferences, but you also don't want to lose the values you hold. It's a never-ending balancing act.

Would your planned entertainment pass the *judgment test* of:

* Having your CEO or director of finance participate?
* Having *all* of your employees participate?
* Telling your family over dinner how you won the business?

Judgment also plays a role in matching the size and nature of the expenditure with the responsibilities and titles of the person being entertained. You don't want to take a client's CEO out for donuts or take a minor official to some posh upscale restaurant, do you?

The entertainment you offer defines you, and your judgment helps your people establish their own judgment skills. Entertainment judgment is about personal choice, about how you choose to be regarded, how you choose to execute your job, and who you choose to be. It is, and always will be, your choice. And remember Janis Joplin's line, "Don't compromise yourself. You are all you've got."

Talk to Jules

At this point Tom has settled on an option. Counsel Jules unambiguously on your policy.

Getting the Message Out

The leaders of any organization establish its judgment guidelines and business tone. Good judgment seeps down from the top over time. An effective sales-unit manager can influence behavior a lot better than dictate it. After setting the example, you can't ignore the example if you think the example becomes personally inconvenient.

Good personal judgment and consistent personal entertainment examples work better than a well intentioned talking-to or policy, but if your company culture is such, put your entertainment policies in writing. If a rep wants to spend his or her own money, that is their prerogative. You can also get the message out creatively. Here is an entertainment self-test.

Entertainment Self-Test—check the box of your choice

Does the entertainment I am planning ooze class?   ☐

Does the entertainment I am planning ooze sleaze?   ☐

In summary, do whatever works for you. Create an effective way to get the message out.

Supporting Actions

Here's a list of tactics that can reinforce your judgment and choices.

- Limit the amount of money that can be spent on entertainment, except for corporate-sponsored events.
- Make suggestions to customers before they make suggestions to you. It is the responsibility of salespeople to balance the places where they would like to entertain with the places that the customer would like to be entertained.

- Sponsor a couple of major events during the year such as golf outings, sailing trips, or banquets, open it for most or all clients, and let that suffice for the year's entertainment.

- Use a national convention or an exhibition for corporate-entertainment events, making it clear that these special events account for your entertainment.

- Use detailed expense-report reviews as a control to shape what is acceptable entertainment.

LESSONS

The benefits of good entertainment judgment include winning business, expense control, solid reputations all around, good use of everyone's time, and professional image.

An overreliance on entertainment weakens a salesperson.

Just as you coach your people on other elements of sales skills and attributes, entertainment etiquette is another skill that needs coaching.

Entertainment is a window for the customer into your company, into its standards and its overall business conduct. Entertainment is a time of relaxation when customers get a truer picture of you—just as you get a clearer picture of them.

Spend company money for entertainment as if it were your own. Judgment, then, becomes much easier.

10–2 THE PROBLEM:
A rep won't accept responsibility for losses.

THE STORY

Larry grimly hung up the phone after speaking with his irate director of technical service. It seemed that one of his account managers was blasting the service department again because of the loss of a major opportunity.

Rob had a reputation of always griping because of service issues, specs not being competitive, prices being too high, or deliveries being too slow. It was time to call him out.

"Rob, I know we lost the Simsbury deal, and service is hot," said Larry. "What happened?"

"We should have never lost it. We have got to do something about the service department. Those people blew it for us," Rob steamed.

This moaning and groaning has reached my limit of tolerance, Larry thought to himself.

TEMPTATIONS

Sales managers are often caught between the need to stand up for their people and the need to step on their people. The tension leads to silly temptations.

Mock pity

"Oh, you poor thing, would you like to borrow my crying towel?"

Join the fray

"I agree with you. Those klutzes can't find their way to the tool room."

Chastise

"Quit sulking, you wimp . . . stand up and get out there and sell!"

Whining over losses can become an infection in a sales unit. It is imperative to stop it.

WHAT HAPPENED HERE . . . ?

The pain and embarrassment of a loss has led to unprofessional judgment.

Rob's pride and self-protection may be at play because he doesn't want to look bad in front of peers. He could have an image to uphold in someone's eye.

Rob may be a poor or average performer afraid of being caught by a reorganization or a sales-channel shift. This problem almost always occurs in poorer performers.

This could have been a complex sale where the team was not identified, ownership not established, roles not clear, strategy not defined or implemented, and with no reviews or oversight along the way.

Someone in service may not have been committed to Rob because he or she had been burned by him in the past.

The business opportunity may have been a visible and strategic situation that management was watching closely. When exposure is high, salespeople are quicker to toss barbs at colleagues.

A strong competitor may be beating up on Rob, and he doesn't want to admit that fact.

Occasionally, salespeople will act this way when they don't understand the job or the expectations. Frustration leads to irresponsible behavior and actions.

Salespeople who are poor listeners often have this habit because they didn't grasp and follow advice when it was offered.

Other business functions or support may have really hurt Rob's sales efforts in the past. You can't discount that possibility, in spite of Rob's track record.

Left unattended, these situations are a bad reflection on the sales manager.

OPTIONS

You don't have any options. You must stop the behavior.

POSSIBLE ACTIONS

Look at Yourself in the Mirror

Do you have an unconscious habit of disparaging other colleagues in the firm when you don't get your way or something goes wrong? If you weren't a part of the strategy development and planning for this particular sales effort, shame on you. Salespeople draw lessons from their manager's actions. Think about these things before counseling Rob's behavior.

Gather Some Facts

The first thing to do is find out who else was involved in the effort and get their quick assessment of the loss. Rob's reputation has likely preceded him, so other people's responses are likely to be tainted by his notoriety. Let them know you're planning a formal loss review.

Think about the relationships between Rob and the other people involved in the sales effort. Is there bad chemistry, a history of poor cooperation, inflexibility, or simply a lack of know-how in working as a team? The answers will help frame your counseling.

Counsel Immediately

Call Rob into the office, after letting him cool down, for a one-on-one discussion. *This is not a loss review*. Site specific comments or behaviors as examples of poor judgment. Tell him the impression that his whining and blaming leaves on others. Use respected sources, documentation, or quotes from others to make your point.

Explain to Rob that his job as an account manager is to manage the sales effort and the resources, not just make the sale. Review that his job is to *lead* the solution of problems, to facilitate teamwork, minimize issues, and ensure that mistakes aren't made. Reinforce that while he is the person ultimately responsible for the win or the loss as the sales-opportunity leader, *teams* win and *teams* lose, not individuals or business functions.

Discuss how much harder future sales will be without the enthusiastic participation of other colleagues who are essential to his success.

Suggest personal apologies to the people involved and leave the execution to Rob.

Communicate the consequences of continued behavior, which could be public embarrassment, reduced responsibility, zingers on his performance appraisal, or turning him into toast. Schedule a personal loss review with him as quickly as possible.

Review the Loss

Treat this one-on-one loss review as a dry run. The primary objective of this review is not the loss itself, but to demonstrate to Rob how his responsibilities and up-front actions could have strengthened the integration of others and eliminated unnecessary placing of blame. Remind him that all salespeople must deal with certain constraints of their employer, disadvantages compared to the competition, and that those are obstacles he is paid to overcome.

Start by reviewing the sales plan and strategy for the sales effort, including a review of all the players involved, the competition, and the customer situation. Find out if he involved the service team before he made the proposal and if he took service management in with him.

It is uncomfortable to relive losses, but that is a fact of sales life. Don't minimize the discomfort. There is a lot of truth in the old cliché, "no pain, no gain." Keeping this dry run between the two of you should minimize defensiveness and rationalizations.

Take a if-we-had-to-do-it-all-over-again-what-would-we-do tack, or a what-should-we-do-if-this-comes-up-again approach. Draw it out on the board or chart pad. Follow your own sales process, dissecting what happened at each step, and discuss the issues and answers all along the way. Project Rob back into the sale by causing him to think about key events and actions. Focus on the planning, the integration, and the application of the people resources he used. Your probing should cause him to call into question assumptions that he may not have previously explored.

Sales-process steps: #1 through *n*	The loss: What *did* we do?	The next opportunity: What *should* we do?
Customer needs and problems		
Our strategy and tactics		
Competitive actions and our responses		
Proposal-and-presentation review		
Issues and answers		
Resources used and roles assumed, etc.		

Build up an appreciation of the roles and responsibilities of others. Use the dialogue to suggest who should have or could have done what. Use the opportunity to suggest how Rob should have coached, monitored, or followed up on other people's actions.

Get the Whole Project Sales Team Together

Now it's time for the formal loss review. Get the other participants and managers together, particularly service management. Limit the meeting to the select few who were involved in the sales effort. Meaningful discussion is inversely proportional to the number of attendees in a meeting, especially a loss review. Have Rob restructure the situation and lead the walk-through, step by step, utilizing the comments and dialogue from your dry-run discussion.

As the sales manager, your job should be to facilitate the discussion and keep it from degenerating into a free-for-all, especially with an account rep of Rob's reputation. Use this loss review to help him resurrect his reputation, as well as review the loss.

Follow-up Coaching

Strengthen Rob's rehabilitation by executing the following activities:

- Spend more time together with him in the field, listening, watching, and coaching.
- Scrutinize his sales plans more carefully.
- Continue to counsel him on tact, discretion, and the reality of office politics.
- Send him to a seminar or a school on team selling.
- Coach him more closely on his next major opportunity, guiding the way.
- Teach him the value of saying thanks and how to express gratitude.

LESSONS

Team selling is a fact of sales life. Many salespeople find it difficult or uncomfortable moving from total responsibility for a sale to being part of a sales team that requires the nurturing of internal relationships. Training in team selling and internal relationship management is essential.

The reality of sales is that support people may let you down from time to time or not meet expectations in spite of your people's best efforts and the support staff's best intentions.

Counsel your people to freely pass out the accolades to celebrate the wins, but to keep disappointment associated with losses in their own pocket.

10–3 THE PROBLEM:

A rep is inflating her expense report.

THE STORY

It was Saturday morning and Leah was reviewing and signing-off on expenses when Michele's report stopped her cold.

"Holy cow! What is this lunch in Atlanta? $147 for two people . . . with a handwritten receipt?" There were also many lunches without receipts below the $25-receipt policy . . . $23.50, $22.95, $24.50, 21.75, $24.00.

"Hmmm . . . I know they don't charge for parking in Centreville."

"A ball game for $233, for three people? Where did they sit, in the dugout?"

"What in the world are these miscellaneous items?"

We need to have a little chat on Monday, she thought as she picked up the phone to leave a message on Michele's voice mail.

TEMPTATIONS

When you discover one of your people abusing her expense privileges you feel a combination of disappointment and anger that can spill over into these temptations.

Compromise

"Oh, well, it's only a little bit. I'll let it go. Besides, she brings in the business, and there were minimal salary increases last year, so this won't hurt anyone."

Hoot and holler

"Damn, Michele, you're a crook! Once more and you're toast."

Hip-shot confirmation

"I always had the feeling Michele was sleazy; now I know it."

Bogus expense-claim control is a part of sales management that demands objective thinking and quick action.

WHAT HAPPENED HERE . . . ?

It looks as if Leah has some hot paper on her hands.

Someone in accounting may have caught some of this stuff in the past and Leah was embarrassed. She looked sloppy and unprofessional and wanted to crawl into a hole, so now she may be doing a more thorough job of reviewing expense reports.

Leah's boss may have come down on her, and now she is cracking the whip in her sales unit. Year-to-date expenses for the sales unit could be over budget.

Sometimes experienced salespeople tend to get sloppy or casual and feel they have earned the right to be creative with expenses, or that they can turn into big spenders.

Michele could be playing catch-up. Salespeople will assume that they have missed some expenses in the past, especially if expenses aren't submitted in a timely fashion, and to even the slate they will throw in expenses to cover a multitude of items they *guess* were not covered in the past. This could be a regular habit, previously undetected.

Leah may have let several items slip through in the past, and Michele keeps pushing and testing for the boundaries of what she can get away with.

Leah may be a new sales manager and is suffering from the fact that her predecessor didn't hold the salespeople accountable for expenses.

Perhaps there is no regular review or discussion of expenses, so the reps may not see it as a priority. New salespeople may not be trained on expense control or Leah's management style may be loose. She may not have a control mentality.

The company may have out-of-date expense policies or no policies at all, or if there are any, no one has been trained on them.

And finally, it may be that all this is legitimate in spite of the bad signs.

OPTIONS

This is simple. You have only one option. Confirm the actions and then stop the cheating.

POSSIBLE ACTIONS

First, Some Questions

Is this the first or the second—or even a third—infraction?

Who committed the infraction? Was this a rookie who doesn't understand or a seasoned pro who should know better? Who committed the infraction should have no bearing on the speed or vigor to address the problem, but it could influence your counseling and discipline. Preferential treatment in regard to expense management is one of the worst things a sales manager can do.

Is this expense report late, or was it submitted on time? Late expense reports add fuel to the suspicion that something may be amiss. Memories are short, and the loss of receipts is more common the older the report.

What is the size of the infraction? Are we talking about one phony lunch or are we talking about a multitude of errors and illegitimate entries?

Does Michele show signs of personal money problems?

Is this a low-level performer nickel-and-diming the company to make up for poor commissions, or a top performer who has learned that lavish spending can be a lazy, expeditious way to get more business?

If the opportunity presents itself, you may want to ask a customer what was discussed during one of those lunches.

Confront

Talk to Michele quickly and firmly, eyeball to eyeball. You will want to see her reactions as well as hear them.

Show her the evidence and explain how it looks to you and why you have doubts and questions. You can't tiptoe through the tulips and neither should you condemn.

For example: "Michele, these lunches are consistently below the receipt level. It appears they may not be real." or "This looks rather high for a ball game." or "Please explain this to me." or "These items look questionable." or "Is this entry inflated?" or "Are some of these entries improper?"

Give her an opportunity to explain and admit her actions. Ask, "Would you like to correct this?" If she concedes, which is highly likely, give the report back and ask for a resubmittal *at a specific time.* Document the incident.

If she is adamant about no foul play on certain items, let them go. You must make a judgment on what is believable and reasonable. The confrontation itself sends a strong message.

Counsel

How you speak is just as important as what you say. This should be a sobering discussion. This is not a time to make light of a serious matter.

Reiterate why expenses must be controlled. Review the company's expense policy. Explain the message that poor expense control sends to others in the company and the impact on personal standing. Indicate that you expect future reports to be timely and squeaky clean.

There is no need for a homily or to spin into a righteous rage. Be quick and to the point, without making the person feel little. The sheer fact that Michele was called in is humiliating.

Don't be surprised if you get rationalizations or policy objections as a self-protection mechanism. Don't let any of that weaken your resolve.

Disciplinary Steps

There must be some level of disciplinary action that accompanies the infraction. Each infraction must have consequences, at an increasingly serious level. Here are some possible approaches:

- If it was just a few small items tell the employee that you expect to never see that happen again. Have the report amended immediately.

- Give a warning that spells out a serious disciplinary step if there is a second infraction.

- Threaten her that future expense reports must be submitted on a certain date or there will be no reimbursement.

- Let Michele know that all expense reports will be thoroughly examined in the future.

- Ask for certain receipts *beyond policy on an exception basis,* or ask for receipts on *all* expenses.

- Tell Michele she will need pre-approval for particular expenses from now on.

- If this is a second infraction, or the expense claims are of such a large size, turn it into an official reprimand and put a letter in the personnel file.

- If the expenses have already been paid, have the correction made on the next expense report or have the money deducted out of the next salary check.

- Termination is a viable option.

Whether this is fraud involving bogus airline tickets or bogus lunches treat it the same. Size of the infraction is not the issue. Repeat offenders should be dealt with harshly. You send a strong message to all with your disciplinary steps.

It's Time to Think

Don't let the event go by without looking at policies and practices that may be contributing to the problem. Consider taking several of the following steps to minimize or eliminate the issue.

How closely have you been reviewing expenses? Look at how you may have created a condition for the problem to exist.

Review your written expense policy with accounting and with your manager. Is the policy out of date? Sometimes written policies languish in old binders for years. You know the ones—they're so old the authors are no longer with the company.

What questions about expenses do you often get from your people? Repetitive questions are signals. If there is always a need to explain something or always the need to make an exception it means there is the potential for abuse. This is a signal to rewrite the policy.

What mistakes are repeatedly caught by accounting? These are also signals that the policy needs to be rewritten—or that *both* you and your people may not understand the policy.

Are you *personally* comfortable with the expense policy? If you're not, suggest modifications. It is very difficult to manage and enforce a policy that you believe is flawed.

What do your people complain about in regard to authorization levels and expense levels? Why? Salespeople will puff up other numbers if they feel there is something legitimate for which they are not getting reimbursed. Perhaps you need to challenge reimbursables.

Look at all expense accounts with *equal* scrutiny and compare the expense reports of everyone in your unit. The items expensed and the amounts should generally be the same. Exceptions will jump up and bite you. React to them.

Look at your personal behaviors in regard to other administrative matters. Lack of scrutiny on major items such as forecasts and reports are implicit signals that expense reports will get the same lax treatment. You must be consistent.

Watch your language. Simple off-the-cuff comments such as, "Hey, I'll handle it, put it on your expense report" are subtle signals that anything goes.

Set an example. When you travel with your people pick up receipts everywhere, note your mileage, be conservative with spending, note your tips, be prudent with your restaurant and hotel selections, and pay for personal items out of your own pocket. When someone gives you a blank receipt to fill in on your own, ask the vendor to fill it in, circumstances permitting. It sets a good example. Let your people see you keeping records and keeping your receipts organized.

Have your sales unit's travel arrangements made through a travel agent.

Assign an expense budget and let people manage their own expenses, then recognize good expense management. Provide a bonus to people who come in under budget. The bonus can be variable depending how far under budget they are. Do this on a quarterly or semi-annual basis for more impact.

Talk to peers. Ask how they manage and control expenses.

Include a provision in your sales-force automation system to track expense. It aids consistency, thoroughness, and timeliness.

Is your compensation competitive, or are you so far off the mark that some people will try to make up for a lack of pay? This is rare, but it happens.

Signals for the Future

Here are some flags to help spot future transgressions.

- Neatness counts. Messy or barely legible reports are often a sign that something is amiss.
- Poor math is a signal that the whole report was executed with the same sloppy attitude.
- The presence of many small nonprovable, nonreceipted items may signal a mentality to go for the "big one" every once in a while.
- Entertainment and mileage submitted in even numbers is not realistic.
- Late reports are often inaccurate because they were done in haste, and haste spawns creativity.
- Missing receipts on a regular basis are a dead giveaway of hanky-panky.
- The miscellaneous column is a euphemism for fudge. Eliminate it.

LESSONS

Good expense management sends a powerful message. It is a small but visible way that the rest of the management team has of evaluating your business skills and your sensitivity to cost control and people management.

Your best weapon against expense-report inflation is consistent scrutiny and discipline.

There is an element of bean counting to sales management. Get proficient at it.

10–4 THE PROBLEM:

A salesperson is making commitments to customers that can't be kept.

THE STORY

Judy looked at the summary of the week's orders and saw one from an out-of-state firm where her company did not yet have trained service people and where the device had not yet been approved to sell. "What in the world is this" she muttered to herself, striding out of the office to find Mel, the rep responsible for that territory.

"It will be months before we can get someone trained for that area. What are we going to do in the meantime? Is the service manager aware of this? How did this get past credit? And furthermore . . ." she blustered.

"Well, no, not really," Mel interrupted. "But I have been after the service manager to get someone trained for that area. I thought this would be a good way to force open that part of our market. You know service is always so conservative," Mel calmly retorted.

TEMPTATIONS

Over-the-line commitments from reps pushing the edge of the envelope probably are one of the leading generators of excess stomach acid among sales managers.

Anger

"Damn! Mel, you bonehead, what's the matter with you?"

Provide air cover

"All right, all right! Okay. I'll go to the service manager and see if I can sweet-talk him, but this is the last time, you hear me?"

Tsk, tsk

"Shame on you, Mel. Don't do that again. By the way, how did you win it?"

Using results to force policy changes is an old sales trick. Who's running the business anyway?

WHAT HAPPENED HERE . . . ?

It seems that Mel's ego is writing checks that the company can't cash. Little white lies have been a fact of sales life since the first human persuaded another to take something in exchange for something else. Improper commitments on delivery, product capabilities, service responsiveness, return policies, product specifications, availability of upgrades, and a host of other sensitive matters are all fair game for some reps.

Perhaps Mel feels that he'll be outta' here in six months on his way to his next assignment because the company is growing very fast and there are opportunities for advancement. Therefore, he doesn't have to worry about living with this situation.

Does Mel feel undue pressure? The pressure to perform, contest or incentive-trip pressure, the boss's pressure, and competitive pressure all cause reps to bend the rules.

Mel's action also puts unwelcome pressure on other parts of his company. Lone Ranger-like antics always have a ripple effect that runs across an organization.

Is Mel a new rep ignorant of the service-support situation? This could be simple rookie enthusiasm run amok. Commitments are often made because a rep wrongfully assumes something.

Customers contribute to some of these situations by not asking questions, particularly of new reps. Reps with a tendency not to ask second- or third-level questions because they are afraid of the possible answers also contribute to the problem.

Tough buyers can also put the fear of God in some reps, who then erroneously fail to serve up distasteful facts.

Mel may have a desire to be liked by the customer or to please a certain decision maker. The desire to gratify is a powerful and dangerous motivator.

New salespeople are sometimes misguided and think that they should tell clients *anything* to close a deal. Those impressions can come from something he read, a misapplied idea from a seminar, watching too many old sales-related movies, or a bad lesson by a veteran during his training. There is no shortage of bad examples out there.

Maybe Mel is not saying some things because he knows it invites negative responses. Omission is just as bad as *commission*. In the customer's mind an omission is just as much a commitment as an explicit promise.

Many reps sell their creative commitments to weak or vacillating managers. Reps can assess their manager's willingness to condone tainted orders. Every sales manager has a tolerance level for questionable business, especially at the end of a fiscal period, during a contest, or when business is bad.

Orders for products that are very difficult to sell, particularly from tough prospects, that are brought in with uncharacteristic ease are also dead giveaways of potentially questionable commitments.

Constant questions about "Can I do . . . ?"—or—"Do you think we can get so-and-so to accept . . . ?" are dead giveaways to reps that have a predisposition to be overly creative or have a vulnerability to misrepresentation. A sales manager that lets her rep do it to her once will be put in that box numerous times.

This problem can really get complicated when the manager is a willing accomplice, assisting with the commitment inside, fabricating cover stories. Managers often cloak their complicity by creating tales of competitive horrors, citing the strategic value of a customer, or the vital nature of the business. Therefore, second- and third-level sales managers and other department managers see a more insidious version of this problem.

OPTIONS

Your options depend on answers to two questions.

1. Is this a first-time offender or a repeat offender?
2. Is this blatant misrepresentation, or was it a dumb, overaggressive mistake?

   You then have four options.

First-time offender, outright misrepresentation	Repeat offender, outright misrepresentation
Counsel the rep and put a letter of reprimand in the personnel file. Consider probation or termination if the misrepresentation was particularly egregious. Company policy should be your guideline. Misrepresentation can't stand without severe action.	If there have been previous written and verbal warnings, then terminate the rep. Tendencies to misrepresentation are often incurable. Termination also sends a proper message to the rest of the sales unit. If there are extenuating circumstances, soften the verdict by letting the rep resign.
First-time offender, dumb mistake	Repeat offender, dumb mistake
Counsel the rep, provide incremental training, increase the frequency of joint field travel, and provide careful coaching.	Is the employee hiding behind dumb? Playing dumb is an old trick. Has this same error occurred before, or is this a different mistake? A series of dumb mistakes is usually a signal to counsel this person out or ask him to resign. The rep may be in over his head.

The option you pick *may* be influenced by a third question: Do you want to keep Mel because he is a valued member of the team, or is this a marginal employee in other regards?

POSSIBLE ACTIONS

Dig fast and deep into the situation because these problems are most often cross-functional problems. Many people are likely affected.

Talk to Your Rep

You need to find out *exactly* what was told to the customer. Go over all aspects of the sale, being particularly thorough with product and price elements that are traditionally troublesome, or regularly raise thorny questions or objections. Your knowledge of your employee, his track record, and especially his integrity with expense reporting, forecasts, and periodic sales reporting will be your guide in this discussion.

Review copies of correspondence, proposals, and quotations associated with this customer.

The issue here is not the order. The order is irrelevant. Under *no circumstances* should you let Mel interpret your words or actions as concern for the order. Your words and actions—with *all* parties—should be about your concern for his reputation and career, concern about the customer, concern about your firm's relationship with the customer, and concern about your co-workers in service and other affected departments. The discussion about the problem and the solution *must* be in that context or your credibility and integrity are irreparably compromised.

In your best nonaccusatory, problem-solving tone ask:
"What happened? Let's review all the meetings and presentations."
"Exactly how did you represent our service capability?"
"What did the customer ask or assume about service?"
"What are the customer's expectation's with *all* aspects of our product and services?"

Ring the Alert

Alert your boss and alert human resources (and legal department, possibly) if this was misrepresentation to ensure your counseling and actions are in accordance with company policy.

Alert the service manager and make it clear you didn't condone your rep's action. The service manager, in an attempt to be a team player may opt to support the situation, especially if business is bad. However, this help may be more of a hindrance, because it sends a message that the rep was right in the first place. This is where the pressure on you may get intense.

Alert the customer. Jointly meet with the customer and allow Mel to do the talking, correcting his own mistake. If a personal meeting is impractical, conduct a conference call. Do not vindictively embarrass the rep or try to make yourself or your company look virtuous. Don't leave it to Mel to clean up the mess by himself, or you are inviting an incomplete or exacerbated story. You could ask the customer to delay the entry of the order until service people are trained, saying that Mel had misunderstood that training had occurred. If the customer wants to cancel the order, let him cancel it without argument.

Alert payroll. Put a stop on the commission payment, or have it reimbursed back to the company via the next paycheck.

Halt the Infection

Making overzealous commitments is a communicable sales disease. Your actions need to be loud and clear. Reps who overcommit typically do not go around bragging about it, but word does leak out. You need to proactively raise the subject by reiterating the relevant policy.

This Is an Integrity Check

Make sure that your words and actions throughout the process can withstand the test of disclosure throughout the company and with the customer.

Implications

In cases of misrepresentation, reps who have been found out understand that their future with the firm has likely been short-circuited. You will probably be asked the question, "Does this affect my future here?"—or—"Can I still expect a career here?"Your best approach is to be candid, not soft-soaping your remarks. Your own judgment, coupled with your understanding of corporate policies will be your best guide. Please be honest with the rep.

You can expect that Mel's motivation will likely flag during the time after the event and he may even start to look around. You'll end up with a warm body going through the motions. Increase your personal time with him. If this is an employee who made a mistake and you believe has learned from it, then you need to be genuinely supportive.

LESSONS

Extensive time with your people witnessing substantial numbers of sales interviews and presentations, listening to how they answer objections and questions, and coaching them on their efforts is still the best way to spot and eliminate this problem.

Tainted business stains don't wash out. There is no detergent strong enough to remove the stains from anyone associated with business that is obtained dishonestly and allowed to stand.

Other managers, superiors, and customers draw conclusions about your leadership, style, ethics, and support from your tolerance and handling of such problems. You can never recover from having your ethics questioned. Once you're soiled, you're always soiled.

10-5 THE PROBLEM:
One of your reps proposes an illegal action.

THE STORY

Patrick leaned back, feet up on the desk, and listened to Greg's tale of woe. Greg was one of Patrick's most aggressive account managers and was relating how he had been trying, to no avail, to crack a large account, Sincore, for over a year. They were both at wit's end.

Today's strategizing session was a little different because Greg was clearly excited, as if he had just found the golden egg.

What he discovered, he said to Patrick with obvious pride, was that their company was one of Sincore's largest customers. Greg's plan was to tell Sincore that his company would begin to buy from Sincore's competitors if they did not start buying from him. What a plan! They both smiled with self-satisfaction.

After Greg left, the smile dimmed as Patrick thought more about it but, what the heck, he thought.

TEMPTATIONS

Frustration over a long period of time can get many salespeople to consider questionable or illegal actions—whether they admit it or not. In most cases reason prevails, but occasionally an equally frustrated and willing accomplice can be found.

Roll the dice

"Hey, sounds good, let's see if we can get away with it. I'll talk to one of our newer people in purchasing to get their help."

Play poker

"Our purchasing people will never go along with this, so let's just *imply* to Sincore that we would do this. Sincore may fall for it."

Plant seeds of destruction

"We can talk to our users of the Sincore product and have them question why Sincore doesn't use any of our products. That'll create some back pressure."

Patrick's moment of pause has put him on the right track.

WHAT HAPPENED HERE . . . ?

Greg has come up with an idea that may potentially raise serious implications for Patrick and his company. Reciprocity, that is, the use of your company's purchasing power to gain sales, may violate the U.S. antitrust laws.

When salespeople and sales managers are faced with seemingly insurmountable obstacles their creative juices can cross the line into improper and illegal alternatives. It sounds as if neither Greg nor Patrick is aware of the potential implications associated with their temptations.

Top management in the firm may not have a sensitivity or awareness of the potential of problems associated with U.S. antitrust laws. It may be that Patrick and his staff have never received any training on antitrust.

The company may not have internal counsel or an independent attorney with whom it has a close working relationship and who would have proactively raised the issue.

The fact is, the United States has a private and free-enterprise economy that depends upon competition to determine what goods and services will be produced and sold and at what price. The antitrust laws preserve this free-enterprise system by attempting to maintain competition and by stopping business practices that could inhibit or destroy competition.

It is important for sales managers and their staffs to understand the essence of the U.S. antitrust laws and to ensure that their actions and the actions of their sales units do not violate these laws. It is also imperative that Patrick and his people understand his company's policies and practices in support of those laws.

OPTIONS

There is one clear option. Patrick must seek guidance from his company's legal department or outside counsel to ensure that neither he nor Greg violates antitrust laws. He then needs to have himself and all his people trained on the antitrust laws and have his entire staff become familiar with his company's policies regarding compliance.

The alternatives for lack of understanding, and for antitrust violations may include personal and corporate consequences up to, and including, substantial fines, penalties, and/or jail sentences.

POSSIBLE ACTIONS

There is a great deal of legislation, both state and federal, that affects sales practices, and it has grown over the years. The purpose of the legislation has been threefold: to protect companies from each other, to protect consumers from unfair business practices, and to protect the interests of society from unrestrained business behavior.

Some of the laws that affect sales and marketing include the Sherman Antitrust Act (1890), the Clayton Act (1914), and the Robinson-Patman Act (1936).

As stated by the Supreme Court of the United States, antitrust laws were "designed to be a comprehensive charter of economic liberty aimed at preserving free and unfettered competition as the result of trade."

There are many other laws that could affect your industry. Sales managers must know the federal, state, and local laws that affect their sales unit's activities.

There are several important federal regulatory agencies that help to enforce the laws. Some of them include the Federal Trade Commission (FTC), the Food and Drug Administration (FDA), the Interstate Commerce Commission (ICC), the Federal Communications Commission (FCC), the Environmental Protection Agency (EPA), and the Office of Consumer Affairs (OCA). These agencies, and others, can have an impact on your company's sales and marketing practices and performance. Patrick's attorney will be his best guide. Patrick should ask his attorney what laws and regulations, including and beyond antitrust, his sales unit should be aware of and have the sales unit briefed on prohibited practices and language.

Critical Antitrust Elements

The following is a list of questionable and illegal practices that relate to antitrust.

MONOPOLY. A company monopolizes a market when it improperly gains and/or maintains a dominant market share so that is has the power to control prices or virtually eliminate competition. An attempt to monopolize may be found when a company engages in predatory or exclusionary conduct with the specific intent to control a market, drive a competitor out of business, or prohibit a competitor's entry into a market.

AGREEMENTS. The antitrust laws prohibit agreements that unreasonably restrain competition. These agreements between suppliers need not be in writing. Agreements may even be implied from how you and a competitor or you and a customer act. A good rule of thumb is simply to avoid contact with your competitors and if approached by competition, no matter how casual, to remove yourself from the encounter.

AGREEMENTS WITH COMPETITORS AFFECTING PRICE. Agreements between competitors that affect price or the terms and conditions of a sale are illegal. Price-fixing is per se illegal, meaning there is virtually no defense. Salespeople must not make any agreements with competitors or resellers concerning the final prices of goods or services.

ALLOCATIONS OF CUSTOMERS OR TERRITORIES. Competitors may not agree to divide a market or to refrain from selling to certain customers or groups of customers. Likewise, competitors may not agree to share a customer's business.

AGREEMENTS ON RESALE PRICES. It is illegal to require a customer to resell your company's products at a particular price or to reach an agreement with a customer on prices at which your products will be resold. You may suggest resale prices to your customers, but the customers must always feel free to reject these suggestions and independently determine their own resale prices.

BOYCOTTS. It is unlawful for competitors to agree not to buy from particular vendors or to not sell to particular customers.

AGREEMENTS TO LIMIT PRODUCTION. Competing firms may not enter into agreements or understandings that would limit or increase either company's production.

BUNDLING OR TIE-IN AGREEMENTS. Bundling occurs when a seller refuses to sell a customer a desired product unless the customer also purchases a second less-desirable product. Bundling is a violation of the antitrust laws and is presumed to have a substantial anticompetitive effect in situations where the seller has sufficient economic power in the market for the desired product to force a purchaser to buy another product that the purchaser does not want to buy or would prefer to buy from another seller. In other words, if you have a hot product and a dog, it is not appropriate for you to refuse to sell your hot product to a customer unless they also buy the dog.

This listing of illegal practices is meant to be illustrative. Sales practices and prohibitions vary by industry and by jurisdiction. Your attorney's familiarity with your industry and the laws applicable to any particular transaction will ensure that your sales unit is briefed on additional matters to ensure compliance.

Raise the Flag

The first thing for Patrick to do is to set up a meeting with his legal department or independent counsel to discuss his company's policies regarding the antitrust laws and to explore his doubt about Greg's suggested action. Greg's participation can confirm what has or hasn't been said or done to date, and the corrective measures, if needed, can be implemented.

Train the Troops

Patrick must schedule a formal training session for his salespeople. The session *must* be led by his legal counsel. It ensures accuracy and thorough answering of questions. It is important that the attorney describe the laws using everyday language and incorporate examples that specifically relate to the company's products, customers, sales-channel partners, and competition.

Some practical points to include in the training might include:

- Avoid overzealous statements that may suggest an intent to control or dominate a market or to drive out or eliminate competition from the market.

  For example, a sales manager to his sales rep: "I do not care what you have to do, but do not let Acme win any more business in this city."

- Avoid directly or indirectly requiring or requesting a reseller not to pursue a particular business opportunity. Further, absent a properly drafted contract, any restriction of the geographical territories to which distributors may resell, as well as the classes of customers to which they may resell, may be found illegal if it inhibits a substantial amount of competition. Therefore, be careful not to either require or imply such restrictions.

  For example, a salesperson to a dealer: "Hey, Louise, I will take this one direct. Back off. Don't continue your sales effort."

- Never dictate the price at which a business partner is to resell your products.

  For example, a salesperson to one of her retailers: "Naomi, we sell our products at list. I have noticed that you have been winning through discounting. I want that practice stopped, or we'll pull our line."

- Avoid discussing one reseller's pricing or selling actions with another business sales-channel partner.

  For example, a salesperson to one of his distributors: "Harry, we have been working well together, and I want you to get this deal. One of our other distributors is offering a 15 percent discount. You need to step your discount up or you will lose the deal."

- Never terminate an existing relationship with a customer, business partner, or supplier at the suggestion of a third party.

  For example, a customer to a sales rep: "Larry, as one of your largest customers I'm telling you that we will continue to do business with you only if you stop selling to one of our competitors."

- Avoid granting arbitrary price concessions or engaging in price discrimination that lessens competition or is injurious to one customer at the expense of another. Sellers cannot charge competing buyers different prices for essentially the same products if the effect diminishes competition. It is important to use established discounting and allowance procedures in these situations.

  A bad example, "Discounts, Harry? Sure! What do you need to win?"

- Never try to use your company's purchasing power to influence a customer.

  For example, "Listen, my company is your largest customer. That could change if you don't buy this product from us.

- Never threaten to terminate a reselling customer because of price cutting.

  For example, a salesperson to a dealer. "Arnold, you're toast if you don't get your prices back up where they belong."

- Avoid arrangements that prohibit customers from purchasing or dealing in a competitor's products or that require customers to purchase all of their requirements for a particular product from your company, as such arrangements could be illegal.

  For example, a salesperson to a distributor: "Harriet, if you don't buy all your pipe from us, don't expect to buy any of our special connectors."

- Avoid tie-in or bundling requirements.

  For example, a liquor salesman to a store manager: "Yes, Harry, I know you want to buy only our Chardonney. It is the best seller on the market. However, my company offers it only in a package that includes the purchase of one case of our newly introduced Merlot along with every two cases of Chardonney purchased."

Your attorney's understanding of your business will let him or her customize the training to meet your needs. Your own sales experience has likely included situations that you recognized as improper. Sharing those real-life stories and how you handled them is also a highly effective training aid.

Competitive Contact

Since many violations involve agreements between competitors, Patrick's training session should remind his people to never discuss the following with a competitor:

- Pricing policies, terms and conditions, or prices at which products are sold to third parties
- The amount of a bid or the intention to submit a bid

- Profits, profit projections, profit margins, or costs
- Unannounced products or your intention to enter or exit a particular product market
- Market share or production capacity
- Distribution practices or the selection, rejection, or termination of customers or suppliers

Again, Patrick should have his attorney confirm this list and discuss the consequences of any improper sharing of information.

Generally, an antitrust training and compliance program should:

1. Inform your sales personnel how to perform the functions of their job without violating antitrust laws.
2. Continually assist your sales staff in resolving antitrust questions as they may arise.
3. Continue to monitor your business activity to ensure compliance.

LESSONS

It is imperative that you understand the U.S. antitrust laws and other federal, state, and local laws affecting your business. It is equally important that you understand your company's policies and procedures in support of those laws. Pressure to bring in the business creates pressure to compromise. Be particularly vigilant in times of business duress.

Restrictive agreements between your company and its customers or suppliers may violate the antitrust laws if they unreasonably restrain competition. Certain behavior is so anticompetitive that it will rise to the level of per-se illegal. Proposed sales practices should be individually examined by your legal counsel before any action is taken. The best rule is that whenever there is *any doubt* about an intended sales action, contact your manager or attorney.

Conduct a legal-issues training session at least once a year to review laws and regulations appropriate to your business and create a process that documents and tracks suspected questionable contacts. Having a strict training, disclosure, and documentation policy is a good sales-department business practice.

The discussion in this problem is not intended to completely cover U.S. antitrust laws, but rather to stress the importance of antitrust awareness and issue-sensitivity training.

Additionally, businesses that operate in the international arena should be aware that conduct occurring in other countries that impacts competition in the United States is actionable under U.S. antitrust laws. Moreover, international business operations should familiarize themselves with the antitrust laws of foreign countries that may be applicable to sales activity abroad.

10–6 THE PROBLEM:

You become aware that a foreign sales agent has used part of his commission to bribe an official.

THE STORY

Ned, one of Matt's new regional sales managers, just got back yesterday from a three-week trip to Central Asia and the PacRim, and he has come in to give Matt a verbal trip report of his activities and results. As the VP of Sales, Matt is excited about the fact that his firm has decided to expand internationally and pleased that there have been early successes.

As Ned enthusiastically recounts his activities, he notes that one of the firm's authorized sales agents has had to grease a certain government decision maker's palm. The sales agent indicated that his contact would "take care" of some people in the appropriate ministries. Matt doesn't really like that idea, but he knows that business practices are different all over the world.

TEMPTATIONS

The only way to penetrate many foreign markets is to utilize the services of a local sales representative or a commercial agent in that market. In consideration for a commission based on a percentage of the sales in the market in question, the agent helps win the business.

Matt is lucky that Ned shared this with him, but he may be tempted to let this slide.

Look the other way

"Other countries play this game. It's unfair to us not to be able to do the same."

Ignorance

"Seriously, Counselor, I had *absolutely no idea* that was not permitted."

—or—"Our constraints pertain only to certain bad countries, like those terrorist places, right?"

Close your door

"Just a second, Ned, I don't want anyone else to hear this. So what else did he tell you?"

Don't be stunned by this revelation. This kind of activity is commonplace in numerous markets around the world. All of these temptations can get you into serious trouble.

WHAT HAPPENED HERE . . . ?

The risk of imputed liability under the Foreign Corrupt Practices Act (FCPA) for illegal payments may be the single most troubling problem in using foreign sales representatives to promote export sales.

The fact that the firm is new to export suggests that it hasn't done its front-end homework in regard to legal matters. Top management may have left this up to Matt, assuming that he knows what he is doing. The supposition and lack of oversight is dangerous.

It may be that Matt, Ned, and the senior management team are unaware of the details and significance of the FCPA because there has been no training offered or executed by the firm's internal or external legal counsel.

It may be that Matt's firm has no protocols or code of business conduct. The story suggests that the firm may not even have retained counsel.

Perhaps neither Matt nor Ned understands the implications of the situation, or if they do, their priorities are severely out of tune.

The sales agent may not have had any experience dealing with American firms and is therefore unaware of the FCPA and its restrictions.

A good sales agent can provide a supplier with a competitive edge in a particular market by identifying business opportunities and customers, by actively promoting the supplier's products, by advising the supplier of local customs and trade usages, and by assisting in developing a marketing program for the local market.

OPTIONS

You have only one option. The risks are too big and the penalties are too stiff not to do anything else. Individual violators are subject to personal fines of up to $100,000 and/or imprisonment for up to five years. Corporate violators are subject to fines of up to $2,000,000.

Matt should talk to the company attorney, preferably outside counsel, in order to keep the discussions legally confidential. The attorney will need to conduct an internal investigation to assess the extent to which the company knows there is a violation or has authorized a corrupt payment. Top management and the attorney can then formulate the appropriate course of action.

POSSIBLE ACTIONS

The Reality of the Situation

Unfortunately, sales agents have often served to channel sensitive payments or bribes to foreign officials. In response to U.S. companies admitting questionable payments to foreign government officials, Congress enacted the Foreign Corrupt Practices Act in 1977. It is a complicated area of law. Because the Act is ambiguous, it is imperative that you have capable legal counsel aid you in understanding its provisions and provide guidance in your sales and marketing actions. It is a criminal offense for any U.S. person or business entity to make or authorize certain types of payments.

The Act prohibits publicly held companies from *corruptly* making payments to officials of any foreign government or political party, candidates for foreign political office, foreign political parties, and any other person (and here is where the sales agent comes in) where the payor (you) knows that the person will pass some or all of the payment on to one of the foregoing. The Act also requires publicly held companies to maintain records that accurately reflect all payment transactions and controls to prevent falsification of books and records.

Payments to intermediaries are prohibited where the payor knows that the payment will be forwarded to a foreign government official. It is not necessary that you have actual knowledge of the corrupt payment, however, to be liable for the acts of your sales agent. If you believe that the bribe is substantially certain to occur, or there is a high probability it will occur, you must take action to satisfy yourself that it will not occur. Payments and kickbacks to officers, employees, and agents of commercial enterprises that are owned by foreign governments are also subject to this antibribery legislation.

The Act is aimed at attempts to obtain business through influence buying abroad. As a result, only payments that are intended to assist the payor in obtaining or retaining business are prohibited by the Act. The *purpose* for which the payment has been made is therefore critical in determining whether the Act has been violated.

Few companies volunteer to make such payments. Instead, payments are customarily made in response to some indication from a foreign official that such payments are required.

In the end, the sales agent can do whatever he wants. It's his money. But if you become aware of it, it is now your problem.

What's Permitted

Payments by you or your sales agent to foreign officials that are intended to encourage those officials to perform their regular duties unrelated to obtaining new business or retaining existing business, often called "grease," "facilitating," or "expediting" payments are not prohibited. Payments to clerical-level officials in order to expedite the processing of an application, the issuing of a license, or the clearing of goods through customs may be done—but extreme caution is suggested. Attorneys' opinions on both U.S. and foreign law should be obtained.

Action to Take

- Understand your responsibilities, and those responsibilities are to not pay or authorize any other person to pay to any foreign official anything of value to obtain or retain business.
- Do what the law requires. Understand that the law requires you to disavow and repudiate any unauthorized payments made by others that come to your attention and take steps to prevent any such future payments. If the internal investigation indicates

that such payments were authorized by your company you should consider making a voluntary disclosure to the U.S. Department of Justice.

A liberal reading of the Act indicates that it prohibits persons and firms from *corruptly* making payments to sales agents where the payor knows that the sales agent will forward all or part of the payments to foreign government officials. Thus, a corrupt motive or intent on the part of the payor is a necessary element of any offense under the Act. If this were the proper interpretation, U.S. firms would have little to fear with respect to payments made to foreign sales agents, so long as the U.S. payor *does not itself* have a corrupt motive or intend the payments to be passed on to government officials. Under this interpretation of the Act, U.S. firms could remain blissfully ignorant of their foreign commercial agents' questionable, unethical, or wrongful conduct. But, the U.S. corporation *cannot escape liability* by ignoring the sales representative's misdeeds. The definition of "knowledge" in the Act includes conscious disregard, willful blindness, or deliberate ignorance. If you fail to make a full inquiry into your sales agent's activities, under circumstances that would lead a reasonable person to make such an inquiry, and if in fact the agent is making payoffs, you and/or your firm may be criminally liable under the Act.

Local country laws may be broken also. Your legal counsel needs to brief you.

In Matt's case he should consult the company's attorneys, preferably outside legal counsel in order to maintain legal confidentiality, and conduct an internal investigation under the supervision of the attorney regarding the extent of the company's knowledge.

Train your sales agents and inform them of U.S. laws.

Train your own people and execute a yearly refresher course.

Some facts and circumstances that should cause you to be alert include:

- The reputation of the particular country in question
- Personal or professional ties with government officials
- Requests for abnormally large commissions
- The sales agent asks that third country payment arrangements be made
- The sales agent asks you to over-invoice so that the overage can be used to "take care" of a foreign official.

Preventive Steps for Next Time

Any U.S. firm that elects to use independent foreign sales representatives to promote export sales must exercise the utmost caution in selecting its sales representatives and should carefully monitor the sales representatives' activities. Your foreign sales-agent selection process should be executed with the highest level of diligence. Apply the lessons of Problem 9–1 and then brief your foreign sales agent on FCPA provisions as part of your orientation and training practices.

- Build understanding of business practices in the countries in which you are engaged. The U.S. Department of Commerce could be a good starting point.

- Develop internal policies and procedures, such as business conduct guidelines.
- Check your sales agent's reputation and keep your eye on conduct.
- Put FCPA covenants and representations in your international sales-agent agreements. Your legal counsel can assist.
- Be wary of relationships between agents and officials
- Compare your sales commissions to the market value of the services you are getting.
- Be suspicious of cash, third-party, and third-country payments
- Don't participate in questionable meetings or phone calls.

In the end, you may need to terminate agents whose behavior is questionable, but do so only in conjunction with the advice of your legal counsel.

LESSONS

You and all the people who report to you who are involved in international sales and marketing must understand the provisions of the Foreign Corrupt Practices Act.

You must have a good and open relationship with your in-house legal counsel or with your company's outside law firm. It is a good practice to have your attorney brief you and your people on *all* legislation and legal matters that may be of importance to your international business. If your products have or need copyright, patent, trademark, and/or intellectual property protection, it would behoove you to have your counsel train your sales and marketing staff on those matters at the same time.

Business practices are *not* the same around the globe. New markets are coming on the scene all over the world. Many new and emerging economies are frontier economies with Wild West rules and discipline. The problem is a growing—not a declining—business risk.

10–7 THE PROBLEM:

Management wants you to do things that are
in conflict with your values.

THE STORY

"We want you to keep squeezing and pressing until they buy or until they die. Never give up and don't stop. Promise whatever it takes. Anyone not following this policy is outta here. Does everyone understand that?" roared Bud, the national sales manager.

"Another thing," he went on, "I want you to inform your people to tell the prospects that they'll get the new model. Most of them are dumb enough not to understand the difference between the old and the new, and the new safety feature is no big deal, so don't worry about it."

As Sean sat listening, he knew Bud was serious and meant every word. This had been the usual rough-and-tumble quarterly sales meeting. This was an exciting, lucrative business to be a part of, but there were costs. Sean was becoming tired of paying "the bills."

TEMPTATIONS

There aren't any snappy enticements with this problem, except possibly some mock enthusiasm and one-liners to keep your game face with your peers. Instead, there are four nasty and insidious temptations.

The gut-level nature of the problem takes Sean right into some heavy thinking.

Moral laziness

The anticipated emotional and mental work turns you into a moral couch potato.

Moral schizophrenia

You are inconsistent because you have a flip-flopping standard to suit your selfish convenience.

Moral cowardice

Standing up and standing out is risky. As a Japanese proverb goes, "The nail that sticks up gets hammered down."

Creeping compromise

The rush of negative reaction and the desire to do something to change the situation are softened over time by a tendency to gradually accept the new reality.

WHAT HAPPENED HERE ... ?

Bud touched a deep nerve.

Sean's integrity, values, and style are being challenged. It is pretty clear he doesn't want to manage the way Bud is encouraging.

Sean is uncomfortable, possibly embarrassed, and may not be able to operate with full enthusiasm for this latest sales initiative, as much as he may want to.

Sean may not want to set a precedent that would be difficult to alter. Management may ask him to do other things with which he would be even more uncomfortable.

You send messages about yourself to those closest to you through your actions. Sean may be uncomfortable with that prospect.

Bud's edict strikes at Sean's core beliefs and values. When passionately held and voiced values such as Bud's conflict with values that Sean holds, something has got to give.

The most intimate part of Sean's mind, his conscience, his personal sanctuary, has been touched. Conscience is the knowledge or feeling of right and wrong, the faculty or principle of a person which decides on the right or wrong of his actions with a compulsion to do right.

And finally, sometimes a deep protest against a situation arises in us, and we really don't know why.

OPTIONS

There are three options with these situations.

1. Stop and say, "That's it. I can't handle this environment any more."
2. Compromise your values. Play the game and go along with the crowd. Handle the heat in your conscience kitchen with your best facade.
3. Comply with your values. Stand up for what you believe in and take steps to constructively alter the situation and be willing to bear the consequences of your courage.

POSSIBLE ACTIONS

Call a personal time out to get away from the office to discern the situation. Go outside for a walk or find a special spot that you can go to. Problems like this may take you on a few long walks.

At times like this you learn a lot about your inner strength and about how strongly you feel on certain matters. However, feeling and doing are two entirely different things.

Think

There are many subjects to contemplate in these situations. This internal fight may take more time than you like, but that is a measure of the seriousness and depth of your feelings. The following ideas and questions will help you focus.

- As the subordinate, you can expect that management will likely hold fast to its position, unless there are others of your ilk who share the same feelings. Then the concentration of forces can have a bigger impact. (Look for allies.) In the end, if there is anyone who is going to have to compromise, it will probably be you.
- Do you have a covenant with your sales unit? Is the relationship with your direct reports such that compromise on your side tears apart the fabric of your sales unit?
- There are occasions when disobeying a directive is appropriate. Ethical situations meet that criteria.

- What leads someone to stand up for something they believe in? Courage? Conviction? Faith? Intensity? What is leading you to stand up at this particular time on this particular issue? Articulate it.

- Your values and conscience are never a finished product, but a continuing rough draft. The draft ebbs and flows based on your decisions and actions. You are about to alter the draft. Will you be pleased with the prospects of the outcome?

- What are the most important things in your life? How do you want to live, and how do you want to feel about yourself?

- Everyone compromises his or her values in work life to a greater or lesser extent. Not all compromise is pejorative, but compromise in this case may be. How much pejorative compromise, if any, are you willing to tolerate?

- What does the word "enough" mean to you? It means "sufficiency," as in, "That's it, I've had enough."—or—"I can't take, nor do I want any more of whatever is being doled out." When does enough of what management is asking, get to be enough for you?

- If you ultimately decide to walk away from this situation you may have to divest yourself of things you value highly, such as a job, income, or security. When do you walk? Are you prepared to walk?

- Do your words and actions offer evidence of your core beliefs? Would your staff and colleagues listening and watching you understand what you believed in? Would the lessons they draw be lessons that you would want to teach?

- Are you severely or slightly preoccupied with this anxiety? Can you live with this anxiety? Can you be as effective as you like working with the anxiety?

- People who have strong values and beliefs seem to be universally admired. If that is the case, why do many people not try to emulate the strength? Why do others so quickly say, "Oh, I could never do that"? Well, you *can* do that because you have an opportunity staring you right in the face.

- Listen to the messages that are coming from inside of you. Is the little voice whispering at you or screaming at you? Only you can hear it. What is your tolerance for that little voice? You can't make it go away.

The best thing to do at this point is to take your thoughts, in whatever shape they are, to someone with whom you can have a deep, thoughtful discussion in order to firm up your conclusions and potential actions.

Talk to a Confidante or Mentor

You likely have one or two unusually close relationships in the business. Whether or not you go to particular colleagues at decision moments like this is a measure of the relationship.

Go to a moral counselor outside the firm, someone who can give you an ethical response. The objective of going to someone not involved with the business is objectivity, fresh perspectives, reawakening of self, reinforcement, and courage. It is a good idea to link up with someone like this a couple of times a year to revitalize your inner self, regardless of problems.

None of these contacts should be people who are going to tell you what they think you want to hear. A side benefit of this sharing is that it reinforces those relationships.

Speed Is Good

Quick reaction to problems of this nature sends a more convincing message to management. Don't dawdle, in spite of the complexity and personal nature of the subject.

Decision Time

It's time to fish or cut bait.

How do you normally make a decision on a matter of great personal import? Treat this the same way, which may mean including additional friends or family members, thinking how those you hold in highest esteem would opt, recalling results from previous similar decisions, and observations surrounding the decisions of others. The extent of your decision process obviously depends on the ease or difficulty of the problem and how deeply your conscience has been touched.

Make your decision.

If your personal circumstances are such that you *must* hold to your situation, do it with one hand while you hold fast with your other hand to those foundations in your life in which you are rooted.

Talk to Your Boss

This may not be easy, but remember, an attribute of great sales leaders is courage in relationships. Share you thoughts and feelings and make suggestions. Just like any other sales-management problem, don't walk in on the boss without any suggestions on how to handle it. Be candid, focused, and detailed. Let the boss know what you plan to do or what you would like him to do. Part of that may be compromise. Remember that compromise is adjusting and settling a difference by *mutual agreement* with concessions on both sides.

Thank You, but Now Let's Get Back to Business

The talk is just about over. Now the rubber is about to meet the road.

"I hear you and understand you, but are you threatening to leave? Is that what you're telling me?" says Bud. "Is this an excuse for your performance, or are you just going soft on me?" he continues.

What do you do or say next? You need to be prepared for this final stage. You have choices that reflect the options.

- "No, I haven't gone soft, I just wanted to let you know how I felt," Sean continues.

  "Okay, you've let me know. Now let's get back to work. Don't worry about it Seanny, you'll be okay," finishes Bud.

- "No, I've decided that harassing and being dishonest with customers is not the right approach," says Sean.

   "So you're gonna leave?" Bud responds.

   "No, I'm going to stay, but I really feel my approach is better for business. If it doesn't work we'll both know it quickly, and I'll be out of your hair in 30 days. If it works, I'm asking you to let me take my approach to the whole team for implementation. Okay? Do we agree?"

The ball is now in Bud's court.

If Bud is open to your alternatives, go ahead and execute your approach. If it is clear Bud will not change then exit with dignity and with your values intact.

Hold Fast

Behavior is the ultimate score card. You can't claim feelings, or posture high and mightily, and then act another way.

A final thought: "On some questions, cowardice asks the question, is it expedient? And then expedience comes along and asks the question, is it politic? Vanity asks the question, is it popular? Conscience asks the question is it right? There comes a time when one must take the position that it is neither safe, nor politic, nor popular. But he must do it because conscience tells him it is right." Dr. Martin Luther King, Jr.

LESSONS

You learn much about yourself with this type of problem. It helps you articulate your values and recommit to living them. You learn how much personal cost you are willing to bear for your values. Any decision of conscience involves sacrifice. That is the biggest lesson.

Integrity is the core of effective sales management. If you compromise your integrity, there isn't much left. You form your destinies through your choices.

Great sales managers want to be committed to things worthwhile, rewarding, and beneficial. Conquering this problem can reconfirm your authenticity as a great sales manager.

part eleven

TROUBLESHOOTING PROBLEMS CREATED BY YOUR MANAGER

11–1 The Problem:

Your boss regularly bypasses you to get information.

The Story

"Hey, Lilly, why is your boss always coming to us?" asked one of Lilly's salespeople. "What is the matter?"

"I'm not sure," Lilly responded. "What was Troy asking about this time?"

"It's hard to say. We talked about the forecast and the Whichard account. He didn't explain."

"I could have given him a complete update," Lilly said. "Next time Troy asks, tell him I have the whole package."

"Okay, but he seems so uptight."

What in the world is with that guy, Lilly thought. I don't have a problem with anyone talking to my people, but this is getting to be too much. I've got to do something.

Temptations

Good sales managers have a sense of pride and ownership. When bosses start buzzing around too closely it is easy to get nervous and twitchy.

Get mad

"Troy, what is this [expletive]. Am I the sales manager or not?"

Whine

"Hey, Troy, come on, you're making me look bad, cut it out, what's going on?"

Tell your people to keep quiet

"When that guy comes around I want you people to be *very* careful what you say."

In spite of the feeling of disappointment respect the fact that your boss has a job to do. He may not be motivated for it, good at it, or qualified for it, but you have to support him.

What Happened Here . . . ?

Expected communications protocols are out of sync. Sales organizations thrive and depend on constant and rapid communications. Sales cultures are contact- and relationship-intensive, and when something doesn't match expectations it comes across with the subtlety of a cannon. Excess contact by the second-level manager can create apprehension in the minds of some reps because it is abnormal behavior. They ask themselves, Why is Troy doing Lilly's job?

Troy may not trust Lilly, the relationship between the two may be bad, or Troy is quietly building a case against her.

Troy may have his eye on someone in Lilly's sales unit for a promotion and doesn't want to tell Lilly. He wants to personally evaluate Lilly's people.

Troy may simply be numb and insensitive to reporting relationships and business courtesy, or Lilly is being overly sensitive herself.

In today's environment speed is everything, and Troy may feel he can't be bothered by going through Lilly. Troy may be so smart and so fast that he has no patience or tolerance for lines on the organizational chart.

The boss's boss will often be told some things that the first-line manager wouldn't be told simply because of rank, and Troy probably knows that. Several of Lilly's people may spill everything because they want to look good to the boss's boss. They may provide more information than is needed, possibly embarrassing Lilly.

Maybe Troy doesn't want filtered information. Lilly may have filtered something, unintentionally or intentionally, in the past, and Troy was embarrassed. He doesn't want it to happen again. Or Troy's own boss is putting the pressure on him.

Sometimes managers don't like to ask certain questions of their manager subordinates because they don't want to leave an impression that they don't know something basic.

And finally, Troy may be a charismatic manager who enjoys talking to the troops and getting direct feedback.

OPTIONS

You have two options

1. Let it go. Do nothing. Tolerate the intrusion and let it roll off your back.
2. Address your discomfort.

POSSIBLE ACTIONS

Don't lose any sleep over this one because it is easily addressed.

Roll This Over

How much of Troy's running around you is too much? That's a question only you can answer. Try to objectively understand why Troy is behaving this way. Most of the reasons should be readily apparent because you know what he's been looking for. Make notes to yourself so you can prepare for a one-on-one.

Talk to your peers guardedly. Depending on your geographical dispersion, it may or may not be easy to determine if other sales managers get treated the same way. Keep an eye out for how Troy communicates with the staffs of other sales managers, and with the managers themselves.

Are you doing *everything* that you should be doing? Are you proactively taking information to Troy? Is your performance above reproach? If you are a performance problem or a poor communicator yourself, you have little reason to be complaining about anything.

Make a phone or personal appointment to discuss the subject with Troy. Don't just walk in, because you want to give Troy the opportunity to think about the issue. Say something like, "Troy, can I stop back or call back at three? I'd like to discuss your contact with my staff, because they and I both have questions." You don't want to make a mountain out of a molehill, but this is good business courtesy.

Talk to the Boss

Be candid. Tell him that several of your people have approached you. Share your feelings on how it looks to your staff, yourself, and presumably to other managers. Cite examples of specific incidents, and offer alternate approaches. Ask him to share why he is contacting your folks in the manner and with the frequency that he does.

- Ask about his information needs and priorities. You may have some better ideas on how to get that information to him.
- Ask if your reports are meeting his needs.
- Ask if there is something bothering him that you can correct.
- Ask if you can change reporting systems, forecasting systems, or other processes.
- Ask if he is aware that much information he seeks is available through the company's sales-force automation system (which he may not have been trained on).
- Ask if there is something related to personnel issues that he can share.
- Ask if he trusts that you can do the job according to his expectations.
- Ask if he has an issue with the way you've been executing any aspect of the job.

Be Prepared for a Shot in Return

Expect that your manager will react and not just sit there and absorb your counseling. Expect that this will be a give-and-take. Some comments may include:

- "I like to keep in touch."
- "Frankly, you could be more proactive in giving me information."
- "I don't want to bother you. I know you're hustling. Keep doing what you're doing."
- "It gives me a sense of how people feel."
- "I like to have a relationship with everyone in the sales organization."

Accept the comments and don't get defensive. A little, "Oh, thanks, now I understand a little better," won't hurt you either.

He may or may not say it, but he'll respect your feeling of ownership for your sales unit.

Make It Easier for Your Boss

Help him. He may have been reticent to ask for help. You may frighten or intimidate him because of your experience, style, skills, or charisma. Help make his approaches less clumsy.

- Invite him to attend your meetings on a regular basis. Ask him to address issues of strategic and current importance when he is there.
- Set up a formal schedule where he can rotate field-customer contact time with your sales unit if he would like to meet key customers from time to time. Agree on a certain number of days per month or days of the week for him to travel.
- Invite him to sit in on strategy-and-planning discussions for major opportunities and the win/loss reviews associated with those opportunities.
- Obviously, he should be a part of your interview cycle when you're hiring someone.
- Set up a formal schedule when the two of you meet for an hour every week or month to discuss current activities and priorities.
- Ask him to share a copy of his expectations and his priorities with you and your sales unit.
- Include him in lunches, dinners, or other entertainment with customers and sales partners.
- Always ask him what other activities he would like to engage in with your sales unit.

Turn the problem into an opportunity. Remember that your boss is a resource who probably has good sales and relationship skills. Turn his interest to your advantage by having him help you win business. Turn the energy to your benefit.

LESSONS

Taking the initiative to keep your boss regularly involved in your sales unit's activities helps build a solid business and personal relationship. Relationships aren't automatic. They take effort. You get to understand your boss's priorities, concerns, and worries—and to share yours with him—in the process. Sharing builds understanding, confidence, and respect.

Anticipating your manager's information needs by proactively challenging and modifying existing information systems and processes sends a message to your manager that you are alert, sensitive, and responsive. The value of your stock as a manager and a team player goes up.

A major lesson of this problem is that you have to communicate up as well as down. How much up depends on the style of your manager. Be flexible.

Many managers, at all levels, like to manage by walking around. It works. Don't feel threatened if that's the style of any executive in your firm.

11–2 THE PROBLEM:

Your boss is consumed with how he looks to top management.

THE STORY

"Claudia, you need a spreadsheet format for the plan. It's the way Kirk likes it. I put all my plans in that format," Alan advised. "And change the font to Times New Roman. He likes that."

"But, the . . . ," Claudia started to counter. Claudia sighed and gave up. Alan had that glazed anxious look on his face whenever there was any work to be done, or contact with, the division VP.

As Alan pored over the details of Claudia's sales unit plan, the phone rang. It was Kirk.

"Yes, yes," Alan stammered and then bolted out of his chair saying, "Kirk, has a question, I'll be right back—don't leave—keep studying that," as he rushed out the door.

Damn, Claudia thought. This guy doesn't have a mind of his own.

TEMPTATIONS

When you see that a senior executive has a fearful grip on your immediate manager it makes you shake your head in wonder. It tempts you to act in some very nonprofessional ways.

Laugh

"What a way to run a business. This is crazy. I wonder if he asks for permission to go to the men's room."

Contempt

"What a weakling." or "He's an embarrassment to the profession."

Gossip

"Wow, wait until I tell the rest of the sales managers about this latest episode."

The temptations are mutually damaging. The answer is good judgment, support, and respect.

WHAT HAPPENED HERE . . . ?

You have a boss who has an unnatural relationship with his superior. This is primarily his problem, but it cascades down to you, making it your problem as well.

All sales managers have a directional bias.

- Some sales managers concentrate on looking down, focusing on their people, coaching and managing intensely for the salesperson's and the sales unit's benefit. It's fun and rewarding to work for a manager who has a deep and sincere interest in you.
- Some managers' bias is upward, being primarily centered on their superior for their own survival and ambition. It is not nearly as enjoyable to work for anyone who has this bias.
- Some managers' bias is lateral, a clubbish attitude toward his peers because the manager is comfortable in his niche and plans to stay there for the long haul. These kinds of bosses can be fun, but don't expect to learn much from them except a lot of old war stories.

All three of these biases can be overdone. A good sales manager, at any level, *balances* his or her interests, relationships, and responsibilities, but has a downward focus. After all, a sales manager is paid to manage a sales unit, not paid to charm a boss or amuse peers.

Alan's performance may be below standards, and he is under pressure. Perhaps Kirk's personality and style intimidate him.

Alan may be a political animal, supersensitive to events around him, driven to advance at all costs, stepping all over those below him to achieve his ends. A promotion may be in the wind, and he's absorbed with that possibility.

Kirk may be a new VP, and Alan is anxious to impress him. Alan may be new in the job himself. New managers tend to be sensitive and insecure, overly responsive to their superior, and not confident of their own opinions or positions.

This may just be Alan's personal style. Some sales managers are naturally anxiety-ridden. His mind may be consumed with approval: How will this look to Kirk? or How will Kirk like this? Everything is done in the context of pleasing Kirk. Claudia wins or loses based on Kirk's approval, which is not the best position to be in.

The fallout of Alan's behavior is that Claudia doesn't get proper attention, she may suffer from a lack of support, she may unnecessarily get blamed for things, her development and career may not get the attention it should, she may end up doing some of the boss's politically risky work, the boss may not have her best interests at heart, and the boss doesn't really listen to her.

OPTIONS

You have three options in this situation.

1. Quit. Keep your eyes open for another assignment in the company or get your resumé out on the street if this is really bothering you. This option is probably a bit extreme.
2. Tolerate the situation and go about your work until there is a staffing change—until one of you moves on to something else. Of course, that could be an awfully long time.
3. Get close to Alan, find out what's going on and try to help him out—helping yourself at the same time. This option requires some effort, but may have long-term benefit.

The intensity of this problem obviously has a lot to do with which option you pick. Is this a minor irritation, or is this really getting in the way?

POSSIBLE ACTIONS

Assuming you want to stay where you are, be patient, understanding, and alert.

Look in the Mirror

Evaluate your strength in the company. Are you an experienced top performer? If you are well entrenched and well perceived you have more leeway and can probably make a contribution to minimize the problem. Alan *needs you* for his own performance insurance if you are doing a good job.

If you are a new manager, a middle-of-the-pack manager, or a performance problem, your personal risk is greater. In this case, you must get your act together quickly and perform flawlessly. And you better watch closely for changes in attitude and attention toward you because changes can be signals of impending serious trouble. A senior sales manager like Alan, under pressure, is more likely to make quick sacrifice of a lesser-performing junior manager.

Try to Grasp the Senior Manager's Agenda

Build an understanding of what Kirk values and of his expectations.

By working on a relationship with Kirk, geography permitting, you may be able to strengthen your own position, and pick up useful hints to pass on to Alan. But be careful. This association should *always* be secondary to your loyalty toward Alan. If Kirk is not accessible, Alan's comments about Kirk will have to suffice.

It is always helpful to look two levels up and try to get a sense of style and priorities because it helps frame your responses to your own boss. *Do not* misconstrue this action as running around Alan or kissing up to Kirk. That's asking for trouble. The suggestion is simply to be alert and take advantage of every opportunity to get to know Kirk and his values.

Grasp Your Manager's Situation

In your regular contacts and conversation with Alan, listen and observe to find out what feeds this consuming behavior. Try to understand his worries and priorities.

At an appropriate time tactfully raise the subject by sharing your observations. "Alan, I've noticed that you are very concerned with Kirk's feelings and ideas about such-and-such. What can I do to help you?" The opening may relieve Alan and let him feel that he can confide in you. You may need to probe more than once. Once the door is open and there have been a few exchanges Alan may feel that he can trust you more. Your inputs and suggestions will then become more valued and your position more powerful. *Never, ever betray this confidence to anyone.* What you are doing is turning yourself into an adviser or confidante.

Continue the dialogues in an easy, helpful manner. The sensitivity of your comments and questions can deepen over time. *Your understanding and your contributing suggestions to your boss's priorities are the best policy for any manager at any level.*

Adopt These Tactics

The best defense is a good offense.

- Execute your job to perfection, being current and thorough with all your assignments. Help your manager achieve his business and personal goals just as you help customers achieve their business and personal goals. Offer to help on projects and staff work to strengthen your manager's results. Provide prudent business advice, becoming a trusted counselor. This approach will enable you to stay close to your manager and make life more bearable. Be prepared to accept the fact that your advice may be unceremoniously rebuffed from time to time. Also be prepared to accept the fact that the benefit and glory associated with your suggestions may be absorbed by your manager. Don't expect many kudos.

- Use your understanding of Kirk to strengthen your relationship with Alan by discretely feeding Alan observations and tips on what might help position him with Kirk. It's a play that most managers appreciate. Alan will be savvy enough to know what you are doing.

- Overcommunicate with Alan, but do not take the tact of delivering only information that you believe Alan wants to hear.

- Make sure that your sales unit understands both Alan's and Kirk's priorities without going into any unnecessary explanations. Whatever the priorities of those two people, make sure everyone in your sales unit addresses them. Their priorities should *always be* your priorities.

- Do not under any circumstances try to usurp any of Alan's relationship with his boss. That's cutting your own throat.

- Be able to live and work with the paradox of staying close and simultaneously keeping your distance because you can never tell when things will unravel for Alan.

Think of This Effort as an Investment

All of this extra effort and dialogue with Alan consumes extra time and energy that you probably don't have, but you'll find that you'll have the benefit of access to information you normally wouldn't. Being a team player and lending a helping hand to the boss always pays dividends.

LESSONS

The relationship between your manager and his direct superior has a major influence on the quality of your work life, your personal life, and your future. The tone and content of relationships and expectations *always* trickle downhill. The good news is that you can influence the relationships.

Your manager will tend to manage like his immediate superior. The values and style of your second-level superior also cascade downhill, unless your manager is a very powerful personality and very well positioned on his or her own.

By understanding the values and priorities of your manager's manager you can bias your actions and responses to position yourself more favorably and make your job more enjoyable.

11–3 THE PROBLEM:

Yours and your boss's leadership and management styles are different.

THE STORY

As a district sales manager, Henry prided himself in his organization, his management processes, his coaching skills, and his plans. He felt he had a reputation as a real pro.

His boss was an entirely different matter. Rolf was a charismatic guy who had a lot of sales-management experience and was loved by the president who had brought him into the firm a few years ago. Many thought he was a throwback. Rolf didn't work that hard, prided himself in his four-handicap golf game, and held staff meetings that were largely BS sessions.

Rolf did some things that Henry felt were borderline unethical, such as cutting deals outside of policy, deals that Henry and the other sales managers often had to clean up. Henry always had the feeling that he and the other sales managers were always being manipulated.

Henry knew that the chemistry wasn't great and that something had to change.

TEMPTATIONS

Sales managers run into a wide variety of superiors throughout their career. In the end, tolerance may give way to one of these temptations.

Throw in the towel

"This guy is a nut case. I'm hurting my future potential. I'm outta here."

Hibernate

"If I stay out of the office and stay out of his way I'm sure things will be easier."

Engineer his downfall

"I won't say anything bad about him, but I'll never say anything good or supportive."

The relationship with your manager is a critical element of personal and professional growth and mental health. Life is too short to just stand by.

WHAT HAPPENED HERE . . . ?

You're very uncomfortable, and this situation is really gnawing at you. It is rare to have a manager who shares your leadership and management style. You can expect to have managers in your career who are incompetent, insensitive, selfish, lack integrity, are manipulative, and have other negative characteristics. No one is perfect. Including yourself.

The president may tolerate Rolf like an old pair of shoes because he may have a following in the industry and the president doesn't want him running off to competition.

It is highly probable that Rolf didn't hire Henry or promote him into his current position.

Maybe Rolf quietly admires Henry and appreciates the job he is doing. The story alludes to Henry and the others as essentially being used. Rolf can have a good time while the sales managers do the bull work.

Henry probably doesn't feel like an insider or feels that he has no future with this firm any more. He may envy Rolf's relationship with the president.

This is a situation reminiscent of Felix Unger and Oscar Madison from the famous *Odd Couple* TV series, but this situation is not humorous.

The two managers just don't click. Someone's got to give. (Guess who.)

OPTIONS

You've got two choices:

1. Treat this situation as a problem. Within that choice you have two options.

- Be stubborn, turn this into a competition, and vow to do things your way. If you are a superstar in your own right and feel that you have more staying power than the boss, this may work.

- Execute a well-planned job change, either in or out of the company. If this is a deep style or chemistry issue and you absolutely cannot tolerate this personality don't aggravate yourself any more and leave. A fact of sales-management life is that there are a few people with whom you will be exceedingly uncomfortable. No sense frustrating yourself.

2. Treat the situation as an opportunity. Within this choice you have two options. You've got to decide how much change *you're* willing to make, because you're likely to have to compromise your values or style. The degree of change can vary from small modifications in your behavior all the way up to and including the prostitution of your core values.

   - Be flexible, modify your style, and meet your manager on his turf. Learn absolutely everything you possibly can, both good and bad, that this manager has to offer. Live with the situation and contribute to the growth and goals of the company, participating fully and enthusiastically while holding tight to your core principles and values.

   - Trash your style, and make yourself over into a mirror image of the boss. As severe as this sounds, some people do it in this situation.

Some people have little strength of conviction, and others have a lot. How strong you feel about certain things will ultimately help you decide which of these two opportunity options you choose. Always back your convictions regardless of the consequences.

POSSIBLE ACTIONS

Throughout this struggle perform your job to the highest level of your capability.

Facts of Life

Don't lose sight of these immutable realities.

- Your manager is not going to change. Rolf has been around the block and is set in his ways.

- The lack of a leadership and management style match has an impact on your performance, in spite of your efforts to minimize it. Philosophical conflict consumes some energy whether you like it or not.

- Respecting and liking your boss can enhance your performance. It is human nature to go the extra mile for someone you hold in high esteem.

Think About the Situation

Ask yourself the following questions. The answers often shed light on possible actions and help you decide what to do.

Is the problem a difference in core values, as opposed to work habits or personal style? How deep is this? Differences that run deep are not as nearly reconcilable as style issues.

What are your boss's strengths? What can be learned from this guy? Is there a way you can use Rolf's unique talents and style to your sales unit's benefit and to your personal benefit?

What weaknesses or needs does Rolf have? Just like a customer, if you understand his needs, it's easier to offer solutions and help. Can you volunteer to do some work for him or fill some gaps and solve some problems on behalf of his sales unit and the company? The experience can be of great value.

When you look closely at other executives at Rolf's level, and the president, how do they work with him? Can you learn anything from their interactions?

Take a look at how your sales-manager peers work with Rolf. Is this problem just you, or is it others as well? If Rolf is not a problem for others, then this problem becomes even more personal, and you need to take a harder look at yourself.

What do other people say about you? Are you characterized as rigid? Are you dogmatic? Are you a process or culture zealot? Maybe it's time you lightened up a little bit.

Are you refusing to admit that your boss is doing some things right? Are you being stubborn? Are you being too critical? Are you suffering from a holier-than-thou attitude?

Are other managers on the staff fueling your feelings, or are these your own feelings? Sometimes others try to pull you down with them, or try to recruit you into nasty plots. You have to be careful that you aren't being unwittingly dragged into some distasteful collusion.

Are you intolerant of diversity?

There is a lot to think about. You must be an honest judge of yourself.

How Do You Think the Boss Feels?

Rolf has been watching and listening. He is not asleep. He probably knew you were uncomfortable with him before you knew it yourself. This may not bother him at all. He may be waiting for you to loosen up or rustle up enough courage to do something or come and talk to him. As long as you're hitting the numbers he may not care how you feel.

Seek Contact

Avoidance exacerbates the problem and strains the relationship. Communication helps to build understanding and is a great healer. Use casual contact, ad hoc meetings, regular business-review meetings, or career-counseling sessions as forums to build the relationship, lay out your frustrations, and make suggestions.

Ask Rolf to share his impressions of your work, and ideas to improve.

Probe Rolf for strategy, organization, deployment, and sales tactic ideas.

Inquire how Rolf feels about certain activities that are going on in the business.

Explore to find out what kind of help Rolf needs, or if he has any suggestions how the two of you can better work together.

Ask Rolf to share his expectations if you don't already know. Inform him how he can help you.

If there are certain things going on that you don't like or you believe are detrimental to the business or your people, say so, indicate why, and offer alternatives. Stand up for yourself.

Throughout all the exchanges listen closely and act on Rolf's suggestions. This may not be easy at first because it is not as comfortable talking to people who are not like you. *You may never get close, but you'll get closer, and that's all you can ask for.*

If you run into a manager who isn't willing to give you an ear or regularly gives you the cold shoulder, then you'll feel more comfortable making a decision to leave.

Decision Time

If you plan on treating this as an opportunity, stick with these guidelines

- Always be respectful in all your interactions.
- Be candid, letting your manager know quickly when something doesn't seem right.
- Reach out to keep your manager involved in your sales unit's activities.
- Execute your job with vigor to the best of your ability and display initiative to contribute to enterprise-wide problems.
- Use mirroring with your boss to the same extent that you are comfortable using mirroring when you are in sales situations.
- Engage in the activities that Rolf enjoys, to the extent that you're comfortable.
- Drop a pleasant word of acknowledgment when Rolf does something that is consistent with your way of thinking or doing things. Thank him for ideas that you have found helpful. And compliment him for actions that aid the business.
- Use humor to your advantage.
- Bend a little.

If you plan on treating this as a problem . . .

Remember that you work for *both* the company and the man, so give the job a full go all the way until you leave.

LESSONS

It is rare to find a manager with whom you totally click. Those situations are often enjoyable because they lack conflict. But the lack of diversity often inhibits personal growth. Don't confuse the comfort level you have with your manager with the value of working for someone you may not like, but from whom you can learn much.

Good or bad, you'll learn from everyone you work for. There is value in variety in management and leadership styles. Think of the discomfort as a reminder to look at yourself, assess who and what you are, and as a force to modify your capabilities and add to your repertoire of management and leadership skills.

11–4 THE PROBLEM:
You are being micromanaged.

THE STORY

Nils was having dinner with his family and not enjoying it, because it had been another tough day at the office. Nils's boss, Martin, the VP of Sales, had been all over him again that day.

Nils was saying, "The guy questions every move I make. He criticizes my plans and our presentations. The guy is always interrupting whatever is going on with these minutiae-loaded questions. I can't escape him by being in the field because my voice mail gets loaded with his messages, and my need to return the calls slows down our travel. He is always in my face. My people are beginning to wonder what's going on. I don't have time to go to the men's room."

Nils's wife had been hearing this for several weeks and was growing weary of this tale of woe.

TEMPTATIONS

It is never comfortable when you are under the microscope. The overbearing scrutiny creates many nasty temptations.

Aggravate him

"I'll just feed him a little less a little later than he expects, and then play hard to find."

Get mad

"Martin, this is a waste of time. Why don't you pound sand and just let me do my job?"

Bad-mouth

"This guy is a turkey." or "This guy got his management training out of a catalog."

Have you ever noticed that if something is chasing you, when you suddenly stop, turn around, and confront it, the chasing stops?

WHAT HAPPENED HERE . . . ?

First, let's first make sure what micromanaging is and what it isn't. Virtually all sales executives and managers were in sales positions at one time or another. One of the reasons people gravitate to sales is because of the independence associated with the job. Most sales executives and managers retain that independent nature. Micromanagement occurs when an independent sales executive gets in the independent manager's hair more than the independent manager likes or can tolerate—squeezing that independence. The perception is that the boss is getting involved in infinitesimal little things that he shouldn't be concerned with.

Don't confuse micromanaging with coaching or good management. What's micromanagement to one manager may not be micromanagement to another. Everyone has a different level of scrutiny that he can comfortably tolerate. Scrutiny is part of an executive's job. Some executives scrutinize more than others. If you have trouble with *any level* of scrutiny perhaps you should be in business for yourself.

Is Nils a performance problem? If he is, then he may be getting what he deserves. He may not be meeting expectations. Martin may believe Nils is not competent.

It may be that Martin doesn't trust Nils, or trust people in general. Maybe he's not a people guy. They're out there.

Martin may believe that his job is to do exactly what he is doing. Perhaps he doesn't know any better, or *his* manager isn't coaching *him*.

Perhaps Martin came from Nils's position and just can't let go of the old job. That is a common problem.

Perhaps Martin doesn't understand his own job. Oftentimes people don't realize the change in priorities and activities that accompany second- and third-level sales-management positions. If Martin is new at his position, the different level may require different work and a different style. Maybe he doesn't know how to manage, coach, or lead at that level.

Perhaps Martin lacks confidence in himself and naturally is drawn to work with which he is more comfortable. He may like to do Nils's work better than his own.

Perhaps Martin is under great pressure from above. His boss may be squeezing him for information and results. Martin may also be trying to look busy to his boss.

As far-fetched as it sounds, maybe Martin was neglected by *his manager* when he was in Nils's position, and he is overcompensating. It happens. People react to the strengths and weaknesses of their former managers.

Some managers have an arms-length philosophy, and others have a I'd-rather-be-close style. Nils is obviously dealing with someone who likes to be close. Martin's style may be different from Nils's former manager's style.

And finally, Martin may be trying to send Nils a message to leave. Pressuring him out could save Martin a lot of termination-documentation grief, and at the same time he can build up an understanding of Nils's team and his market.

OPTIONS

You have three options in this situation.

1. Tolerate the situation. Are there any light moments in the midst of the micromanagement to lessen the strain? Maybe you can put up with this behavior until one of you moves on.

2. Quit. You can quit by getting yourself moved to another position in the company or start to search for a new employer. The option seems extreme, but it may be the only choice in certain circumstances.

3. Address the issue and solve it. If you like what you're doing, like where you're living, and like the company, stop, put together an action plan, and confront the problem.

POSSIBLE ACTIONS

Take a time-out from throwing micromanagement darts until you've executed this critical first step.

Carry out your job *to utter perfection* using the company's priorities, your manager's objectives and hot-buttons, and your own goal sheets as a yardstick for a reasonable period of time, like a couple of months. Engineer some successes to see how your manager reacts to potential recognition, if at all. Provide *absolutely no reason* for complaint, then ask yourself what happened. Record some examples of interactions, questions, and micromanagement that bothered you during this brief test period. Was your manager's behavior the same, or did it change? If it changed then maybe you were the problem to begin with. If it didn't, then you must put your action plan into gear.

Self-analysis

Study the way your peers work with the boss and resist the temptation to criticize their actions. Their behaviors should tell you some things. They must be doing something right. Ask them about their working relationship with Martin. Ask for tips and tricks that they have found helpful. It's a good bet that you know what the other managers are doing but that you have a hard time bringing yourself to do the same things.

Examine your own priorities, management processes, and style to ensure that your behaviors are consistent with Martin's. It's a good bet that you haven't been totally aligned.

Has Martin's scrutiny resulted in positive changes in the way you do some things? It's a good bet that you have to reluctantly say yes to that question.

Through careful listening and observation, reconfirm Martin's priorities and problems, to make sure you haven't missed or minimized any. Read and listen between the lines on the boss's comments, memos, and E-mails to pick up insights. You may have been interpreting your boss's style or intent erroneously. There may be some things about Martin that, frankly, aren't that bad.

Ring the Bell

When your self-analysis is complete, ask Martin to talk. Request and schedule a one-on-one with enough time to give you both an opportunity to prepare. It doesn't take much to open the door. For example: "Martin, I'm not comfortable. Can we talk?" or "Martin, things aren't feeling good. I think we need a little talk to discuss what I'm perceiving." or "Martin, I think I have a problem."—or—"Martin, I have the feeling I'm not meeting your expectations."—or—"I think I must be doing something, or several things, wrong?" Now is not the time to back down and disguise or minimize your concern or get mushy. Tell him, "I feel that I can't turn around without having you examine or criticize every little thing I do. Can we get together tomorrow morning at eight?"

Discussion Time

This is a problem-solving session.

Keep it private. There is no need to broadcast this around the office. There will be only one loser if you're out there painting your boss unfairly, and that's you.

Be objective and keep your emotions out of the discussion. A thoughtful approach is more likely to draw respect and consideration. Provide examples of Martin's actions that you were uncomfortable with or didn't understand. Make some suggestions that, from your point of view, would be mutually beneficial. Listen hard in return to Martin's reactions and suggestions.

You should be able to anticipate your boss's reactions and questions, so you should be able to prepare some answers. Since you understand your own performance, there should be no performance-related surprises but, rather, expect that the *intensity* of things that you thought petty are major in Martin's mind.

Ask for candid feedback, but recognize that sometimes a boss has trouble being candid. You may have done something minor that he doesn't want to turn into a major issue, or you may have a small irritating habit that he doesn't want to admit really bugs him. You probably understand what he's trying to get at, so react just as you would in trying to understand a customer's problem. Get confirmation to ensure understanding and don't get defensive.

Thank Martin for his past involvement and cite examples of what worked, not to stroke him, but in recognition of the fact that, frankly, some of his involvement was helpful.

Finally, ask how you can help him. It's a good way to help diminish the problem, and it will elicit the response, "How can I help *you*?" Listen hard and take notes as necessary.

Get Agreement

Agree on any action plan, if required. Perhaps you can agree to a regularly scheduled meeting and agenda to discuss items of mutual interest.

Agree on systems, processes, and information needs that you will honor. Martin will probably try to meet you partway. The dialogue will remind him that the members of his staff have different styles and needs.

Overcommunicate

For the future, provide more information and proactively seek more contact than ever before. Many managers absolutely love to coach and share and are thrilled to have their people seek advice. Many others like to control their organizations closely. A select few basically don't trust anyone. Fewer still are paranoid. All of those types of managers will seek contact on their own if they feel they are being avoided.

LESSONS

Managers on the receiving end of intense inspection and scrutiny most often deserve it, so look at your own actions and performance first before claiming micromanagement. Sales executives and managers who practice micromanagement do it for a reason. Managers subject to this behavior must try to understand the underlying reasons in order to help, not hinder, their immediate superior.

Dialogue almost always clears the air, and you and your manager will both know a little more how the other thinks, feels, and works.

Expectations identification is also key to this problem. Understand what your boss expects from you and understand what you should expect from your boss. A good sales executive will openly share and discuss his expectations with his staff.

Ask *your own people* how you can better work together and support each other as a team. The micromanagement problem can occur both up *and down* an organization.

part twelve

TROUBLESHOOTING INTERNAL MANAGEMENT PROBLEMS

12-1 THE PROBLEM:

Your sales automation effort is frustrating everyone.

THE STORY

"It's crazy, don't you agree?" said Carol when she stuck her head into her sales manager's office. "What are they trying to do with all this computer reporting and information I don't need? We have enough to do, without any more senseless bureaucracy, don't you agree, Dan?"

Dan shrugged, "Hey, let's give it a chance. It's right for us. Stick with it."

"Who was this stuff designed for anyway?" Carol continued. "Who am I working for, the sales department or the MIS Department? This is absolutely insane!"

Dan's sales-force automation (SFA) project was just getting started, and he wasn't completely happy with it either. It's falling apart, he thought to himself, shaking his head.

TEMPTATIONS

Sales-force automation has the benefit of giving everyone in the organization more information about customers, sales partners, and sales efforts. The technology can be scary and frustrating to many salespeople and can cause sales managers to yield to foolish temptations.

Bring the hammer down

"You don't like it? There's the door! Sayonara, baby!"

Throw in the towel

"I think we made a mistake." or "We weren't ready, let's set it aside temporarily."

Scream at your vendor

"You idiots said this would be simple, now you get your butts in here and fix it!"

These temptations hurt, rather than help, the sales challenges your sales force faces.

WHAT HAPPENED HERE . . . ?

The SFA effort seems to be bogged down to the point of potential rebellion. Something about it is adversely affecting the staff.

The story implies that the sales department didn't have a major role in the initial needs analysis, validation of the design, prototype evaluation, acquisition, or testing of the systems—but there could be a lot more at play here.

Many salespeople and sales managers are intimidated by these systems at first. It forces people out of their comfort zones. Dan's staff may be uncomfortable with using computers and technology, and it is one more thing to learn, on top of so many others. Perhaps Dan has moved forward too quickly or did not train his people sufficiently.

The fear of "big brother" also seems to be at play. "They" are trying to keep track of "us," or "they" are checking up on "me." Maybe Dan's people think this is electronic eavesdropping.

Finally, the team may not yet have come to grips with the realization that the environment for today's salespeople and sales managers includes the qualities of being a microbusiness manager first, living in a data- and statistics-intensive environment, mastering change-management skills and electronic communications skills, and living with constant learning.

OPTIONS

You have three options with this problem.

The first option is to stop in your tracks *if* the system really wasn't designed with the sales force in mind. Simply drop the idea. It's happened. However, this may not be feasible because of investment, momentum, and management's expectations.

The second option is to press forward, as is. Change is a challenge, and bellyaching is a fact of sales life. Firm resolve and time have a way of straightening things out. The size and scope of the problem will tell Dan whether this is a viable option.

The third option is to call time-out, back up, and reexamine the situation. This option lets Dan correct flaws before they escalate and lets him and his people come up to speed quicker.

POSSIBLE ACTIONS

Calm your people down and remind them there is no stepping backwards in this game.

Regroup

Dan must get the sales unit together, let them vent, and then seek positive suggestions.

He should talk to the marketing and MIS managers, and other managers, share the sales unit's feedback, and put together a revitalization plan. *Dan must also get his vendor involved.*

A willingness on the part of management to change some preconceived ideas, step up communications, and rebuild around the following actions may be the best approach.

Reconsider Some Early Assumptions

- Did you appoint a make-it-happen, knock-down-the-hurdles sales or marketing leader to head the project, or did you appoint a bit-head manager for political reasons?

- Was there sufficient collaboration with all affected parties from the beginning?
- Did you select a vendor that had a track record of service, support, and innovation, or did you go with the low bid? Is it too late to make a change?
- Did you factor in the modest capability of your sales force to grasp these new methods, or did you try to simplify this effort in order to make your case in the first place?
- Did you focus on information that is vital to enhance customer values and sales-force values, or did too much secondary management stuff sneak its way onto the agenda?
- Did you set reasonable expectations and goals or did you inject a lot of sizzle and pop around overly ambitious objectives in order to rationalize the investment?
- Did you take a measured, stepped approach to implementation, rolling it out in phases, or did you try to do it all at once?

Remind Everyone What This Is All About

It would be a good idea for Dan to remind everyone in the sales unit the reasons that the firm has chosen to invest in SFA systems. The overall goals must remain in sight.

- Remind and show the team that the systems are intended to reduce business costs in order to improve competitiveness.
- Remind the team that technology enables faster sales cycles, shortens the order-fulfillment process, adds customer value, and helps hold customers.
- Remind the team that your SFA strategy integrates with your mainframe strategy so the team can get data they need, but previously could not.
- And finally, remind the team that the systems are intended to help them make an extra buck or two.

Reiterate the Priorities

Make sure the spotlight is focused in the right place. Top-notch SFA systems should satisfy three target groups, in this priority order:

1. Customers, clients, and sales partners (#2 being a distant second).
2. Your sales and value-delivery team, which includes internal sales staff, telemarketers, customer service, technical service, credit and collections, delivery, and others.
3. Sales management, followed by marketing management, followed by other managers.

Someone needs to keep his hand on these priorities because there are dark forces that cause these priorities to drift.

Reconfirm Everyone's Values

Just as in selling, identify the values that SFA can facilitate for each target group. Start with your customers. Research may be needed to confirm what it is that customers want or value in every step of the transaction process. The transaction process includes all pre-selling and postsales activities, often accomplished by people in functions other than sales. A customer-first approach with SFA helps you keep your eyes and ears on your most important business asset—your customer base. Customer values should always serve as an anchor point.

1. From the customer's vantage point, SFA systems can and should enhance values such as complete answers to questions, getting things right the first time, faster responses than anticipated, follow-up ahead of schedule, fixing problems beyond expectations, and being easy to do business with. Is your SFA system designed to meet your customer's values?

Only when you know your customer's values can you begin to make any decisions about the applicability of technology. A periodic reaffirmation of customer values can help you keep all your sales and technology processes relevant and on-target.

2. The next step back from the customer base is all the people who touch the customer on a regular basis. That's the sales force and various internal staff from many functional areas. Research and confirm what information all these people would like to have at every step of the sales and transaction process. Omitting the identification of these people's needs is one of the major reasons for SFA-project failure.

From the sales force and internal staff's vantage point SFA systems can and should enhance things that are important to them such as personal credibility, delivering differentiating presentations, enhancing their image, increasing income, making better use of time, exceeding customer expectations, personal achievement, feeling good about themselves, feeling good about working for a progressive firm, and feeling more connected to the organization. Is your system meeting these values?

Sales forces are by nature skeptical, but they will adopt your agenda if they are convinced that a technology or process will help them do their job and make an extra dollar. Conversely, they will find reasons to discard or disregard your agenda if their values are not addressed.

3. The final step back from the customer is management, and their values must also be a part of the initial needs analysis.

From management's vantage point, SFA systems enhance such values as access to previously unavailable information, better decision making, reinforcing the quality message, cost reduction, customer retention, threat identification, forecast accuracy, critical activity tracking, productivity, measurement of additional marketing variables, and rapid reaction to market conditions. (These points should also be important to the sales unit because in their own territory, salespeople must deal with the same factors.)

Dan must communicate these three value sets as program objectives to the sales unit.

Reignite the Synergy

$1 + 1 + 1 = 4$. Your marketing and sales strategy is the first 1. Your sales process is the second 1. Your SFA system is the third 1. The complementary nature of the three is powerful and satisfies the values of the three target groups.

Dan should demonstrate to the sales unit how the three are complementary. For example, a marketing strategy based on product customization, supported by a sales strategy of comprehensive product knowledge, framed by a sales process designed for complex sales can be nailed with an SFA system that delivers detailed product updates, specifications, and drawings.

The sales process is often the weak link in the equation. A good SFA system can act as the glue and strengthen it. Sales processes are the methodologies that your firm utilizes to sell. Sales processes offer a common vocabulary, a logical sales cycle, guidance for what salespeople should be doing, and a backdrop for sales managers to coach against. For sales processes to be effective tools, there must be disciplined usage.

When reigniting SFA systems, provide a refresher of your sales process and the marketing and sales strategies and make sure both are supported by the SFA system and vice versa.

Retrain the Troops

As you know, all of your competitors can acquire the same hardware and software. The trick lies in getting the sales unit to use everything to its *full advantage*, and that's where training comes in. The initial goal for SFA training should be buy-in and comfort. Enthusiasm for the technology will come later.

- Understand your audience. Remember that most salespeople and sales managers are pragmatists. Pragmatists value facts and matter-of-fact training.
- Get a cross section of your sales unit to participate in the design of the training. Ask what they would like or need.
- Make the training session design a mirror image of the real world.
- Execute a pilot training program, incorporate the feedback, and tune the final program.
- Build interest in the new system prior to training via bulletins or newsletters. This also helps to squash rumors and diffuse negative talk about the system's intent.
- Build an answer to the following question, that is specific to your business, into the training: "How can an SFA system help me win more business and retain more customers?"
- Flush the bit-head vocabulary out of the training program.
- Demonstrate to everyone in detail where in the entire presale- to post-sales-transaction process the technology will be used and how it helps the customer and helps them.
- If you wrap this technology training in vision schemes a savvy sales organization begins to sniff BSing. Talk about productivity or enhanced profitability strengthens the signal that the shoveling is about to begin. Instead, show them how the system alleviates *their* pain and contributes to *their* success.
- If practical, conduct the training face-to-face. Alternatively, provide one-on-one training in the form of CBT (computer-based training), CD-Rom, or video/multimedia that allows remote students to learn and to be tested.

- Make sure the SFA system is complete and working flawlessly before any training begins.
- Put together an ongoing technology training camp to include all types of hardware, software, communications devices, and presentation technologies. This investment helps embed the current, and future, technology initiatives into your sales culture.

Rebuild Compelling Reasons for Usage

Find or create several reasons that *force* usage of the system by the sales force. Mandate that the *only way* a certain task can be accomplished and submitted is through the SFA system. A monthly forecast for example. Or expense reports. Or customer complaints. Make sure you back up the mandate with training so there is ability to do the job.

Remerge the System into Your Operation

Make the system a regular part of meetings, planning, forecasting, and other activities; provide a hot line and a help desk just as the vendors do; bury some personal incentives in the daily messages that go on-line; and share success stories of usage.

Recommitment from Up Top Is a Requisite

Encourage executive management to use its PCs, laptops, applications, E-mail, Internet, and communications devices. If possible, make it the only way they can get to information.

Behavioral changes by sales organizations will be replicated when modeled by changes at the top. Management must commit themselves with sleeves-up involvement, not just dollars.

LESSONS

The inability to gain rousing acceptance for new technology can have far-reaching negative effects in today's business environment. SFA-systems implementation are a real test of teamwork and project-management skills. The cultural adjustment is a challenge to your change management and training skills.

Success or failure has to do with committed leadership and understanding management, not with technology.

12–2 The Problem:

An overzealous product manager regularly butts in.

The Story

"Oh, it's *you* again," said Jed, the sales manager, looking up to see Lionel, his least favorite product manager.

"I want to know why the forecast is low," Lionel announced. "And I want to travel with some of your people next week, as well."

"I want product in inventory, first," Jed shot back.

"And why aren't the new models moving," Lionel continued.

"Because you're an inept product manager, you bonehead," countered Jed. "And who stacked all these boxes of product brochures in my office, uninvited?"

Jed just shook his head disgustedly as Lionel walked out.

Temptations

Aggressive encroachment can get your hackles up real quick, and the temptations are many.

Hide

"Tell Lionel the only time I can meet is at McDonald's at 6:00 A.M. And it's on him."

Take a powerful pharmaceutical

"This guy gives me a headache whenever I hear his name."

Chastise him

"You're kidding, Lionel, get serious, I don't have time for your crap. Why don't you read my monthly report or phone these 243 prospects yourself to get some feedback."

The perception of intrusive behavior is usually lost on the intruder.

What Happened Here . . . ?

You have a clueless pain in the butt who is driving you nuts.

Lionel could simply be selfish and self-centered, lacking sensitivity and being numb to other people's feelings and agendas. This guy may be flat-out abrasive and obnoxious.

Lionel could be under severe pressure to get the job done, or maybe he is being told by his boss to hound you.

Lionel may be new to the job, and what Jed is experiencing is puppy-dog excitement and youthful exuberance.

Lionel may not know how to influence peers, or know how to work in a matrix environment. He may be a guy just trying to do his job the only way he knows how.

Lionel may not trust Jed, may not believe that Jed will do the job for him because Jed has given him reason to be suspicious.

Someone may have told Lionel that persistence pays off, and he is going to employ the squeaky-wheel theory on Jed. He is going to wear him down one way or another.

This could be a simple chemistry issue—two people who simply don't like each other.

In the end, one of the two is going to have to step up and lead the management of the relationship.

OPTIONS

You have three options with this problem:

1. Distance yourself further from Lionel if the situation in your judgment is simply intolerable, while executing all that is required with Lionel's product line.
2. Tolerate him as he is, grit your teeth, and march on.
3. Embrace Lionel, and turn his energy, his know-how, and his momentum *to your advantage*. Make Lionel's zealous approach work for the both of you.

You can stretch out a hand or you can walk on by.

Key point: The option you choose, and the vigor with which you execute it may be affected by Lionel's personal status, power level, and the relative importance of his product line in your business. But is it right to let those things influence you? Think about it.

POSSIBLE ACTIONS

Relax. This can be a rewarding problem if you like to mix it up with people and if you are tolerant and understanding. If you're not, this will be a lesson in patience.

First: a Self-test

Are you oversensitive, overprotective of your turf, or not the team player that you like to make yourself out to be? Are your *own* interpersonal and teamwork skills suspect?

Size up Lionel

Make an assessment of Lionel. What is he good at? What skills and knowledge does he possess that can augment your sales-unit competencies? Never underestimate the capabilities of your colleagues. They just may surprise you with facets of business knowledge or insight.

Where does Lionel need help on both a business and personal level, and where can you help him? What motivates him? You are not his manager, but you *are* a team member.

Watch how the other people in marketing or other sales managers deal with him. What can you learn?

From a sales manager's perspective, here is a tongue-in-cheek characterization of the two varieties of staff-support managers.

Theory S Staff Managers	*Theory M Staff Managers*
Cooperative, friendly, energetic, open, trusting, knowledgeable, responsive, interested, ambitious, great attitude, energy-giver, makes you comfortable, runs fast, and turns everything into a war on competition.	Self-centered, cautious, devious, untrusting, crafty, entrapping, measured, political, energy-taker, makes you uncomfortable, whiner, and turns everything into a war of the wills

---

Theory-S staff people can get a ton of cooperation out of sales managers. When working with Theory-S managers you can concentrate on looking forward. With theory-M managers you always have to look in the rear-view mirror.

Lionel sounds like a theory *M*, and you'll hope that Jed is a professional who can influence Lionel to change and grow. (*M* stands for "maverick," and *S* for "supportive," by the way.)

Chew on These Points

Remember the following when working with overzealous colleagues:

It is not a sign of weakness to accede to a bothersome colleague's wishes. Cooperation in the face of frustration communicates personal strength, confidence, and understanding.

Deep down in your management consciousness admit to yourself the fact that colleagues, however they might frustrate you, can be of great value to your sales unit. Another pair of eyes and ears, and another mind, can yield ideas that may be unobtainable by you alone.

Recognize and accept your professional gaps. Don't assume that you are so tough or gifted that you can run alone. Employ the willing assistance of your equally tough and gifted colleagues.

Your people learn a great deal about you and they form their own interpersonal styles as they observe your interactions with everyone. What kind of message do you want to leave them about teamwork and adaptability?

In spite of quizzical behaviors, your co-workers are inherently capable and willing to aid the common cause of sales growth and company success.

A sales manager who responds to tactless approaches with a tactless attitude always loses.

Talk It Out

Share your frustration candidly with Lionel and ask him to share his in return. Don't be surprised if it takes more than one discussion to get everything on the table.

Talk about specific roles and responsibilities, mutual expectations, define the help you would like to receive, and ask Lionel to define the help he would like to receive.

Establish simple rules of contact, unmistakable protocols so no one is mucking around uninvited in the other person's sandbox. In time, as respect grows, you can be more flexible. Show each other the impact of encroachment on each other's responsibilities. The intent is not to build walls, but to establish discipline and embed common courtesies.

If Lionel has any sense of humor at all, share the Theory-*S* and the Theory-*M* sales-management guidelines. (But first make sure *you* are a Theory *S* yourself.)

Don't document anything, or you'll only reinforce the lack of trust.

Reach out and Set an Example

Help Lionel to be a big winner.

- Tell everyone in your sales unit to cooperate fully with Lionel. Civility begets civility.
- Ask Lionel for help, don't just be reactive to *his* wishes. For example, could he execute a special project for your sales unit, such as a mailing, an open house, or a seminar?
- Invite Lionel to sit in on training sessions you sponsor and ask him to contribute.
- Ask to be a part of his product-planning committee, sit in on a focus group, help with a survey design, contribute to strategy development, or assist with sales-aid creation. Your contribution will show Lionel that *you* also have something to offer.
- Ask to have one of your customers be a pilot or beta site for one of Lionel's new products. The effort accelerates personal interaction and can actually be fun.
- When you create your own travel, meeting, and training plans, give Lionel the opportunity to schedule his participation on your sales unit's calendar.
- Ask Lionel for opinions on matters outside his direct control or interest. The questions imply that you value his opinions—and you should.
- Dole out the accolades in recognition of Lionel in situations where his contribution was a factor.

Get on with Your Job

Give it time and understand that things won't change overnight. Keep your personal example of work habits and teamwork at the highest level and keep that hand stretched out.

Lessons

You send a team-player message about yourself all across the organization chart.

The most effective way to motivate others to help you fulfill your goals is to help them fulfill *their* goals.

Work is a more enjoyable environment, in spite of contention, when you take the responsibility to lead or heal cooperative efforts. When you're working for the benefit of *others* you're more likely to be a vibrant, energetic contributor.

There are only two stupid ways to lose business: by your own lack of effort or by your reluctance to collaborate with colleagues.

12–3 The Problem:

You have an adversary on the sales staff.

The Story

The staff meeting was getting nasty for Leon—again!

"That approach is fundamentally flawed," Earl shouted.

Earl was the business development manager, and the target of his abuse was Leon, a relatively new region sales manager. Both Leon and Earl reported to the VP of sales and marketing.

They didn't agree on the new compensation plan proposal, didn't agree on new distributor policies, and didn't agree on the whole meeting agenda. Leon felt as if he'd been in the gym rather than the conference room for the past two hours.

The constant sniping and innuendoes were driving Leon up the wall. Man, I've *got* to do something about this, he thought to himself.

Temptations

When you regularly have to deal with someone who drains your mental, physical, and psychological energy and raises your anxiety level, it can foster absurd temptations.

Hurt him

"I think I'll withhold this competitive information from him."—or—"It's time to launch a counter-defamation campaign against that jerk."

Gossip

"Did you hear how Earl screwed up in last week's presentation to the GM?"

Rancorous language

"That was a totally asinine idea that Earl whimsically threw against the wall today."

Don't exacerbate the problem by fueling the fire.

WHAT HAPPENED HERE ... ?

You have an enemy. This is nasty stuff, and certainly not a healthy situation.

Disagreements or tension occur in all sales units, and it is to be expected from time to time. It is not necessarily bad, but it can get to be destructive if not contained and managed.

Earl may not respect Leon. He may not think Leon is qualified for the job, or Earl covets Leon's job. Leon may not meet Earl's view of what a region sales manager should look like.

Leon may be one of those MBA hot-shots who didn't come up through the school of hard knocks, doesn't have the same background as Earl, and is therefore not in the club.

Perhaps Earl sees Leon as a direct competitor. Maybe they're both on a track for the same job.

Perhaps this is simply grandstanding and positioning. Some managers act like that in group situations, for reasons known only to themselves.

Leon may have done something to really hurt Earl, make Earl look bad, or Earl may have picked up something erroneous on the grapevine.

Earl may not like Leon's style or approach to the business. This could be a classical chemistry problem.

The culture of the company may be very political or may foster combative behavior. There are some executives who like to let their people duke it out.

Earl may feel jealous because he is out of the mainstream in a special staff position. He may have the feeling that a macho, self-serving approach is the way to make his presence felt. This could also be immaturity, insecurity, or even emotional instability on Earl's part.

Finally, Earl may just be a classical loose cannon.

OPTIONS

Question: Is this a competent person or someone with a personal problem? If Earl is a stable, solid contributor then you have two options.

1. You can decide to tolerate it and coexist because of special circumstances, politics, or because you simply choose not to engage.

2. You can decide to do something about the situation because this is more than a bothersome little tic—it's driving you crazy. You can choose to mend the relationship.

If this is an incompetent, insecure individual (and they're out there), then it may be best to just indulge him, let nature take its course, and go about your job to the best of your ability. This is similar to option one, but amounts to little more than humoring the antagonist and letting management deal with him.

POSSIBLE ACTIONS

Leon has a job to do. It's time to stop fretting and start acting. Leon's on the same staff so he has to work with Earl. The reality of this becoming a close relationship may be unlikely, but that's not a reason to back off.

Why Would You Want to Do Anything with This Situation?

The answers may be obvious, but it's a good question to start you thinking about an approach to Earl and how you choose to manage relationships with peers.

- Teamwork is imperative in today's sales environment.
- The relationship gets in the way of your individual and sales-unit productivity.
- Your have your own reputation, career, and future to think about.
- You want to set a good example for your own people.
- You want to take a professional approach to conflict management.
- Your own physical and mental health are consequential.
- Your responsibilities are mutually supportive.
- And it's the right thing to do.
- Why else would *you* want to resolve this? _____

The bottom line is, it's clearly worth the effort because those are good reasons. We raise these reasons because the confrontational nature of the problem creates a secondary temptation to cop out and tolerate the situation. Your list is meant to help steel your resolve.

Analyze the Signals

It helps to recount the signals of the deteriorated relationship because they help you pinpoint the environments or circumstances that feed the issue, define its depth, and give you a sense of what needs to be addressed. It also helps you spot other relationships that may need some work.

- Do you have make-believe defensive conversations with Earl? Admit to yourself if Earl intimidates you and admit the reason why.

- In a group, does Earl act as if you're not there? Does he refer to you as "him"? Does he not look you in the eye when he talks to you? Do *you* intimidate *him* without knowing it?

- Does Earl challenge *all* of your initiatives and efforts or just some of them? The answer may reveal his agenda.

- Do you feel anxious when you get a phone message from Earl or see him come around the corner? Could it be that he rightfully challenges you because you're not doing a thorough job in his eyes, and down deep inside you know it, but don't want to admit it?

- Are you disappointed when you are put on a team with him? Could it be that you know he'll look better than you? Do others like him or respect him more than they like or respect you?

- Do you find yourself wondering what he is thinking, or what he'll say next? Could it be that you have trouble admitting that someone else's ideas are better than yours?

- Do you feel deflated when he walks into the room? Does it change the atmosphere and your natural style? Could it be that you're not prepared to the same level he is?

There are two sides to every relationship problem. It helps if you have the courage to honestly admit to things *on your side* of the ledger.

Think About Current Connections and Contacts

Here are some things to think about that may help you focus your corrective actions. Again, be honest with yourself.

Who is better positioned politically on the staff, or has more position power? The answer may impact your approach. In virtually all cases the antagonist is better positioned or equal, which is one of the reasons that this is a problem in the first place. If Earl has more muscle, you may have to be more accommodating.

Is this a topic problem that relates simply to activities or ideas? Is this a relationship problem that relates to areas of joint interest and impact? Is this a personal problem that relates to you or Earl as individuals? The answers will tell you if logic or emotion is your best response.

Have you attacked a pet idea of Earl's in the past? Is there an apology overdue?

Are you stepping on Earl's perceived or real responsibilities by accident or on purpose?

Is Earl trying to create a faction within the sales unit to isolate you? Does he want you out for some reason?

Is the relationship just cold, or is it antagonistic? Cold implies a simple chemistry mismatch; antagonistic implies a deeper agenda.

Is Earl jealous of you? Do you have something—a skill, contacts, abilities, something about you personally that he admires and wishes that he possessed? Can, or would you share it?

Are you shining too much, tooting your own horn, getting too much press, taking the spotlight off Earl, and maybe rubbing it in?

Would Earl be reading this problem with the same intensity that you are?

The idea behind this introspection is to force personal candor. The exercise also has the effect of shedding light on answers.

Your Manager's Role

Your mutual manger will have spotted the contentious relationship. Like all managers, he will have a threshold of tolerance for conflict in his organization. You can bet that he will intervene when *he thinks* it's necessary. You can engage your manager, while not appearing to be a whiner, by simply asking for suggestions that *you* could take to improve the relationship and leave it at that.

Watch and Listen

Watch how others on the staff deal with Earl. What are Earl's values? What does he seem to enjoy about his relationships with others? Use all this to your advantage.

Talk to Earl

Give him a call. (This is a sales call you're about to arrange. Schmooze him a little bit.)

Say that something is bothering you, and you'd like to get it off your chest.

Say that you'd like to know how you can support him better.

Say you're not feeling comfortable with the relationship.

Say you have a feeling that something is bothering him.

Say you'd like to clear the air.

It takes nothing more than a simple statement like that to get the ball rolling, but *speed* is of the essence because Earl is spreading this all over the office and conflict festers over time.

Use the thoughts and answers that came out of your introspection to start the discussion.

Ask questions and listen, don't get defensive, and remember, it's not just what you say but how you say it. What you want is to start regular, casual dialogue.

Take the High Road

As the relationship moves forward, set an example and take these ten courageous steps to keep the ball rolling.

1. Laugh at yourself if you've earned it.
2. Be supportive of Earl's initiatives, to the extent that your basic principles permit.

3. Keep Earl scrupulously informed on your work that affects his unit.

4. Share your expertise as one coach talking to another coach.

5. Ask Earl for opinions on matters of mutual importance or on matters on which he possesses expertise, build on the ideas, and let Earl know you used his inputs.

6. Sit down with Earl one-on-one frequently, share a couple of lunches, and slowly increase the trust level of communications.

7. Sincerely compliment Earl for his work and don't forget to say thanks for contributions to your sales unit. And celebrate together if an opportunity permits.

8. Be respectful of Earl's personal and business sensitivities.

9. Keep your eyes open for an opportunity to adopt a goal similar to one of Earl's goals.

10. Treat Earl as a customer.

It's a great example for your team, and your initiatives won't go without notice across and up the organization chart.

While this discussion presented no responses from Earl as Leon moved forward, the reality of the situation is that Earl *will* respond, perhaps cautiously at first, but it's a good bet he'll meet Leon partway.

LESSONS

There will always be staff associates with whom you don't click.

Stop the seething and needless energy consumption when these situations are small. All relationships can be improved to a lesser or greater degree. It just takes some candid thinking and courageous action.

Your own relationship-management efforts will serve as a great school so that you can guide your own people in similar situations.

Adversity can turn into opportunity and yield some of the strongest relationships you ever imagined if you work it.

12–4 THE PROBLEM:
You must convince other managers to support a major sales initiative.

THE STORY

Carlos had just been appointed the new sales director for Latin America, leading the firm's first committed thrust into offshore markets.

His VP had been behind this initiative and was convinced it was time to go global and had tossed Carlos this hot potato. The president had bought into the idea, but the rest of management was lukewarm. Some quietly complained that there were higher priorities.

Carlos was running into grief from the finance people because of longer terms and letters of credit, with the production people because of design changes, with the shipping people because of the warehouse in Miami, and with marketing communications because of translations, and on it went. He couldn't win.

TEMPTATIONS

When you are the one out on a limb by your lonesome, it's not hard to yield to these temptations.

Grovel

"Jerry, please, I really need your help here. If you support me on this issue, I'll stand behind you on that equipment you're campaigning for, or whatever else you need."

Fight

"Hey, I don't need your dumb hassling Thelma. I'll tell you what I think of your two-bit group."

I'll do it myself

"I don't need these lazy, uncooperative people. I know exactly what needs to be done."

When you are pioneering, keep your heart and one hand firmly around the organization.

WHAT HAPPENED HERE . . . ?

There seems to be mushy commitment to this major sales initiative.

This problem is typical of situations where a sales manager has been given (or taken) responsibility for a project or initiative that is new, different, or inconsistent with the run-of-the-mill business.

Who is given the task says a lot about the company's commitment to the effort. Since everyone understands the informal organization chart, other managers can all tell from the outset whether they need to get behind an initiative. That's an important lesson for the executive who assigns a manager to an initiative. *How* and in *what forum* and with *what resources* that initiative is announced also has a major effect on its buy-in and outcome.

There is a big difference between launching an initiative with a memo and a minuscule budget versus launching one with a corporate staff meeting and deep-pocket support.

Other initiatives such as national-account programs, the introduction of new sales channels, introduction of a new product line, and use of new technologies such as sales automation often share the same issues.

In the story, the VP may feel that Carlos has the consensus-building skills and is up to the challenge. On the other hand, he may also feel that Carlos's level of inexperience and naiveté will help him accept the challenge. It may be that Carlos is being used. The VP may know that other sales managers may not have been willing to accept the personal risk associated with such an assignment.

The chances of success of new ventures are better if there is a balance of power between the responsible manager and other managers.

OPTIONS

Carlos was handed a hot potato. Remember in the game of hot potato, the objective is to hold the potato for as little time as possible. The same is true in sales management. This is one of Carlos's options. Do a superficial job on this assignment and get himself out of it as quickly as he can. That is a conflict-minimizing approach, in essence, doing enough to get the ball rolling, but then handing it off to another unfortunate manager. Some people do that.

The second option is to accept the challenge, and bake the potato, serving it with all the condiments Carlos can find, making it *so appetizing* that everyone wants a piece of the job now and in the future.

If an initiative has a godfather, as is the case in the story, Carlos might be wise to pursue the project with the same intensity that the godfather has for the initiative.

POSSIBLE ACTIONS

Seize the opportunity. It is a subtlety that won't be lost on other managers.

Understand Your Colleagues

Understand their fears and concerns. Understand that they may be worried about costs, lack of time, business risk, extra work, the need to learn new things, having their current priorities diluted or interrupted, uncertainty of the outcome, and self-proclaimed sacred cows.

Understand their measurements and how the efforts associated with your initiative may impact their measurements.

Understand the detailed sales history, if any, associated with this initiative (the good, the bad, and the ugly). Those facts and fictions may be thrown at you in times of disagreement.

Take a look at what worked in the past with other business initiatives and try to learn something from them. Contact the folks who led those initiatives if they are still available.

Identify the antagonists who are likely to give you trouble. Recognize from the outset that you may never be able to get everyone totally committed, but the best you can hope for is to neutralize them.

Plan

Create a personal, written internal sales plan, akin to a political campaign, whose objective is to create buy-in, allay fears, support everyone's measurements, and bury the legends and old emotions. A plan will also ensure that you don't lose sight of all the following actions.

Take the High Ground

Be sensitive to profits, margins, return-on-investment, expenses, and other key business indicators as you move forward. No one can argue with a top-down, business-first mentality, as opposed to parochial, personal-agenda approaches that doom most initiatives to failure.

Take a Savvy Approach

The activities you execute should be aimed at building consensus, relationships, and credibility. The campaign should never be considered over until you are safely ensconced in a different responsibility. Here are 12 proven campaign tactics

1. Make sure that you personally exhibit detailed knowledge of the depth, scope, and challenges of the initiative. Do extensive research on the initiative you're leading. Become an expert on the subject. Expertise is hard to fight. But don't embellish and enlarge the initiative, pompously making it into something it isn't, because you'll lose credibility.

2. Have modest and realistic goals in the beginning. Meet those goals, to establish credibility, then raise the goals at a rate commensurate with your resources and the goals of the firm and the comfort level of the management team. Engineering some quick, modest successes will establish a positive track record.

3. Lead from personal strength at the outset, executing those activities with which you are comfortable, well versed, and in which you have a good reputation.

4. Consider creating an advisory team, made up of representation from different business functions. Have them contribute to policy- and business-practice formulation associated with the initiative. Meet regularly to discuss issues and progress.

5. Integrate your people, processes, reports, and numbers into the mainstream. You'll want to use superglue to cement yourself to the core business, not stand alone. Any perception of the establishment of a personal principality invites attack. Integration minimizes differences.

6. Look for and nurture internal champions and sales agents at all levels and in all functions and departments. Get some people informally working for you who will stand up for the initiative in your absence.

7. Constantly ask your colleagues if they have any questions or concerns about what you are doing. If they don't raise any, then the monkey is on their back. If they raise questions, address them concisely and candidly.

8. Look for ways to tie your work to the *personal* as well as the professional interests of any antagonists.

9. Build consensus and support from the bottom up in organizations that are led by doubters.

10. Build a file of extensive data, exhibits, and proof statements as you go forward. Document demonstration of the *real* benefits to the business, and benefits to individual business functions. Use this ammunition with discretion.

11. Promote or relocate some of your people to positions inside other business units. Seeding your people within tough constituencies can help garner support from the inside out.

12. Use the initiative's godfather with discretion to knock down hurdles. Overuse will become obvious and dilute the impact of the godfather.

Take on a Professional Air

Style counts when leading new initiatives. Don't point fingers for lack of support, but be quick to acknowledge assistance. Don't sugarcoat anything, especially setbacks.

Build trust, which is obtained through consistent performance, equal treatment of others, and integrity of your actions.

Be an open book, sharing information as requested, providing detailed explanations and data as needed. Playing your cards closely can arouse suspicions.

Be willing to accept revision in form and detail as you go forward, especially respecting the inputs from others and executing your actions with impeccable precision.

Proceed slowly and respectfully, but understand that there will be times when you have to pick up speed and plow ahead. After all, you're the one being compensated and measured.

Take a Participatory Tact

Getting others in the boat with you goes a long way. Engineer some well-executed involvement. Here are some ideas:

- Take other executives out in the field with you so they can see and listen for themselves.
- Take the antagonists to trade shows, seminars, and conferences so they can witness reality.
- Include difficult managers in your training sessions so they can see the extent of your efforts.
- Have colleagues from other departments speak at your meetings.

- Volunteer to speak at their meetings and special events, so you can update their staffs.
- Ask others to give talks at seminars and conferences that relate to the initiative.
- Pair off an antagonist with a supporter at meetings or special functions.
- Get your outside contacts involved with the doubters when they come to visit. Walk key contacts around and introduce them to all your colleagues. Openness breeds comfort.
- Include skeptical colleagues in big, tough negotiations.
- Get the doubters involved in the interviewing process when you're hiring additional staff.
- Ask about promotion-ready candidates on their staffs that you can bring onto your team.

Be creative. The list of possibilities is virtually limitless.

Keep the Reinforcements Coming

Information is key. Provide copies of articles from business dailies and the trade press. Detailed and informative action reports work well. Storytelling is an effective way to describe your unit's activities. Communicate competitive initiatives going on in parallel to your initiative.

Inform everyone about the impact of your effort on the company's performance. Discuss the implications of the sales volume on employment, on the factories, on profits, on market shares, on strategic positioning, and so on.

Make sure everyone always understands "what *we* need to do" in order to continue to be successful with the initiative.

Make sure no one loses sight of the *imperatives* that led to this initiative in the first place. The initial rationale often gets lost.

And help make it happen for *other managers* and *their* programs. Reciprocity works.

Get Tough When You Have To

There are times, in spite of everything you do, that you are going to have to stand up for what you believe. Strength of conviction and action are musts. You get no points for being a marshmallow.

Recognize Good Support

Provide recognition up and down and across the organization as the project moves forward. The following points have all proven to be successful.

- Thank-yous at the grass-roots level and the midmanagement level are often worth the most, and don't forget the folks in remote locales who bought into and supported your efforts.

- Schedule a lunch for a management group and give a short talk with emphasis on thanks.
- Use trips to major conferences and meetings as recognition for lower-level people.
- Send letters and E-mails of appreciation, and for extraordinary effort above and beyond, write commendations, copying the contributor's boss and personnel file.
- Establish a formal recognition program.
- Give small gifts to folks in the office who helped with your efforts.
- Write and place articles in the company newsletter.
- Get coverage in the annual report for people who made a major impact.
- Use a press conference or press releases to gain wider impact.

And finally, don't be afraid to blow your own horn from time to time, with the same energy that others blow theirs.

LESSONS

The manager of a major initiative always has a bigger internal than external selling job.

Managing a new initiative is basically change management. If done well, you'll build a reputation for yourself as a business builder, a market-development expert, a consensus builder, and as a good leader and manager.

There are many positive benefits that flow from leading such initiatives. You'll make several new friends in the process, and you'll get grudging respect from even the most hardened colleagues. The biggest lesson is that you will learn things about your business and associates that you never knew before. Your personal confidence will take a great leap forward. You'll also learn the value of a godfather.

There are also risks. If not done well, you can hurt yourself. If you're not the type of person who is comfortable with risk, shy away from pioneering initiatives.

12–5 THE PROBLEM:

A customer's unusual request has corporate-wide implications.

THE STORY

Cookie, the district sales manager, and one of his account managers were in the midst of a heated meeting with the GM of operations, the vice president of finance, the president, the VP of sales and marketing, the MIS director, and others. The subject was a presentation the two salespeople had made to a longtime customer yesterday. It seems that Cookie had been asked if his firm could meet a demand that represented about 40 percent of his company's capacity.

The GM of operations adamantly wanted nothing to do with it, and neither did his cohorts. He was already working the lines two shifts and was not about to blow up the factory. The finance manager didn't like the idea either, and the president was "sort of" lukewarm.

Cookie thought to himself, "Here I am, hanging out, being grilled, for something I thought was a great deal for the company. I don't understand."

TEMPTATIONS

A sales manager's dream about a big hit can fuel contentious bickering and sniping when the request hits a brick wall. The heat of the moment can generate silly temptations.

Strut

"We did it! We brought in the BIG one! Aha! Aren't we something?"

Brawl

"Hey, Mr. Complacency, I'm bustin' my butt to bring in the business, and you're sitting there like some pompous judge. Come off it."

Play politics

"I'll position myself behind the President. That way I can't go wrong."

You will always run into widely divergent opinions and agendas within your management team on unusual customer requests. This is a time for listening and objectivity.

WHAT HAPPENED HERE . . . ?

A dream opportunity came your way. A good customer thought enough of you to ask for something special—but he wants it "My Way," as the famous 1969 Frank Sinatra song goes.

Customers make unusual requests because they want to either reduce costs or do something that ultimately differentiates themselves in the market.

First off, this meeting occurred very quickly, and that could be part of the problem.

Cookie may not understand that unusual requests play havoc with existing customers and sales partners, shattering production schedules and lead times. Spiked growth or a resource-consuming departure from the mainstream can be devastating.

Cookie's dream request could also have an impact on emotional soft stuff like executive incentives, financial forecasts, and limitations on other opportunities or pet projects.

Unusual requests cause changes, which often cause an unwillingness to cooperate. Unusual requests can disrupt people's comfort level, provoke more work, cause unplanned investment, siphon valuable time from employees, generate onerous processes, and offer no perceived advantages in the minds of a few key players.

Some of the managers in our story's conference room may understand that today's business environment is a *less certain* environment than in years past. Unusual requests made in less certain environments often imply a bigger risk.

In the absence of a crisis, with the numbers looking good, arrogance can also get in the way of accepting major customer initiatives.

Finally, sales may be viewed as always trying to enrich themselves at the expense of others and to get things *their way.*

OPTIONS

The company has options, a multitude of business alternatives that can range from politely declining the opportunity to a piecemeal approach to snapping up the opportunity in toto, to forwarding the request to another component of the corporation.

Cookie's options as a sales manager have more to do with role. Here are three option possibilities:

1. Hands off because this is too big and complex. Not a likely option, but possible.
2. Play a supportive role with the account manager as the people responsible for leading the customer interface. This is most likely.
3. Participate fully in all aspects of the business decision and all follow-on actions. This is what Cookie would like.

POSSIBLE ACTIONS

Step up and call time-out.

Get Your Act Together First

Cookie shouldn't expose himself to a further onslaught of questions or embarrassment without obtaining additional information. Some detailed documentation to build everyone's understanding may be called for.

- Gather all your current sales data on the customer. Write up a thorough assessment of the customer, the customer's long-term quantity needs, and the customer's markets.
- Ascertain the competition's position and efforts within the account.
- Put together a history of your firm's relationship with the customer.
- List all executive and operational contacts, their roles in this situation, and your current relationship with all of them.
- Identify recent sales and marketing actions that you have undertaken with this customer.
- Document the receivables history and current balances.
- Provide copies of all contracts or agreements to everyone involved in this discussion.

For the next meeting, Cookie should develop a list of answers to questions such as: "Specifically, what was asked for?" "Who was at the meeting?" "What is the reason for the request?" "When do they want the product?" "What are the probabilities?" "What price do they want?" "Is this funded or are they just kicking tires?" "Where does this *take* us?" "How does this position us?" and so on. For the future, he can turn these expected management questions into a checklist for everyone in his sales unit to use for other unusual requests.

If needed and feasible, he can take another respected nonsales manager with him to revisit the customer as a part of an expanded fact-gathering mission. The presence of a nonsales manager sends a strong message of interest to the customer, helps probe for relevant information, and helps with the inside selling job back home.

Kick off a Benefit/Risk Comparison

Cookie should initiate a benefit-risk comparison to which other staff executives can contribute, giving them a prepared track to run on. The fact that he started such an analysis sends a strong message about his personal objectivity. These ideas are intended to get you started. Complete the comparison on your own.

Benefits: "Why should we do this" or "What will the company get out of this deal?"	Risks: Why shouldn't we do this" or "What are the consequences of not doing this deal?"
• It gives us a cushion and could lock-in our financial projections for the next few years.	• We could spend a lot of time on this and still not get the order.
• The situation offers future partnering opportunities.	• The effort will keep us from working on something more important.
• The request is an opportunity to establish new relationships at new levels in new departments.	• The customer's new product could bomb, leaving us with excess capacity.
• It gives us an opportunity to broaden our internal process expertise by doing something new.	• We could be perceived as arrogant or self-satisfied if we turn it down, and then lose everything!
• The benefit of incremental (profitable) business.	• Etc., etc. . .
• It offers a competitive advantage, and will aid customer retention.	
• Our participation sends a message to the market about our responsiveness, hunger, and innovation skills.	
• The volume will help reduce out unit costs. Etc., etc. . .	

Unusual requests are often hidden messages. The marketplace could be telling Cookie's firm to do something new and different. Savvy executives usually pick up on this fact.

How to Encourage Buy-in

- Communicate the request in the context of your firm's overall business and marketing strategy as opposed to a random happening and present the opportunity as *consistent* with corporate strengths and capabilities. (If, in fact, it is.) A sales manager who can present an opportunity in that light comes across as a solid businessperson, not a sales opportunist.

- Be honest and candid with your personal assessments. Subjective sales-ey embellishments reduce credibility.

- Commit personal financial resources and organization to the effort so it doesn't look as if you are the brazen recipient of a gift. Be willing to share the pain as well as the gain.

- Be patient—these internal business decisions take time. The customer understands the complexity of their request.

- Sell the customer on participating fully as a partner in *executive-level discussions* from the beginning. Turn this into an institutional opportunity and relationship instead of a transactional opportunity. Your top brass will appreciate this.

Plant Some Seeds

Management may already be doing the following, but be ready to offer these suggestions.

Suggest a coalition of stakeholders to evaluate and guide the request. By suggesting a coalition, you ensure that you are a part of it or that the sales unit's interests are represented. The coalition should contain various functional expertise, plus position power. Perhaps you can be so bold as to suggest a leader to head the coalition. For the future, suggest that the firm turn this into a standing rapid-reaction team to handle other unusual requests. Asking the customer to reciprocate with a team of their own would help cement this relationship.

Your rapid-reaction team then has the responsibility of executing a quantitative business analysis, qualitative market-impact analyses, issue identification and resolutions, trade-off analyses, implementation plans, customer-communication plans, and process management of the unusual request.

Define the Role You Play Before One Gets Defined for You

Stay intimately involved while the company makes a go–no-go decision, and then have your account manager and/or yourself coordinate the communications as the order unfolds and the project is totally implemented. Arm's-length participation leaves a bad taste in the mouth of the rest of the management team and can negatively influence a future request.

Political Tips to Bias the Go–no-go decision

- Look for subtle ways to enhance the interests of affected operations or departments.
- If possible, on an individual basis, and without being patronizing, communicate to all participants how they can obtain some kudos in the process and help their personal agendas. You can bet that their wheels have already been turning. Oil the wheels.
- Keep your eyes and ears open for a godfather or godmother to influence the request.

LESSONS

Handling this kind of problem builds your understanding of the capabilities and long-term interests of your company. You should be able to articulate those capabilities and interests to customers, so that you are able to discern what's possible and what's not possible within broad guidelines before you bring *anything* through your front door. When you do bring in something special, have it nicely packaged before you lay it on the table.

Prompt your people to keep their eyes, ears, and minds open to unusual customer requests. Yes—you have to sell what is on the shelf, but it is also your responsibility to stir up and bring forward new ideas. Those initiatives make the sales unit a more valued asset to the business.

Execute unusual requests brought to *you and your team* when the shoe is on the other foot. A cooperative attitude engenders reciprocity.

12–6 THE PROBLEM:

Other managers give you no respect.

THE STORY

The staff meeting broke up with laughter. The marketing manager had been all over Len for information he wanted, the accounts-receivable manager was upset with Len about average days to pay, the service manager had been complaining that Len's people were not selling extended warranties, and the engineers were scoffing at Len's requests for product-spec changes. It seemed as if every time Len opened his mouth, he got criticized or shouted down. He was mad and tired of the barbs and being the butt of jokes.

He went back to his office drained. It had not been subtle.

The messages were loud and clear. He felt like Rodney Dangerfield.

TEMPTATIONS

This is an emotional problem that strikes at your self-esteem and self-worth. These temptations will get you nowhere.

Curl up and hide

"Let's see, it's 10 o'clock. That means Anna is in the regular MIS meeting, so I can walk through her department without being assailed or glared at."

Rationalize

"Those poor slobs don't understand what sales is all about. They're *lucky* they have someone like *me* to keep this business afloat."

Lash back

"I'll rip into them at the next meeting, those jerks."—or—"We won't push the new products and that will fix that marketing manager's butt."

Approval, deference, and courtesy are natural managerial expectations, but they require nurturing and maintenance.

WHAT HAPPENED HERE . . . ?

It is hard to do a difficult job when you're not taken seriously. You always feel deflated.

Len's business culture may be ambivalent toward sales, or it may be internally focused.

Business may be so good that management has gotten lax about caring for its customers and, therefore, the sales organization by extension.

Perhaps Len is seen as a self-absorbed prima donna, and not a company man. People may have trouble with his laser-like focus on his own agenda. His aloofness may invite disrespect.

Len may exhibit no sensitivity to profits and margins, only to raw sales numbers. He may be a poor negotiator and has shown his willingness to give away the store, therefore seen as not having the company's interests at heart.

Maybe Len doesn't meet the ideal spec, or expectation for a sales manager that other people feel his position demands. For example, the finance manager may consider him far too young, or lacking solid business experience.

Len's work habits may be questionable. The time he comes to work, the time he leaves, or the thoroughness of his reports, plans, and documentation may have a bad reputation.

Len may stick up too aggressively for his own people, in spite of the fact that they cause problems for other departments. He may be seen as having a lack of sensitivity to other parts of the business.

Len may be humorless, a consummate BSer, or a shopworn sales Neanderthal.

Colleagues' behaviors are always invited. They don't happen on their own.

OPTIONS

First, are you looking for *respect*, looking to be *liked*, or both? The two don't necessarily have to go together. An overconcern with being liked is transparent and often impacts respect.

Respect is binary: You either have it or you don't.

Len's three options are to do something crisp and definitive about this problem, succumb to living with it, or playing with some half-hearted measure that frankly, is as good as doing nothing.

POSSIBLE ACTIONS

Respect grows. It *can* be nurtured. The opinions of others *can* be changed. The good news is that this is a *manageable* problem, but the bad news is that Len has to admit to himself that he probably needs to alter some of his behaviors and invest some time and effort in a personal sales campaign.

The Seeds of Respect

Respect is based on extensive knowledge, consummate skills, the height of your expectations, the accountability you demand, the discipline you enforce, the sensitivity you display, and the integrity of your actions. These seeds need to be nurtured through personal commitment and performance.

Think About This

Have you been nurturing those seeds, or have you been a milksop, too defensive, too casual, too brash, too easy, or too lackadaisical?

Did you invite this disrespect by your actions and demeanor?

Did you feed this disrespect by exercising poor judgment in what you say?

What styles and values do the other managers and the salespeople in your enterprise respect? Not what *people* do they respect, but what *activities and approaches* to day-to-day work do they respect? Your objective should be to meet or exceed those styles and values—those activities and approaches.

Get Some Advice

Talk to your manager, your mentor if you have one, someone in HR, or even a close associate outside the company.

You need to find out the cause of the disrespect, why some people feel the way they do, and get some candid feedback. Admittedly, this is tough question to explore. Try something like this:

"Ernie, do you have any ideas how I can turn off the heat?"

"Ernie, I always seem to be catching a lot of heat, and I'm not sure why."

"Why am I not taken more seriously, Ernie? How have I teed these people off?"

You may want to go to some of your detractors or those who you sense are not in your camp and ask for suggestions. Confront the other manager with your issue. He or she may feel initially uncomfortable, but your forthrightness will be respected. For example:

"Tom, I'm always open to ideas on how we can work better together. Any suggestions?"

"Tom, it's clear something I've done is bugging you. What's the issue?"

"Tom, what's irritating you? Let's clean it up."

Build Some Bridges

Look for some ways to build relationships and work together.

- Listen more.
- Provide the highest level of support that you can to other managers. Don't be afraid to ask, "Can I help you with that?"
- Find out what another manager's biggest problems are and try to help solve them. Try to contribute to both the professional and personal goals of that person.
- Be genuinely supportive of initiatives from people you're having trouble with.
- Volunteer to be a guest speaker at another manager's meeting.
- Invite other managers to your meetings or customer presentations. Ask certain managers to make a presentation to your team.
- Do some lunches with other managers. Don't always be so formal. Lighten up.
- Get yourself placed on a team or work group with specific colleagues.
- Volunteer some ideas or pass on some newspaper or trade-journal clippings.
- Ask another manager for advice or opinion on something you believe he or she can genuinely help.

Change Some Approaches

Here are some positive behaviors to exhibit.

Do your job well, being thorough and precise, not leaving any room for outside criticism.

Prepare for contacts with other managers. Anticipate their questions and issues, not leaving anything to chance. The action spurs respect.

Be consistent in promises made, setting and fulfilling realistic expectations, saying no when you should, and honoring your commitments as responsibly as possible.

Follow company policies rather than looking for ways to duck around them. A company's policies affirm the core values of the enterprise, and those who hold to them inspire respect.

Don't let other managers see you putting them and the company at risk through poor judgment or flamboyant schemes. If your actions can withstand the light of open disclosure and scrutiny, you'll inspire respect.

Letting other managers see you hold your people accountable and to high performance standards fosters respect.

Display an interest in other aspects of the business, aside from sales. It builds respect.

Occasionally yielding your position in a fight for resources, letting the other guy or gal win one, builds respect.

Have a tennis game or a jog together to build relationships. Let other managers see you as a whole, balanced person. It spurs respect.

Here are some negative behaviors to eliminate.

Behavior that provides perceived personal gain at the expense of other employees or the company does not foster respect.

While striving to achieve outstanding sales results, understand that winning at any cost by any means does not inspire respect. Or put another way, managing and leading from the school of do anything to get the deal done will not help your position.

Attempts to deceive, exploit, or manipulate anyone on sales matters does not inspire respect.

Continual extremism on business-issue solutions invites taunting and disrespect.

Finally, admit that you or your people were *outsold* in certain situations. When you stop and think about it, most losses occur because someone outsold someone else, but how often do you hear a sales manager admit to that fact? Quit blaming price or product specs or terms of sale all the time and throwing those things in the face of other department managers. True, those things do contribute to losses, but stand up and absorb your share of the blame. Admitting to shortfalls or lapses shows you as human.

Watch What Happens

There is no doubt you'll get positive reactions—smiles, comments, and winks. Acknowledge them politely and keep plugging along. Give it time.

LESSONS

You are the guardian and gardener of your respect. Work at it.

part thirteen

Troubleshooting Problems Created by Corporate Actions

13–1 THE PROBLEM:

You must reduce the size of your sales force.

THE STORY

Jordan's firm had slipped significantly over the past few quarters. The company's revenue picture was not good. Rumors of layoffs have been flying fast and furious. However, Jordan has not paid much attention to the rumors because why would any company reduce its sales force when they need revenue, she thought.

Well, surprise! Lara, the national sales manager and Jordan's boss, just had a conference call with all the sales managers to inform them that a 15 percent staff reduction was required by a certain date, and she gave Jordan and the other district managers their quota.

Lara said the chief operating officer had met with the senior staff, including Lara, earlier in the day to announce the company's plans. Lara repeated the details and spoke in terms of changes in the market, the necessity to reduce costs to remain competitive, and survivability. It was a textbook pitch that nevertheless created a mood of anxiety.

TEMPTATIONS

Reducing your selling force is one of the most difficult and emotion-laden jobs a sales manager has to do. It can lead to wild statements and temptations.

Push back

"No way! We're already abused children. I'm running a bare-bones, morale-wracked, fatigued team as it is. We'll get a mass bailout."

Offer up sacrificial lambs

"I will just get rid of my secretaries, administrators, and trainees. That will do it."

Offer up your friends

"Toss out the whole marketing-communications group. We can outsource that stuff."

Reductions executed in a responsible way are more apt to have long-term benefit to all parties. Top management needs Jordan's principled leadership right now.

WHAT HAPPENED HERE . . . ?

Revenues were below expectations and the firm probably sees no relief on the horizon, so is looking to reduce costs in order to preserve itself. Dramatically reduced profits and profit forecasts may be the underlying issue.

This is not an unusual situation in today's economy. Companies need to constantly adjust their operating model to reflect realities. In the case of a revenue shortfall, it seems counterintuitive to downsize your selling force. The metaphor *never shoot your farmers when you are starving* always comes to mind at these times, but sales cutbacks happen anyway.

Unfortunately, in times of work-force reduction, large, homogenous organizations, such as sales, often get hit hard. The thought process is that even at a reduced size, sales will continue to sell, and the remaining people can be directed and managed to be more profit oriented. On the other hand, smaller more specialized functions are often left pretty much alone because reductions could seriously impact their viability.

Jordan's firm could have grown too fast, gotten into products, product-line extensions, or services that were much more than it could handle. A series of bad business decisions—some bad calls—could also have led to this problem.

The company may be planning to move some of its selling effort to outside sales channels, such as reps. Direct response marketing, websites, and other internal-marketing formats can also win business and reduce reliance on territory selling.

Maybe Jordan's company is going to be sold and wants to make itself look more attractive to suitors.

The fact that many firms now choose to buy from only one or two vendors means fewer salespeople are needed. This could be a factor in Jordan's industry.

Whatever the reasons, Jordan is faced with a difficult task.

OPTIONS

Your options really depend on the directives you receive from corporate.

You might be asked to reduce your force over an extended period of time. If so, a *hiring freeze* and *attrition* may be your options and may solve your problem.

If, on the other hand, the reduction needs to be immediate, your options become *termination,* or possibly *golden-parachute deals.*

Another option is *redeployment* of people. Downsizings sometimes result in unexpected openings in other parts of the business for which some of your people could be well qualified. Close contact with your manager and Human Resources can help facilitate such moves.

An additional option is offering to expand the boundaries of your current responsibilities. If certain sales-support or marketing functions cease to be of critical mass they are sometimes completely eliminated. You could offer to salvage and manage that reduced function, suggesting that your targeted employees *take on new responsibilities.* Bending over backwards for creative ways to salvage your staff helps keep morale up.

A final option, as a last resort, may be offering certain people a *part-time* role, maintaining their employment continuity and bringing them back full-time when business picks up.

POSSIBLE ACTIONS

In spite of the tension and emotion that accompanies this challenge, Jordan must maintain her poise and objectivity.

What Is the Magnitude of the Hit

Downsizing requests come in two flavors, dollars and people.

Corporate sometimes makes this easy for you by requesting that you reduce your force by a specific number of people. (Jordan has already been given a number.)

At other times corporate will ask you to reduce your operating expenses by a specific amount and stop your capital spending completely. Downsizings from a expense-reduction perspective give you a little more flexibility. It allows you to consider such things as:

- Trimming travel expenses
- Canceling a major sales meeting
- Delaying a new hire until later in the fiscal year
- Eliminating planned sales promotions

In virtually all cases, after you have gone through a cost cutting exercise, you will still need to reduce your head count by some amount.

Communications Effort

The company is likely to have a carefully crafted external and internal communications effort to announce the downsizing. Top management, legal, human resources, and finance have likely turned over every stone, and Lara was most likely a part of the effort. Jordan must understand the messages and processes thoroughly because her people will want to know exactly what happened, where they stand, and what's next. The rationale, or why, for the reduction needs to be clearly communicated to all. Customers and sales partners must also be given consistent messages. Competition can be expected to make hay with the downsizing, claiming to one and all that "you are in big trouble."

Being open and candid at times like this is imperative. It cuts rumors and stories and needless worrying. It also helps keep up performance while all this is going on. Jordan must let her sales unit know a number to be cut as soon as she is authorized to say so.

Her people will approach her individually, searching for more details. They will assume that she knows more than she actually does. She must be scrupulously consistent and prepared to get additional answers as needed. If asked to speculate about the future, Jordan must refuse. Speculation fuels anxiety.

Criteria

Depending on her role and the size of her firm, Jordan may or may not be asked to create strict criteria, or set of guidelines, for determining who stays and who goes. Performance will be the likely decision guide. Past appraisals, rankings, and personnel files will be called for. Jordan may be asked to create a new stack ranking based on specific quantitative and qualitative measures. She may be asked to quantify certain qualitative performance information. Throughout it all she should expect close oversight.

Criteria may include possession of specific technical skills, capability in certain markets or with certain customer segments, or special knowledge. Top management must ensure that the criteria be able to stand up to challenge. The reduction cannot be viewed as being discriminatory or haphazard.

Specific candidates for termination will be identified, but not notified, at this point.

The Work to Be Done

With a reduced organization and with likely changes in other support functions and departments, Jordan can expect that the work to be done by her sales unit *may* change. Roles may need to be redefined. Goal sheets and objectives will change.

Sales processes may need to be altered. This is certainly a big opportunity to make increased use of sales-force-automation capabilities. Jordan will be in the middle of all this, being expected to contribute and to grab the changes with a can-do attitude.

Design Your New Organization

Since Jordan now understands the extent to which she must reduce her sales unit and the redefined work to be done, she must now design her new organization and deployment before taking any action with her people. Fundamental rethinking, or taking a clean-slate approach, will be to her and her people's benefit. This can get complicated. Cooperation with marketing, MIS, finance, other key functions, plus her peers and Lara will ensure that Jordan's decisions are based on hard market facts, prior sales data, and the objectives and constraints of the new corporate structure. Redeployments must be logical and consistent with the firm's new strategy.

Staff the New Organization

Jordan's task is to now assign her remaining people to positions in her new organization.

If she knows her people as she should, she'll know from whom to expect push back. Even in times like these, a few people, lucky to be survivors, can still be expected to appeal for most-favored status.

Delivering the Message

The formal notification process will likely be orchestrated by HR and top management, but Jordan, with another manager in attendance, will be the likely messengers of termination.

The loss of self-esteem and depression are often bigger hits than the economic blow at times like this. As a result, Jordan may also want to have an exclusive discussion with each of her departing people, sharing personal thoughts, voicing appreciation for past efforts, and giving assurances of personal help or references as needed.

Jordan should reinforce to the departing people whatever exit training is available, identifying outplacement services, offering help in preparing resumés, offering help with interviewing skills, and aiding in identifying new opportunities to the best of her and the firm's ability. She should encourage them to take advantage of everything the firm offers.

Hug the Remaining People

Downsizing is difficult for everyone involved. This includes those who are left in the organization. Once Jordan has actually terminated those who must leave, she must immediately pull her new team together. She should let them know that it was a difficult task for her, that she realizes that they have lost some friends and peers, and that she understands the pain.

She should share again with them what is going on in the company, why this move was necessary, and the changes that have occurred in other departments. Jordan may also want to share the process used to select who was to be terminated because she doesn't want people to think it was random.

Once she has done this, she must lead the team forward.

- Share the deployment, assignments, and plan for the new organization.
- Tell all her people where and how they fit in and what corporate's and her new expectations are.
- Announce the revised compensation, bonus, or stock-option plan if they were a part of the changes.

Let the staff know that there *is* a future and that they are an integral part of it. Trust with the remaining sales force will be a challenge. The surviving members of the sales unit will have lingering effects to work through in their own minds. The answer is close, comprehensive communications in the time after the reduction to make sure everyone is "okay."

Get Ready for a Ripple Effect

A stone has been tossed into the organization pool. Jordan must be ready for some problem ripples. It is her job to discern whom the ripples may touch. For example:

- Top people may decide to leave on their own. Carefully crafted assignments, compensation stability, discretionary perks, and realistic assurances of advancement may minimize this ripple.
- Salespeople and staff will complain about more work or new work they don't understand. It will affect their morale and productivity. Sales-process and management-process improvement, training, and technology may be the key to minimizing this ripple.

- Salespeople may compete rather than cooperate because of fear that they can be hit again, that the downsizing is not finished. Leadership, numerous team activities, and Jordan's trust-building efforts can keep this ripple under control.

LESSONS

You should be able to anticipate downsizings. Just look around you at the state of the business, the markets, the industry, and the financials. Don't wait for the bell to ring. Start thinking about the points made in this discussion when you see the indicators swing south.

Always know who your top performers are. Stack-rank your people and then make sure that the performance ratings you assign properly represent that stack ranking.

Keep your sales unit lean and mean at all times. If management sees you as sensitive to costs you may not have to contribute as much as a department that is loaded with fat.

It is difficult to keep all of your good people when your company goes through a downsizing. Your good people would rather choose when they leave rather than letting you do it. You cannot guarantee lifetime employment to anyone. You can, however, guarantee that you will invest in your people through training and other means so that they will be the best they can be. This will help make them employable, which is the best you can do in today's world.

13–2 THE PROBLEM:

A merger demands blending two sales forces into one.

THE STORY

Takashi, the vice president of sales, walked into Zack's office and opened with, "Zack, I'd like you to quickly read and sign this nondisclosure agreement." Needless to say, Takashi had his district sales manager's attention. As Zack reviewed it, Takashi added that their firm was finalizing a merger with KTO Corporation, a noncompeting manufacturer with which Zack was familiar. This was to be a merger, not an integration or an acquisition.

"Am I *in* or am I *out*?" came the expected question from Zack.

"Right now, *in*, Zack, but none of us can be 100 percent certain," Takashi candidly said.

"I need you to start thinking," Takashi continued. "You know something about KTO's products and distribution. How many people could we operate with? What level of sales could we achieve? What would the distribution channels look like? What might we save in capital and operating expenses? You know, everything."

No, I really don't know, Zack thought to himself, but he was still too shaken to ask.

TEMPTATIONS

This is a problem where the temptations are all a variation of the same theme, as the story has already revealed.

Bail out

"It's over. It's been a nice ride. Time to take the next bus out of town."

There are also other reactions that race through one's mind at times like this as your survival instinct kicks in. "Merger anxieties," instead of temptations, may be a better label. Where will I end up? Will I still have a job? Who do they have on their team? Are they really good? Who will I be working for? What will happen to my people? Doubt, questions, and uncertainty gnaw at you constantly. It is not clear who, if anybody, can protect you or is willing to risk his or her own neck for you.

Then the mind becomes amazingly uncluttered as "merger revelations" come to the fore. Honest recognition of your own clout and power suddenly becomes obvious. You now have the capacity to recognize, with incredible clarity, how you stacked up in your pre-merged company. You rationalize the special talents and knowledge you possess, agreeing with yourself on why they need me. You make a quick assessment as to the nature of the future you may have in the new enterprise. You know in a heartbeat for what processes, materials, and facilities you will lobby hard. All this in a matter of seconds or minutes. It is remarkable how honest you can be with yourself at times like this.

The anxieties and revelations naturally bring some people back to the singular temptation. The better answer is to begin thinking about what your boss has asked you to think about, not resisting the changes, viewing things objectively, being as realistic as you can, and guarding against being political.

WHAT HAPPENED HERE . . . ?

Zack doesn't feel comfortable and probably won't for some time. There are only five things of which Zack can be certain at this moment.

1. The first certainty is that an executive in one of the two firms crafted an aggressive-growth strategy, was concerned about the survival of his or her business, had a long-term positioning vision, saw the synergy of complementary products and services, was astute enough to smell a good deal, could see how the new entity could be more powerful than the two individual firms, or a combination of any or all of the above. A savvy broker, banker, or major investor could have fueled the situation just as well. Someday Zack and his people will hear a laundered version on how all this got started.

2. The second certainty is that the top management of Zack's firm and KTO have likely met on several occasions. There may already be a small army of bankers, lawyers, and

consultants involved. The discussions to date have likely focused on strategic matters, major objectives, new corporate structure, skeletal organization outlines, market coverages, and major synergisms. Zack's boss, Takashi, was probably a part of most or all of these discussions, and Takashi has probably been told to share some, but not all, of the facts with his staff.

3. The third certainty is that the past is the past. The entity that Zack has been a part of for X years will be no more. It will be like going to an old-time hardware store to buy a customized gallon of paint. The clerk will start with a gallon can of one color, pour in a little bit of another color, and slowly stir it with a stick. There will be streaks and swirls of the original colors for some time because the process is slow. That is what is going to happen to the two companies, and it will impact Zack. It doesn't matter if he was originally a part of the gallon can or the added color. The end result will be brand new, but it will take time for the two corporate cultures to blend into a new color.

4. The fourth certainty is that Zack's next several months, and possibly much more, depending on the size and complexity of the two firms, will be a flurry of activity on top of his normal responsibilities. Zack is going to be a busy man.

5. The fifth certainty is that the rumor mill will be rife with possibilities.

OPTIONS

You have four major options with this problem.

1. Bail out. If Zack doesn't want to be a part of the new color, now is the time to leave.
2. Wait to grab the gold ring if an attractive package is offered. There's nothing wrong with seizing a good deal if you have an attractive alternative.
3. Play wait-and-see. Zack could decide to mechanically go through the motions, to see who and what shakes out. It's a bit of a risk because management may pick up on his attitude, but his anxieties may leave him feeling that this is a good option.
4. Leap into the process with gusto. Grab hold of reality, take the initiative to help fill the new voids, and make yourself a highly valued player. Mergers are loaded with opportunities, as well as with risks.

POSSIBLE ACTIONS

If you can put aside Machiavelli's reputation, a quotation from the sixteenth century Italian statesman should help set the tone "There is nothing more difficult to take in hand, more perilous to conduct, or more uncertain in its success than to take the lead in the introduction of a new order of things."

Takashi and the rest of top management will be looking for Zack and his peers to exhibit the following five imperatives when the deal becomes known and the new order must be created.

1. *A sense of urgency.* Management will be looking for the merger to be accomplished as quickly as can be. They want to get on with the business of the business.
2. *Understand the dynamics of change.* Zack can expect that someone on the management team or a consultant will lead a discussion on change management. If not, there are several good books on the subject.
3. *Openness to ideas.* The lid is coming off the paint can. Don't hang onto the past, but be synergetic and adaptable, willing to accept the other firm's policies or processes.
4. *Innovative contribution.* Vigorously offer ideas and initiatives to help shape the future enterprise. Don't ruminate about what was or sit back and wait to be spoon-fed.
5. *Leadership.* Zack's role will consist of aligning his people through his communications and actions, motivating them to follow, helping them to manage stress, and accepting the responsibility for implementing all the nuts and bolts.

Zack may not yet realize that he is a key player, not a pawn, in this scenario. He will be called upon to help design and implement the new order and must help sell the new vision.

In response to Takashi's instruction to start thinking, here is an outline of what should be going through Zack's mind to make this problem easier.

Major Expectations

- Mergers can take many months or a year or more to complete, depending on the size of the organizations. It takes time for the people and processes to settle down. In spite of the desire for urgency, management may want to go slow in certain areas.
- Top management will be operating under the assumption that there is synergy under every rock. Synergy results in either reduced costs, incremental revenues, or both. Zack and the rest of the sales management team will be asked to help identify both.
- If functions overlap anywhere, there will be a winner and a loser. Those decisions will be made by the executive team facilitating the merge. Support staff will probably diminish.
- Zack may or may not be invited to all the meetings. It doesn't necessarily mean he is in trouble. It probably means that the subjects to be discussed don't affect him.
- It is not unusual to see a drop in productivity during a merger, so Zack will be expected to manage against it.
- Zack should expect to be immersed in new data and analysis and measurements and dimensions beyond what he has ever experienced.
- Zack will be asked early-on to make estimates of cost savings and new-sales forecasts in numerous what-if scenarios.
- Zack should be prepared to give presentations on people, markets, processes, and mechanics. He'll get questions such as, "How will we do this?" "When will we see the benefit of the merge?"—or—"How will the customers react?"
- Executives leading mergers understand that considerate and thoughtful people management is a key to success. Whether or not that approach cascades down to Zack, he should pass a caring attitude down the line.

- There will be contested turf and contention over many philosophical and practical matters, but Zack will be expected to reach out to the people from the other company.
- Zack may get a new boss and have to learn his or her style and expectations.
- Throughout it all, until the actual consummation of the deal, Zack should expect tight security while the process unfolds.

Phases of the Sales-Force Integration

Zack can anticipate many intense planning and implementation phases as the integration unfolds. The phases may be called information gathering, planning, rationalization, decision making, communications, training, implementation, and team building. Each phase will be packed with a variable number of major subjects and milestones. He should expect to be heavily involved as a team member in some phases and minimally involved in others.

Mechanics and Processes Need to Be Rationalized

The many strategic and tactical reasons the merger took place should permeate every action associated with the blending of the two sales forces. Zack will be called upon to build an understanding of the other company so as to take advantage of their core competencies and to help identify and eliminate redundancies.

Zack will likely be asked to help set criteria and evaluate and make decisions on literally every mechanical and process aspect within the sales function. When Takashi said start thinking, he meant that everything was on the table. Here is a sample listing.

- Management principles, expectations, and philosophies must be discussed and standardized.
- Major markets and micromarkets need to be identified and rationalized.
- Territories must be revamped and rationalized.
- The sales methodologies and processes, if they are different, must be evaluated for fit and merged.
- Definitions of key words, jargon, and measurements must be standardized.
- Major attention must be devoted to integration of administrative data and computer systems.
- Sales-automation software and selected hardware may need to be made compatible.
- Competitive actions and statements in regard to the merger must be anticipated, and counter messages and actions suggested.
- A well-crafted communications plan associated with informing the sales force, customers, and sales partners is critical.
- The new identity for the new enterprise must be firmed up and the sales staff trained on how to portray it.

- Sales-unit strategies need to be crafted or reformulated.
- National-account and major-account programs must be blended.
- Pipeline management and forecast methodologies must be reviewed.
- Sales-partner-communications programs and support toolboxes need to be revalidated.
- Quotation and proposal processes and policies, review procedures, and authority levels need examination.
- Sales-partner agreements, franchise agreements, and government contracts need review for possible novation.

The list will be long. A clean slate is an opportunity to create optimal processes.

Personnel Questions Must Be Filled in

Zack will probably be asked to help create a standardized assessment checklist to be used on sales staff in both companies. He should be prepared to make objective people recommendations that will make the new organization strongest. It is also likely he may be asked to update his own resumé for review by top management. In spite of management's contention that all positions will be filled on merit, the process may get political. How political depends on your existing corporate culture and executive leadership.

The compensation plan, policies and procedures for personnel integration, appraisal-and-measurement processes, titles and job responsibilities, severance plans, and recognition programs will all be on the table.

When the Whistle Blows

Once the merger is consummated, Zack will be expected to start acting on all the aforementioned issues and keep the ball rolling. He becomes a morale manager who can't let the colors in the paint can separate. He'll be asked to firmly fix the new vision and processes in the culture. The sooner he gets his people mentally and operationally aligned with the new reality, the better off they all will be.

Zack will be asked to generate some wins as fast as he can so that the benefits of the merger can be publicized to fuel momentum.

He must be careful of letting himself and others declare that everything is complete prematurely. The details with mergers keep coming and coming and coming. He must be mentally prepared for it and not let it frustrate him or his sales unit.

LESSONS

Merging two sales organizations is not a perfect process. It comes down to leadership, teamwork, and sweat.

Keep your performance and execution at high levels. Continued high performance is necessary but not necessarily sufficient for survival in mergers because you may not be able to control the politics or other exogenous events. Mergers are difficult because job security and many sensitive egos and psyches are involved, and realistic people will realize that there will be winners and losers.

You can count on mergers being stressful. Stressful situations always hone your survival skills. They teach you a lot about yourself and the people around you.

The rigor of the experience has the effect of making you a stronger leader and manager.

13–3 THE PROBLEM:
Availability of products or services has deteriorated.

THE STORY

"Boss, I need your help," Luke pleaded over the phone. "All of a sudden I hear we can't deliver our number-one product. This is craziness! I have already gotten some cancellations."

"Yes, I know, I'm hearing it from everyone," Cas, the general sales manager, responded.

"I don't have all the details yet," Cas went on. "You know how paranoid they are over at the plant, they're afraid word will leak out. We always seem to get a laundered version of the real story. I have a meeting with the general manager in an hour."

"Damn, and here we are near the end of the quarter struggling to make plan. This will absolutely kill us—and our bonuses," Luke reminded Cas.

Cas did his best to assure Luke that he would get the real story.

TEMPTATIONS

Frustration can grow quickly and lead to temptations that don't make sense when you are in an embarrassing predicament outside your control.

Point fingers

"Those people in production are clueless. We'll blame them for missing the sales goal."

Be arrogant with customers

"Quite frankly, you people are lucky that you are getting any product at all."

Concoct a story

"Let's tell everyone we discovered some tainted material and we're saving everyone from a catastrophe."

The times when corporate actions create problems are the times when the enterprise needs to band together to support one another. Adversity must breed increased creativity and solidarity.

WHAT HAPPENED HERE . . . ?

The production lines coughed. The shelves are barren. The back room is empty. And everyone is catching an earful from irate customers. In these times of sophisticated inventory-management programs a supplier can severely damage his customer's business.

The first thing the sales managers need to do is look at themselves. Luke and the others could have done a bad job of forecasting, or Cas's corporate-wide forecasting process could be broken. In the same vein, pipeline management may not happen or is executed poorly.

From a sales-and-marketing-management perspective:

- The marketplace may have gone absolutely bonkers over your product.
- A positive story in the press or on TV may have fueled demand. A celebrity endorsement or use of the product in a hit movie may have excited consumers.
- An ad campaign could have been far more effective than anticipated.
- Customers could have come up with creative new applications.
- Usage of Luke's products by a couple of high-profile customers may have incited demand.
- A competitor could have gone out of business.

These are pleasant availability problems, aren't they? You could call some of them a sales manager's dream. Isn't it easy to explain them? That's the point. Capture the feeling that accompanies explaining these problems and transpose it to the following, uglier realities.

From a production or operations management perspective:

- Your purchasing, raw materials, or operations functions may be poorly managed.
- Mistakes by production planners could be the problem.
- It may be that the company's suppliers cannot provide components needed to produce the amount of product required due to issues of their own.
- Difficulties with your own production processes, such as trouble installing new production equipment, safety violations that need to be cured, quality that may have drifted out of bounds, an accident that shut down a line, or new robotics that don't work as anticipated are all possibilities.
- Strikes, weather, or natural disasters could be affecting deliveries of raw materials.

The possibilities are lengthy. Understanding the realities is the major element of managing this problem because Luke, Cas, and the others will need to explain it to their salespeople, and they in turn will need to explain it to their customers.

OPTIONS

There are two options with this problem, and they both relate to positioning, or where you place yourself and your sales unit in relation to your customers.

1. You can take an outside-in stance, offering *explanations* and imaginative solutions from the customers' perspective. To explain means to make plain, clear, or intelligible; to clear of obscurity. You can manage the problem on behalf of your customers, as if you truly worked for them. (Which you, in fact, do.)

2. You can take an inside-out stance, offering *excuses* and cover stories to protect yourself and your colleagues and to keep internal confrontation to a minimum. To make an excuse means to minimize, apologize, or justify.

The spoken difference between explanations and excuses can often be subtle, but which do you prefer when *you* are a customer?

POSSIBLE ACTIONS

Customers generally understand that availability problems can occur, and they will work with you toward resolution. One key is to keep them in the loop.

Confirm What Happened

Cas must find out *exactly* what is going on and obtain a best estimate as to when the problem will be resolved and when customers can expect to see product flowing normally. The management team must size the problem. Are we talking days, weeks, or months? A day's delay for certain businesses can be a disaster.

Cas and other staff managers should work to articulate the problem in the simplest way possible *and, most important, place themselves in the shoes of their customers, anticipating questions and problems and beginning the generation of solutions.*

Communicate

Once Cas and Luke have the correct story and the probable time frame, they must communicate it clearly to their salespeople. The best way to do that is eyeball-to-eyeball in a meeting or via video conference, if at all possible. The salespeople must see management explaining the problem, and they must have an opportunity to ask questions and get clarification. These sessions almost always generate new questions, so Cas must be prepared to get additional answers quickly.

Luke and Cas need a communications plan, not a story. The message must be consistent. You can never tell whose phone will ring, so delivery of the message must be consistent at all levels. A written copy of the explanation for the sales staff, to use as an explanation guide, can help. Management should tell the sales staff *how* to explain the problem, not just toss them some words or a cheat sheet. This comes back to the fine points between explanations and excuses and taking an outside-in problem-solving approach.

> Explanations are characterized by sincerity, facts, and brevity.
>
> Excuses are characterized by shading, rationalizations, and rambling monologues.

Personal communications by sales management to the largest and most important customers and sales partners is often best. Let them know you realize that the company's delivery schedule is causing them a problem and that you will come up with solutions.

Constant communication via sales-force-automation systems, if available, must keep the field and inside sales organization updated on availability changes and progress.

Look for Solutions

The second key is to think outside the box. Sales management should use this communications session to stir everyone's problem-solving facilities. There are many clever things that can be done to help customers cope.

• You can offer to substitute products that are deliverable for those that are not.

• If possible, you could offer a free upgrade to an alternative product until the shortage subsides.

• Reduce prices on alternative products or services.

• Place alternative products in customer or partner inventories on consignment.

• Change shipping modes to something that is much faster and absorb the difference in costs.

• Purchase goods from a competitor, repackage them, and sell them as a short-term alternative to your own products. (And don't hide this approach)

• Suggest a competitive supplier for emergency quantities. This suggestion may jolt both the customer and the competitor, but the action creates an implicit responsibility to return to you when the problem subsides. The risk is usually minimal.

• If deliveries are stretched out your delivery-time commitments must be flawless. If you promise to deliver at 4:10 on the eighth it MUST be there at 4:10 on the eighth.

• Introduce a special rebate promotion on alternative products.

• Include presale or post-sale services, for which you normally charge, at no cost.

• Ship incomplete products or systems at a discount and provide guidance to the customer how to complete or finish the product. Do the same thing with bundles of components, or kits.

• Suggest that one customer or partner source directly from another customer or partner's inventory. Publish a list of inventories for everyone so they can see who has what.

- Sell your quality rejects or *B* inventory at big discounts, identifying the problems with what you ship.

- Extend warranties or the length of service contracts on alternate products.

- Offer your customers temporary loaners of alternate products, if the nature of your business permits.

- Manage customer inventories on your own, taking it upon yourself to move goods from one location to another.

- Look for off-shore suppliers that don't sell in the United States. Make a one-time buy to cover your shortfall.

- Scour the market for used products, refurbish them, and sell them at cost or at minimal markup.

A good way to come up with additional alternatives is to gather the sales and marketing teams together a second or third time to brainstorm additional ideas. Experience in handling a few customers will cause new ideas to be generated. Don't discard anything. What may seem to be impossible to apply across the company may be an ideal solution for a single customer.

Make operations or production a part of all this brainstorming. Inclusion is critical for people or functions who may have contributed to the initial problem. It's healing. Oftentimes they will bend over backwards to create alternatives. Expect that they will also offer alternatives no one from sales or marketing could ever have imagined.

Once alternatives have been identified train the sales staff on where and how to offer the alternatives. Expect that customers will ask to tweak and twist the alternatives. Salespeople will need a hotline to get answers to those questions, and management must manage the alternatives so they don't get out of hand. Management should encourage sales staff to bring forward alternatives that customers suggest to them, or empower the sales staff to make certain decisions and commitments on their own. The best salespeople will work to resolve these problems by themselves, taking the initiative, and not dumping everything back on the plant.

It is not unusual for solutions created during availability crunches to become regular offerings. There *is* a serendipitous side to this problem.

Manage the Allocation

The third key is to have an allocation system. Cas and the sales managers must take charge of the product flow into the territories. In order to determine which customers get what product when, Cas and the rest of the sales managers should develop a process to determine which customers have the greatest short-term needs. Allocation criteria could include percentage of product previously taken, size of customer's existing inventory, the presence or lack of alternatives, geographic balance, and so on. One starting point is to ask customers to specify bare-minimum requirements, letting them know what will be done to fulfill those requirements.

Cas must be continuously advised by operations on the status of product and then needs to become a referee who will make decisions about what goes where. Once he allocates down to the sales units, sales-unit managers such as Luke must allocate further down the line.

Luke and his people must constantly communicate with customers in a timely fashion. Luke must be careful to treat customers who are in competition with each other on even terms, avoiding help to one at the detriment of another.

Set Future Expectations

Luke must make sure that his sales unit communicates realistic delivery expectations on future sales of the affected product and of all products. Customers become more sensitized to delivery quotations and actual delivery times when they have lived through this problem. This is not the time for anyone to make overaggressive compensatory commitments.

Clean Your Own Linen

Finally, this problem should remind Cas, Luke, and the rest of the sales-management team to clean up their act with planning, pipeline, forecasts, and market-information processes. This availability problem can serve as a practical teaching tool for the entire sales organization.

LESSONS

This problem drives home the importance of good information processes, internal relationships, and internal communications. It also teaches you to appreciate the issues the rest of the business must deal with, and it teaches you to respect the difficulties faced by colleagues in other functions. It emphasizes the necessity of salespeople to understand how their company operates.

Build strong relationships with customers and sales partners. Those relationships can transcend delivery and other operational problems and carry you over hard times.

Another big lesson is providing explanations and solutions to customers, not excuses. Explanations and solutions are for customers' benefit and protection. An excuse is self-serving. Salespeople must be trained to offer explanations and be empowered to create and offer solutions.

13–4 The Problem:

A change in sales channel strategy alters your sales unit.

The Story

When Mary, who was a district sales manager, heard the news she went ballistic. Her firm, which had long used dealers to handle low-end products, was now planning on transferring some of the bigger-ticket items to these VARs (value-added resellers).

"We're being whipsawed again," she fumed. "It was all right when they took some of those small products out of our hair. They consumed as much time and effort as the big ones, and there wasn't much money in it for us. But this is a totally different matter. I don't want to see these products go away." She was in her boss's office in a heartbeat.

"Jim, this will kill us. My best people will leave. Are we being phased out?"

"Hold on," he said. "Don't worry. It is not a fait accompli."

Worried? I'm frantic, she thought to herself.

Temptations

Changes that alter the basic nature of your work are always cause for alarm and conjecture. It is easy for the mind to run wild with preposterous temptations.

Load 'em up
   "Let's nail as many prospects as we can and let the VARs clean up the mess."

Move
   "I'm going to apply for the job of VAR district manager. It is obvious that is where the action is going to be."

Quit
   "It is obvious this company is no longer committed to its direct-sales organization."

Instability in the environment makes rational leadership all the more essential.

What Happened Here . . . ?

A sales manager got an unwelcome surprise and now the whole staff is uptight. A product is threatened to be walled-off. No one wants to experience a loss of stature or income.

Mary's firm has probably made a decision to reduce the cost of sales. The company may feel it must focus on the most profitable products and customer classes and leave other products and customer classes to alternate sales channels. The company may also have felt that it was imperative to make changes because of yet-to-be-announced product offerings, the growth and maturity of markets, and changes in customer buying behaviors and needs. Additionally, competition may have taken steps, and the company must react to protect itself.

Fear can run rampant during transition periods. There is a growing level of mistrust and anxiety. Mary and her people may also see this as an erosion of account control or possibly having their jobs eliminated.

The company may be taking the fun stuff, a prestigious product line, away from the direct-sales force. The comfort zone is being disrupted.

Mary and her people may see the other sales channel as second-class and don't want to see it enhanced.

The company's move could be seen as a desperation move by Mary and the other sales employees. Salespeople have little patience with being jerked around by changes in corporate strategy.

Mary may fear the loss of customers and relationships that her people have worked hard to develop, and there is an unwillingness to write off all those personal investments.

And finally, expanding the use of alternate sales channels *is* becoming an increasing fact of corporate life.

OPTIONS

Since the word is already out, the only options deal with communications. The decision has probably been made in spite of Jim's protestation to the contrary.

1. Jim can send out a memo, broadcast a fax, and send out an E-mail, all of which will probably create a tidal wave of retribution.
2. Jim can execute a comprehensive communication plan that puts the changes in context and addresses everyone's questions and anxieties.

POSSIBLE ACTIONS

Relax. Jim knows that someone should have thought of these questions before this point, but he's got to grit his teeth and get on with stabilizing his sales units.

Assemble a Team

Get a diverse group of managers and individual contributors from pertinent departments together to formulate a change plan. Sales-and-marketing management, key sales and marketing people, credit, collections, operations, and human resources are obvious.

Jim needs to prepare a communications blitz. Detailed and candid explanations of the changes is the best technique for achieving cooperation. He should make full disclosure the rule.

Jobs, Money, and Control

Inform the sales staff of the effect the new strategy changes have on The Big Three.

Confirm, first and foremost, that no one's job is at stake if that's the case. If jobs *are* at risk or are planned to be eliminated or reduced through normal attrition, say that.

Confirm that compensation is safe. Tell the sales staff, in detail, about any changes in the compensation plan and how the company has ensured that they remain whole. That may mean double-crediting the sales, altering compensation on other products, or altering salaries. Comp drives selling behavior for all, motivation for many, and retention for the $-obsessed.

Confirm who will have control over the accounts. An informal hierarchy is always in place when you sell through multiple channels. One channel or organization is assumed to be more important than another, thus an informal pecking order develops. When changes occur the stature of one channel challenges the stature of another channel. If the direct sales-organization is still top dog, say it.

Anticipate Other Issues and Questions

The sales organization will have additional questions regarding the changes. Prepare for them.

- "What do I as a salesperson lose and what do I gain as a result of these changes?"
- "What additional work will this change cause for me?"
- "Will I have to learn anything new? Does this mean any new processes or software?"
- "How will prospects and transactions in process be handled?"
- "How should we answer customer questions regarding these changes?"

Show 'n' Tell

It is imperative to share the details why this new approach is being instituted. Understanding will aid your salespeople in buying into what you are trying to accomplish and keep you from losing them. Make sure the staff sees that this is not an arbitrary decision. Confirm that the firm is not out to get the sales force, but rather to strengthen its profitability and survivability.

- Show people what is going on in the market, including the facts, figures, research data, and customer-interview comments that supported the changes.
- Tell the sales staff what forces instigated the change, including buyer preferences, competitive actions, changes in technology, and new product and service offerings.
- Show them the objectives of the changes, what the changes are intended to accomplish, and how it will ultimately benefit them.
- Tell everyone the company's business strategy and marketing strategy and the resultant sales-unit strategy, so that their actions can be consistent and supportive.

- Show them the risks associated with the changes and how their individual actions can help minimize the risks.
- Tell them what other people and departments in the company will be doing in support of the changes.
- Show them the media messages the company will be using to make customers comfortable and to short-circuit misinformation that competition will likely spread.
- Tell them the downside of what would happen if the firm did nothing in regard to sales channel changes.
- Show them the competitive situation and how the company's actions will make their jobs easier against competition.
- Tell them what products they will and won't be allowed to sell and what customers and prospects they will and won't be allowed to call on. Explain why.
- Show the sales unit how the entire customer base will be covered.
- Tell them how you will provide incremental training for the products and technology on which you are now asking them to focus.
- Show the sales unit how you have modified and prepared the internal-sales-support infrastructure to integrate with these changes.
- Tell the staff that you are willing to accept revisions by being open to their questions, objections, and suggestions. Reacting to valid input makes good business sense.

Sales managers must step up their field travel and coaching assistance during times of transition to ensure that salespeople have in fact heard and understood the changes so that their messages to the market are consistent and complete.

Keep the Sales Unit Up to-Date with Sales Channel Dynamics

Do they really care about this? Not about the details, but they *do care* about working for a company in which they have confidence.

Sales channels is becoming a more important subject for salespeople to understand. While the majority of salespeople are aware of different sales channels, they may not understand the rationale or the strengths and weaknesses of each channel or the channel dynamics underway in your industry. A brief tutorial conducted by sales and/or marketing management from time to time can put your market dynamics in focus. A discussion of why and where sales channels are proliferating can set the stage for future changes in your sales organization.

The discussion of sales-channel options, even the channels the company is not using, builds a sense of where the sales unit fits and builds respect toward management and makes everyone feel that the company is alert and knows what it is doing.

One net effect of these communications is to enable your salespeople to tell prospects how and where to get information on the firm's products and services and the available alternatives where they can buy. Sales staff must represent *the entire company*, not just their own parochial interests. Nothing aggravates prospective buyers more than salespeople who say, "That is not my responsibility" in answer to an inquiry.

Warning Signs to Determine if Your Salespeople Aren't Making the Shift

If people are having difficulty adapting to alterations in sales channels or are uncertain what to do, expect to experience the following symptoms.

- Your reps complain a lot.
- You will be asked about other job opportunities in the company.
- There are numerous conflicts to resolve about who is to do what.
- You get stupid questions.
- You receive complaints about compensation.
- A top performer will leave.

If the warnings occur on an exception basis, treat them that way. If otherwise, reignite your communications effort and send the marketing staff back to the drawing board.

LESSONS

Nothing lasts forever. Your company will decline if it does not continuously adjust its sales channels to the changing reality of the marketplace. Expect changes in channels the same way you expect changes in products. Smooth transitions with sales-channel changes occur if detailed communications and training accompany the implementation. Salespeople who see changes executed in the context of a total marketing strategy rather than a short-term opportunistic whim are more likely to support the effort.

Don't diminish monetary and psychic rewards when you alter sales channels.

13–5 THE PROBLEM:

Your reward and recognition programs are not competitive in the market.

THE STORY

Ryan had been struggling for a couple of months trying to hire a couple of new salespeople. Two of his top people had just left because of attractive offers that Ryan couldn't counter.

Ryan's employer was a small company that had been growing slowly but surely.

He was sharing this dilemma one day over lunch with Hieu, the director of finance.

"I know this business is going to take off, but right now, it sure is hard to draw good people and keep them. I can't compete with the big guys. Wow, you should hear some of the offers and compensation that's out there. Damn. I had no idea."

"What are you going to do?" asked Hieu. "I'll be happy to help you look at the numbers and see if I can give you any suggestions. Have you talked to HR?"

"Yes, of course, they are trying to help, but I'm out of ideas."

TEMPTATIONS

When you are asked to do the infeasible with the insufficient the atmosphere can grow intolerable in a hurry.

Play scapegoat

"The president is a bean counter and doesn't understand the sales culture."

Make promises you can't keep

"I'll just tell the candidates to trust me, that I'm working on a revised comp plan."

Compromise

"I give up. Hey, I'll just take the next two warm bodies that come along."

Sales executives must do everything possible to make salespeople and sales managers want to join and stay with a company. They need an acquisition plan and a retention plan just as sales reps need a plan to acquire and retain customers.

WHAT HAPPENED HERE . . . ?

You don't have deep pockets. This problem is a two-edged sword—recruiting and retention. In the current free-agent world the competition for talented bodies is fierce.

Quality people are more vulnerable to turnover because they are a desired commodity and they are rooted out by search and contingency firms.

Ryan's firm could be in financial trouble. Top management may be trying to keep the lid on costs. This could be a low-margin business that can't afford to pay much.

What worked for years reward- and recognition-wise may have become obsolete.

Pay scales throughout the company may be low. Sales can't outstrip other functions. Management has to be sensitive to balance.

The problem may be more than Ryan's recognition and reward programs being non-competitive in the market. It could be that the image of Ryan's firm, the work environment, and the sales culture is not attractive. Compensation becomes an easy scapegoat when neither applicants nor employees perceive or receive other tangibles and intangibles important to them.

OPTIONS

Ryan has three options with this problem.

1. He could put an argument together intended to make the compensation plan more attractive. This can work. Armed with good market data, he can convince HR and the president of the reality of the market and the need to make some changes.
2. Innovate. Ryan can position himself as providing a differentiated sales culture and values that candidates find attractive. This can often work better than option #1.
3. Ryan could execute a combination of both.

POSSIBLE ACTIONS

If you reward and recognize them they will come. A reward-and-recognition program must be a match between what you can create and offer and what candidates and employees want or draw satisfaction from. Money is only one of many keys to attracting and retaining people.

Two Goals

Sales managers want people to feel good about acceptance decisions and where they are working.

1. Ryan wants job candidates to be able to go home, lay an offer letter on the table, and feel good about it.
   - The first question the candidate is likely to get is: "Did you get the job?" The desired answer, offered with a big smile: "YES, I got it!"
   - The second question: "How much?" The desired answer, with a bigger smile: "Look at this . . . ," at which point he or she hands over a detailed letter that summarizes all the opportunities and rewards of being a part of Ryan's firm. Ryan's job is to make that letter strong enough so that the response is . . . "WOW!" A candidate must be able to stand there confidently proud of what he or she has just accomplished. He or she has to protect image and ego. No one wants to defend an acceptance decision.
2. Ryan wants existing employees to be able to go home and say, "You'll never guess what I had an opportunity to do today!" "WOW, that's neat," is again the targeted response.

Don't Chase What You Can't Catch

Many salespeople and sales managers are motivated primarily by money. That's fine, but identify them early in the screening process. Early questions and comments are dead giveaways. Be candid and tell those people that you may not be the right firm for them.

There is a huge pool of salespeople and sales managers who are motivated, and draw satisfaction, from other things. Chase what you can catch.

Question Yourself

Ryan must ask himself why he decided to stay with this firm. What return on investment did he receive? Why has he been happy? What can he learn from his own experience? He should share that with candidates and existing employees.

Trade-Offs

Ryan's big issue is dollars. If there is only X amount of dollars in the budget, is it feasible to pay 12 people well, rather than 14 people not so well? Can the comp for two heads be divvied up and spread around? Are there other trade-offs with other expenses that can be made?

Dig a Little

How do you know your reward and recognition programs are not competitive in the market? Are you saying that solely because applicants turn you down and people leaving puff up their offers? Don't take that level of analysis up the line.

Interview ex-employees, sometime after they leave, and determine what led them to leave. Ask them what suggestions they would make to strengthen the culture. Do the same thing with people who have turned down your offers, at a comfortable time after the turndown. A few people will be expansive, most won't. It's worth a lunch or a phone call.

Think Team

You can't expect to draw and hold many *top* salespeople in a sales department if you have dogs in other departments. Does your firm have only dogs? Highly unlikely. Your firm has a sprinkling of top engineers, top marketers, and top accountants. Identify them. Use their names and reputations to draw and hold others. Top people tend to draw more top people.

For example:

- "Our president formerly served in the Commerce Department under President Bush."
- "Our director of marketing is the author of a bestseller on marketing research."
- "One of our engineers was part of a team at Northwestern that developed this technology."

Do you think a top wide-receiver free agent wants to sign with a team that doesn't have a top quarterback? Not likely. Superstar players move to teams where they think they can win Super Bowl rings and their buddies tell them they'll like the coach's system, not always to the team that makes the best offer. Design and offer the ring and the system. The ring is the recognition you provide and the system is your sales culture.

Establish a Differentiated Culture

Create a cultural difference that is in demand and that you can preserve. The sales culture becomes a major part of your reward and recognition programs. There are many famous corporate sales cultures out there, Xerox, Northwestern Mutual Life Insurance, Mary Kay, Hewlett-Packard, Motorola, and Proctor & Gamble, to name a few. They were built over time by managers like you, but you don't have to be big to have a differentiated sales culture.

People buy into cultures. However, cultures must be able to be seen and felt before they are claimed, otherwise the claim is just smoke. So build it before you start talking about it. In time, employees and candidates will see and feel it. It is possible to have a culture within a culture, as you're aware. Many successful sales managers who are a part of big organizations do it all the time by creating a special aura in their sales units.

For a salesperson or a sales manager to be able to say that he or she is a part of a respected sales culture is a reward in itself. Here are three examples:

IMAGE.   How do you look? This doesn't necessarily mean white shirt and rep tie. It means the sharpness, order, and cleanliness of everybody and everything about your business. Image sends a message of professionalism. Image can help you recruit and retain.

What is the image when someone drives up to your front door and walks through that door? Do you think they would be proud walking their family and best friends through that door? How do your corporate press clippings look? Do they turn people on or off?

RIGOR.   Create an elitist atmosphere by building a tough sales unit. Make the training and the management processes the most demanding in the industry. Establish such a rigorous reputation that people scramble for the few available slots. People don't join the Marine Corps or the Navy's Seals for the pay. It's tough to get in, many are cut, but the psychic rewards are priceless. Look around you at other rigorous organizations and reap the lessons of their ability to attract and retain the best. Rigor can be found in teaching-hospital medical staffs, upper-echelon symphony orchestras, amateur sports teams, and prestigious law firms.

ALIGNMENT.   Make candidates and employees aware of the fact, that while you may not have deep pockets, your firm is intellectually rich and has aligned itself with all the latest business concepts and technologies. People want to be a part of organizations that are on the leading edge.

Create an *enriching* culture with any or all of these three and other cultural attributes of your choice. People want to be enriched in more ways than just in the pocketbook.

CAVEAT.   Sales cultures come, and sales cultures go. Cultures take work to build and maintain.

Engineer Reasons to Stay

Make some decisions, create some policies, and execute some exceptions that make people feel good and permit them to say nice things about stuff that is important to them. For example:

- *Trade shows:* "We get to stay at the Ritz-Carlton in Chicago for the annual trade show." If everyone stays at Motel 6 and Red Roof Inns normally, why not?
- *First-class air travel:* "I don't travel that much, but when I do, I get to fly first class." If flights are infrequent, why not?
- *Computers:* "I get to use a great laptop. PC World rated them #1." If you can make some trade-offs and cut a deal, why not get the best?
- *Education:* "I got to attend a special program at Stanford." Can the folks attend a top-notch program once every two years?
- *Executive contact:* "Guess whom I had lunch with today?" Why let the boss eat alone?
- *Car:* "My car? Oh, it's a Cadillac." Nothing wrong with leasing a previously owned luxury car.
- *Club membership.* "I get to stay in shape by playing racquetball one day a week with clients." Not expensive, and certainly a healthy investment.
- *Spouse participation:* "My wife really enjoyed the Labor Day picnic in the president's backyard." Not expensive, and a great way to build home-front buy-in.
- *Quality recognition:* "Did you see my picture in the paper last week?" If you're going to give a plaque, make it a PLAQUE, and present it in style.
- *Timing:* "We get commission payments a week after the order." If you can't pay much, at least pay early.
- *Impact:* "People actually listen to me, and have implemented some of my ideas."

You're paying for the latent creativity, so you may as well use it.

Listen for the Little Things

Casual statements and small requests are all simple signals that, if acted on, can satisfy needs and desires and keep people motivated and comfortable. For example; "It sure would be nice if I had a 17-inch monitor."—or—"It would be great to get availability reports from production control on time."—or—"I don't understand why my direct-deposit check doesn't hit the bank every fourth Friday."—or—"That's twice in a row the product manager has canceled out of a sales call."—or—"I was never told my idea wasn't considered."You get the idea.

Virtually all comments you hear will be sensible. You may not be able to respond to 100 percent of them, but you can't let *any* of them go by. You retain people the same way you retain customers, by consistently exceeding their expectations with the little things.

In Summary

Lead and manage as if you were playing a game called "Interview." When you conduct an interview do you spend most of the time talking about compensation? No. Rather, you talk with the candidate about what he did, what she's learned, what he accomplished, whom she worked with, what kind of training he experienced, challenges she attacked and solved, teams on which he worked, and noteworthy achievements that were attained. Isn't that right?

Let your existing people and candidates see, *through your actions and through your words,* that working for your firm and your sales unit will prepare them for their next interview.

Reality Check

In spite of the creativity, Ryan will still probably lose more candidates and employees than his deep-pocketed counterparts do, but his hiring hit rate and his employee retention will improve. As in selling, you can improve your candidate close rate and retention rate by delivering and maintaining value.

LESSONS

Treat this as a corporate problem utilizing the talents and know-how of HR and other managers. Concentrate on building a sales culture that has one of the finest reputations in the industry, a sales force to which people *want* to belong.

You don't have to throw a lot of money at this problem. Not all top salespeople take jobs just for money. Throw what the applicants and employees would like to catch and can use to their future benefit.

Present your reward and recognition programs positively and matter-of-factly. Don't be defensive or apologetic. Be honest, thorough, and exhibit pride in your programs.

part fourteen

TROUBLESHOOTING YOUR OWN PERSONAL PROBLEMS

14–1 THE PROBLEM:

*You're not sure if you've got what it takes
to be a "great" sales manager.*

THE STORY

Art has been a regional sales director for a year. Somehow, he had thought that the skills and capabilities that had made him an award-winning area sales manager would carry him to the same level of recognition in his bigger job. So far it hasn't worked out that way. He has begun to doubt himself, his abilities, and his future. He has been looking around and has been awed by what others seem to be doing so naturally. Frankly, it is a little scary. He is beginning to ask himself if he has what it takes to execute this job at the level to which he has grown accustomed—and that level is to be *great*, not just good.

TEMPTATIONS

You may have asked yourself this same question. Don't let these be your answers.

Quit

   "I think it may be time to start reading the Mart Section of the *Wall Street Journal*."

Agonize

   "What am I going to do? This is terrible. I don't think I'm going to make it."

Grope for pats on the butt

   "Boss, I'm doing okay, aren't I? Aren't I? Boss, did you hear me?"

Experiencing a hunger to be reassured of your capabilities and effectiveness is natural.

WHAT HAPPENED HERE . . . ?

Stop worrying. Everyone has moments of self-doubt. It goes with the territory.

There is no flawless formula to sales-management greatness. There is no way of totally knowing if you've got what it takes before you take that next leap upward. What it takes depends on your environment, the level you're at, your experience, the skills and aptitudes you already possess, the support you get, and your own gumption.

Art may have thought that this regional spot was just a simple ticket to be punched on the way up the ladder—that it would be a no-brainer. He may have wrongly assumed this was going to be a piece of cake.

Like others in many of today's fast-moving companies, Art may have been swept along in a tide of people needed to do the job with little forethought from management on his readiness.

It may be that Art is not getting any feedback. Feedback is important. Art should ask for it, if he's not receiving it, although Art's expectations for feedback should be cut back the higher he goes.

Perhaps Art hasn't received any formal training for this job, or the powers-that-be felt he knew what to do.

Maybe Art was put into this job a little too early. That does happen. Rising stars catch someone's eye, and they are dropped into the deep end of the pool prematurely.

Whatever led to this question and Art's current discomfort, the fact that he is stewing about it says a lot of positive things about his personal motivation.

OPTIONS

First, what is "great." Great is in the eyes of the beholder. Great probably means that the headhunters are looking for you, that you are on your firm's high-potential list, and that you consistently lead or are near the top of your region, division, national, or worldwide standings. It also means that you probably get called on to join committees or speak at special functions and conferences and that you are regularly sent to the best company schools, development programs, and conferences. Great means that you're promoted on a regular basis or that the track record of your responsibility has continued to get bigger and broader.

First, a question: You need to decide if you want to *find out* what it takes to be great. That may sound strange, but finding out is self-inflicted pressure, and you may not want that. If you don't want that pressure, stop here and go on to another problem.

Second, your one option:

- You have only one decision to make. You must decide whether or not to make the commitment and the investment to *be* great.

Remember, the problem is deciding to do what it takes to be *GREAT*, not just good.

POSSIBLE ACTIONS

Get to Know Yourself

The first step is self-awareness, understanding where you currently stand. Assess your present capabilities by sitting down and writing out your strengths and the areas needing improvement. Think about all the appraisals, performance reviews, feedback sessions, career-development sessions, formal and informal dialogues, and off-the-cuff made-in-jest comments that you have heard about yourself in the past. Being honest with yourself is the most important thing to do.

Change in your supercompetitive business environment demands commensurate personal changes for those who wish to be great. Yet change without a firm understanding of *what* should be changed or added to your personal inventory is folly.

Because you continue to evolve over time, whether you try or not, this self-assessment and personal inventory *is a continuing step* on your path to greatness.

> Self-assessment is very tough. If there is any way possible to get outside counseling assistance, Art should make every effort to try and take advantage of it.

Talk

Talk to your boss, and to your mentor, if available. Share your feelings. Ask for their recommendations. If you don't have that level of relationship established, find a friend, neighbor, or family member who is or was in sales management. Talking is a continuing step to greatness. Continuing to bounce thoughts off of personal backboards helps keep you focused.

Where Are You?

The next step is understanding *what it takes* to be great.

Different levels of sales management require different levels of knowledge, attributes, and skills to be great. While there are subtle differences in various business sectors and around the world, the following foundation imperatives can serve as a guideline to greatness.

The Ten-Common Threads of Greatness:

First Level Sales Manager	Mid-level Sales Director	Top-level Sales Executive
1. Integrity	1. Impeccable uprightness	1. Deep-seated principles
2. Strong relationships with key customers	2. Strong relationships with sales partners	2. Strong relationships with strategic partners
3. Good judgment	3. Solid judgment	3. Impeccable judgment
4. Sets a good example	4. Sets a solid example	4. Sets an outstanding example
5. Inspiring leadership	5. Quiet leadership	5. Respectful leadership
6. Strong understanding of sales skills and tactics	6. Strong understanding of sales processe	6. Strong understanding of the sales profession

7. Strong work ethic	7. Disciplined work ethic	7. Balanced work ethic
8. Team player	8. Team manager	8. Team leader
9. Perseverance	9. Courage	9. Mature resolve
10. A track record of sales success and market-share growth	10. A track record with launching new products and services and countering competitive threats	10. A track record with changing and emerging markets and channels

It is sometimes hard to distinguish the fine line of intensity and depth from one level to the next, but you know the difference when you see it.

Additional Differentiators

First-Level Sales Manager	Mid-level Sales Director	Top-level Sales Executive
Knowledge	*Knowledge*	*Knowledge*
• Outstanding understanding of the company's products, services, and technologies	• Outstanding understanding of business processes, company policies, and company practices	• Outstanding understanding of the corporation and the industry
• Excellent understanding of customers, sales partners, market segments, and territories	• Excellent understanding of internal business functions and trends	• Excellent understanding of marketing and finance; a businessperson above everything
• Local-market focus	• Regional- or national-market focus	• International-market focus
• Competitors and communications devices	• Networks	• Technologies
Attributes	*Attributes*	*Attributes*
• Ego drive, strong competitive spirit, great attitude entrepreneurial, empathetic, risk taker	• Observant, analytical, organized, intrepreneurial, patient, invigorating, focused, responsive, risk manager	• High credibility, tact and diplomacy, inspiring, well balanced, supreme confidence, maturity, open, risk controller
• Strong drive for sales results	• Strong drive for balanced excellence	• Strong drive for profitability

Skills

- Outstanding coach; ability to impart knowledge and sales-skill techniques

- Strong capacity to communicate to a wide variety of salespeople and customers

- Sensitive to sales personnel needs

- Great recruiter; possesses the ability to find and hire the best sales talent

- Motivator

- Strong execution skills

- Sales-opportunity strategist

- Outstanding tactical planner, shorter term in outlook

- Works outside with correctness

Skills

- Outstanding manager; very capable with controls and able to apply proper level of scrutiny

- Strong capacity to communicate effectively up and down and across the organization

- Sensitive to home-office and interdepartmental needs

- Great developer of management talent

- Consensus builder

- Strong implementation skills

- Conceptual strategist

- Outstanding interorganizational planner

- Works inside with exactness

Skills

- Outstanding leader; a highly articulate visionary with strong personal presence

- Strong capacity to communicate at the highest corporate and customer executive levels

- Sensitive to senior-management and director-level agendas

- Great organization management and deployment acumen

- Charismatic leader

- Strong innovation skills

- Business strategist

- Outstanding strategic planner, longer term in outlook

- Works topside with precision

The Nine Operational Requisites for Greatness . . . at All Levels

1. Lead with courage and discipline . . . to attain quality in all things
2. Set goals and expectations . . . that challenge the sales unit
3. Create and execute plans . . . to achieve outstanding results
4. Build a great team . . . without compromise
5. Train fanatically . . . to keep your people growing all the time
6. Focus on $-producing activities . . . that lead to profitable business
7. Engage your resources . . . inside, outside, and at all levels
8. Manage relationships . . . first with customers and sales partners and then inside
9. Work with upbeat intensity . . . to set an assumptive winning attitude

Think of all these foundation elements in the context of the old Chinese proverb, "Even the highest towers begin from the ground."

Analysis

After the self-assessment and input from others you should know where you stand. The ten common threads; the knowledge, attribute, and skill differentiators; and the operational requisites describe your destination. The delta represents the gap to be filled to achieve greatness.

Final Step

Now that you know what it takes to be great, crank it up a notch and begin investing in yourself. Put yourself in environments where you can learn and grow.

LESSONS

This problem causes you to measure *yourself*, the most critical appraiser you'll probably ever face, and think about what actions you should take for your own self-development.

Only a few people seem to come by the attributes of greatness naturally, in this and in many other professions. Don't let the lack of natural talent deter you or lead you to believe that you can't be a great sales manager. Most great sales managers have made themselves into what they are.

This problem should stimulate a willingness to experiment, to invest in yourself, to persevere, and to make mistakes. A manager learns from his or her own successes and failures as well as from those of others.

Your own thoughts on the subject of greatness should be a reminder, regardless of your level, to give feedback to your people on what it takes for them to be great *at their level*, because some are chewing on this question just as you are.

14–2 THE PROBLEM:
You're anxious to get promoted.

THE STORY

Elizabeth had been an area sales manager for 18 months. She made the President's Club her first year, which was no small feat, considering she had taken over a pretty bad sales team. She was working hard, but for the past few months she had been getting antsy about moving on and had even made some informal comments to her boss about additional responsibility and more training. Everything had been great, but she felt her ticket had been punched in this position, there was no more to learn, and it was now time for the next step.

Additionally, a couple of calls had come in from headhunters with some pretty attractive offers that fueled her fire. Some of those situations sounded really exciting.

Elizabeth was thinking about pulling the plug if nothing happened soon.

TEMPTATIONS

Success spawns these feelings, and everything you read about reduced loyalty makes it sound like the right thing to do. Your career deserves more than these temptations.

Grab the first opportunity

"That recruiter sounded sincere. And the bucks are great. I'm going to take that job before anyone else does. Good-bye, suckers!"

Compromise

"This ad sounds pretty good, in spite of having to move out to L.A., and I'm sure I'll learn to love selling the strange little products they're talking about."

The urge to get ahead is random and fickle. You never know when, or how hard, the promotion bug will bite. Start thinking and preparing before it happens.

WHAT HAPPENED HERE . . . ?

Something deep inside is agitating Elizabeth to move on to something else. Maybe she is just impatient.

Elizabeth may not understand how much more there is to learn, or maybe the job content is not challenging. This position could be too easy, or she hasn't worked the position to its full potential. An inflated opinion of herself could be contributing to these feelings as well.

Perhaps Elizabeth's goals and results to date have been a fluke. Her manager may have given her low goals and she lucked out. Elizabeth may understand that fact, so she figures she'll get out while her track record looks good. That frequently happens.

It could be as simple as Elizabeth's firm having no current openings and Elizabeth feeling that 18 months amounts to being stuck in this spot for too long.

Maybe Elizabeth is being held in her current position because the firm *needs* her there. While that does occur in many cases, her tenure seems too short for that to be realistic.

Perhaps the firm and Elizabeth's manager are not committed to people development and growth. Sales managers can pick up those vibes.

Her firm may have a traditional time-in-grade mentality. They may feel that X number of years are a requisite, and Elizabeth hasn't gotten that check mark next to her name yet.

Maybe Elizabeth and her manager haven't developed a target-position plan or growth plan for promotion. The lack of sharing expectations is a major contributor to this problem.

A peer may have moved on rather quickly, and it has whet her appetite. That is common.

OPTIONS

First, are there opportunities where you are? Just because you don't *see* the opportunities doesn't mean they aren't there. Promotion opportunities are like icebergs—most are beneath the surface. So the first action item is to confirm or deny the existence of short- and long-term opportunities with your manager (or mentor, if available) about your career aspirations.

Then you have two options

1. You can start looking on the outside if you don't like what you hear.
2. You can stay and put together a campaign to move yourself forward where you are.

These are personal and serious decisions that should be given time, and Elizabeth should take advantage of the opinions and advice of others, both inside and outside the firm.

POSSIBLE ACTIONS

The President's Club plaque is still warm, so let it cool down.

Consider These Points

Has someone in or out of the company been plying you with platitudes, unjustly inflating your ego? It is okay to feel good about yourself, but you have to be realistic at the same time.

Look around you at other possible candidates for promotion—who should be easily visible. Can you *differentiate* yourself from them? What do *they* have that you don't have?

Is what your manager and the HR people are telling you about your potential said with conviction and sincerity? Don't deceive yourself and don't let their comments get you all misty-eyed. Remember, they don't want to lose any good people. As a sales-management professional your personal radar is probably pretty good, so read between their lines.

Hiring managers never want to defend a choice, look bad after the fact, or hurt themselves. Are you carrying any baggage? Do you have any deficiencies? Other managers probably know you better than you realize.

Eighteen months of performance does not make a hall-of-famer. Do you want to put yourself on the market with a 1–0 record? In the major leagues that doesn't count for much. *Consistent* excellent performance reads better on any resumé.

Readiness Check

Are you *really* ready for a promotion? A manager who is aspiring to get promoted is often, but not always, mentally ahead of her employer. Your assessment of readiness and your manager's assessment of readiness can be two different things. If there is a disagreement on readiness, you need to find out what is lacking, what steps need to be taken to get ready for that next spot, and agree on an action plan and on a general time frame to make it happen. *But remember, there are no guarantees with these plans, and don't ever expect any.*

There are three major aspects to promotional readiness.

1. *Sales.* This is the easy part, the basic requisite. This includes the ability to demonstrate competency with sales results. Sales managers often rely too much on their numbers. Don't dwell on your numbers because it smacks of shallowness. Good numbers are *expected* and are only the ticket to let you walk through the door to be considered.

2. *Management.* This is the harder part. Have you been sufficiently baptized by the fire of personnel issues, terminations, promotions, conflict management, dispute settlements, contract negotiations, expense cutbacks, downsizings, and customer complaints? If you have had reasonable experience with these issues, dwell on them because they showcase you as a problem solver. If you haven't, perhaps you are pushing your position too quickly.

3. *The intangibles.* This is the hardest part and what ultimately differentiates the winners from the losers. The most important readiness criteria are often softer attributes such as work ethic, teamwork, integrity, maturity, strategic thinking, the ability to tolerate ambiguity, the ability to embrace change, comfort level with diversity, organization skills, integration skills, innovation skills, platform skills, personal presence, and so on. These intangibles relate to leadership. Hiring managers are sometimes reticent to talk about these soft attributes because they are difficult to explain, difficult to quantify, and difficult to defend. They tend to talk about the easy quantifiable stuff that wrongly feeds the younger manager's expectations. Think how the intangibles come into play when *you* make a hiring decision. It is no different for someone that you want to go and work for. A good promotion campaigner will make the soft stuff their trump cards. Dwell on those intangibles during a campaign because they showcase you as a leader and a mature businessperson who will fit in the new position.

Synchronize Your Watches

Your career clock and the company's career clock tick at different rates. It should be obvious that the company will not adjust their clock very much, except in the face of circumstantial needs. So you are left with the choice of making a decision to wait or to move.

What is the return on investment of X amount of additional time in your current position? Have your manager answer that question. If you're the manager being queried, you better have your ducks in a row on this one.

Set Yourself up for Success

Put together a personal promotion campaign that contains some of the following:

- Look at the last couple of people who were promoted into the job that you would like to have. Find out what their credentials, experience, and performance were at the time of their promotions and integrate those elements into your promotion plan.
- Volunteer for a project or a special assignment, a study group, or a quality team that will put you in contact with people for whom you would like to work. If you are smooth about it, you may be able to demonstrate your skills and capabilities to the point where they *request* you to be a part of their team.
- Ask for a collateral assignment, indicating how your capabilities will strengthen the effort. While some collateral assignments may be fun, they may not showcase your skills. Look for assignments that are high visibility and that tap the passion of top management.
- During your annual-review process, discuss your career desires with your manager. The secret to that meeting is being well prepared, not just saying, "Boss, I want to move." Initiate follow-up discussions to drive the process. Don't rely solely on the annual review.
- Build a familiarity with the requirements of the position you want, particularly its issues and challenges, and be ready to indicate how you would tackle those challenges.
- Be able to answer the questions:
  "What makes you think you're ready for the next step?"
  "Why are you interested in that particular position?"
  "Why are you the right person for that job?"
  "What will you bring to that position?"
- Build a relationship with human resources and acquaint them with your desires.
- Consider the idea of creating your own job based on the needs you see around you.
- Begin to train yourself for the job you want. Investigate what seminars or schools you can attend to prepare yourself for the next step.
- Talk to people who are in the job that you would like to have in order to familiarize yourself with job content.
- Think about whom you might recommend to backfill your current job. You don't want your manager to hold you back because of fear of an open slot.
- Build a relationship and plant an awareness of your capabilities and interests with your manager's manager. That person has a broader view of corporate needs and opportunities. *But be careful*, because you don't want any perceived end runs.

Keep Plugging

Execute your current job *beyond* expectations. Take it up another notch—another level.

If your manager is savvy, he or she will keep the promotion issue on the front burner and through specific actions regularly demonstrate to you that your desire is uppermost in his or her mind. He or she may have you interview another department manager, ask you to act in his or her absence, or give you a special assignment that puts you in contact with other business functions or divisions. Persistence should pay off.

LESSONS

The first day you step into a new job is the day you start your campaign to get your next job because timing is an element you can't control. That mentality will help ensure excellence in your current position, and your readiness to fill positions of opportunity.

Engage in regular discussions with your manager about your desires and opportunities.

The actions of people who launch promotion campaigns only when an opportunity comes into view are often transparent. A good hiring manager, upon seeing these spurts of frenzied positioning, will ask himself or herself, "Where have you been . . ." It doesn't play well.

Your personal feelings about promotion are a reflection of how many of your people feel about *their* careers. Many are chafing at the bit the same way you are. Just like you, if their goals aren't realized they may be out on the market sniffing around. Give them the candid career guidance and counseling that you yourself would like.

Things turn out best for people who make the best of the way things turn out.

14–3 THE PROBLEM:

Your boss is dissatisfied with your performance.

THE STORY

Ted's sales unit was having another bad month. As he was poring over the figures, his new region sales director, Helen, quietly walked into his office and closed the door.

"Ted, what's the problem?" Helen said in a clipped tone. Ted had been a sales manager for several years and *never* thought he'd be on this end of this kind of discussion.

"Ted, I'm not happy with what I see," Helen continued. "This can't go on much longer—you're digging a hole."

Helen went on to make a couple of other observations about the way Ted was managing his people and about his people's work habits.

Ted had nothing substantial to offer and was left to stew about his poor performance.

TEMPTATIONS

Nothing can grab your attention like a rifle shot from the boss that you're in trouble, and nothing spurs self-protecting temptations faster than the threat of dismissal.

Cheat

"I'll throw in some soft orders and hope we can firm them up."

Challenge

"Boss, you're wrong! Let's look at the facts! You're not being fair."

Hide

"I think I'll just stay out of her way and see if I can weather the storm."

This is an emotional time. And it's decision time. Helen certainly has Ted's attention.

WHAT HAPPENED HERE . . . ?

Something, or everything, about Ted's performance is subpar. A file is probably being built. The bell is about to toll.

Ted may be in over his head. The job may have become more than he can handle. As times have changed, jobs and expectations have grown. The bar is now a lot higher, and Ted may not be prepared for today's reality.

Ted may have neglected his own personal development and is now about to pay the piper.

Optics may be an issue. Ted may not be an effective ambassador for his boss. A senior manager wants to feel comfortable and confident that a subordinate will show well. Other people draw conclusions about your boss based on your actions and style. Ted may not be a good or positive deputy.

Helen may have been directed to get tough. She could have been told to flush out her bottom 25 percent as part of a downsizing effort.

Helen may not have been able to describe exactly what she wanted from her people, or not communicated her expectations at all, and Ted has been trying to satisfy a virtually invisible yardstick. It happens.

Helen could have ambitious personal plans and doesn't see Ted as being able to contribute to her planned rocket ride up the organization chart. She considers him expendable in satisfying her own agenda.

Because Helen is a new manager she may be operating from hearsay regarding Ted's past performance and potential. She may not have given Ted a sufficient chance to prove himself, or she may lack confidence in his ability to ever become a top performer. And you can't overlook that maybe Helen has a little bit of a problem providing leadership and direction.

OPTIONS

First, three BIG questions.

The first big question: Do Ted and Helen both sincerely agree that this is a salvageable situation, or would it be a waste of both of their time? In order to successfully turn around the situation they both must be *brutally honest*. Lack of candor wounds everyone.

The second big question: Is Ted willing to change his work style and compromise some of his beliefs? In order to turn around Helen's opinion he must *overshift*. Any stubbornness would be tantamount to cutting his own throat.

The third big question: Is Ted willing to make a wholesale investment of time and effort? In order to turn around Helen's opinion he must *over correct*. He can't let his ego lead him to do things incrementally.

If Ted gets a positive answer from all of the big questions he should get to work.

If he gets a negative answer from any one of the big questions then he needs to get his resumé in order.

POSSIBLE ACTIONS

Ted is in the position he is in because of habit and style choices he has made in the past. It is time to make some new and different choices to get out of this predicament.

Look in the Mirror—It's Self-assessment Time

One of the biggest problems with turning around dissatisfaction is flawed self-assessment. Ted must admit to himself that his self-view is skewed, wrong, incorrect, in error, overstated, or inflated. Scream it out. *I am wrong about myself.* He must exorcise the old self.

He needs to ask himself if he is working up to capacity and if he is doing things he should be smart enough to avoid. Is he creating opportunities for Helen to criticize him? What current written goals and objectives are on target, what's off the mark? Are his preconceived notions about acceptable performance obsolete? Are there principles at stake here that strike at personal integrity issues and may be worth disagreement? Is he blinded by his past evaluations? If he distorts reality for the sake of his own comfort it is impossible to take corrective action.

Honest self-assessment is liberating and is in his best interest. He must talk to the person, or people, in his life he trusts the most to help free his personal candor.

Glance Around—It's Environment-Assessment Time

How well does this job fit Ted, and how well does he fit this job? Is he miscast?

His problem may be because he has chosen a career in sales. Should he even be in sales management? Has he chosen the wrong company to work for? Would Ted be better off in another business function and another role? He must declare his answers. Life is too short and the options too attractive to tolerate compromise.

Try This Litmus Test

Watch the body language, listen to the vocabulary, and observe the ambiance Helen displays around her best performers. The extent of the *deviation* from that behavior to how she behaves around Ted should give him a rough indication how far he is from being perceived as a long-term player on her team. This simple inspection can tell him where he stands.

The Relationship

Mutual loyalty and respect *must* be the basis of the relationship. Ted doesn't necessarily need to be comfortable and cozy working for Helen. Liking doesn't have to be an ingredient in the relationship. Boss-subordinate relationships are not intended to be mutual-admiration societies.

Look at Your Boss and Assess What Makes Her Tick

Before Ted has a discussion with Helen he must try to understand the business and personal motivations, and the values, fears, worries, and anxieties of his manager. What causes her to lose her temper? To whom is she very sensitive? Does she keep herself to a tight calendar and schedule? Is she naturally competitive? How does she relate to her superior? Ted must analyze her as he would analyze a prospect. Understanding is built though observation and listening.

Talk to Others

Ted should go to another manager or to his mentor (if he has one) to get an indication of what Helen is looking for. He should watch the conduct of his peers, listen to their comments, and judge what he can pick up to make his behavior more acceptable.

It's Time to Talk to the Boss

Make an appointment so that both of you have a chance to prepare. If Ted takes the initiative with this discussion it will be to his benefit because it puts him more in control.

Consider these sample questions to open the dialogue and clear the air.

- "Helen, we agree that things aren't going as we both would like. May we talk about it?"
- "Can you share some suggestions?"
- "Have you seen anything that you think I need to change?"

- "What would you like me to do that I'm currently not doing?"
- "What do you recommend I do to change the situation?"

If the responses are positive and expansive, keep going down this track. If they are superficial or lack encouragement, switch to this track.

- "Do I have a future in your sales unit?"
- "Would you like me to resign?"
- "Should I start looking for another job?"

It takes courage to ask these questions, but that's how to get results. It's like asking the customer for an order—and Ted should certainly be comfortable with those situations. Asking candid questions engenders a cooperative attitude and creates respect in Helen's mind.

These discussions *almost always* involve more than the numbers. Helen may have trouble being candid and expansive about soft subjective matters, not because she doesn't want to be candid, but because it is difficult to deliver critical feedback of a *personal* nature. Ted should help if he must by asking questions.

- "Is there something about my style that bothers you?"
- "Do I have a habit that makes you uncomfortable?"
- "Have I unintentionally stepped on someone's toes?"
- "Is there something missing from my leadership approach?"
- "Am I not seeing something basic and obvious?"

He should ask Helen to review her expectations and make sure he understands them.

It doesn't matter if Ted agrees totally with Helen's suggestions or expectations. Concentrate on how Helen feels and thinks. Don't argue. If Ted gets defensive he only digs his hole deeper. *A sales manager earns the right to argue*—and Ted hasn't earned anything yet. Ted must admit it if he doesn't know what to do to eliminate certain dissatisfactions. The worst thing he can do is say, "Yes, I understand, I'll fix the problem."

Ted can tell if Helen is sincerely interested in his improvement by the depth and detail of her suggestions and by the presence or absence of a supportive, coaching manner.

In the end, agree and document what needs to be done.

Action Time

Ted's primary job becomes one of doing everything possible to recover his standing.

He shouldn't take any of his frustration out on his sales unit. They probably know that Ted (and some of them, by extension) are in trouble. These situations are never secrets.

Adopt a Strategy—and an Attitude

This is a sales campaign. The product is *Ted* and he needs a 3D recovery strategy based on *d*ifferentiation, *d*ominance, and *d*emand, similar to Problem 2–4. After talking to

Helen, Ted should know what she *demands*. He should *dominate* by working on a process or activity high on Helen's agenda that sets a benchmark of performance that is useful to her organization. And finally, Ted should execute the process or activity by exhibiting behaviors that are clearly *differentiated* from his old behaviors. For example, his strategy could be to execute sales plans that set an example for the entire company, far superior to anything he has ever submitted.

If he adopts a heightened, make-it-happen outlook and enthusiastically champions Helen's agenda he will be more apt to turn around her dissatisfaction.

He shouldn't *tell* Helen what he plans to do, or tell her what he has done, but rather make sure she *sees* him doing the things she suggested. Actions speak volumes.

Secrets to Re-earning Confidence

Here are a dozen suggestions to help get out of the hole.

1. Nail the next forecast. The bottom line is Ted's most powerful weapon.
2. Help make the boss look good by contributing solutions to her biggest problem.
3. Exhibit a sense of urgency in all matters that is *in excess* of the boss's own sense of urgency on those matters.
4. Keep your eyes open for a highly visible, extracurricular task. Volunteer to participate or lead and then do a superb job.
5. Execute a public appearance, such as a staff meeting presentation, that is squeaky clean.
6. Seek contact with Helen. Reaching out communicates desire and commitment.
7. Seek group contact. Inject yourself into activities and engage your peers because withdrawal from the mainstream reinforces rumors and exacerbates the problem.
8. Set day-to-day performance standards for yourself that are consistent with Helen's advice, and measure yourself against them Bias your day-to-day work actions and priorities to mirror Helen's.
9. Embrace Helen's advice; don't just accept it. Managers love flexibility, a willingness to listen, and enthusiasm for their ideas.
10. Ted should visibly change the way he works. Get to the office at 6:30 in the morning. Reorganize his workspace. Write crisper, more creative documentation. Dramatic *visible changes* imply that activity that can't be readily observed is also being changed dramatically.
11. He must become his own PR agent by diplomatically sending positive messages about his sales unit up the line.
12. He must visibly and sincerely confer his respect and loyalty.

Look Forward to the Future

If Ted *accelerates* his pace and *embeds* his new habits as he comes out of this dissatisfaction problem the momentum will help keep him at a new level of performance. As Mary

Pickford said, "If you have made mistakes, even serious ones, there is always another chance for you. What we call failure is not the falling down, but the staying down."

LESSONS

Always try to be the first to react to dissatisfaction, in spite of the fact that you know it's tough to do. Be honest and courageous. *You know* if you're in trouble. As an example, imagine your feelings if one of your people walked in to talk to you, versus you walking in to talk to them, about performance. It's a big difference, isn't it? It takes guts, but it works. The time to take action with a performance problem of your own is at the first, tiniest inkling that something is out of tune. Your manager will respect your candor and your call for help.

Experience teaches sales managers to minimize certain tasks and to prioritize other tasks, to utilize what works for them and to discard what doesn't. That is how management styles develop. When styles run into changes in the environment and in bosses, and a sales manager doesn't proactively adapt, dissatisfaction often develops. If you get a new manager it behooves you not to take anything for granted. Do not assume that your existing style will satisfy the new manager. Be ready, willing, and able to change and the faster the better.

You learn a lot about yourself, relationships, and people by escaping a near-death management scenario. These experiences, as uncomfortable as they are, create learning and growth. "There is no education like adversity" is the way Benjamin Disraeli put it.

14–4 THE PROBLEM:

It is time to decide whether to stay or move on.

THE STORY

David had been in his current job for eight years, gone through three presidents, four different bosses, and the company had just been purchased by a foreign firm with a heavy handed notoriety. David had always been a good performer, so much so that he felt he could do the job blindfolded. He did have a reputation as a bit of an agitator, but it had never hurt him, as far as he knew. On the personal side his one child had just graduated from high school.

Sitting on the airplane one day gazing out the window and contemplating these facts, it struck him that maybe it was time to do something different. A business story in the airline magazine and the executive ads in the newspaper stirred his mind. He thought about this during the whole flight, and when he got off the plane it was really gnawing at him.

TEMPTATIONS

These thought processes can be emotional and consuming and can easily lead to irrational reactions.

Retire in place

"Hey, I don't have anything to worry about. I'll just throttle back and cut coupons."

Leap at the first opportunity

"This ad looks good to me. I'll send them my old resumé in the morning."

Let depression set in

"Oh my, what am I going to do? I don't have a future. I waited too long."

For sales managers who help other people make career decisions day in and day out it is interesting to see how casually they often approach personal decisions of their own.

WHAT HAPPENED HERE . . . ?

David has ants in his pants either because there has been pressure slowly building that he now feels for the first time, or he is squirming in place because there has been a single and powerful event that grabbed his attention, or a combination of both.

The pressure *to make a decision* is fed by numerous factors—some that pressure him to move on, others that pressure him to stay. This problem emerges when the factors that prompt moving on begin to outweigh the factors to stay.

There are so many potential factors beyond the story that David should create two lists to keep track of the possibilities. These examples should help stir your own thinking.

Factors that lead to a decision to move on	Factors that lead to a decision to stay
• There is a threat that you will lose your job.	• Extended family considerations are important
• Big money has been offered to you.	• You don't want to move the children out of the area.
• More responsibility has been offered to you.	• Your spouse has a great job and enjoys it.
• You're no longer learning anything where you are.	• You like where you live.

- Your boss or mentor, whom you respected, quit.
- There is a threat of a downsizing or reorganization.
- You were not selected to attend a prestigious training seminar.
- You were snubbed by a top executive.

- You have been bitten by the entrepreneurial bug.
- The work environment has changed because of new management.
- The work environment is expected to become unbearably intense because of cost-cutting.
- You have heard and read about great opportunities in other industries or companies.
- You saw an attractive ad in the newspaper.
- There are other things in life that you'd like to do.
- You have been courted furiously by another firm.
- You have been in the position for a long time, and your prospects for growth or change are bleak.
- You no longer feel a sense of loyalty or pride in your employer.

- Your firm is rumored to be downsized.

- The signals you're picking up from your manager are not positive.
- The technology or product you're involved with is no longer on the leading edge.
- You've overhead a negative conversation about yourself.
- Your friends have left, and you hear others talking about leaving.

- Security associated with your current job is good.
- You have tenure that results in extra benefits.
- You have acquired a great deal of product or technical expertise.
- You are in the process of finishing a degree program.
- You thoroughly enjoy colleagues at work.
- You are very proud to work for this company.
- You make good money.

- There has been a promise of change, growth, or advancement.
- You like and respect your boss.
- You have the respect of the management team.
- Friends and family live in the area.

- You have a lot invested in this company.

- Affiliation with the current employer has value in the industry and in your professional community.
- You're scared to move or apprehensive of change.
- You love your office.

- You love your job.

- You find your work satisfies your need for achievement.
- You work in a resource-rich environment.

- Sales channels are changing to your disadvantage.
- Your last salary increase was well below expectations.
- Your values and/or motivations have changed.
- You recognize that moving up in today's business world often means moving on.
- The work is no longer exciting or stimulating.
- Someone junior to you got a promotion over you.
- You're not one of the stars, and you think you have a better chance of being a star elsewhere.
- You can't penetrate the tight relationships and old-guard organization infrastructure.
- You have become bored with your work, doing the same stuff over and over again.
- Your personal responsibilities have changed, freeing you up to do other things.

- You have status in your current position.
- You feel you can weather the current hard times where you are.
- You have responsibilities that you absolutely love.
- You've been told you're badly needed.

- Certain powerful people have asked you to stay.
- You are respected and admired.

- You are having fun.

- The outlook for yourself and the company looks good.
- You can personally influence your course and your future.
- You are making a valuable contribution.

There are subtle nuances on the list, but it is often the subtleties that make the difference in these decisions.

What's happening here is an internal struggle between the two columns of factors. Change precipitates these struggles. All these factors come and go because you work in a dynamic sales world. There are big factors and there are little factors, and what is big to one sales manager may be little to another. It is not just the number of factors, but the intensity of the factors that come into play. Some create heavy pressure and others create only light tension. Stay or move-on decisions are always fueled by a combination of objective and subjective factors, some of which are significant and others of which would seem inconsequential to another manager. No sales manager, in the face of a challenging question on this subject, should ever feel defensive or embarrassed about his or her list.

OPTIONS

First, some definitions.

Stay. Stay doesn't necessarily mean staying in the same job. Stay could be a different sales-management job in the same firm, the same job in a different division or subsidiary, or a switch to marketing or operations in the same firm.

Move on. Move on doesn't necessarily mean joining a different firm. Move on could be retirement, a new profession, starting a business, going back to school, or taking a leave of absence for a volunteer program.

Since this is an either-or problem, your options relate to *how* you will make the decision.

You have two choices.

- A *snap decision.* Yield to pressure and emotion and make the decision on your own.
- A *thoughtful decision.* Withstand the pressure, take your time, and seek guidance and counsel.

In spite of the pressure you may be under, a thoughtful decision obviously has long-term value.

POSSIBLE ACTIONS

Relax. These feelings and decisions are very common.

What Is the Short-Term Goal?

This is the crux of the problem. What does David want to do? Where does he want to go? David needs to identify his goal before he can relieve the pressure. The goal could be a specific target such as job *x* or income *y*, or it could be a combination of many factors from his list.

What Is the Ultimate Goal?

Will *stay* or *go* do a better job of getting David to his final destination? The reason for stopping to think about the longer term goal is to ensure that the shorter-term decision will help him get to the ultimate goal as well.

What Do You Bring to the Table?

Whether or not David is aware of another opportunity, he needs to appraise himself in order to make a better decision. Once he does that he'll have a clearer idea of how movable or marketable he is. An assessment will also identify gaps and holes he needs to fill. Because honest self-assessments are difficult or nearly impossible, David should use his resources.

Share your struggle with your boss (if feasible), mentor, human resources, colleagues, family, and friends to get their ideas. They can help create clarity and objectivity through the questions they ask. Confide in these resources at the first twinges of discomfort. The longer you wait the harder it is to listen because you'll be under greater pressure.

Armed with an assessment, you'll be better able to decide where you fit.

Where Do You Fit Best?

In what type of environment would you feel most comfortable? And how would you like to be managed? When you look around you, look backward into your past and look inside yourself—what cultures and what managers do you respect and make you feel most comfortable?

Here are examples characterizing cultures and managers. Create a chart for yourself.

Where I fit best

I prefer a culture that looks like:	*I prefer a manager that looks like:*		
• Achievement is recognized in a big way.	**Values:** What the manager believes in	**Style:** The way the manager operates	**Skills:** What the manager is good at
• The company atmosphere is friendly.	• Integrity	• Has a control mentality	• Strategic thinker
• High standards and quality are the focus.	• Values people	• Is approachable	• Good coach
• The company is intellectually curious and open to new ideas.	• Trust	• Shares opinions	• Leaderships skills
• There are people around me who are honest, no games.	• Honesty	• Is structured and organized	• A good communicator
• ?	• ?	• Is competitive	• ?

What are the values where you are? If you don't share the values of the culture you're in, or the values of management you work with, continuing pressure and discomfort are inevitable.

Managers come and go, but cultures are more enduring. Assuming you joined a new company and the hiring manager were to leave the company the day after you joined, would you be able to survive in that environment? Would you be comfortable and able to operate at your full potential?

Don't let dollars overshadow your analysis. If you don't fit, it doesn't matter how much money you make. You'll end right back where you are.

What About You Affects Your Fit?

Think about how your predispositions fit in the current situation and think about how they may fit somewhere else. Candid answers to these questions can help shape your decision.

- Are you a conceptual or a pragmatic person?

- Can you let go of things, or do you have to control everything?
- Do you thrive on intellectually stimulating environments, or is that not important to you?
- Are you a transformer who likes to churn things, or are you a great soldier who is an outstanding implementer?
- Do you tend to cling to processes, or can you extemporize and be flexible?
- Are you a culture zealot, or are you open and accepting?
- Can you tolerate experience linearity, or do you always have to be doing something different?
- Can you tolerate ambiguity, or do you prefer structure and precision?

Use this partial list of questions to prime the pump of other values and predispositions. The answers help reveal your preferences.

Timing Is Critical

Windows of opportunity open and close in a hurry. Like playing the lottery, if you happen to be in the right place at the right time, the factors line up loud and clear and fit looks good, you can win big. But those cases are rare. You'll still need to create a decision matrix for yourself.

Decision Time

Most people make decisions in their mind, making it difficult to keep track of all the variables and criteria that have come out of the previous analysis. Writing the factor and fit variables down helps you focus, helps you not to forget anything, and aids in sharing with your resources.

Here are some examples. Create a matrix with your own factor and fit variables. Remember that nothing is inconsequential, so plug in all your thoughts.

What I GAIN by moving on	What I GAIN by staying
More independence and more responsibility	Better positioning for an even more attractive opportunity in the future
Fresh ideas and new market challenges	Additional experience
Reduction of stress	No hassle with moving
A firm with deeper pockets and more resources	?
An innovative atmosphere	?
A much bigger team to manage	?
A feeling of excitement	?
?	?

What I LOSE by moving on	What I LOSE by staying
Good and respected friends, the camaraderie	Expanding my sales-management skills
Being associated with a market leader	A sense of excitement
?	New and expanded contacts
?	?

Make your decision!

LESSONS

Today, more than ever, you have to look out for yourself and be your own career manager. There is a tendency to assume that because you are currently doing a good job you will be taken care of. That may not be a good assumption. Self-direct your career.

Understand where it is you want to go with your career and make your decisions in the context of those objectives, always trying to keep yourself in positions where you fit best. Good fit facilitates good performance, and good performance takes the pressure off stay-or-go decisions.

Become an expert sales manager, not necessarily an expert food-and-beverage sales manager, or chemicals-sales manager, or office-products sales manager. Focus on the functional expertise. And know yourself well. A solid command of who you are and of sales and sales management can open up more doors.

A key lesson of this problem is to seek out the opinions of others and not to try to make these decisions on your own. There is too much at stake.

A Problem-Solving Checklist

Scan this list of 21 thought processes and action items as a reminder of additional matters to consider. You will find the checklist helpful in ensuring clarity and completeness as you develop possible actions.

❏ State the problem simply and clearly. Separate the real problem from the apparent problem because everything is not always as it seems at first glance.

❏ There are always stories attached to problems and always those with more than one side that needs to be understood.

❏ Ask questions and gather facts. Assumptions will falsely color your actions.

❏ To the best of your ability, uncover all the"what happened here . . . ?" ingredients that may have contributed to the problem.

❏ Use your people resources—managers, peers, and subordinates; plus customers, clients, and sales partners—to clarify the problem, consider options and actions, and frame implementation of your decision. Resource utilization often takes courage, but you will find your actions more thorough, effective, and respected.

❏ Look at yourself. A candid self-assessment of your role and predispositions contributes to the credibility and the integrity of your actions. Your actions must be consistent with who you are.

❏ Hold yourself to high standards. You'll feel better, and your people will rise to meet your expectations.

❏ Have the courage to admit to your own role in creating a problem. The acknowledgment will draw respect and attract staff members to buy-in to the solution.

❏ Identify your primary options and as many variances to those options that you can.

❏ Write things down. The physical action will force precision and completeness. Trying to keep everything in your mind contributes to stress and inconsistencies.

❏ Take time out to think and synthesize along the way to your final actions. Respites stimulate better solutions.

❏ Create a logical flow of possible actions that you will follow.

❏ Don't be deterred by what others will think of you. There will always be negative, compromising forces that will try to draw you off course or diminish your standards.

❏ Never look for blame or place blame. The effort is always counterproductive.

❏ Consider what can be done to prevent the problem from happening again. Make those steps a part of your solution and implementation.

❏ Ensure your possible actions meet the test of being conceptually consistent.

❏ Make a decision that can withstand the scrutiny of the question, "why"? Say the answer out loud to help test its credibility.

❏ Act crisply and decisively, in accordance with your personal values, guiding principles, and company policies.

- ❏ Remember that you have a responsibility to safeguard company assets and reputation, to coach and counsel your staff, to exceed company sales expectations, and to stand up for the needs and rights of customers, clients, and sales partners.
- ❏ Think of all the people who were involved in the causes and the ramifications of the problem and make sure they are all touched by the solution.
- ❏ Always pause to look for and file lessons drawn from the experience.

Your Feedback-and-Input Opportunity

Your ideas can be included in the next edition of *The Sales Manager's Troubleshooter*.

We would appreciate your input and suggestions regarding Temptations, What Happened Here . . . ?, Options, Possible Actions, and Lessons for any of the problems discussed in the book.

Your proposal for new and additional problems to address are also welcomed.

Dear John and Charlie:

I would suggest that you add the following to Problem #_____.

_____

_____

_____

I would suggest that you address the following Problem in the next edition.

Problem:_____

_____

_____

Name (optional) _____

Title_____

Company _____

Phone: (   ) _____

Please fax your suggestions to 703-591-2849, or E-mail your suggestions to jcebrowski@salesbuilders.com

We will recognize accepted suggestions to current problems and ideas for new problems in the next addition. Thank you for your contribution.

John Cebrowski   Charlie Romeo

INDEX

C